The Free Inquiry Papers

The Free Inquiry Papers

Edited by
Robert Maranto, Catherine Salmon,
Lee Jussim, and Sally Satel

AEI PRESS

Publisher for the American Enterprise Institute
WASHINGTON, DC

ISBN-13: 978-0-8447-5067-5 (Paperback)

Library of Congress Cataloging-in-Publication Data have been applied for.

© 2025 by the American Enterprise Institute for Public Policy Research. All rights reserved. No part of this publication may be used or reproduced in any manner whatsoever without permission in writing from the American Enterprise Institute except in the case of brief quotations embodied in news articles, critical articles, or reviews. The views expressed in the publications of the American Enterprise Institute are those of the authors and do not necessarily reflect the views of the staff, advisory panels, officers, or trustees of AEI.

Publisher for the American Enterprise Institute
for Public Policy Research
1789 Massachusetts Avenue, NW
Washington, DC 20036

Printed in the United States of America

Contents

PART I. THE NEED FOR FREE INQUIRY 1

1. The Free Inquiry Papers: Why Now? 2
   Robert Maranto, Catherine Salmon, Lee Jussim, and Sally Satel

2. Why Democracy Requires Free Inquiry 5
   Graeme Auton, Robert Maranto, and Catherine Salmon

3. Why Free Speech? 21
   Jonathan Zimmerman

4. Why Social Justice Requires Free Inquiry 28
   Akeela Careem and Lee Jussim

PART II. THREATS TO FREE INQUIRY 47

5. The Rise of Self-Censorship in America 48
   Joseph L. Sutherland and James L. Gibson

6. How Institutional Speech Erodes Academic Freedom 62
   Aaron Saiger

7. Academic Freedom and the Social Media Veto 82
   *Chad G. Rusthoven, George Yancey, Patricia Nayna Schwerdtle,
   and Donald Alexander Downs*

8. Do No Anti-Racist Harm: Medical Education Under Threat 104
   Sally Satel

9. Lysenkoism Then and Now: A Cautionary Tale of Censorious
   Social Norms 130
   Catherine Salmon and Lee Jussim

10. Ostrich Syndrome and Campus Free Expression 143
    *Sean T. Stevens, Nathan Honeycutt, Komi Frey,
    and Andrea Honeycutt*

v

vi THE FREE INQUIRY PAPERS

11. Examining the Tensions Between Free Markets and
Free Speech 168
Brian Knight

PART III. KEEPING FREE INQUIRY ALIVE 183

12. Mobilization for Academic Free Speech:
The Wisconsin Model 184
Donald Alexander Downs

13. Make a Bureaucracy to Beat a Bureaucracy? Free Speech
Bureaucracies and How to Get Them 203
Robert Maranto

14. Can Intellectual Diversity Be Recovered in Academia? 219
George R. La Noue

15. Merit, Fairness, and Equality: An Alternative to Diversity,
Equity, and Inclusion 234
Dorian S. Abbot, Iván Marinovic, and Carlos M. Carvalho

16. Rhetorical Jujitsu: Leveraging Campus DEI to Promote
Ideological Diversity 247
Richard E. Redding

17. Fighting the Good Fight in an Age of Unreason:
A New Dissident Guide 267
Anna I. Krylov and Jay Tanzman

PART IV. LOOKING FORWARD 305

18. Free Speech Advice for the President of Hypothetical U 306
Greg Lukianoff and Adam Goldstein

19. Beyond Free Speech: The Constitution of Knowledge 321
Jonathan Rauch

20. Conclusion: How to Bring Back Free Inquiry 333
Robert Maranto, Lee Jussim, Catherine Salmon, and Sally Satel

About the Authors 345

Index 357

PART I.
The Need for Free Inquiry

1

The Free Inquiry Papers: Why Now?

Free inquiry is under attack in the United States and other English-speaking nations as never before in living memory.[1] Although challenges from populist elected politicians exist and receive considerable attention from scholars and journalists,[2] the most consistent and thoroughgoing threats to free inquiry in the United States currently originate within elite institutions, particularly higher education.[3]

This collection of essays, written by scholars with different academic backgrounds, experiences, and political perspectives, documents what has happened in these institutions and in society more broadly and proposes remedies to restore healthy free inquiry. Its starting point is a discussion of the importance of free inquiry itself. Surveys indicate that most students, university administrators, and political leaders no longer understand *why* free inquiry matters; many actually reject it outright. The essays in Part I illustrate free inquiry's importance for individual justice, science, and democracy itself.

Part II chronicles lessons from past efforts to suppress inquiry in the US, Russia, and China. The authors in this section also describe threats to free inquiry on campuses today and how they now extend into the worlds of business, science, and medicine. The authors describe the many ways free inquiry can be restricted, such as through personnel decisions, the retraction of published peer-reviewed papers, and deplatforming.[4]

Parts III and IV explore immediate and long-term strategies for the restoration of free inquiry and offers actions and tactics for legislators, alumni, and higher education leaders to produce lasting reforms. Many of the authors in this section have been in the trenches themselves, fighting protracted battles against suppression. Much of the wisdom they impart in these chapters comes from their experiences and their successful attempts to challenge restrictions on free speech and produce a healthier climate for freedom of speech and inquiry on their campuses. The final chapter summarizes the contributors' prescriptions for policymakers, educators,

THE FREE INQUIRY PAPERS: WHY NOW? 3

administrators, students, and free speech activists who want to restore free inquiry to academia.

Recent decades have seen a severe free inquiry recession on campuses and elsewhere in the United States despite a robust free speech tradition. Much has been written about this topic, but this volume is the first effort to provide a comprehensive look at the situation and suggest remedies across different disciplines.

We have many to thank for this book, starting with our colleagues in the Society for Open Inquiry in Behavioral Science, whose support was vital. Assembling a monumental collection that brings together scholars from many fields was challenging. We are grateful to the authors who have contributed, but especially to AEI Press and a team of talented editors who have made this volume compelling as a whole. Sarah Bowe, who leads the editorial team at AEI, has brought meticulous attention to each new iteration of the chapters, and her patience with many inquiries and revisions has been remarkable. Finally, we are grateful to AEI for understanding the importance of this volume and especially to Matthew Continetti, director of Domestic Policy Studies, for giving us the green light to move ahead on the project.

Robert Maranto, Catherine Salmon,
Lee Jussim, and Sally Satel

Notes

1. Robert Corn-Revere, *The Mind of the Censor and the Eye of the Beholder: The First Amendment and the Censor's Dilemma* (New York: Cambridge University Press, 2021); Claire Lehmann et al., eds., *Panics and Persecutions: 20 Tales of Excommunication in the Digital Age* (London: Black Spring Press Group, 2021); Greg Lukianoff and Jonathan Haidt, *The Coddling of the American Mind: How Good Intentions and Bad Ideas Are Setting Up a Generation for Failure* (New York: Penguin Press, 2018); and Sean T. Stevens, Lee Jussim, and Nathan Honeycutt, "Scholarship Suppression: Theoretical Perspectives and Emerging Trends," *Societies* 10, no. 4 (December 2020): 82, https://www.mdpi.com/2075-4698/10/4/82.

2. Anne Applebaum, *Twilight of Democracy: The Seductive Lure of Authoritarianism* (New York: Doubleday, 2020); and William A. Galston, *Anti-Pluralism: The Populist Threat to Liberal Democracy* (New Haven, CT: Yale University Press, 2018).

4 THE FREE INQUIRY PAPERS

3. James R. Flynn, *A Book Too Risky to Publish: Free Speech and Universities* (Washington, DC: Academica Press, 2020); and Stevens, Jussim, and Honeycutt, "Scholarship Suppression."

4. Eric Kaufmann, *Academic Freedom in Crisis: Punishment, Political Discrimination, and Self-Censorship,* Center for the Study of Partisanship and Ideology, March 1, 2021, https://www.cspicenter.com/p/academic-freedom-in-crisis-punishment; James D. Paul and Robert Maranto, "Elite Schools Lead: An Empirical Examination of Diversity Requirements in Higher Education Job Markets," *Studies in Higher Education* 48, no. 2 (February 2023): 314–28, https://www.tandfonline.com/doi/full/10.1080/03075079.2022.2134334; and Stevens, Jussim, and Honeycutt, "Scholarship Suppression." Regarding elite media, see Batya Ungar-Sargon, *Bad News: How Woke Media Is Undermining Democracy* (New York: Encounter Books, 2021).

2

Why Democracy Requires Free Inquiry

Graeme Auton, Robert Maranto, and Catherine Salmon

> Aggressive and even violent protests have erupted at some of the country's most progressive schools. . . . Are these schools brutal and toxic environments for members of various identity groups? Or has a set of new ideas on campus taught students to see oppression and violence wherever they look?
>
> —Jonathan Haidt and Greg Lukianoff[1]

> Convictions are more dangerous enemies of truth than lies.
>
> —Friedrich Nietzsche[2]

As we write, highly autocratic Russia is invading a highly corrupt Ukraine that has struggled with democracy since claiming independence in 1991. It is an unequal conflict epitomizing one of Jonathan Haidt's moral foundations, *liberty versus oppression*, and the moral desire to root for the underdog.[3] We believe that "oppression," which describes a fundamental reality of human history, is now a much-overused term in US higher education, often invoking a panoply of imagined insecurities and involving such matters as practically imperceptible microaggressions or even such transgressions as failing to impose detailed administrative regulation of Halloween costumes.[4]

At many American universities, it is common to hear that "words are violence" and unwanted opinions are acts of aggression.[5] In dramatic contrast, since spring 2022, on our computers and television screens, we have seen each day what real oppression and violence look like. The leveling of Mariupol has nothing in common with the sensitivities of faculty and

6 THE FREE INQUIRY PAPERS

students who believe that someone else's exercise of free speech is a threat to their well-being.

Democracy is fragile. Like in any political system, outcomes are shaped by the people in charge, and as a result, democracy is subject to (and can be a source of) military threat—hence the continued relevance of military alliances such as NATO to protect us from invasion and project our values. Yet, of 51 state (including the District of Columbia) public school civics and social standards, only 12 mention NATO, and only one (New York) explicitly mentions the USSR's mass murder of Ukrainians in the 1932–33 Holodomor famine. Indeed, for the progressive left, memory of the USSR has become something of an inconvenience that will die off with the boomer generation, just as the reality of Josef Stalin's very real oppression was an inconvenience for the American left in the 1930s, as detailed in Richard Crossman's edited volume *The God That Failed*.[6]

If democracy's opponents have the will and resources to use force, and democracy's defenders do not, we know who will dominate. And yet we confront the reality of a university-educated elite in the United States that does not believe traditional democratic values are worth defending. This is a perennial shortcoming of the academic elite.

In the US and perhaps much of the West, we no longer teach young people about democracy's value and how it rests on open-society values such as free inquiry rather than centralized power strongly "nudging" if not coercing "right" thinking. Indeed, though academia goes to tremendous lengths to deny the reality of what it is doing, universities have, courtesy of an overwhelmingly "progressive" academic administrative class and faculty, significantly ceased to be *academic* institutions committed to the open exchange of competing ideas. They have instead become the guardians of a secular political religion that bears an uncanny resemblance to the radical left ideology of those who condemned capitalism and admired Stalin's brutal excesses before World War II.[7] What are we to make of this?

The importance of free inquiry to democracy is similar to the importance of free speech. Free speech is essential to democracy's success because free and open debate will usually lead to the best options being considered and dangerous and damaging errors being avoided. Moreover, because democracy is a system in which power is supposed to be derived from the people, it relies on knowledgeable citizens who are free

WHY DEMOCRACY REQUIRES FREE INQUIRY   7

to criticize government officials and policies. Parenthetically, this is a key difference between Israel, where citizens can and often do criticize government, and Gaza, where Hamas ruthlessly punishes dissent; yet few if any journalists covering the current conflict have noted that their Gazan interviewees cannot speak freely.

A citizenry cannot be knowledgeable without access to uncensored ideas, data, and opinions. Government should not collaborate with social media giants, for instance, to censor ideas or information it does not want the people to have (as occurred in the lead-up to the 2016 and 2020 presidential elections in the United States). Doing so impinges on not only free speech but also the free inquiry required for the people to have solid knowledge on which to base their opinions and political choices.

You cannot know the answer if you cannot ask the question, or even know which questions are relevant. When questions about decisions and the evidence behind them are censored, citizens no longer have access to knowledge, because free inquiry has been restricted, undermining the credibility and ultimate legitimacy of a political system.

As Haidt points out, there is something unnatural about democracy.[8] We evolved in small tribes in which loyalty to one's own group and leadership increased success in competition with other tribes. Indeed, given their shared history, Russians likely see Ukrainians not as fighting oppression but as disloyal to Russian *authority*, to invoke another of Haidt's moral foundations. Democracy contradicts this natural order since, like science, it rests on *fallibilism*, the idea developed by philosophers dating back to Aristotle but perhaps best captured by Karl Popper in *The Open Society and Its Enemies*.[9]

Fallibilism holds that no person or movement holds a monopoly on truth. All are fallible. Hence, we should not limit the search for truth by killing or marginalizing dissidents, promoting fundamentally ad hominem arguments (a species of fallacy now tremendously popular in higher education), or otherwise imposing standard beliefs. We should hold even knowledge produced by scientific processes as tentative. Yet the present academic environment manifestly does not do this. Much of it has instead become an incubator for what Eric Hoffer called "true believers."[10]

Holding knowledge as tentative and leaders as fallible rather than divine is deeply unnatural—and accordingly contested by fundamentalists of all

8 THE FREE INQUIRY PAPERS

kinds, religious and secular. Much ink has been spilled regarding the cognitive closure in some religious faiths, yet, with a few exceptions,[11] far less work has explored secular fundamentalism on the left of the sort that now dominates US academe. For this, one must consult classic and now largely forgotten works such as Hoffer's *The True Believer* and Crossman's *The God That Failed*.[12] In a revealing essay in the latter, Arthur Koestler recalls giving a 1938 speech on the ongoing Spanish Civil War shortly before he broke with the Communist Party. Koestler's talk

> contained three phrases, deliberately chosen because to normal people they were platitudes, to Communists a declaration of war. The first was: "No movement, party or person can claim the privilege of infallibility." The second was "Appeasing the enemy is as foolish as persecuting the friend who pursues your own aim by a different road." The third was a quotation from Thomas Mann: "A harmful truth is better than a useful lie."
>
> That settled it. When I had finished, the non-Communist half of the audience applauded, the Communist half sat in heavy silence, most of them with folded arms. This was not done by order, but as a spontaneous reaction to those fatal commonplaces. You might as well have told a Nazi audience that all men are born equal regardless of race or creed.[13]

It might be instructive to give a similar speech today before student activists, faculty, and administrators at elite colleges and universities and watch the reactions. Structural leftist fundamentalism is now deeply ingrained in the institutional policies and curricula of most American colleges and universities, but the last thing administrators and faculty want to confront is a candid observation of just what they are doing to subvert the integrity of the institutions for which they have become responsible. Their first instinct, again, is to deny their own project. Doing otherwise would subject them to a dialogue that they at all costs seek to avoid, as becomes obvious in their assertion that any hint of disagreement constitutes "violence."

Academic Priorities Can Clash with Democratic Ones

Like prior versions of Marxism, and indeed like premodern tribal societies, the postmodern approaches common in higher education now resemble fundamentalist religions in three respects. First, they define people primarily as members of groups rather than as individuals. Relatedly, they hold Manichaean approaches to truth, with clear divisions between good and evil thoughts and people. This mindset lends itself to cognitive closure, censorship, and repression.

They also prize theory more than either scientific empirical testing or practical experience.[14] Finally, like Marxism, Hegelianism, and Platonism, and resembling early 20th-century American progressives such as Woodrow Wilson, they harbor a deep-seated distrust of pluralism, the distribution of authority, and a democratic public's judgment.[15]

As Vincent Ostrom details, Wilson advocated centralizing power in the presidency and the bureaucracy, thus overcoming federalism and the constitutional separation of powers, on the theory that bureaucratic experts could best run government.[16] Similarly, postmodernism prioritizes planning by distant ideological or bureaucratic elites, not the more flexible wisdom of direct service providers and communities. Wilsonians,[17] 1970s planners,[18] and postmodern progressives[19] have proved wildly inaccurate (and not a little bit ignorant of history) regarding the ability of intellectual and bureaucratic elites to understand and manage real-world events. It is as though the 1980s collapse of the Soviet economy, with its overwrought emphasis on central planning, never happened.

In addition, academics, both faculty and administrators, are as prone as politicians and the rest of the population to virtue signaling. Virtue signaling is typically used to enhance one's standing in a social group by expressing moral views or opinions prized by that group.[20] Much of the research on virtue signaling has grown out of earlier work on sexual signaling and honest signals, such as fitness in animals in the context of mating.[21]

Just as these physical signals may convey information about being a good mate, signaling shared moral positions conveys allegiance to a group. Unfortunately, there is often a degree of moral hypocrisy, such that people may verbally (or online or via signs on their lawns or vehicles) proclaim their moral positions but not have much follow-through. Driving

10 THE FREE INQUIRY PAPERS

Hummers or flying private jets to climate conferences are common examples of "do what I say and ignore what I do."

In a largely progressive postmodern academic setting, virtue signaling and groupthink mostly silence alternative viewpoints via "cancellation" and sometimes the threat of job loss and reputational damage. Laura Kipnis's experiences with student protests and administrative investigations at Northwestern University over an opinion piece in the *Chronicle of Higher Education* is an excellent illustration of this and can be read in full in her book.[22] The message is clear: No ideas outside the mainstream ideological narrative should be publicly discussed. Those who dare, as Kipnis did in her essay on sexual paranoia on campus and critique of sexual harassment policies, should prepare for student complaints and demands for investigation by often biased administrators. In Kipnis's case, the investigations resulted in Northwestern eventually exonerating her. Yet the Obama (and then Biden) Department of Education's embrace of "subjective" standards for sexual harassment make such official harassment common, as Melnick details.[23]

The academic establishment's priorities sharply contrast with democratic systems as we know them. Democracy assumes that no one entity, whether a party as in Koestler's day or bureaucratic rule makers, as often happens in our day, holds a monopoly on truth or wisdom.[24] Thus, democracy requires free-flowing ideas, with different policies introduced in the provision of government services and then tested when put before voters. Democracy requires a commitment to policy flexibility rather than policy rigidity, with input from citizens and policymakers periodically reevaluating what they have done rather than, as bureaucracies often do, reflexively defending existing practice.[25]

In the academic world, this commitment to openness is embodied in "academic freedom," a concept now considered quaint and outmoded by an academic bureaucracy that is deterred from its authoritarian impulses only by its frequent losses in the courts. A recent example can be seen in the overturning of the termination of an award-winning associate professor of psychology at the University of Central Florida. Charles Negy dared to tweet an opinion that didn't fit the current narrative, one about "black privilege." As a result, he faced a Twitter mob demanding his termination. The university's president immediately denounced Negy and launched an investigation designed to justify firing him. The arbiter begged to differ with the investigation and the president, ruling in Negy's favor, and he was reinstated, but only after suffering a painful two-year process. The university president paid no such toll, continuing to enjoy his $525,000 annual salary undisturbed.[26]

Instead of democratic sensibilities, we have witnessed a growing commitment to rigid fundamentalism and the proposition that there is only one acceptable definition of truth or reality, particularly when it comes to social policy questions. Such fundamentalism is *by definition* inimical to intellectual diversity or the free exchange of ideas. It is not only authoritarian but also thuggishly anti-intellectual. In the long run, it impedes change rather than promoting it.

Elite Politics, Suppression of Free Inquiry, and the Collapse of Democracy

In Britain, parliamentary democracy with periodic national elections practically assures change—sometimes too much of it—guaranteeing that dominant groups sometimes lose and subordinate groups and individuals sometimes work their way into power. Political change from parliamentary elections sometimes reflects ideology but also, as in the US, reflects perceived performance, with matters such as inflation, unemployment, and foreign policy success affecting the ability of incumbent parties to retain power. In the same way that economic markets send signals about what goods are desired,[27] political markets can send signals about what public policies are needed, with elections and bargaining playing key roles in translating perceived needs to policy.

These processes of change are thus central to how democracy operates in the UK and the US.[28] But, as we have argued, change requires more than one set of voices. It requires *intellectual diversity* of the sort that dies when public discourse is monopolized by privileged elites, movements with only a single overarching agenda, or political forces that justify ideational coercion in the service of "social justice."

Peter Turchin's structural-demographic analysis of American history highlights the role played by elites (and particularly the overproduction of elites, much of it now fueled by universities) as an increasing number of aspiring elites compete for the limited supply of elite positions of power.[29] Increased competition among elites leads to the formation and intensification of rival networks of allies (or political coalitions) vying for the rewards of state service.

The result is a divided elite class characterized by substantial rivalries and increasingly isolated factions that can no longer work together. Turchin details how this process leads to sociopolitical instability as the population at large picks a faction or seeks a new system entirely, as during the French Revolution. Elite expansion, seen in increasing numbers of elites and their increasing incomes, is one of the most reliable predictors of state collapse and high political instability.[30]

Turchin highlights three conditions that can lead to the end of democracy and civilizations more generally.[31] The first is the previously mentioned problem of the elites—in particular the bloated elite classes experiencing increased competition for limited elite positions. The second is declining living standards for the population in general (the non-elites). The third is state insolvency, in which the government can't cover its financial debts and its reckless spending and borrowing lead to high inflation and other economic woes.

Does this sound familiar? The typical response of the elites (whether ideological or economic elites) is to try to pacify the people with handouts, and when those run out, suppression of dissent is sure to follow. Can our democratic system avoid this path? Not without free inquiry and the ability to recognize problems, ask tough questions, and do the research to get an array of answers.

Despite their well-recognized flaws, the US founders set up systems in which the relatively powerless could seek change, and sometimes obtain it, due to the limitations and fragmentation of state power.[32] Particularly in *Federalist* 10, James Madison advocated a large and thus socially and economically diverse republic so that no one faction could attain a sufficient majority to oppress others. The separation of powers advocated in Madison's *Federalist* 51, assuring multiple access points for a range of interests, also limits coercion, reinforcing this flexibility and making bargaining and compromise central to policymaking.[33]

This understanding of pluralism (including ideological pluralism) as key to US government, contrasting with many foreign governments, became American elites' central value by the 1950s.[34] Later, in the post–Cold War period, "exporting democracy" (often through ill-advised policies of "regime change") became an explicit goal of US foreign policy, if not always a priority.[35] On the state and local levels, limited government and decentralization allowed for local experimentation, often reflecting local values while fostering multiculturalism. More successful innovations were (and are) copied widely, if unevenly. This was in sharp contrast to centralized systems, which empower "experts" whose value is often exaggerated and who are all too willing to take power away from a democratic public.[36]

Perhaps nowhere is this tension more pronounced than in raising and educating children, with some educational and political elites now calling for a presumption that centralized bureaucracies rather than parents and local teachers should have dominant authority regarding education. Indeed, respected experts and public intellectuals like Harvard Law Professor Elizabeth Bartholet now call for presumptive bans on home education and school choice generally,[37] which sharply contrasts with evidence that education experts are in fact highly inexpert[38] and contradicts long-standing US legal and social norms empowering families and private schools with rights protecting some degree of autonomy.[39] In most cases, these arguments involve not only a defense of "expertise" but also an insistence that children be inculcated with particular ideological dispositions, often in disregard of constitutional protections of speech and conscience.

Indeed, one of the hallmarks of the contemporary academic left, in addition to its intolerance, is its increasingly anti-constitutional temper. We have no doubt that many academic colleagues on the left would echo the sentiment expressed on a popular television show by Elie Mystal, a legal correspondent for *The Nation*, that the US Constitution is (to quote Mystal) "kind of trash," since it was crafted by white male slave owners with no input from black slaves, Indigenous people, or women.[40]

Christopher Caldwell reminds us of the world that was lost with the rise of political correctness, "principled" intolerance, and the new anti-constitutional temper:

14 THE FREE INQUIRY PAPERS

Traditionally there had been expressive freedom in the United States. "Free speech, free press, free exercise of religion are placed separate and apart," wrote Supreme Court justice William O. Douglas. "They are above and beyond the police power; they are not subject to regulation in the manner of factories, slums, apartment houses, production of oil and the like." This conception of First Amendment freedoms was being eroded.[41]

Douglas was articulating his dissent in *Beauharnais v. Illinois*, in which the Supreme Court *upheld* an Illinois law making it illegal to publish or otherwise express "depravity, criminality, unchastity, or lack of virtue of a class of citizens of any race, color, creed or religion."[42] It sounds strange today to hear a lion of the progressive left such as Douglas adhering to such an absolutist stance on the First Amendment and free speech.

Threats to Democracy, Free Speech, and Inquiry in the West

We see three key, understated threats to democracy in the West related to free speech and inquiry. First, as Eric Kaufmann details, if cultural elites who dominate academia, media, and government bureaucracies decree that some policies are "sacred," and thus not amenable to questioning, voters are alienated, particularly when those sacred policies contradict mass values, have significant costs, and violate long-agreed-on political rules of the road.[43]

Given broader democratic traditions,[44] Kaufmann argues that when academic, media, and political elites prevent policy debates from reaching the political agenda, the result is democratic failure. As Turchin argues, the elites' divisiveness as they jockey for power and social position also contributes to sociopolitical instability and puts democracy at risk.[45] Thus, Kaufmann points out that, in the US, whites and minorities largely agree on matters such as modifying affirmative action and maintaining strong national borders, yet, ironically, elites denounce such ideas as "racist," keeping them off the political agenda.

In response, populist political entrepreneurs like Donald Trump have arisen to meet public demands, with similar dynamics occurring in Europe

WHY DEMOCRACY REQUIRES FREE INQUIRY 15

and Latin America. Witness the 2016 Brexit vote and the rise of Fidesz and Viktor Orbán in Hungary, Prime Minister Giorgia Meloni's Brothers of Italy party, Nayib Bukele in El Salvador, Javier Milei in Argentina, and—earlier—Jair Bolsonaro in Brazil. More recently, the June 2024 European Parliament elections resulted in significant gains for moderate conservatives and the populist euroskeptic right, with the moderate conservative European People's Party gaining 14 seats to become the biggest single bloc (a total of 190 seats) and the right-wing European Conservatives and Reformists (a seven-seat gain, to 76) and Identity and Democracy (a nine-seat gain, to 58) both benefiting from the shift in European popular sentiment. The results sufficiently distressed French President Emmanuel Macron that he called for a snap parliamentary election, while in Germany, Olaf Scholz's Social Democrats registered a historically poor showing.[46]

The success of conservative and euroskeptic or nationalist parties was attributed to four factors: inflation (the rise in the cost of living), concerns about illegal migration, the cost of the "green transition," and the war in Ukraine.[47] Before the June 6–9 election, it had become increasingly clear that popular European concerns did not necessarily coincide with those of the European Union's political elite and that popular anxieties were sometimes best distilled in the agendas of conservative, nationalist, euroskeptic, and populist movements. While Kaufmann generally favors such movements, William A. Galston, Cas Mudde and Cristóbal Rovira Kaltwasser, and others fear that populism could itself undermine democracy by weakening democratic institutions.[48]

Of course, if those institutions limit policy debate, arguably they have undermined their own legitimacy, making populist attacks predictable and even useful (so long as they are nonviolent). When higher education and aligned bureaucracies impose policies that not only align with their sacred values (and budgets) but fail in practice for decades, and then they marginalize or terminate dissenters, they undermine legitimacy and fuel populist attacks on traditional institutions.

Second, virtue signaling shuts down free speech and free inquiry by shaping a culture, currently facilitated by social media, in which people who express a differing opinion—the *wrong* opinion—are the targets of attempts to censor, cancel, or otherwise ostracize. As Geoffrey Miller wrote in his book *Virtue Signaling: Essays on Darwinian Politics & Free Speech*,

16 THE FREE INQUIRY PAPERS

> It drives social justice warriors to take over media, academia, and corporate life, and to impose their ideology of "diversity, equity, and inclusion" on everyone through enforced conformity of thought, inequity in hiring and promotion, and exclusion of heterodox thinkers from any positions of power or influence.[49]

Vivek Ramaswamy has written about the impact this movement has had in the corporate world,[50] and it can be seen every day on multiple social media platforms, including Twitter (now X). Users have been called out for virtue signaling, and the platform itself has been accused of censoring certain tweets that deviate from the accepted ideological view. If people are not free to discuss controversial topics in which the data are not conclusive, they can hardly be the informed citizenry needed for democracy to be successful.

Virtue signaling can be absurdly misleading, as when one-sided anti-Israeli activism on university campuses criticizes Israel's human rights record while ignoring the bloody record of the country's enemies. It can also be self-defeating, as when university trustees and administrators insist on divesting in certain industries for environment, social, and governance reasons that are not guided by any true concern for an institution's financial health.

Third, most governance happens far below the elite level of media attention and debate, such as in bureaucracies, public education, and higher education.[51] John McWhorter argues that for decades, education "experts" have imposed on US public school systems methods of teaching reading that have cemented rather than closed achievement gaps, assuring high levels of social inequity.[52] E. D. Hirsch and, separately, Robert Maranto and Jonathan Wai portray this as part of a larger pattern of academia that encourages education bureaucracies to impose practices that undermine academic achievement and then exiles the critics of such policies.[53]

For example, as the research summary by Musa al-Gharbi shows, diversity training does not work, or at least not in the forms that currently exist.[54] R. Shep Melnick details the same dynamic regarding bureaucratically imposed sex- and gender-related policies in K–12 and higher education.[55] Yet routinely, those in higher education who question such practices face isolation or termination.[56] Even as we write this, there is a legal dispute over the University of North Texas's decision to terminate a faculty member who questioned the concept of "microaggressions," even though considerable evidence calls into questions that concept's usefulness.[57] As Chapters 4 and 10 show, such legal disputes have now become common, and intolerant institutions often find themselves on the losing side.

If we terminate those who point out policy failure, how can academia and democracy function? Quite simply, democracy cannot work without flexibility, bargaining, and the ability to revise and even repeal existing policies. If cultural elites, the academic establishment, or bureaucratic "experts" make large policy areas sacred, beyond question, democracy cannot endure. The *Washington Post* adopted the slogan "Democracy Dies in Darkness," but Bill Maher also recently pointed out that "Democracy Dies in Dumbness" when cancel culture shuts down not only free speech but also the free inquiry required for a knowledgeable citizenry.[58]

Notes

1. Jonathan Haidt and Greg Lukianoff, "Why It's a Bad Idea to Tell Students Words Are Violence," *The Atlantic*, July 18, 2017, https://www.theatlantic.com/education/archive/2017/07/why-its-a-bad-idea-to-tell-students-words-are-violence/533970.

2. Friedrich Nietzsche, *Human, All Too Human: A Book for Free Spirits*, trans. R. J. Hollingdale (Cambridge, UK: Cambridge University Press, 1996), 179.

3. Jonathan Haidt, *The Righteous Mind: Why Good People Are Divided by Politics and Religion* (New York: Pantheon, 2012).

4. Bradley Campbell and Jason Manning, *The Rise of Victimhood Culture: Microaggressions, Safe Spaces, and the New Culture Wars* (New York: Palgrave McMillan, 2018), 265; and R. Shep Melnick, *The Transformation of Title IX* (Washington, DC: Brookings Institution, 2018).

5. Haidt and Lukianoff, "Why It's a Bad Idea to Tell Students Words Are Violence."

6. Richard H. Crossman, ed., *The God That Failed* (New York: Harper & Brothers, 1949; New York: Columbia University Press, 2001).

7. Crossman, *The God That Failed.*

8. Haidt, *The Righteous Mind.*

9. Karl R. Popper, *The Open Society and Its Enemies* (London: Routledge, 1945).

10. Eric Hoffer, *The True Believer* (New York: Harper & Brothers, 1951).

11. John McWhorter, *Woke Racism: How a New Religion Has Betrayed Black America* (New York: Portfolio, 2021); Helen Pluckrose and James Lindsay, *Cynical Theories: How Activist Scholarship Made Everything About Race, Gender, and Identity—and Why*

This Harms Everybody (Durham, NC: Pitchstone Publishing, 2020); and Ilana Redstone and John Villasenor, *Unassailable Ideas: How Unwritten Rules and Social Media Shape Discourse in American Higher Education* (New York: Oxford University Press, 2020).

12. Hoffer, *The True Believer*; and Crossman, *The God That Failed.*

13. Arthur Koestler, untitled essay in Crossman, *The God That Failed,* 15–75.

14. McWhorter, *Woke Racism*; and Pluckrose and Lindsay, *Cynical Theories.*

15. Popper, *The Open Society and Its Enemies.*

16. Vincent Ostrom, *The Intellectual Crisis in American Public Administration* (Tuscaloosa, AL: University of Alabama Press, 1974).

17. Robert Maranto and Jonathan Wai, "Why Intelligence Is Missing from American Education Policy and Practice, and What Can Be Done About It," *Journal of Intelligence* 8, no. 1 (January 2020), https://www.mdpi.com/2079-3200/8/1/2.

18. Charles E. Lindblom and David K. Cohen, *Usable Knowledge: Social Science and Social Problem Solving* (New Haven, CT: Yale University Press, 1979); and Theodore J. Lowi, *The End of Liberalism: The Second Republic of the United States,* 2nd ed. (New York: Norton, 1979).

19. Melnick, *The Transformation of Title IX.*

20. Marc Orlitzky, "Virtue Signaling: Oversocialized 'Integrity' in a Politically Correct World," in *Integrity in Business and Management,* ed. Marc Orlitzky and Manjit Monga (New York: Routledge, 2017), 172–87; and Geoffrey Miller, *Virtue Signaling: Essays on Darwinian Politics & Free Speech* (Las Vegas, NV: Cambrian Moon, 2019).

21. Amotz Zahavi and Avishag Zahavi, *The Handicap Principle: A Missing Piece of Darwin's Puzzle* (New York: Oxford University Press, 1999).

22. Laura Kipnis, *Unwanted Advances: Sexual Paranoia Comes to Campus* (New York: HarperCollins, 2017).

23. Melnick, *The Transformation of Title IX.*

24. Lowi, *The End of Liberalism*; and Melnick, *The Transformation of Title IX.*

25. Lindblom and Cohen, *Usable Knowledge.*

26. Robert Maranto, Catherine Salmon, and Lee Jussim, "Cut Their Pay and Make Them Teach," RealClearEducation, June 9, 2022, https://www.realcleareducation.com/articles/2022/06/09/cut_their_pay_and_make_them_teach_110737.html.

27. Milton Friedman, *Capitalism and Freedom* (Chicago: University of Chicago Press, 1962).

28. Bernard Crick, *In Defense of Politics* (Chicago: University of Chicago Press, 1982); and James Q. Wilson and John J. Dilulio, *American Government,* 9th ed. (Boston, MA: Houghton Mifflin, 2004).

29. Peter Turchin, *Ages of Discord: A Structural-Demographic Analysis of American History* (Chaplin, CT: Beresta Books, 2016).

30. Peter Turchin and Sergey A. Nefedov, *Secular Cycles* (Princeton, NJ: Princeton University Press, 2009).

31. Turchin, *Ages of Discord.*

32. Peter Turchin and Sergey A. Nefedov, *Secular Cycles* (Princeton, NJ: Princeton University Press, 2009); and Jill Lepore, *This America: The Case for the Nation* (New York: Liveright, 2019).

33. Clinton Rossiter, ed., *The Federalist Papers* (New York: Signet Classics, 1961).

WHY DEMOCRACY REQUIRES FREE INQUIRY 19

34. David B. Truman, *The Governmental Process: Political Interests and Public Opinion* (New York: Alfred A. Knopf, 1951).

35. Stephen M. Walt, *The Hell of Good Intentions: America's Foreign Policy Elite and the Decline of U.S. Primacy* (New York: Farrar, Straus and Giroux, 2018); John J. Mearsheimer, *The Great Delusion: Liberal Dreams and International Realities* (New Haven, CT: Yale University Press, 2019); and for a positive view, Joshua Muravchik, *Exporting Democracy: Fulfilling America's Destiny* (Washington, DC: AEI Press, 1991).

36. Philip E. Tetlock, *Expert Political Judgment: How Good Is It? How Can We Know?* (Princeton, NJ: Princeton University Press, 2017); and Ostrom, *The Intellectual Crisis in American Public Administration.*

37. Elizabeth Bartholet, "Homeschooling: Parent Rights Absolutism vs. Child Rights to Education & Protection," *Arizona Law Review* 62, no. 1 (2020): 1–80, https://arizonalawreview.org/homeschooling-parent-rights-absolutism-vs-child-rights-to-education-protection.

38. Maranto and Wai, "Why Intelligence Is Missing from American Education Policy and Practice, and What Can Be Done About It."

39. Robert Maranto, "Between Elitism and Populism: A Case for Pluralism in Schooling and Homeschooling," *Journal of School Choice* 15, no. 1 (2021): 113–38, https://eric.ed.gov/?id=EJ1292468.

40. Andi Ortiz, "'The View': The Nation's Elie Mystal Calls US Constitution 'Kind of Trash' Since 'Slavers' Wrote It (Video)," The Wrap, March 4, 2022, https://www.thewrap.com/the-view-constitution-trash-elie-mystal-video.

41. Christopher Caldwell, *The Age of Entitlement: America Since the Sixties* (New York: Simon & Schuster, 2020), 158.

42. *Beauharnais v. Illinois*, 343 US 250 (1952).

43. Eric Kaufmann, *Whiteshift: Populism, Immigration, and the Future of White Majorities* (New York: Abrams Press, 2019).

44. Crick, *In Defense of Politics*; and Wilson and Dilulio, *American Government.*

45. Turchin, *Ages of Discord.*

46. See Jan Strupczewski, Sudip Kar-Gupta, and Ingrid Melander, "Far-Right Advances in EU Election, France Calls Snap National Vote," *Reuters*, June 10, 2024, https://www.reuters.com/world/europe/european-parliament-poised-rightward-shift-after-final-voting-2024-06-09.

47. Strupczewski, Kar-Gupta, and Melander, "Far-Right Advances in EU Election."

48. William A. Galston, *Anti-Pluralism: The Populist Threat to Liberal Democracy* (New Haven, CT: Yale University Press, 2018); and Cas Mudde and Cristóbal Rovira Kaltwasser, *Populism: A Very Short Introduction* (New York: Oxford University Press, 2017).

49. Miller, *Virtue Signaling.*

50. Vivek Ramaswamy, *Woke, Inc.: Inside Corporate America's Social Justice Scam* (London: Hatchett UK, 2021).

51. Lowi, *The End of Liberalism*; Jonathan Haidt and Greg Lukianoff, *The Coddling of the American Mind: How Good Intentions and Bad Ideas Are Setting Up a Generation for Failure* (New York: Penguin Press, 2018); and Melnick, *The Transformation of Title IX.*

52. McWhorter, *Woke Racism.*

20 THE FREE INQUIRY PAPERS

53. E. D. Hirsch, *The Schools We Need and Why We Don't Have Them* (New York: Doubleday, 1996); and Maranto and Wai, "Why Intelligence Is Missing from American Education Policy and Practice, and What Can Be Done About It."

54. Musa al-Gharbi, "Diversity Is Important. Diversity-Related Training Is Terrible.," Minding the Campus, November 6, 2020, https://www.mindingthecampus.org/2020/11/06/diversity-is-important-diversity-related-training-is-terrible.

55. Melnick, *The Transformation of Title IX.*

56. McWhorter, *Woke Racism.*

57. Craig L. Frisby and Robert Maranto, eds., *Social Justice Versus Social Science: White Fragility, Implicit Bias, and Diversity Training* (New York: National Association of Scholars, 2024).

58. Real Time with Bill Maher, "New Rule: Democracy Dies in Dumbness | Real Time with Bill Maher (HBO)," YouTube, June 17, 2022, https://www.youtube.com/watch?v=5tu9JGK_yH0.

3

Why Free Speech?

Jonathan Zimmerman

Why is free speech under fire on American campuses? And why should we care about it, anyway?

A few years ago, I invited Mary Beth Tinker to speak at my undergraduate course on the history of American education. Tinker is an important historical figure in her own right: She was one of several students at Warren Harding Junior High School who wore black armbands to school in Des Moines, Iowa, in 1965 to protest America's involvement in the Vietnam War. Sent home from eighth grade as a punishment, she sued her school district on First Amendment grounds. *Tinker v. Des Moines* wound its way up to the Supreme Court, which ruled in her favor in 1969. In a ringing decision, the Court declared that neither students nor teachers "shed their constitutional rights to freedom of speech or expression at the schoolhouse gate."[1]

My students loved Tinker's story, and who doesn't? Adorable 13-year-old confronts Big Bad Authority. Adorable 13-year-old wins. Cut to the credits.

But when our class discussion turned to the present, the mood changed. Students insisted that schools and universities should prohibit hate speech, which hurts innocent people. Tinker was fighting the good fight against the war in Vietnam. But racists, sexists, homophobes, and transphobes are different, my students said. They cause harm, offense, and even trauma in their victims. We need to shut them down.

Tinker wasn't having it. At her middle school in Des Moines, she said, there were students who had fathers, uncles, and brothers who were fighting in Southeast Asia. Don't you think they were offended and hurt by a snotty-nosed kid whose armband suggested that their loved ones were risking their lives for a lie?

Of course they were. Speech hurts, which is why censors across time have tried to stamp it out. So if you're going to prohibit speech that hurts someone, well, forget about Tinker's armband. Forget about free speech. Period.

My students took this in, and then they tried another tack. Wasn't free speech really just a tool of the powerful? That's why white men like it so much, of course. It lets them have their say, while it harms (there's that word again) people with less status and influence in society.

Tinker wasn't having that either. In 1965, she told the class, she was a 13-year-old girl. Free speech was the only power she had! Take that away, and she would have nothing at all.

Indeed, free speech powered every great movement against oppression and injustice in American history. My students have been socialized to view free speech as hateful or at least as "conservative"—something that helps people at the top maintain their power and privilege. That's exactly backward. And it's why we need to look at history, which can remind us about the radical purpose and potential of free speech.

Let's start with American anti-war resistance, which is as old as America itself. From the struggle with France over seafaring in the 1790s to the conflict in Vietnam, anti-war activism has been heavily censored. Tinker was hardly the first dissident to condemn US military policies and practices. But her generation was the first to win the legal right to do so.

The most famous free speech case in the United States involved a socialist, Charles Schenck, who was arrested during World War I for distributing pamphlets that urged men to resist conscription. In a 1919 Supreme Court decision, Oliver Wendell Holmes declared that Schenck's speech was tantamount to falsely shouting "fire" in a crowded theater; it posed a "clear and present danger" to the nation, Holmes wrote, so it should not be permitted.[2] He would soon come to regret that ruling, which could be used to muzzle any kind of speech that government authorities declared dangerous.

Indeed, a few months later, the Court upheld the jailing of radicals who had distributed leaflets condemning the American military intervention in Russia and other efforts to impede the Bolshevik Revolution. This time, Holmes took the side of free speech: The leaflets were written in Yiddish, he argued, and they presented no significant obstacle to the American war effort. Instead, the real danger lay in efforts to suppress them. "Persecution for the expression of opinions seems to me perfectly logical," Holmes

WHY FREE SPEECH? 23

warned, dissenting from the Court's decision. "If you have no doubt of your premises or your power and want a certain result with all your heart you naturally express your wishes in law and sweep away all opposition."[3] All of us have a will to censor, in short, which is precisely why we need to resist the temptation.

Holmes is venerated for this opinion today, so it's easy to forget that it remained a minority one for a half century. During World War II and the Cold War, thousands of American teachers, civil servants, and other citizens were harassed, hounded out of their jobs, or imprisoned for prior or current affiliations with the Communist Party.[4] The justification was the same one that censors always use: There's a war going on, and we can't let anyone on our side play for the other team.

Only in 1957 would the Supreme Court strike down the laws banning Communist organizational activity. And it wasn't until the early 1970s that the Court fully protected anti-war expression. Two years after it allowed Tinker's armband protest, it overturned the arrest of a 19-year-old man for walking into a courthouse wearing a jacket that bore the words "Fuck the Draft."[5]

It's easy to forget how recently you could be jailed for simply speaking your mind about America's foreign entanglements. Thanks to the courage and sacrifice of the free speech warriors who came before us, we can finally criticize our wars—and the government that conducts them—without fear of punishment or retribution.

We can also denounce racial and sexual oppression, which likewise has relied on fear and suppression to sustain itself. The first mass censorship campaign in American history was engineered by slaveholders in the South, who sought to ban abolitionist literature from the US mail and even the floor of Congress following Nat Turner's rebellion in 1831.[6] That's why antislavery activists were also ironclad supporters of free speech.

The great African American abolitionist Frederick Douglass called free speech "the great moral renovator of society," because nobody could challenge slavery if their tongues were silenced.[7] "Liberty is meaningless where the right to utter one's thoughts and opinions has ceased to exist," Douglass told a Boston audience in 1860, on the eve of the Civil War. "There can be no right of speech where any man . . . is overawed by force, and compelled to suppress his honest sentiments."[8] Douglass wanted America to hear *his* honest sentiments: that slavery was a moral and political abomination, a violation of the nation's best ideals, and a sin before God. And nobody would hear him unless he had freedom of speech.

Campaigns demanding suffrage rights and birth control for women also suffered enormous repression and censorship. Before women won the right to vote in 1920, government officials shut down suffragist protests or looked the other way when mobs threw lit cigars and apple cores at protesters. Likewise, Planned Parenthood foremother Margaret Sanger was indicted on four counts of obscenity for publishing information on contraception.

Sanger fled the US in 1914 for England and returned a year later, after the charges were dropped. But she continued to face threats to her freedom of speech, which made her an international cause célèbre and—ironically—helped popularize the birth control cause. (Planned Parenthood has recently distanced itself from Sanger, who invoked eugenic arguments for birth control: It would reduce the number of non-white babies.) When police tried to shut down a scheduled 1921 address by Sanger at New York City's town hall, the crowd lifted her onto the stage while chanting, "Defy them!" Two officers grabbed her arms and pulled her out of the hall, as the crowd broke into a chorus of "My Country 'Tis of Thee." The next morning, newspaper accounts of the imbroglio placed "birth control"—a formerly tabooed term—in bold headlines.[9]

An even stronger taboo was attached to gay and lesbian Americans, who were routinely harassed, brutalized, and jailed because of their sexual orientation. Their underground newspapers and magazines were banned from the US mail on the same grounds as the censorship of Sanger: They were ruled obscene. In the 1950s, federal authorities confiscated one magazine for printing a short story about a lesbian relationship; they also seized copies of a bodybuilding magazine because it was popular among male homosexual readers. But the Supreme Court intervened, declaring that authorities had violated the free speech rights of gay-themed publishers.[10] That was a boon for America's LGBT communities, which used their newfound First Amendment freedoms to demand the other rights they'd been denied for so long.

WHY FREE SPEECH? 25

It's simply impossible to imagine the movements to legalize same-sex love—and, ultimately, same-sex marriage—without the right to free speech. It was the precondition for every other form of progress.

And so it remains. If you want to make America more just, more equitable, or more peaceful—more *anything*—you need free speech.

Have Americans used free speech to inject hate into the public sphere? Of course they have. At the January 2021 insurrection at the Capitol, for example, some protesters wore Nazi and Confederate regalia. But the answer to hateful speakers is to raise your voice against them, which is a vital exercise of free speech in its own right. Trying to muzzle them will simply make them martyrs, providing precisely the publicity they crave. And whatever restrictions you establish to silence them will eventually be used to silence others—or, maybe, you.

Witness the now-famous 1987 speech code at the University of Michigan, which barred "any behavior, verbal or physical, that stigmatizes or victimizes an individual on the basis of race, ethnicity, religion, sex, sexual orientation, creed, national origin, ancestry, age, marital status, handicap or Vietnam-era veteran status."[11] Sounds good, right? Wrong. Over the next 18 months, whites charged blacks with violating the code in over 20 cases. One African American student was punished for using the term "white trash."[12] I wouldn't call that racist, myself, but that's the whole point: We disagree about what constitutes offensive or hateful speech. And once you concede that any set of ideas should be banned as too harmful to say or hear, the people with the most power can impose their ideas on you.

Consider the recent spate of bills Republican-led state legislatures proposed to limit critical race theory, the 1619 Project, and other instruction about racism and sexism. Of the five states that had passed such measures by the end of June 2021, four barred lessons that would give rise to "discomfort, guilt, anguish, or any other form of psychological or emotional distress on account of that individual's race or sex."[13] Try holding a full and honest classroom discussion on those terms! You can't. There are many legitimate grounds for criticizing the 1619 Project, which has drawn fire from some historians for distorting the past. But it should be debated on its scholarly merits—whether it is accurate, reasonable, and persuasive—rather than whether it might make someone feel bad.

In the guise of protecting students' psychological health, these state measures effectively put difficult parts of our past and present—especially slavery and white supremacy—out of bounds. Will addressing the Tulsa Race Massacre of 1921 or contemporary police brutality cause feelings of guilt and anguish in students? It's hard to know, so K–12 teachers will avoid or downplay these topics. It's too risky. Happy faces only, please.

Over the past few years, colleges and universities have employed the same logic to exact penalties for discomfiting speech. The speech codes of the 1980s have mostly melted away, but new forms of restriction have arisen in their place. Dozens of institutions have promulgated lists of tabooed microaggressions, defined as small and often unintended slights that nevertheless take a lasting psychological toll on their targets. The results have been predictable: People are biting their tongues, if they know what's good for them.

Similarly, students have demanded that professors issue trigger warnings for sensitive course content that could harm listeners. At the University of Southern California, most notoriously, Professor Greg Patton was removed from his course in 2020 for using a Chinese term that sounded like the N-word in English. "Our mental health has been affected," a group of Patton's students complained in a letter to their dean. "We would rather not take his course than to endure the emotional exhaustion of carrying on with an instructor that disregards cultural diversity and sensitivities and by extension creates an unwelcome environment."[14]

Tinker couldn't have put it better herself: Speech hurts. But if my liberal colleagues continue to restrict it on those grounds, they won't have a leg to stand on when GOP lawmakers do the same thing. We need to let everyone speak their minds, no matter what feelings might be provoked. Period. The alternative is a land of dueling grievances, in which we all try to silence each other because of the alleged injuries we have suffered. That's not a country I care to live in. And I'm guessing it's not one you care to live in either.

Why free speech? Because it lets the least among us have their say. Because it's the only way to fight all the injustices and inequities that continue to mar America. And because we are stronger than the censors think we are. Speech hurts, but we can handle it.

Let free speech ring! Anything less will diminish us all.

Notes

1. *Tinker v. Des Moines Independent Community School District*, 393 US 503 (1969).

2. *Schenck v. United States*, 249 US 47 (1919).

3. *Abrams v. United States*, 250 US 616 (1919).

4. Ellen Schrecker, "Blacklists and Other Economic Sanctions," in *The Age of McCarthyism: A Brief History with Documents* (Boston, MA: St. Martin's Press, 1994), https://writing.upenn.edu/~afilreis/50s/schrecker-blacklist.html.

5. *Cohen v. California*, 403 US 15 (1971).

6. Michael Curtis, *Free Speech, "The People's Darling Privilege": Struggles for Freedom of Expression in American History* (Durham, NC: Duke University Press, 2000).

7. Frederick Douglass, "A Plea for Free Speech in Boston (1860)," National Constitution Center, https://constitutioncenter.org/the-constitution/historic-document-library/detail/frederick-douglass-a-plea-for-free-speech-in-boston-1860.

8. Douglass, "A Plea for Free Speech in Boston (1860)."

9. Peter C. Engelman, *A History of the Birth Control Movement in America* (Santa Barbara, CA: Praeger, 2011), 125.

10. Carlos A. Ball, *The First Amendment and LGBT Equality: A Contentious History* (Cambridge, MA: Harvard University Press, 2017), 15–16.

11. *Doe v. University of Michigan*, 721 F. Supp. 852 (1989).

12. American Civil Liberties Union, "Speech on Campus," December 18, 2023, https://www.aclu.org/documents/speech-campus.

13. PEN America, "Joint Statement on Legislative Efforts to Restrict Education About Racism and American History," June 16, 2021, https://pen.org/joint-statement-legislative-efforts-restrict-education-racism-american-history.

14. Conor Friedersdorf, "The Fight Against Words That Sound Like, but Are Not, Slurs," *The Atlantic*, September 21, 2020, https://www.theatlantic.com/ideas/archive/2020/09/fight-against-words-sound-like-are-not-slurs/616404.

4

Why Social Justice Requires Free Inquiry

Akeela Careem and Lee Jussim

Universities have long been a bastion of free and open academic inquiry and discourse. Recently, however, an increasing number of attacks on free inquiry and free speech have occurred on university campuses nationwide. These attacks come from multiple directions, including both sides of the political spectrum and within academia itself. What is especially disturbing is that many of these attacks are carried out in the name of social justice.

Books have been removed from libraries, schools, and university campuses because they are considered offensive or harmful.[1] Politicians and state governments are seeking to ban the discussion and teaching of topics like critical race theory, institutionalized racism, and ideas deemed to be "divisive" in K–12 schools and, in some cases, even universities.[2] Controversial speakers are being shut down on university campuses before they even have a chance to share their ideas.[3] Research papers have been retracted, not because of issues with the data or conclusions, but because academic outrage mobs have decided that certain ideas should not be studied or discussed.[4] Many academics are increasingly finding themselves afraid to speak up about difficult topics or even conduct research on these topics for fear of being censured, "canceled," or, even worse, fired.[5]

In the first part of this chapter, we review some of the justifications social justice advocates have presented for limiting free inquiry. In the second part, we review history, social science evidence, and current events to argue that those attempts to limit free inquiry are misguided and that social justice does in fact require free inquiry.

A Note on Free Expression, Free Speech, Free Inquiry, and Academic Freedom

The terms "free expression," "free speech," "free inquiry," and "academic freedom" are distinct, yet related, concepts. These terms are often used interchangeably, but it is worth taking a moment to clarify how they differ.

Free expression includes not only free speech but other forms of expression such as works of art, flag-waving, flag burning, book burning, and hanging in effigy. When we refer to free expression, we adopt a modified version of Sean T. Stevens, Lee Jussim, and Nathan Honeycutt's definition: "the refusal to allow individual expression or thought to be controlled, without consent, by an external authority"[6]—(to which we add) *or any person or group with the potential power to suppress it*. An external authority generally refers to *a specific, single authority* (such as a government official or academic administrator). We add "any person or group with the potential power to suppress it" to include pressure groups and even mobs. The "heckler's veto"—when a mob prevents some speech or discussion from taking place through threats, harassment, and violence—is a well-known example of a large group exerting power to suppress expression.

People often seem to believe that free speech refers only to legally protected speech, but this is not the perspective taken here. Although the government is one possible external authority that might restrict speech, there are, potentially, many others (e.g., employers, media executives and editors, and professional organizations). Although there may be no laws preventing one's employer from prohibiting certain types of speech, such prohibitions nonetheless constitute an attempt to control speech and expression by an authority external to the person or group wishing to engage in that speech or expression.

We use the term "free inquiry" to refer to the ability to explore, study, or investigate any topic without fear of being punished by some external authority. As such, it is a subset of free expression and can apply to anyone.

Finally, "academic freedom" refers to protections that apply to scholars at academic institutions and grants "scholars the freedom to research, teach, or communicate facts or ideas without fear of suppression or censure, job loss, or imprisonment."[7] The concepts of academic freedom and

30 THE FREE INQUIRY PAPERS

free inquiry are essential to academia because they allow scholars to pursue their work without fear of retaliation and without outside suppression.

The Social Justice Case Against Free Inquiry

Social justice advocates rarely argue explicitly against free inquiry. Instead, they often make statements such as "free speech and academic freedom are important, *but*," followed by arguments framed in socially benevolent terms calling for restrictions. For example, a recent editorial in *Nature Human Behaviour* began, "Although academic freedom is fundamental, it is not unbounded," and then later it declared, "There is a fine balance between academic freedom and the protection of the dignity and rights of individuals and human groups."[8] Three major arguments social justice advocates present for limiting free inquiry are that it can cause harm, that those engaging in this inquiry are biased, and that inquiry has always been limited by certain values anyway. We review these arguments next.

Avoiding Harms by Limiting Free Inquiry. One of the main social justice arguments against free inquiry is that certain ideas are harmful to goals of equality and egalitarianism.[9] A common concern motivating censorship is that ideas, including scientific research, may be appropriated by malevolent actors to support harmful policies and attitudes.[10] The idea here is that some forms of expression and even scholarship are too dangerous to pursue and that much contemporary scientific censorship is aimed at protecting groups perceived as vulnerable.

Some have argued that scientists should consider the consequences of the types of inquiry they pursue.[11] Science is inherently a value-laden pursuit, they argue, making the pursuit of truth only one among many other contending values. Because science does not exist in a social, cultural, or political vacuum, they say, academics should also consider the impact of their work on society.

One example is the investigation of racial differences in intelligence. Historically, research on intelligence has been deployed to advance social Darwinism, eugenics, and theories of racial superiority in the service of malign agendas, causing great harms (such as the rise of Nazism).

Therefore, the argument goes, the potential for such research to cause great harm needs to be weighed against the potential benefits, and in many cases, the potential for harm so exceeds the potential for benefit that the work should not be conducted at all. If it is conducted, it should not be admitted into the avenues of acceptable scholarly discourse (such as peer-reviewed journals). Similar arguments can be made regarding research on sex differences, cultural differences, transgender issues, the effectiveness of diversity initiatives, policing, and almost any topic related to egalitarianism.

Academic Inquiry Can Be Biased. Another important consideration in this debate is that academic inquiry can be biased.[12] There is inherently a subjective aspect to academic inquiry, especially in the social sciences. Researchers' biases can influence research questions, methods, and the interpretation of findings. Authors may interpret their research findings in ways that further an agenda, rather than furthering the truth.

In some cases, academics arguing for the right to free inquiry may actually be arguing for their right to advance biased views. If free inquiry can mask ax-grinding agendas intended to harm marginalized groups, the argument goes, then the benefits to censorship vastly exceed the costs. Eliminating, as much as possible, propaganda designed to cause harm masquerading as science is an unmitigated good, according to would-be censors.

Academic Inquiry Is Already Restricted. Another social justice argument against free inquiry is that academic inquiry has always had restrictions. Journals do not publish every submission, for example, and funding agencies do not fund every proposal they receive. "Anything goes" has never been how science is conducted or scholarship produced. Therefore, restrictions on free inquiry are nothing new.

Furthermore, even science has never been a value-free endeavor.[13] The only difference now is that rather than advancing the values championed by those with greater political and social power and status, a more socially beneficial set of values is being advanced—namely, those emphasizing the experiences and perspectives of those who once were and often still are marginalized.[14]

32 THE FREE INQUIRY PAPERS

Thus, according to these lines of argument, professional societies, journals, and funding agencies have not just the right but the responsibility to weigh scholarship's potential contributions to knowledge against the potential to cause social injustices and harms. And if the scales tip toward harm, it is better not to publish or fund the research.

In summary, then, the case against free inquiry that some social justice advocates make is primarily based on protecting marginalized groups. Consequently, according to this perspective, free inquiry must be limited to prevent societal harms. These arguments, when presented in isolation, may seem compelling. In the next section, however, we argue that they are not as compelling as they may seem and that they are, in fact, dangerous *even and especially for advancing social justice*.

Why Social Justice Requires Free Inquiry

In this section, we argue that free inquiry is actually necessary to advance social justice. We review relevant history, current events, and arguments that illustrate that restrictions on free inquiry are harmful to social justice causes.

Restrictions on Free Inquiry Are Bad for Social Justice. History demonstrates that many important social justice movements have used free speech and free inquiry to advance their causes. The most obvious case is the civil rights movement of the 1950s and 1960s. Martin Luther King Jr. proclaimed in his clarion call: "Somewhere I read of the freedom of assembly. Somewhere I read of the freedom of speech. Somewhere I read of the freedom of press. Somewhere I read that the greatness of America is the right to protest for right."[15]

In his famous "I've Been to the Mountaintop" speech, King did two related things: (1) He drew on the legal protections for free speech and expression that were enshrined in the Constitution to protect the right of his movement to advocate for civil rights, and (2) he *reminded* Americans of their commitment to the bedrock protection of free speech and expression rights as one of the greatest of American accomplishments. By doing so, he sought to strengthen those protections so that he, and the civil rights movement more broadly, could draw on them for protection when engaging in protests to advance social justice.

Free speech and expression were also crucial to social justice fights well beyond the civil rights movement. Such protections were crucial to all sorts of protest movements, including protests against the Vietnam War, protests for gay rights, protests against Donald Trump's Muslim ban and border policies, and protests against racial injustice following the police murder of George Floyd. The principles of free inquiry and discourse were essential to defending and supporting these groups as they fought for social justice.

History is riddled with instances of the government and society attempting to suppress the fight for social justice on grounds that certain ideas were "harmful." In 1933, the Nazi law banning political meetings and demonstrations was called "Decree for the Protection of the German People."[16] In the antebellum American South, state legislatures routinely banned "incendiary" literature, which usually referred to pamphlets, articles, and books arguing for the abolition of slavery.[17] Violators could be jailed or executed. Ironically, given modern discourse that often conflates violence, harm, and offense,[18] Southern politicians often justified bans on abolitionist speech on the grounds that they were malicious and injured Southerners' feelings.[19] Thus, there is a long and ugly history of seeking to "protect" people, and even their "feelings," from speech they oppose by using censorship.

But censorship as a method of oppressing minorities was not restricted to the antebellum South. Long before King's clarion call for free speech, Frederick Douglass, responding to a Boston mob that shut down an abolitionist meeting, strongly proclaimed the need for free speech, especially for abolition:

> Liberty is meaningless where the right to utter one's thoughts and opinions has ceased to exist. That, of all rights, is the dread of tyrants. It is the right which they first of all strike down. They know its power. . . . Slavery cannot tolerate free speech. Five years of its exercise would banish the auction block and break every chain in the South.[20]

Almost a century later, the second Red Scare of the 1940s evoked a slew of repressive measures, generally described as McCarthyism after the demagogue senator who led a witch hunt for Communists. These witch hunts created a generally chilling effect for leftists and nonconformists, so that the civil rights movement was effectively put on hold for fear of being labeled Communist.[21]

Even more important, as the Red Scare subsided in the late 1950s, a series of landmark civil rights cases established, entrenched, and expanded federal protections for free expression.[22] In response to a now more-active civil rights movement, Southern states and municipalities passed a slew of laws and ordinances that were ostensibly content neutral (such as prohibiting protests or handing out leaflets in public places) but were specifically designed to suppress the civil rights movement.[23] In 1961, the Supreme Court overturned Louisiana's laws preventing black protestors from peacefully engaging in a sit-in at a segregated restaurant.[24]

One of the great legal accomplishments of the marriage between free speech and civil rights emerged from *New York Times v. Sullivan* in 1964.[25] Civil rights leaders bought a *New York Times* advertisement that exposed and decried some of the terrible treatment of civil rights leaders in the South, including by certain police departments. The problem was that some of their claims were erroneous and exaggerated (e.g., overstating how frequently King had been arrested). The Montgomery Police Department sued for defamation and received a half-million-dollar award by a lower court. Unfortunately for them, however, the Supreme Court overturned the decision on the grounds that defamation required demonstration of actual malice and not just error.[26] Even more important with respect to free speech, the Court stated:

> Thus we consider this case against the background of a profound national commitment to the principle that debate on public issues should be uninhibited, robust, and wide-open, and that it may well include vehement, caustic, and sometimes unpleasantly sharp attacks on government and public officials.[27]

Thurgood Marshall, the Supreme Court's first black justice, believed that the First Amendment advanced equality and social justice because it ensured the voices of the marginalized an opportunity to speak and be heard.[28]

History demonstrates that, far from accomplishing the often-stated goal of preventing harm, censorship has often been the leading edge of authoritarianism, sometimes a brutally lethal one. But even short of mass murder, restricting free inquiry to prevent harm often causes more harm than it prevents. One of the many dangers of restricting free inquiry is the "who decides?" problem. The answer is, inherently, whoever has the power to decide.

This renders definitions of harm entirely a function of power. Whether those in power truly believe in the high moral purposes they use to justify censorship, or cynically justify capricious exercises of power in the name of morality, hardly matters. Once what can and cannot be stated or investigated becomes determined by power, rather than bedrock protections of human rights, these restrictions could one day come back to hurt the very people and groups whose protection is sought. As science historian Michael Shermer explains:

> The justification . . . that people might be incited to discrimination, hate, or violence if exposed to such ideas fails the moment you turn the argument around and ask: What happens when it is you and your ideas that are determined to be dangerous?[29]

Today, the need to protect free inquiry is still a pressing issue, not a hypothetical one relegated to the evils of the past. The modern and real manifestation of this issue involves efforts by a number of Republican state governments to regulate speech involving critical race theory or other "divisive" concepts, even at state colleges and universities. For example, the Florida state legislature, with the active support of Gov. Ron DeSantis, passed House Bill 7 (a.k.a. the "Stop Woke Act") in 2022, which bans teaching about racial privilege or the ways in which the concept of merit has been used to justify and sustain racist and oppressive hierarchies.[30] A federal judge blocked enactment, and the governor is considering an appeal.

Similar bills have been passed by 18 states and are under consideration in 10 more.[31] For example, Oklahoma passed a bill in May 2021 banning public schools from teaching certain ideas about race and sex that the state believes are related to critical race theory.[32] Oklahoma teachers could lose their licenses, and schools could lose their accreditation if the state believes they have violated this law; schools have even had to cut classic works of literature that deal with racial topics from their curriculum out of fear of violating this law.[33] In April 2022, Georgia passed legislation banning the discussion of "divisive concepts" about race in schools, including ideas that "the United States is 'fundamentally racist' or that . . . individuals 'should feel anguish, guilt or any other form of discomfort or stress' because of their race."[34] These are just a few examples of recent "anti-woke" legislation that Republican-controlled states across the country have passed, and these laws have had a chilling effect on academic discourse and freedom in the affected states.

More important, these examples illustrate the extreme dangers posed to social justice by using "perceived harms" as a justification for restricting free inquiry. Harm is almost entirely subjective, absent being able to draw straight lines from ideas to some form of measurable damage, something that is rarely done. One person's great ideas are another's "harm." Those who advocate that harm is a legitimate basis for restricting free inquiry open the door for their opponents to suppress *them* on the grounds that *their* ideas cause harm.

Some of the state government responses to intellectual currents designed to be liberating and anti-racist are disturbingly similar to the attempts common throughout the antebellum American South to suppress expression of abolitionist speech. Nothing is more emblematic of the need for social justice movements to embrace the endorsement of free speech by such historical icons as Douglass, Marshall, and King than are these attempts by Republican state governments to suppress expression of ideas targeting racism and oppression.

Restricting Free Inquiry Harms Social Justice Efforts. Restricting free inquiry could lead to the suppression of research and discussions that actually help social justice causes. In recent years, researchers have made enormous strides in important topics such as prejudice, racism, sexism, and LGBTQ issues. For example, consider legal interventions designed to reduce discrimination by first changing implicit biases.

The logic appears compelling: People hold unconscious racial bigotries, and by changing those, there should be less bigotry in the world, an unmitigated good. Unfortunately, both parts of this claim are erroneous:

The main measure of supposed unconscious bias, the Implicit Association Test (IAT), is not unconscious,[35] and changing IAT scores has no effect on discrimination.[36] A system that effectively suppresses research on grounds that unconscious racism is bad so anyone not wanting to change it must be a white supremacist would be a dysfunctional system indeed, one in which effective programs could not be readily distinguished from ineffective ones. A similar analysis could (and, in our view, should) be applied to any social justice issue, including decolonizing education,[37] treating people manifesting aspects of gender dysphoria, maximizing diversity in college admissions, addressing climate change and climate justice, and closing gender gaps in STEM and corporate boardrooms. If free inquiry is restricted, it may become difficult—or worse, impossible—to conduct research that uncovers methods that do and do not advance social justice.

Restricting Free Inquiry Could Give Power to the Wrong Groups. When freedom of inquiry is restricted, this power is removed from the individual and given to some authority to decide what inquiry is "permissible." If free inquiry is restricted, who gets to say which types of inquiry are permitted? Should it be the government? Many would argue that it is dangerous to give such power to the government, which is exactly why freedom of speech was enshrined in the First Amendment to the US Constitution. Once the government is given the authority to police free inquiry, there is no way to possibly know where it might stop. For example, what if the government decides that research on the impact of abortion restrictions on women is harmful toward unborn fetuses? What if the government decides to clamp down on any research that makes the government look bad? What if the government decides to stifle social justice discussions and research altogether?

If we agree that it is dangerous to give this power to the government, then who should get to decide? Should the public decide which types of inquiry are acceptable? Should the loudest voices on social media decide, even if they do not represent the views of the majority? Should bureaucrats in universities decide?

Whoever one thinks should be given this power, what makes those people qualified to decide what is worthy of inquiry? What keeps those people, whoever they might be, from abusing this power in some way or using it to

38 THE FREE INQUIRY PAPERS

punish those they dislike? What keeps those people from eventually using this power to discriminate against dissimilar others? These questions highlight just some of the many complicated issues that come with restricting freedom of inquiry—and some of the possible harms to social justice that could arise from such restrictions.

Free Inquiry Allows Knowledge to Advance. Free inquiry is an essential and important piece of the search for knowledge and wisdom. Any quest for justice that is based on falsehoods, misinformation, and unwise choices is doomed from the start. Many thinkers and academics before us have argued for freedom of speech and freedom of inquiry, and their arguments continue to hold true today.[38]

John Stuart Mill, for example, made a strong case for free inquiry in his 1859 book *On Liberty*. He argued that we should not silence opinions that we oppose because we cannot know for sure if that opinion is untrue, and further, even if that opinion were actually untrue, we would be assuming ourselves to be infallible by suppressing those ideas.[39] Such an assumption is dangerous to make because no person is truly infallible. Although Mill also recognized that there are no guarantees that the truth will emerge from free and robust public discourse, we concur with his conclusion that by embracing robust discourse, the truth is more likely to reveal itself and can be held more securely.[40]

This latter point is worth spending some time on. Mill argued that even if one is completely right and one's opponents are completely wrong, discussion of the wrong argument should *still* be permitted in public discourse. Unless even correct views are sometimes challenged, Mill argued, the depth of understanding for *why* they are correct can atrophy—potentially leading to the abandonment of true beliefs in favor of false ones that cannot be refuted.[41] One can often see this process firsthand by asking someone to explain how they know the world is round (and requiring the answer to be something other than "because the authorities say so").

Judge Alex Kozinski made a similar argument in the 2010 case *Rodriguez v. Maricopa County Community College District*: "Intellectual advancement has traditionally progressed through discord and dissent, as a diversity of views ensures that ideas survive because they are correct, not because they

WHY SOCIAL JUSTICE REQUIRES FREE INQUIRY 39

are popular."[42] The process of dissent is what allows correct ideas to persist and incorrect ideas to be disproven or corrected, which makes free inquiry all the more important.

Science moves forward through the exploration and debate of different and possibly conflicting ideas. If certain ideas are suppressed, knowledge cannot move forward. Existing knowledge cannot be tested and compared against new ideas, and there would be no mechanism for the correction or updating of existing knowledge. In other words, the restriction of free inquiry would prevent us from ever knowing if our present ideas are incorrect. Although it may sometimes take decades for science to correct false claims, the ideas that are actually true will be able to stand up to criticism and debate because, however slowly, empirical evidence will accumulate supporting them.[43] If society is restricted in the exploration of certain topics, we can never learn more about these topics, discover the truth among competing ideas related to these topics, or learn related information that may benefit society.

Within the social justice context, researchers are starting to realize that the effectiveness of many widely accepted practices meant to advance social justice is actually questionable, yet many are afraid to question these ideas or investigate them further for fear of being denounced for racism, sexism, or some other ism. For instance, recent research has called into question the effectiveness of diversity trainings[44] and implicit bias trainings,[45] yet these trainings continue to be prominent across corporations and other organizations. If one truly cares about advancing social justice, it would be beneficial to vet these programs with skepticism to determine truly effective methods to combat bias.

Self-Censorship by Scholars and Researchers Is Detrimental to Society and Social Justice. Self-censorship occurs when scholars avoid or suppress controversial research questions or conclusions for fear of sanctions.[46] Self-censorship has been rising in the US for decades,[47] and we have little reason to expect scientists to be immune to this broad sociocultural trend. Recent reports suggest that nearly all US scientists self-censor their empirical beliefs somewhat.[48] Mass self-censorship can distort perceptions of scientific consensus on controversial issues and slow or prevent scientific discovery. Self-censorship need not be based on accurate concerns of reputational damage; pluralistic ignorance can create illusions that certain topics are off-limits.[49]

Recent restrictions on free inquiry and attempts (some successful) to punish scholars and researchers for publishing controversial claims have led to self-suppression in the academy.[50] Academic self-suppression could have serious negative outcomes such as important findings never being published and important ideas being left unpursued. These outcomes harm society because they prevent not only the advancement of knowledge but also science's self-correcting mechanisms from functioning.

Social Justice and Free Inquiry Are Not Inherently Competing Values

Most relevant to the present chapter, however, is the premise that the pursuit of truth and the pursuit of justice are mutually reinforcing. As King declared in "Letter from a Birmingham Jail," the first step in campaigns for justice is to get the facts to determine whether an injustice has occurred.[51] If people self-censor because they recognize an ugly history of activists punishing those whom they view as their opponents, they will fail to get the facts, and, even if they do, they may well fear to disseminate them. Thus, fact seeking must be built on a foundation of justice—of protection of the free speech and inquiry rights of all. Similarly, *when there are injustices*, their existence, extent, sources, and remedies can be understood clearly only if free inquiry is protected.

Free inquiry and social justice are not conflicting ideas, as some would paint them to be.[52] They can and should be synergistic. Social justice can continue to use free inquiry as a tool to move forward, just as it always has.[53]

The fight for social justice is long and difficult. Change is often incredibly slow. Minds are hard to change, laws even harder. Progress is sometimes incremental at best and nonexistent at worst. But let us not shoot ourselves in the foot by making free inquiry the enemy when it is one of the most important tools in the arsenal for the fight for social justice.

Notes

1. Jonathan Friedman and Nadine Farid Johnson, "Banned in the USA: Rising School Book Bans Threaten Free Expression and Students' First Amendment Rights," PEN America, April 2022, https://pen.org/banned-in-the-usa; Elizabeth A. Harris and Alexandra Alter, "Book Ban Efforts Spread Across the U.S.," *New York Times*, January 30, 2022, https://www.nytimes.com/2022/01/30/books/book-ban-us-schools.html; and Sarah Wood, "Book Bans: What to Know," *US News & World Report*, May 17, 2022, https://www.usnews.com/education/k12/articles/book-bans-what-to-know.

2. Fabiola Cineas, "Critical Race Theory Bans Are Making Teaching Much Harder," Vox, September 3, 2021, https://www.vox.com/22644220/critical-race-theory-bans-antiracism-curriculum-in-schools; and Jeremy C. Young and Jonathan Friedman, "In Higher Education, New Educational Gag Orders Would Exert Unprecedented Control over College Teaching," PEN America, February 1, 2022, https://pen.org/in-higher-education-new-educational-gag-orders.

3. Jeremy Bauer-Wolf, "ACLU Speaker Shouted Down at William & Mary," *Inside Higher Ed*, October 4, 2017, https://www.insidehighered.com/quicktakes/2017/10/05/aclu-speaker-shouted-down-william-mary; Eugene Kim, "Billionaire Investor Peter Thiel Chased off Stage by Angry Protesters at UC Berkeley," Business Insider, December 11, 2014, https://www.businessinsider.com/peter-thiel-chased-off-stage-by-angry-protestors-at-uc-berkeley-2014-12; Josh Moody, "Law Students Shout Down Controversial Speakers," *Inside Higher Ed*, March 22, 2022, https://www.insidehighered.com/news/2022/03/23/law-student-protests-stifle-speakers-yale-uc-hastings; Madison Park and Kyung Lah, "Berkeley Protests of Yiannopoulos Caused $100,000 in Damage," CNN, February 2, 2017, https://www.cnn.com/2017/02/01/us/milo-yiannopoulos-berkeley; and Allison Stanger, "Understanding the Angry Mob at Middlebury That Gave Me a Concussion," *New York Times*, March 13, 2017, https://www.nytimes.com/2017/03/13/opinion/understanding-the-angry-mob-that-gave-me-a-concussion.html.

4. Colleen Flaherty, "Is Retraction the New Rebuttal?," *Inside Higher Ed*, September 18, 2017, https://www.insidehighered.com/news/2017/09/19/controversy-over-paper-favor-colonialism-sparks-calls-retraction; Lee Jussim, "The Threat to Academic Freedom . . . from Academics," Medium, December 27, 2019, https://psychrabble.medium.com/the-threat-to-academic-freedom-from-academics-4685b1705794; and Lee Jussim et al., "The New Book Burners: Academic Tribalism," in *The Tribal Mind and the Psychology of Collectivism*, ed. Joseph P. Forgas (London: Routledge, 2024).

5. Eric Kaufmann, *Academic Freedom in Crisis: Punishment, Political Discrimination, and Self-Censorship*, Center for the Study of Partisanship and Ideology, March 1, 2021, https://cspicenter.org/wp-content/uploads/2021/03/ESummary.pdf; and Sean T. Stevens, Lee Jussim, and Nathan Honeycutt, "Scholarship Suppression: Theoretical Perspectives and Emerging Trends," *Societies* 10, no. 4 (December 2020), https://www.mdpi.com/2075-4698/10/4/82.

6. Stevens, Jussim, and Honeycutt, "Scholarship Suppression," 3.

7. Stevens, Jussim, and Honeycutt, "Scholarship Suppression."

42 THE FREE INQUIRY PAPERS

8. Editors of *Nature Human Behaviour*, "Science Must Respect the Dignity and Rights of All Humans," *Nature Human Behaviour* 6, no. 8 (August 2022): 1029–31, https://www.nature.com/articles/s41562-022-01443-2.

9. See, for example, John M. Herbert et al., "Words Matter: On the Debate over Free Speech, Inclusivity, and Academic Excellence," *Journal of Physical Chemistry Letters* 13, no. 30 (2022): 7100–4, https://pubs.acs.org/doi/10.1021/acs.jpclett.2c02242; John Horgan, "Should Research on Race and IQ Be Banned?," *Scientific American*, May 16, 2013, https://blogs.scientificamerican.com/cross-check/should-research-on-race-and-iq-be-banned; Sandra Y. L. Korn, "The Doctrine of Academic Freedom," *Harvard Crimson*, February 18, 2014, https://www.thecrimson.com/column/the-red-line/article/2014/2/18/academic-freedom-justice; and Janet A. Kourany, "Should Some Knowledge Be Forbidden? The Case of Cognitive Differences Research," *Philosophy of Science* 83, no. 5 (December 2016), 779–90, https://www.cambridge.org/core/journals/philosophy-of-science/article/abs/should-some-knowledge-be-forbidden-the-case-of-cognitive-differences-research/4D6C6733CC40B5A1646AF90659D07173.

10. Editors of *Nature Human Behavior*, "Science Must Respect the Dignity and Rights of All Humans."

11. Herbert et al., "Words Matter"; and Editors of *Nature Human Behavior*, "Science Must Respect the Dignity and Rights of All Humans."

12. Helen E. Longino, *Science as Social Knowledge: Values and Objectivity in Scientific Inquiry* (Princeton, NJ: Princeton University Press, 1990).

13. Longino, *Science as Social Knowledge*.

14. Herbert et al., "Words Matter"; Korn, "The Doctrine of Academic Freedom"; and Kourany, "Should Some Knowledge Be Forbidden?"

15. Martin Luther King Jr., "I've Been to the Mountaintop" (speech, Mason Temple, Memphis, TN, April 3, 1968), https://www.americanrhetoric.com/speeches/mlkivebeentothemountaintop.htm.

16. Jacob Mchangama, *Free Speech: A History from Socrates to Social Media* (New York: Basic Books, 2022).

17. Mchangama, *Free Speech*.

18. April Bleske-Rechek, "Offense = Harm = Violence," Unsafe Science, May 1, 2023, https://unsafescience.substack.com/p/offense-harm-violence.

19. Mchangama, *Free Speech*.

20. Frederick Douglass, "Plea for Freedom of Speech in Boston" (speech, Tremont Temple Baptist Church, Boston, MA, December 9, 1860), https://lawliberty.org/frederick-douglass-plea-for-freedom-of-speech-in-boston.

21. Mchangama, *Free Speech*.

22. Mchangama, *Free Speech*.

23. Mchangama, *Free Speech*.

24. *Garner v. Louisiana*, 368 US 157 (1961).

25. *New York Times v. Sullivan*, 376 US 254 (1964).

26. Mchangama, *Free Speech*.

27. *New York Times v. Sullivan*, 376 US at 270.

28. Lynn Adelman, "The Glorious Jurisprudence of Thurgood Marshall," *Harvard Law & Policy Review* 7, no. 1 (2013): 113–37, https://journals.law.harvard.edu/lpr/wp-

content/uploads/sites/89/2013/06/The-Glorious-Jurisprudence-of-Thurgood-Marshall.pdf.

29. Michael Shermer, "Giving the Devil His Due: Why Freedom of Inquiry in Science and Politics Is Inviolable," *Journal of Criminal Justice* 59 (November–December 2018): 136–39, https://www.sciencedirect.com/science/article/abs/pii/S0047235217300995.

30. H.R. 7, 2022 Leg. (Fla. 2022), https://www.flsenate.gov/Session/Bill/2022/7/BillText/er/PDF.

31. Schwartz, "Map: Where Critical Race Theory Is Under Attack."

32. Kathryn Schumaker, "What Is Critical Race Theory and Why Did Oklahoma Just Ban It?," *Washington Post*, May 19, 2021, https://www.washingtonpost.com/outlook/2021/05/19/what-is-critical-race-theory-why-did-oklahoma-just-ban-it.

33. Tyler Kingkade and Antonia Hylton, "Oklahoma's Anti–Critical Race Theory Law Violates Free Speech Rights, ACLU Suit Says," NBC News, October 19, 2021, https://www.nbcnews.com/news/us-news/oklahoma-critical-race-theory-lawsuit-aclu-rcna3276.

34. Sharon Bernstein, "Georgia Becomes Latest U.S. State to Ban 'Divisive' Concepts in Teaching About Race," Reuters, April 28, 2022, https://www.reuters.com/world/us/georgia-becomes-latest-us-state-ban-divisive-concepts-teaching-about-race-2022-04-28.

35. Adam Hahn et al., "Awareness of Implicit Attitudes," *Journal of Experimental Psychology: General* 143, no. 3 (June 2014): 1369–92, https://psycnet.apa.org/record/2013-42388-001.

36. Calvin K. Lai et al., "Reducing Implicit Racial Preferences: II. Intervention Effectiveness Across Time," *Journal of Experimental Psychology: General* 145, no. 8 (August 2016): 1001–16, https://psycnet.apa.org/record/2016-29854-001.

37. Judy M. Iseke-Bames, "Pedagogies for Decolonizing," *Canadian Journal of Native Education* 31, no. 1 (2008): 123–48, https://ojs.library.ubc.ca/index.php/CJNE/article/view/196433.

38. Jonathan R. Cole, "Defending Academic Freedom and Free Inquiry," *Social Research* 76, no. 3 (Fall 2009): 811–44, https://www.jstor.org/stable/40972159; Daniel Friedman, "Free Speech Doesn't Protect Nazis. It Protects Us from Nazis," Quillette, July 11, 2018, https://quillette.com/2018/07/11/free-speech-doesnt-protect-nazis-it-protects-us-from-nazis; Jonathan Haidt and Greg Lukianoff, "On U.S. Campuses, Free Inquiry Is Taking a Beating," *Philanthropy*, Winter 2017, https://www.philanthropyroundtable.org/magazine/winter-2017-on-u-s-campuses-free-inquiry-is-taking-a-beating; John Stuart Mill, *On Liberty* (London: John W. Parker and Son, 1859); Shermer, "Giving the Devil His Due"; Stevens, Jussim, and Honeycutt, "Scholarship Suppression"; and Jonathan Zimmerman, *Free Speech: And Why You Should Give a Damn* (Buffalo, NY: City of Light Publishing, 2021).

39. Mill, *On Liberty*.

40. Mill, *On Liberty*.

41. Mill, *On Liberty*.

42. *Rodriguez v. Maricopa County Community College District*, 605 F.3d 703 (9th Cir. 2010).

44 THE FREE INQUIRY PAPERS

43. Abraham Loeb, "Benefits of Diversity," *Nature Physics* 10, no. 9 (September 2014): 616–17, https://www.nature.com/articles/nphys3089.

44. Edward H. Chang et al., "The Mixed Effects of Online Diversity Training," *Proceedings of the National Academy of Sciences* 116, no. 16 (April 16, 2019): 7778–83, https://www.pnas.org/doi/full/10.1073/pnas.1816076116; Patricia G. Devine and Tory L. Ash, "Diversity Training Goals, Limitations, and Promise: A Review of the Multidisciplinary Literature," *Annual Review of Psychology* 73 (2022): 403–29, https://www.annualreviews.org/doi/10.1146/annurev-psych-060221-122215; Frank Dobbin and Alexandra Kalev, "Why Diversity Programs Fail: And What Works Better," *Harvard Business Review*, July–August 2016, https://hbr.org/2016/07/why-diversity-programs-fail; Frank Dobbin and Alexandra Kalev, "Why Doesn't Diversity Training Work? The Challenge for Industry and Academia," *Anthropology Now* 10, no. 2 (September 2018): 48–55, https://www.tandfonline.com/doi/full/10.1080/19428200.2018.1493182; and Elizabeth Levy Paluck and Donald P. Green, "Prejudice Reduction: What Works? A Review and Assessment of Research and Practice," *Annual Review of Psychology* 60 (2009): 339–67, https://www.annualreviews.org/doi/abs/10.1146/annurev.psych.60.110707.163607.

45. Patrick S. Forscher et al., "A Meta-Analysis of Procedures to Change Implicit Measures," *Journal of Personality and Social Psychology* 117, no. 3 (September 2019): 522–59, https://psycnet.apa.org/record/2019-31306-001; Calvin K. Lai et al., "Reducing Implicit Racial Preferences: I. A Comparative Investigation of 17 Interventions," *Journal of Experimental Psychology: General* 143, no. 4 (August 2014): 1765–85, https://psycnet.apa.org/record/2014-10299-001; and Lai et al., "Reducing Implicit Racial Preferences: II. Intervention Effectiveness Across Time."

46. Carroll J. Glynn, Andrew F. Hayes, and James Shanahan, "Perceived Support for One's Opinions and Willingness to Speak Out: A Meta-Analysis of Survey Studies on the 'Spiral of Silence,'" *Public Opinion Quarterly* 61, no. 3 (Autumn 1997): 452–63, https://www.jstor.org/stable/2749581; and Stevens, Jussim, and Honeycutt, "Scholarship Suppression."

47. James L. Gibson and Joseph L. Sutherland, "Keeping Your Mouth Shut: Spiraling Self-Censorship in the United States," *Political Science Quarterly* 138, no. 3 (Fall 2023): 361–76, https://academic.oup.com/psq/article/138/3/361/7192889.

48. Cory J. Clark et al., "Taboos and Self-Censorship Among Psychology Professors" (unpublished manuscript, 2023); and Nathan Honeycutt, Sean T. Stevens, and Eric Kaufmann, *The Academic Mind in 2022: What Faculty Think About Free Expression and Academic Freedom on Campus*, Foundation for Individual Rights and Expression, 2023, https://www.thefire.org/research-learn/academic-mind-2022-what-faculty-think-about-free-expression-and-academic-freedom.

49. Timur Kuran, *Private Truths, Public Lies: The Social Consequences of Preference Falsification* (Cambridge, MA: Harvard University Press, 1997).

50. Clark et al., "Taboos and Self-Censorship Among Psychology Professors."

51. Martin Luther King Jr., "Letter from a Birmingham Jail," April 16, 1963, https://www.africa.upenn.edu/Articles_Gen/Letter_Birmingham.html.

52. Editors of *Nature Human Behavior*, "Science Must Respect the Dignity and Rights of All Humans."

53. Ludy T. Benjamin Jr. and Ellen M. Crouse, "The American Psychological Association's Response to *Brown v. Board of Education*: The Case of Kenneth B. Clark," in *Racial Identity in Context: The Legacy of Kenneth B. Clark*, ed. Gina Philogène (Washington, DC: American Psychological Association, 2004), 231–53, https://psycnet.apa.org/record/2004-14385-013.

PART II.
Threats to Free Inquiry

5

The Rise of Self-Censorship in America

Joseph L. Sutherland and James L. Gibson

Americans today are deeply divided on ideological and partisan attachments, political issues, and values. Indeed, these divisions can extend all the way to whom—or what kind of person—their children should marry. A concomitant of these divisions is that political discourse has become coarse, abrasive, divisive, and intense. When it comes to politics, it is increasingly likely that even an innocent but misspoken opinion will cause a kerfuffle to break out.[1]

It should not be unexpected, therefore, that many Americans engage in self-censorship, electing to withhold their views from others even when presented with an opportunity to express them. In a nationally representative survey we conducted in 2023, we included a question about self-censorship that the famed sociologist Samuel Stouffer first put to the American people in 1954: "What about you personally? Do you or don't you feel as free to speak your mind as you used to?"[2] Although we readily acknowledge the potential frailties of this wording, its utility is that the same question has been repeated in several surveys between 1954 and 2023.

The 2023 results are sobering: Fully 48 percent reported feeling less free to speak their minds than they used to. The findings reflect a slight increase from the level of self-censorship in 2020, up from 46 percent.[3] That so many Americans withhold their views is remarkable—and portentous.[4]

More unnerving, however, is how much the level of self-censorship has increased in the past 70 or so years. In the 1950s, at the height of the Red Scare, when a circumstantial miscue could land a person in jail, Stouffer discovered that only 13.4 percent of the American people felt less free to speak their minds than they had previously; nearly 85 percent said they did feel free to speak their minds. During an era famous for political persecution, few Americans seem to have personally felt the heavy hand of the Republican senator from Wisconsin and his many acolytes.[5]

Figure 1. Change in Levels of Unwillingness to Speak One's Mind, 1954–2023

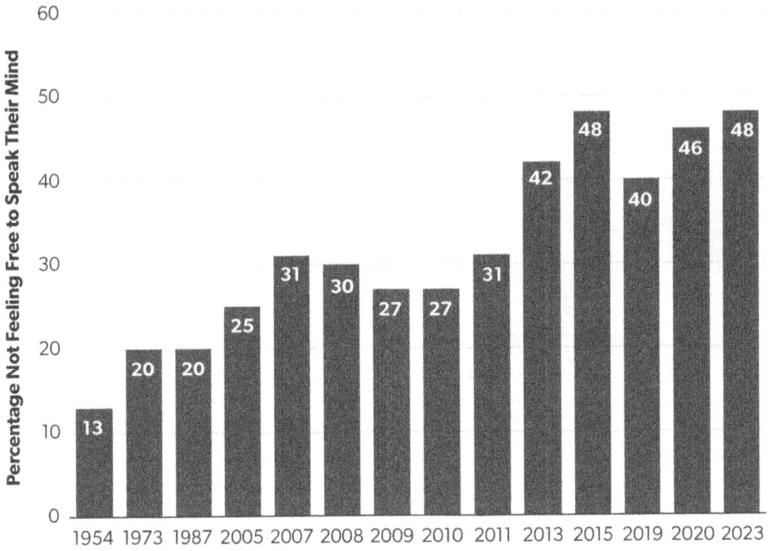

Note: The Stouffer question asks, "What about you personally? Do you or don't you feel as free to speak your mind as you used to?" See the online appendix for a discussion of the sources of these surveys. This figure is based on available survey data; readers should carefully note the survey year on the x-axis.
Source: Sources compiled in the online appendix in Joseph L. Sutherland and James L. Gibson, "The Rise of Self-Censorship in America," American Enterprise Institute, January 11, 2024, https://joesuth.com/assets/papers/SSRN-id4671208-appendix.pdf.

Figure 1 reports the percentages of people from 1954 to 2023 who did not feel free to speak their minds. These data reveal a steady erosion of levels of perceived freedom, although there are two points of significant decline: 2005–07 and 2011–13. Since about 2013, levels of unwillingness to speak one's mind have remained fairly constant, with at least four in 10 Americans feeling unfree to do so.

Public opinion on most matters is slow to change. Yet perceptions of individual-level freedom decreased dramatically from 1954 to 2023. Although some might understand these data to indicate that those with "bad" views no longer feel free to express themselves, which may be a good thing, we have no means of discerning whether the speech lost is "good" or "bad" speech. Given the benefits of deliberation among citizens for democratic politics, most democratic theorists would regard these results as too important to ignore.[6]

Explanations for the Rise of Self-Censorship

What accounts for this remarkable loss of perceived freedom in the United States? Is this loss of free speech a function of the fear of being misunderstood by friends and colleagues, or are the causes more systemic, such as government surveillance of social media, telephone, and email discussions?[7] Is the explanation associated with a culture of "political correctness" that many conservatives rail against, or is the source even more elementary, reflecting growing political polarization, incivility, and political intolerance?

Unfortunately, little recent research has investigated the causes and consequences of changes in levels of political freedom reported by the American people, so we are largely in the dark as to why such a large proportion of Americans do not feel free to express their opinions. Earlier studies examined various aspects of self-censorship, but practically none have investigated change over time. Fortunately, our data enable us to investigate change in levels of self-censorship.[8]

In this chapter, we explore for policymakers and the broader public several hypotheses about the correlates of self-censorship at the aggregate (macro) level. We also include summaries of our findings at the individual (micro) level, recently published in *Political Science Quarterly*, in this chapter's endnotes.[9]

Our analysis here is neither comprehensive nor definitive; we are not making causal claims. When the direction of the relationship is contrary to our stated expectations, we reject the original causal process underlying the hypothesis (with some degree of discomfort). We contend, however, that determining what goes with what—and what does *not* go with what—is a valuable first step in understanding how and why people engage in self-censorship. Given the presumed importance of unbridled political discourse for the health of democracies, our findings raise troubling issues for contemporary American democracy.

Hypothesis 1: Affective Polarization

We first focus on recent scholarship studying affective polarization, a type of division in the mass public in which "ordinary Americans increasingly dislike and distrust those from another party."[10] Taylor Carlson and Jaime Settle conjecture that the increase in self-censorship may be related to increasing polarization.[11] Because people so dislike each other—to the point of detesting each other's views and values—they may perceive a great cost associated with sharing their opinions publicly, with little or no reward. Therefore, they keep their mouths shut and refrain from expressing their true opinions.

Perhaps a saving grace is that people tend to live in politically homogeneous echo chambers and therefore are most likely to encounter mainly like-minded folks, reducing their fear of disturbing the peace if they express their views.[12] Nevertheless, unless one can completely isolate oneself from the toxic political environment of contemporary America, it could be prudent to withhold one's views, at least in certain contexts. Free speech has never been free, but the cost of such speech today seems to have skyrocketed—and, to some, the cost may have become exorbitant and out of reach.

Figure 2 adds to the information in Figure 1 the trends in partisan and ideological affective polarization among the American people (as measured by Jon Rogowski and Joseph L. Sutherland).[13] Note that owing to the unavailability of data between 1954 and 1973, we start this data series in 1973; because new polarization data are not yet available, we terminate this data series in 2020.

At the macro level, there is no obvious one-to-one relationship between levels of affective polarization and levels of self-censorship, but there are substantial interconnections over time, whatever the causal link between these two concepts. As polarization has increased, so too has self-censorship. It seems unlikely that levels of self-censorship have caused levels of polarization because we cannot see how silence would contribute to increases in political differences and animosity.

Although grounded in a small number of data points, the relationship between the two indicators is quite strong: Based on filling in yearly scores using linear interpolation, the correlation of self-censorship with

Figure 2. The Relationship Between Self-Censorship and Affective Polarization

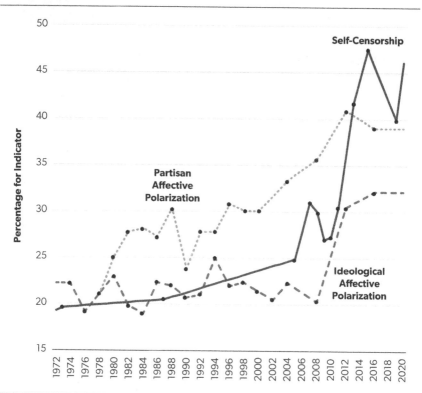

Note: "Self-censorship" is the percentage of people who do not feel free to speak their minds. "Ideological affective polarization" is the absolute value of the average difference in thermometer scores assigned to "liberals" and "conservatives," with higher scores indicating greater degrees of affective polarization. "Partisan affective polarization" is the absolute value of the average difference in thermometer scores assigned to "Democrats" and "Republicans," with higher scores indicating greater degrees of affective polarization. To facilitate interpretation, the figure interpolates the data points between each survey for each variable. (See the online appendix.) Because of the availability of data, the time series begins in 1973. Source: Jon C. Rogowski and Joseph L. Sutherland, "How Ideology Fuels Affective Polarization," *Political Behavior* 38 (June 2016): 485–508, https://link.springer.com/article/10.1007/s11109-015-9323-7.

ideological polarization is 0.91 (N = 48); with partisan polarization, r = 0.86 (N = 43). One concomitant of rising affective polarization may have been the loss of freedom to speak.[14]

Hypothesis 2: Support for Civil Liberties

Polarization is sometimes narratively associated with an unwillingness to recognize the civil liberties of all, especially opponents one considers despicable. Therefore, a reasonable hypothesis is that self-censorship has increased because, nationwide, the reluctance to grant civil liberties to everyone has increased. As it turns out, that does not seem to be so.

Since 1972, the General Social Survey (GSS) has asked in its nationally representative surveys three questions pertaining to civil liberties—that is, queries about three activities regarding various groups presumed to be unpopular with the American people. We created an index of group-based support for civil liberties for each year in the GSS time series. The index summarizes the responses to the five groups and three activities asked about: It is the average response to 15 civil liberties items (after scoring the responses to each item as either supportive or not). The yearly averages are reported in Figure 3, which adds levels of civil liberties opposition to the self-censorship data shown in Figure 1. We also carry over from Figure 2 the measures of affective polarization.[15]

The GSS data indicate a steady and significant *decrease* over the past several decades in opposition to civil liberties for all in the United States. From the data in Figure 3, it is obvious that decreasing levels of opposition to civil liberties cannot easily account for an increasing level of self-censorship. The simple hypothesis that personal political freedom has been lost to the growth in mass unwillingness to grant civil liberties—that is, intolerance—to these groups and groups like these can be clearly rejected.

Yet it may be that national trends are of little consequence because individuals are affected by the intolerance of their local communities, not of the nation. In our recent article, we reported on a mixed-level analysis that links the location of the 2020 Freedom and Tolerance Survey respondents to measures of community political intolerance (drawn from Christopher Claassen and James L. Gibson; the measures index the degree to which a community tolerates politically unpopular views) and tests whether individuals living in more intolerant communities are more likely to engage in self-censorship.[16] We find that little relationship exists between community intolerance and self-censorship.[17] The answers to the empirical puzzle of increasing and widespread self-censorship must be found elsewhere.[18]

Figure 3. Self-Censorship, Opposition to Civil Liberties, Partisan Affective Polarization, and Ideological Affective Polarization, over Time

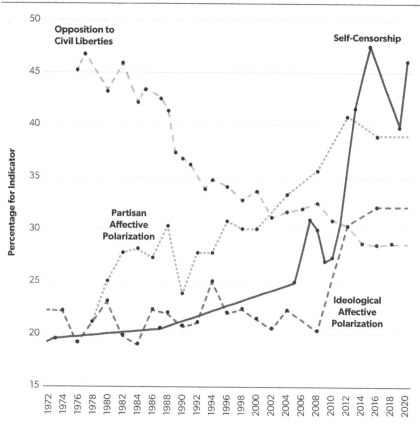

Note: "Self-censorship" is the percentage of people who do not feel free to speak their minds. "Ideological affective polarization" is the absolute value of the average difference in thermometer scores assigned to "liberals" and "conservatives," with higher scores indicating greater degrees of affective polarization. "Partisan affective polarization" is the absolute value of the average difference in thermometer scores assigned to "Democrats" and "Republicans," with higher scores indicating greater degrees of affective polarization. "Opposition to civil liberties" is the average number of "rejection of civil liberties" responses to 15 questions (three activities for five groups). To facilitate interpretation, the figure interpolates the data points between each survey for each variable. (See the online appendix.) Because of the availability of data, the time series begins in 1973.
Source: Joseph L. Sutherland and James L. Gibson, "The Rise of Self-Censorship in America," American Enterprise Institute, January 11, 2024, https://joesuth.com/assets/papers/SSRN-id4671208-appendix.pdf.

Summary and Discussion

When we started this research, we frankly did not expect self-censorship to be so widespread in the United States. We were even more surprised to discover its increase over time—and that it has been a seemingly persistent phenomenon for the past decade.

Widespread self-censorship has important implications for the health of democracy in the United States. If those holding dissimilar views keep their mouths shut, then discourse preserving democratic values may become a thing of the past. As Diana Mutz has written, "Exposure to dissimilar views has been deemed a central element—if not the sine qua non—of the kind of political dialogue that is needed to maintain a democratic citizenry."[19] Explanations for *why* self-censorship is on the rise, however, leave much to be desired.

Macro-level affective polarization may reasonably contribute to increases in self-censorship, and our findings are consistent with this explanation. However, our failure to discover a macro-level connection between an unwillingness to recognize civil liberties and self-censorship was unexpected. In fact, an unwillingness to recognize civil liberties has declined markedly, suggesting that the general political culture may not be the primary source of encouragement to self-censor. Except for the all-pervasive and much-discussed climate of political polarization, the macro-level political environment seems not to be the main source of pressures to self-censor.[20]

It seems likely that people's choices to withhold their views are not necessarily governed by either the macro-level political environment or their micro-level environment[21] but at some level in between: their meso-level environment. The meso-level political environment encompasses a person's social interactions with family, friends, neighbors, and coworkers and other relationships they have created or maintain to get by in life. A person's metropolitan community or their county can be altogether different from their meso-level environment. In fact, the meso-level environment need not be constrained by location, owing to the omnipresence of email, telephone, and social media.

When people are prompted to share (potentially unacceptable) views with others in their meso-environment—those with whom they expect

56 THE FREE INQUIRY PAPERS

routine, necessary, and, in many cases, long-lasting interaction—they may choose to self-censor to avoid creating the distrust and distaste associated with affectively polarized relationships. What constitutes an unacceptable political view is idiosyncratic to this meso-level environment. For instance, in certain circumstances, those who favor abortion keep their mouths shut; in other contexts, those who oppose abortion keep their mouths shut. Context-dependent patterns are generally difficult to discern and analyze with survey data such as these.

Next Steps: A Spiral of Silence?

Elisabeth Noelle-Neumann theorizes that self-censorship drives a "spiral of silence."[22] In a nutshell, the theory hypothesizes that people's willingness to speak their own opinions is related to their perception of the opinion climate around them. They self-censor when they are afraid their viewpoint will be rejected by many of their relations. Insidiously, their own self-censorship prevents others with that same viewpoint from being reinforced in that viewpoint. Without reinforcement, more people remain quiet, establishing orthodox views that ascend into a perhaps undeserved domination.

The spiral-of-silence theory is not a theory of government repression; instead, it is a social theory. Officials are not the source of disapproval; rather, it is one's friends, family, and neighbors. For instance, Jörg Matthes, Johannes Knoll, and Christian von Sikorski find that "expressing dissenting views to family, friends, or neighbors has a stronger effect as compared with strangers, politicians, or the media." They take this finding further, considering Mutz's research:

> When voicing dissent to close others, social accountability is arguably higher compared with voicing disagreement to journalists, politicians, or strangers. Thus, citizens suppress their views to maintain social harmony. In terms of the spiral of silence, this means that disagreement with friends and family may lead to a higher state of fear of social isolation as compared with strangers.[23]

THE RISE OF SELF-CENSORSHIP IN AMERICA   57

We hypothesize it is this social fear that drives self-censorship.

Investigating the influence of social norms on people is by no means easy, especially if placed within the dynamic context of the spiral of silence. Not everyone is aware of norms, not everyone acquiesces to norms in the same way, the sanctions for violating norms are experienced differently by different people, and so on. Designing a study capable of providing an understanding of these processes is difficult and demanding, to say the least.

Our analysis has only scratched the surface in understanding the causes and consequences of self-censorship. Refusing to express what one thinks are unpopular points of view may be good for smoothing social and familial relationships but is, we submit, inimical to a vibrant democracy. Finding ways to lower the costs of expressing dissenting views should be a priority for those who favor the liberal democratic form of governance.

After all, dissent is the essence of democracy. As Chief Justice Earl Warren wrote in *Sweezy v. New Hampshire*, "Mere unorthodoxy or dissent from the prevailing mores is not to be condemned. The absence of such voices would be a symptom of grave illness to our society." That nearly one-half of Americans today are reluctant to express their views is indeed symptomatic of an anemic democracy.[24]

Acknowledgments

The Freedom and Tolerance Surveys on which this chapter partially relies were funded by the Weidenbaum Center at Washington University in St. Louis. The authors appreciate the support made available for this research by Steven S. Smith, former director of the Weidenbaum Center. Additional support for these surveys has been provided by the Law and Social Sciences Program of the National Science Foundation grants (SES-0943389 to J.L.G. and Chintan Turakhia and SES-0553156 to J.L.G.). Any opinions, findings, and conclusions or recommendations expressed in this chapter are those of the authors and do not necessarily reflect the views of the National Science Foundation. The 2020 AmeriSpeak Freedom and Tolerance Survey was also funded by the Weidenbaum Center.

58 THE FREE INQUIRY PAPERS

We are particularly indebted to Professor Jacob M. Montgomery and the American Social Survey, funded by the Weidenbaum Center, for support for our 2022 survey. We are also indebted to Peter Enns and the staff at Verasight for including our measure of self-censorship in one of their 2023 nationally representative omnibus surveys.

Notes

1. For further discussion, see James N. Druckman and Matthew S. Levendusky, "What Do We Measure When We Measure Affective Polarization?," *Public Opinion Quarterly* 83, no. 1 (Spring 2019): 114–22, https://academic.oup.com/poq/article/83/1/114/5486527; and Shanto Iyengar et al., "The Origins and Consequences of Affective Polarization in the United States," *Annual Review of Political Science* 22 (2019): 129–46, https://www.annualreviews.org/doi/pdf/10.1146/annurev-polisci-051117-073034.

2. Samuel A. Stouffer, *Communism, Conformity, and Civil Liberties: A Cross-Section of the Nation Speaks Its Mind* (New York: Doubleday, 1955).

3. James L. Gibson and Joseph L. Sutherland, "Keeping Your Mouth Shut: Spiraling Self-Censorship in the United States," *Political Science Quarterly* 138, no. 3 (Fall 2023): 361–76, https://academic.oup.com/psq/article/138/3/361/7192889.

4. We define self-censorship as "intentionally and voluntarily withholding information from others in [the] absence of formal obstacles," per Keren Sharvit et al., "Self-Censorship Orientation: Scale Development, Correlates and Outcomes," *Journal of Social and Political Psychology* 6, no. 2 (2018): 331–63, https://jspp.psychopen.eu/index.php/jspp/article/view/5065/5065.pdf. See the online appendix for detail on the surveys. The appendix is available at Joseph L. Sutherland and James L. Gibson, "The Rise of Self-Censorship in America," American Enterprise Institute, January 11, 2024, https://joesuth.com/assets/papers/SSRN-id4671208-appendix.pdf. The 2023 Verasight survey asked the Samuel Stouffer question with an explicit "don't know" response option. Because "not knowing" whether one can express one's views without repercussions is likely to encourage self-censorship, we have treated these as "less free" responses. The online appendix addresses several potential threats to the validity of the indicator, concluding generally that, like many, if not most, analyses of change in public opinion over time, the value of investigating how responses to the query have evolved exceeds the question's limitations.

5. Stouffer, *Communism, Conformity, and Civil Liberties*. See also James L. Gibson, "The Political Consequences of Intolerance: Cultural Conformity and Political Freedom," *American Political Science Review* 86, no. 2 (June 1992): 338–56, https://www.cambridge.org/core/journals/american-political-science-review/article/political-consequences-of-intolerance-cultural-conformity-and-political-freedom/75865A16D08974F828D9C8BAD38C8320; and James L. Gibson, "Intolerance and Political Repression in the United States: A Half Century After McCarthyism," *American*

Journal of Political Science 52, no. 1 (January 2008): 96–108, https://www.jstor.org/stable/25193799.

6. See Diana C. Mutz, "Cross-Cutting Social Networks: Testing Democratic Theory in Practice," *American Political Science Review* 96, no. 1 (March 2002): 111–26, https://www.cambridge.org/core/journals/american-political-science-review/article/crosscutting-social-networks-testing-democratic-theory-in-practice/2E570E31F3BB84B723CEF2A48A3C6741; and James N. Druckman, "Political Preference Formation: Competition, Deliberation, and the (Ir)relevance of Framing Effects," *American Political Science Review* 98, no. 4 (November 2004): 671–86, https://www.cambridge.org/core/journals/american-political-science-review/article/political-preference-formation-competition-deliberation-and-the-irrelevance-of-framing-effects/4D4C8A74BC5432BAF8B2BAAD0E800AA7.

7. Rachel Levinson-Waldman, Harsha Panduranga, and Faiza Patel, "Social Media Surveillance by the U.S. Government," Brennan Center for Justice, January 7, 2022, https://www.brennancenter.org/our-work/research-reports/social-media-surveillance-us-government.

8. See, for example, Gibson, "The Political Consequences of Intolerance"; Gibson, "Intolerance and Political Repression in the United States"; and Jaime E. Settle and Taylor N. Carlson, "Opting Out of Political Discussions," *Political Communication* 36 (2019): 476–96, https://www.tandfonline.com/doi/epdf/10.1080/10584609.2018.1561563.

9. Gibson and Sutherland, "Keeping Your Mouth Shut."

10. Iyengar et al., "The Origins and Consequences of Affective Polarization in the United States."

11. Taylor N. Carlson and Jaime E. Settle, *What Goes Without Saying: Navigating Political Discussion in America* (Cambridge, UK: Cambridge University Press, 2022).

12. Kathleen Hall Jamieson and Joseph N. Cappella, *Echo Chamber: Rush Limbaugh and the Conservative Media Establishment* (New York: Oxford University Press, 2008).

13. Jon C. Rogowski and Joseph L. Sutherland, "How Ideology Fuels Affective Polarization," *Political Behavior* 38 (June 2016): 485–508, https://link.springer.com/article/10.1007/s11109-015-9323-7. See also Iyengar et al., "The Origins and Consequences of Affective Polarization in the United States."

14. We also conducted a micro-level analysis using 2020 data from the Freedom and Tolerance Surveys, the source of the 2020 data point reported in Figure 1. We find that those who are themselves more polarized *do not* withhold their views more. There may be several reasons for the lack of relationship at the individual level, but the best explanations most likely have to do with how friends and associates of people *react to* polarization, rather than the degree of one's own polarization. Some who hold polarized views might seek out like-minded friends and therefore feel free to express themselves (as in echo chambers), but others holding such views may not (or are not able to) and therefore do not feel free. Gibson and Sutherland, "Keeping Your Mouth Shut."

15. For examples of over-time analysis of the General Social Survey data, see Dennis Chong and Morris Levy, "Competing Norms of Free Expression and

Political Tolerance," *Social Research* 85, no. 1 (Spring 2018): 197–227, https://muse.jhu.edu/article/692750; Dennis Chong, Jack Citrin, and Morris Levy, "The Realignment of Political Tolerance in the United States," *Perspectives on Politics* (2022): 1–22, https://www.cambridge.org/core/services/aop-cambridge-core/content/view/7813ABE313EC0008AB3E282292A318D7/S1537592722002079a.pdf/the-realignment-of-political-tolerance-in-the-united-states.pdf; and Joshua T. Davis and Samuel L. Perry, "White Christian Nationalism and Relative Political Tolerance for Racists," *Social Problems* 68, no. 3 (August 2021): 513–34, https://academic.oup.com/socpro/article/68/3/513/5810532.

16. Christopher Claassen and James L. Gibson, "Does Intolerance Dampen Dissent? Macro-Tolerance and Protest in American Metropolitan Areas," *Political Behavior* 41 (2019): 165–85, https://link.springer.com/article/10.1007/s11109-018-9444-x.

17. $r = 0.07$, $p = 0.056$, $N = 711$.

18. Following Gibson, we also considered whether people who are more politically intolerant are more likely to engage in self-censorship. Using a "least-liked" measure of intolerance, the data reveal only a weak correlation between intolerance and self-censorship ($r = 0.06$). Gibson, "Intolerance and Political Repression in the United States." For further consideration of this relationship, see Gibson and Sutherland, "Keeping Your Mouth Shut."

19. Mutz, "Cross-Cutting Social Networks," 122.

20. At the micro level, we find few connections. Intolerance in the respondent's local community is a poor predictor of self-censorship. Perceptions of governmental political repression are but a modest predictor of self-censorship. We also report that individual demographics fail to predict self-censorship: Respondents who describe themselves as born-again do not engage in more self-censorship, nor do the more highly educated or strong partisans (though, to the contrary, we do find a weak relationship among strong ideologues). Gibson and Sutherland, "Keeping Your Mouth Shut."

21. We also tested whether respondents who view the government as more repressive—that is, perceive political repression—are more likely to keep their mouths shut. The hypothesis that those perceiving more government repression engage in more self-censorship receives some, albeit only limited, support in the micro-level analysis. A small group of respondents who asserted that the government would not allow political activities engaged in significantly more self-censorship ($r = 0.13$, $p < 0.001$). This does not suggest a causal relationship between self-censorship and perceived repression; it may be that perceptions of government repression cause self-censorship, but it may also be that unwillingness to express oneself produces a tendency to see the government as repressive. Gibson and Sutherland, "Keeping Your Mouth Shut."

22. Elisabeth Noelle-Neumann, *The Spiral of Silence: Public Opinion—Our Social Skin* (Chicago: University of Chicago Press, 1993).

23. Jörg Matthes, Johannes Knoll, and Christian von Sikorski, "The 'Spiral of Silence' Revisited: A Meta-Analysis on the Relationship Between Perceptions of Opinion Support and Political Opinion Expression," *Communication Research* 45, no. 1 (February

2018): 3–33, https://journals.sagepub.com/doi/epub/10.1177/0093650217745429. For a useful depiction of how the decision to self-censor is made, see the scenario described by Carlson and Settle, *What Goes Without Saying*, 109–10.

24. *Sweezy v. New Hampshire*, 354 US 234 (1957).

6

How Institutional Speech
Erodes Academic Freedom

Aaron Saiger

The *mission* of the university is to advance knowledge and transmit it to the next generation. The *method* of the university is academic freedom, a guarantee that members of the academic community can freely express their ideas. A university uncommitted to both method and mission is unworthy of the name. A university that denies academic freedom, even if it nevertheless seeks and transmits the truth, is better characterized as a different kind of institution: a think tank, political party, lobbying firm, or revival meeting.

But what if a university, as an institution, expresses its *own* ideas? Many argue that doing so just adds voices to the mix, supplementing the university's desirable cacophony and silencing no one. But this is wrong. Institutional speech declares official orthodoxy. Such declarations are enemies of free thought. They label adherents as right-thinkers and place actual and potential dissenters on notice that their opinions are not just false but wrongheaded, even evil. This is by design: Universities are urged to state their views on contested topics not simply to rebut bad ideas but to undermine the authority and credibility of those who advocate them.[1] Such acts are inimical to a thriving culture of free inquiry, which must not simply tolerate but affirmatively welcome dissent.

Universities (and subunits of universities, like campuses, schools, and faculties and departments in their corporate capacities) should therefore eschew institutional speech when they can. The ideal of the university as a neutral forum, however, flies in the face of the multifarious scope of the modern university, whose tendrils infiltrate countless diverse spheres of activity. When universities are engaged in their daily business—admitting students, hiring faculty, granting degrees, funding programs, or setting curricula, for example—they have every right and, indeed, obligation to justify their actions. They must execute these functions defensibly, after all. Given that, it is perverse to deny them the right to defend their decisions.

Academic freedom, therefore, requires three principles around institutional speech. First, the university should adopt a presumption against such speech, taking public positions only when doing so is a necessary component of discharging its own functions. Second, when taking a position is necessary, institutional speakers should supplement their own statements with affirmative support for inquiry and for free and robust objection to official positions. And finally, individual faculty should stop seeking, or even desiring, an institutional imprimatur for ideas and arguments important to them. The collective mission of truth seeking is best served by a community of scholars, each stating what they believe to be true without either fear of institutional sanction or hope for institutional endorsement.

Counter-Speech Scenarios and Their Attractions

In 2020—the year when a white Minneapolis police officer murdered George Floyd—many American universities began to opine regularly on matters of race. Universities issued *cris de coeur* reckoning with their own racist pasts.[2] They decried racist and racially inflected incidents on campus. Events off campus also routinely triggered university speech. A police officer kills a black citizen, and everyone in the university receives an email expressing official horror. The officer is indicted (or not) and then acquitted (or not), and more emails flow on the same theme.

Quickly, such official position taking extended beyond race. The Supreme Court decides the Constitution does not protect abortion rights, and a same-day email blast announces that the institution believes, the Court notwithstanding, that the Constitution does. A riot takes place on the US Capitol grounds, and the university sounds an official tocsin bewailing the state of democracy. War erupts, and the university condemns one or another combatant (even as it maintains its silence regarding other conflicts). In this way, today's universities—not individual faculty and students, but the institutions themselves—have come routinely to adopt foreign policies, jurisprudential theories, and domestic policy platforms.[3]

A particular, and particularly problematic, variety of such statements flows from the desks of university deans, presidents, and trustees when some professor somewhere—call her Professor X—opines in a way that university brass considers false, offensive, or incendiary. Internal and external constituencies then demand that the university sack or otherwise punish Professor X. American universities these days accede to such demands with alarming frequency,[4] but many are still able to recognize that punishing speech violates academic freedom. Such universities therefore often respond to disfavored speech not by punishing the speaker but with speech of their own. They claim that doing so reconciles the principle of academic freedom with the desire to oppose inflammatory statements from within their ranks.[5] So the university announces to the community that Professor X's views are insensitive, insulting, untrue, appalling, or racist. The university proclaims it is committed to academic freedom and therefore will not punish the speaker, but it also states to the world that Professor X's views are utterly wrong, morally blind, and inimical to its community's deepest values. In short, rather than punish, the university denounces.

It is in the nature of institutions that once such views are stated, they are developed and embellished. Numerous university schools and academic departments have declared anti-racism, defined in some particular way, to be a foundational principle of their communities.[6] Internal and external pressures to take such stands, about all sorts of moral, political, and social propositions, are strong. As such statements proliferate, universities become like congressional candidates: They are expected to have an opinion about nearly everything.

The few politically labile issues regarding which universities demur from institutional position taking—as this is being written, the most notable are Hamas's October 2023 attacks on Israel and the justice and wisdom of Israel's retaliation—read almost as special cases, hypocritical exceptions to the rule.[7] The Israel-Hamas war, in particular, may ultimately make such selective hypocrisy harder to maintain. In the three years between the murder of Floyd and the murders by Hamas, some university administrators have come to wish emphatically they had stayed quiet more consistently.[8] Nevertheless, institutional speech continues to proliferate.

HOW INSTITUTIONAL SPEECH ERODES ACADEMIC FREEDOM 65

Conflict over university position taking arises in the context of more broadly eroding university commitments to academic freedom in general—across the ideological spectrum. The most consistent and far-reaching attacks on academic freedom in the United States to date have come from the right. Several governors and state legislatures have defiled their state universities by prohibiting them, by law, from teaching critically—a word often sloppily defined—about race.[9] State university officials, unable or unwilling to risk disobedience, are policing compliance in ways consistent with no one's understanding of academic freedom.

But one's outrage at the right's contempt for the freedom of the mind is then immediately whipsawed by the calls of faculty at elite left-leaning universities for the dismissal of colleagues for allegedly racist ideas or the review of their research for impermissibly racist tendencies.[10] Elite university administrators can be even worse. Right-leaning faculty who speak their minds about race and gender have found themselves removed from their classrooms, deprived of teaching assignments, banned from campus, investigated ad infinitum, and even fired on trumped-up pretexts.[11]

All these phenomena—instigated by ideologues of the right and left who share little other than their unwillingness to hear opposing views and then pursued by university leaders who either agree with or fear them—unambiguously violate academic freedom. They are much worse than institutional speech. But they also create the context in which institutional speech operates.

Today, institutional speech on hot-button issues carries the whiff of threat—sometimes more than a whiff. If a university broadcasts to the world that Professor X's ideas are hurtful, vile, and violent, Professor X is wise to wonder whether things will stop there. And even if they do, academic freedom is harmed. This conclusion requires additional analysis of what academic freedom is and what it is for.

Tolerance of Dissent Is Not Enough

Many university administrators take the view that academic freedom requires only that universities refrain from punishing dissenters. On this view, universities can take whatever positions on crucial issues—and, for that matter, non-crucial issues—they like. Such speech neither sanctions nor silences anyone. When the New York Yankees sponsor the playing field at Yankee Stadium, it is not unfair for them to fill the ballpark with home-team fans and home-team logos. Likewise, one of those voices in the multivocal university can be an institutional one, the corporate voice of the university itself. Dissenters are as free to dissent in the presence of that voice as when that voice is silent.

Some will find this analogy compelling, and others will not. Yankee logos at Yankee Stadium may seem unobjectionable, but a line might be crossed were the logos placed on the umpire's uniform. Similar institutional expression is considered to be unfair in other contexts as well. For example, we prohibit political displays and electioneering near polling stations, lest voters feel pressured.[12]

Many universities have long taken the position that it is possible to announce core values that supplement or stand alongside truth seeking. Religious schools have a long history of doing so, but secular universities do this as well. For every *crescat scientia* (University of Chicago), there is a *leges sine moribus vanae* (University of Pennsylvania). There is little reason to object to this when these positions are as general and anodyne as Penn's or as Stanford's *Die Luft der Freiheit weht*.

But, as we have seen, some universities espouse positions that trigger disagreement both reasonable and vehement. For many faculty members and administrators, the university exists partly to further secular ideological commitments other than the usual pursuit and transmission of truth and learning. Many academics argue, for example, that "social justice" is properly the university's mission—not just insofar as truth seeking furthers justice but more directly, in ways sometimes general but sometimes quite specific.[13]

This approach, under which academic freedom permits the university to articulate its own views and requires only that dissent be tolerated, has strong echoes in the First Amendment doctrine that applies to "government speech"—speech by the state in its own name. We understand the Constitution to permit such speech, independent of the nature of its claims or the kinds of disagreements it inspires, because it does not interfere with its citizens' expressive rights to disagree. For New Hampshire to adopt the motto "Live Free or Die" does not derogate the right of

HOW INSTITUTIONAL SPEECH ERODES ACADEMIC FREEDOM   67

New Hampshire folk to prefer life to freedom and to say as much. It just expresses the view of the government of New Hampshire.

The government-speech doctrine applies as a matter of law to public universities but not private ones. Our central question, of course, is not about legality. Rather, the intuition that underlies the government-speech doctrine is deeply relevant to whether declarations of policy by any university are compatible with academic freedom. If you dislike what the government says, the doctrine suggests, your remedy is not to complain that your rights have been violated but to disagree and, if you like, seek to change the government by persuasion, activism, or the deployment of political power. In these activities you are protected. Until you succeed, you are free to dissent; meanwhile, the state can speak as it likes.[14] University speech, whether in response to speech within its community or at its own instigation, likewise does not undermine the freedom of faculty or any other member of the university to disagree or advocate for change.

Why is this wrong? Because rules against punishing or silencing speech are necessary but far from sufficient elements of what is required to avoid the chilling of dissent: a university *culture* of free inquiry.[15] In this key respect, the university is not like the state. The government has no brief to create a culture of inquiry or encourage intellectual exploration. Its duty is to preserve freedom—that is, to tolerate. Universities, by contrast, do undertake to create and maintain a culture of free inquiry. Such a culture cannot be had if an institution labels some speakers as good and others as doubleplusungood. When faculty condemn each other, the process of debate is enhanced, but when the debate sponsors choose a side, academic culture suffers.[16]

The goal of academic freedom is to let professors speak the truth about controversial subjects as they see it, without *fear* of reprisal. Institutional speech, on the other hand, involves the corporate university—the entity with the money, power, and platform—taking a side.[17] Teachers who fear for their jobs, their tenure, their conditions of work, their salaries, their access to funds, or their access to university brands and resources know, in the main, that the best way to protect those things is not to aggravate those who control them. This is true a fortiori when those in control use that control, with some regularity, to punish speech, but it is also true even when the sponsor is scrupulous to avoid silencing and punishment.

68 THE FREE INQUIRY PAPERS

Even a university that never punishes a dissenter can still chill expression by making it feel as if sanctions *might* be applied. And sanction is a plastic category. The working life of even tenured faculty members depends on many decisions that administrators make by grace—leave eligibility, laboratory space, teaching assignments, and, crucially, compensation. It is hard to establish why administrators make these decisions as they do, which motivates faculty to stay on the good side of those administrators. University expressions of institutional opinion therefore legitimately worry nonconformists.[18]

These fears can seem somewhat overwrought. Reprisals, after all, remain rare. But even a small number of reprisals can have a substantial *in terrorem* effect. Reprisal is not the only problem, moreover; it's a problem just to be told that your institution repudiates you. These problems are well-known, of course, to faculty who have long inhabited the fringes of acceptable academic discourse: the anti-Zionists, gender theorists, Marxists, Communists, and occasional right-wing racists who have been marginalized by institutional orthodoxies for a long time. And it is telling, of course, that the dangers of official orthodoxies have come to more prominence only now that such scholars have been joined by political conservatives, classical liberals, and pro-Israel folks. But the dangers are no less for that.

Neutrality Is Ideal—but Often Impossible

If the position that academic freedom demands merely tolerance is fatally weak, the opposite view—that it demands institutional neutrality—is too rigid to implement.

The case for neutrality has never been made more persuasively than it was in 1967 by a committee convened by the president of the University of Chicago. That group has become eponymously known as the "Kalven Committee" for its chair, Harry Kalven Jr. Its brief report insists that a university organized to seek truth must itself be neutral with respect to that truth:

> The mission of the university is the discovery, improvement, and dissemination of knowledge. Its domain of inquiry and

HOW INSTITUTIONAL SPEECH ERODES ACADEMIC FREEDOM 69

> scrutiny includes all aspects and all values of society. A university faithful to its mission will provide enduring challenges to social values, policies, practices, and institutions. . . .
>
> The instrument of dissent and criticism is the individual faculty member or the individual student. The university is the home and sponsor of critics; it is not itself the critic. . . . A university, if it is to be true to its faith in intellectual inquiry, must embrace, be hospitable to, and encourage the widest diversity of views within its own community. It is a community but only for the limited, albeit great, purposes of teaching and research. It is not a club, it is not a trade association, it is not a lobby.
>
> . . . There emerges . . . a heavy presumption against the university taking collective action or expressing opinions on the political and social issues of the day.[19]

This is a compelling vision. The university "sponsors" a playing field. It provides resources and room for members of the community to seek the truth as they understand it and then to say what they find. The sponsor of the field should make sure no side has an advantage; the fix should not be in.

Some portions of university officialdom itself of late have moved toward Kalven's vision of neutrality. One example is Jenny Martinez, then serving as dean of the Stanford Law School (and, at this writing, Stanford's provost). Stanford law students, on some accounts abetted by law school administrators, had disrupted a March 2023 speech by federal judge Kyle Duncan on the grounds that his views regarding sex, gender, and other issues were troglodytic and not worthy of public hearing. In an open letter of apology, Martinez quoted Kalven in support of a promise that her administration would not

> announce institutional positions on a wide range of current social and political issues, make frequent institutional statements about current news events, or exclude or condemn speakers who hold views on social and political issues with whom some or even many in our community disagree,

70 THE FREE INQUIRY PAPERS

because to do these things "can lead to creating and enforcing an institutional orthodoxy . . . at odds with our core commitment to academic freedom."[20] Martinez's commitment was particularly striking because she had announced no institutional position with respect to Judge Duncan. Hers was a proactive recognition that demands for official positioning in general threaten academic freedom.

Martinez found support at other elite institutions. A group of prominent faculty at Princeton urged "universities and their units" to "refrain from publicly denouncing the research or extramural comments of members of the campus community with whom they disagree, lest they create official pariahs."[21] The following year, a blue-ribbon faculty working group at Harvard—a campus deeply shaken by unrest over wartime events in Israel and Gaza—likewise declared that "the university and its leaders should not . . . issue official statements about public matters that do not directly affect the university's core function."[22] The Harvard report engaged with academic freedom and the value of neutrality substantially less directly than Martinez or her counterparts at Princeton,[23] but it did note that institutional speech "may make it more difficult for some members of the community to express their views when they differ from the university's official position."[24] Notably, the working group's report was published simultaneously with a letter from Harvard's acting president and acting provost—individuals "acting" in those roles as a direct consequence of campus foment over free expression—endorsing the working group's recommendations as official university policy.[25] (Several months later, Harvard elevated both leaders to its full presidency and provostship, no longer encumbered by "acting" status.)

These accounts of neutrality are so compelling that it can be hard to see their flaws. How can an institution committed to open debate take a side? But even neutrality's proponents tend to hedge. The Kalven Report, for example, takes the position that neutrality is a "heavy" but rebuttable "presumption." "From time to time," writes the committee,

> instances will arise in which the society, or segments of it, threaten the very mission of the university and its values of free inquiry. In such a crisis, it becomes the obligation of the

university as an institution to oppose such measures and actively to defend its interests and its values.[26]

The Harvard working group likewise asserts that a university "has a responsibility to speak out to protect and promote its core function."[27] In other words, neutrality is the best posture, but *only most of the time*. Sometimes a university must set itself against particular kinds of egregiously baseless or damaging views. The university as an institution must be allowed—indeed, it even has a duty—to stand up for at least some claims about what is good, just, and true.

On the right, this neutrality-as-presumption has been an enthymeme underlying laws prohibiting critical instruction about race. The legislature prohibits such instruction not simply because it is wrong, not even because it is deeply wrong, but because it is *entirely* wrong, damaging to individual students, destructive to the academy, pernicious to the culture, and fundamentally un-American.[28] On the left, many university censors and their backers make the same charges against institutional failures to embrace contemporary racial orthodoxies.[29] Racist claims—and Zionist claims, too, for many—so damage the academic community that they cannot be tolerated, they argue. Some kinds of untruth cannot be expressed in a university devoted to open inquiry. Some issues do not permit "both-sidesism." Some opinions are too grotesque not to reject with full voice. Silence is assent.

These arguments reveal the Kalven Committee's "crisis" exception to institutional neutrality to be, as policy, hopeless. The slippery slopes it creates have no limiting conditions. Who chooses the "values"? Who delineates the university's "core" and its "mission"? Who decides which kinds of issues permit only one legitimate conclusion? Those in power at the university decide—unless, even worse, politicians or other actors external to the university arrogate that role to themselves.

Academic freedom exists as a principle precisely to deny such a priestly class the ability to limit the range of protected dissent. Censors on both the right and left condemn one another without irony because they are all orthodox believers. Challenges to their doctrines don't compute. Permitting such people to define institutional orthodoxies threatens the university's core truth-seeking function.

Principled Neutrality and Its Necessary Exceptions

There is, however, sound thinking behind the Kalven Committee's and the Harvard working group's conclusion that the policy of institutional silence demands exceptions. One reason the government-speech doctrine has developed as it has is that it is difficult to see how an effective state could function otherwise. The state must do too many things that require the expression of opinion to prohibit such expression. It does even more things that necessarily imply such opinions, even if they go unstated. Universities are like this too.

For example, universities are legally required under civil rights laws to restrict harassment based on race and sex, a category that includes some kinds of speech.[30] More broadly, a university that declines to create an undergraduate major in ethnic studies; runs a study abroad program in Moscow, Singapore, or Jerusalem; invests its endowment in fossil fuel companies; lobbies to liberalize visa requirements for international students; refuses to bargain with a graduate student union; or bills the indigent for care received at a university hospital—such a university has reasons for these policies that it can appropriately want or even need to articulate. It is not an option for the university to take no position. It perforce must invest, employ, admit students, bill patients, and run programs; therefore, it must decide how it will do so. It is unreasonable and counterproductive, then, to prohibit a university from justifying the positions it does take.

And this means that a university, with respect to many boiling-hot issues, cannot place itself above the fray. It cannot admit students or hire employees without a position on racism and how it should be mitigated. It cannot conduct research, sponsor journals, or establish campuses abroad without a position on academic boycotts. It cannot decide whether to require vaccination for entry to campus without a position on vaccination.

Universities as institutions—in practice, here I mean university administrators—also shape the intellectual life of their institutions directly, in ways both large and small. When they cultivate donors, for example, they shape present and future academic directions. When they target some academic departments for growth and others for dissolution, they determine the range of ideas discussed on campus. When they invite speakers for graduations and other events, award honorary degrees, or set summer reading assignments for incoming students, they center certain issues and brush others aside.

The best response to these needs is to categorize them as exceptions to a policy of institutional silence. In the formulation of the Harvard working group, universities "must speak out on issues directly relevant to the university's operation."[31] The problem, of course, is what counts as "directly relevant."[32] Put differently, the problem is to determine what issues are *not* relevant.

Contemporary developments in university life magnify the potential reach of a "university operations" exception manyfold. As Craig Calhoun notes, "Many universities have in effect become conglomerate corporations" whose endeavors include "managing giant laboratories seeking to innovate in dozens of different fields; running hospitals, radio and television stations, housing facilities, publishing companies, and semi-professional sports teams; . . . [and] providing extension services to agricultural producers."[33] Davarian Baldwin has shown that universities play a central role in their local economy, in their variegated capacities as landlords, property developers, job creators, gentrifiers, providers of physical and cultural infrastructure, and lobbyists.[34] These sprawling universities are at work in the world. Each operation that Calhoun and Baldwin describe, like the core academic functions of admissions and hiring, perforce involves missions, principles, and policies, all of which can demand justification.

The academic freedom of faculty is particularly threatened by the growing precarity of faculty positions and the exponential growth in administrative jobs.[35] Most university teaching is done by adjunct faculty who work without tenure, the possibility of tenure, or even a realistic expectation of continued employment. This applies especially to adjunct faculty whose employment is at will but also to the minority protected by union contracts. Even unionized adjuncts reasonably fear visibly departing from official positions.

As university administrators make more of the faculty adjuncts, moreover, they also employ growing armies of subdeans, administrators, and other bureaucrats, who are expected to amplify or at least not work against institutional values.[36] These staffs, who like adjuncts are often employed at will, can dwarf faculties in size and influence, a phenomenon decried on the left as the "neoliberal" or "corporatized" university and on the right

74 THE FREE INQUIRY PAPERS

as the "bureaucratized" one. Under either label, university administrators accustomed to a structure where they lead a large staff in a particular direction can sometimes forget that academic freedom is a value at all. And these staffs exert influence largely via institutional speech.

This is especially concerning with respect to two species of staffers. The first are the "student services professionals" who have increasingly penetrated the sphere of instruction—often under the rubric of "orientation" or "training"—that one might have thought was the province of the faculty.[37] The second are the denizens of "communications" offices,[38] paid to shape and broadcast institutional messages.[39] The work of these groups gives institutional speech, in addition to institutional prestige, institutional reach and power. A dissenting faculty member takes on not just a university leader but a leader backed by a squad of trained communications professionals.

The issue of precarity also highlights how institutional judgments about the content of its members' academic speech are unavoidable. Personnel decisions are the most crucial way that administrations influence academic discourse. Since long before the Kalven Committee, the intellectually critical processes of hiring and tenure decisions involved the institution's explicit consideration of the content of faculty expression. It asks: How smart is this candidate, how creative, how cutting-edge? How would this candidate advance the goals of the department or unit?

Universities as institutions also have—as Kalven recognized—not only the right but the duty to police (to some extent) instructor speech in the classroom. It is a university's obligation to demote or fire a physics professor who teaches that the earth is flat. (For this reason, bans on teaching critical race theory *in the classroom* threaten academic freedom less than blanket prohibitions on its discussion elsewhere in the university.)

The interpenetration of administration into faculty life brings to mind another analogy to constitutional doctrine, that of checks and balances. The executive branch does not and may not legislate, but it is given discrete but important legislative powers, like the veto and rulemaking, to check legislative excess or incapacity. So, too, hiring and tenure decisions about faculty and presidential and decanal selections must allow for institutional opinion about academic matters, including a candidate's ideas, thoughts, and public statements. And in many contexts, opacity regarding institutional opinion is highly undesirable, which necessitates institutional speech. At the same time, the interpenetration of administrators and faculty into academic life demands rigorous policing of other boundaries, lest the boundaries between faculty and the administration dissolve before the reality of administrative power.

The Anti-Racist University

Allowing speech to trump neutrality when related to university operations creates its own slippery slope. Perhaps the leading justification for institutional speech about race in progressive universities is that it is necessary to educate racially diverse student bodies. Even if—especially if—racially explosive speech cannot be punished without violating academic freedom, such speech undermines students' education by making them feel disrespected, unwelcome, alienated, and outside. Learning is at risk under such circumstances. To counteract these feelings, and therefore to discharge its core educational functions, many argue that students can and should expect to hear their universities commit to principles of anti-racism or inclusion and denounce opposing views as racist and wrong. And so, in service of their core goal of transmitting knowledge to contemporary students, many universities newly trumpet their devotion to cultivating in all community members feelings of "inclusion" and "belonging"—even at the cost of marginalizing dissent.

This pedagogical justification for institutional speech in this area has substantial force. It cannot be dismissed because it is about student feelings. To be sure, some have objected to this elevation of emotion. Many right-leaning voices mock the "snowflake" students of the left, so in thrall to (and often "exhausted" by) their emotions.[40] But, without apparent irony, not a few of those dismissive voices then welcome legislative bans on critical teaching that makes students feel "uncomfortable" or "guilty" because of their race.

Everyone should recognize that maintaining a culture of academic freedom is itself fundamentally *about* feelings. Heterodox faculty who fear reprisal for speaking freely are complaining about their own emotions. Fear is no less an emotion than alienation or guilt.

76 THE FREE INQUIRY PAPERS

Ultimately, however, a university cannot meet demands or expectations that it establish orthodoxies to promote feelings of belonging or inclusion. The desire for a reassuring orthodoxy that mitigates feelings of exclusion is, ultimately, the desire to teach and learn in an environment where dissent is disparaged and, inevitably, at least to some degree, suppressed. The comforts of orthodoxy are exactly the comforts that the university is committed to refusing to provide.[41] If an instructor expresses an opinion that makes a student feel disrespected or like they don't "belong," how can that be a reason, in an academic community, not to express such an opinion? And if expression of opinion is proper, then respect for diversity of opinion is necessary. Rejection of diversity of opinion cannot be an element of respect for diversity of membership. The whole enterprise of the free and freewheeling search for truth requires that we re-understand the latter not to derogate the former.

A Modest Program to Promote Academic Freedom

Although the Kalven Committee was right that neutrality is not always possible or appropriate, it missed the mark when it identified the proper scope of exceptions as those required by "crisis." Rather, universities should limit their position taking to those areas where their own activities make it necessary to take a side. The problem this raises in turn is that universities' immediate incentives will often lead them to enlarge the set of activities that they understand to involve such necessity. This conclusion commends a three-point program of action.

First, universities should adopt as a presumptive policy the position of the Kalven and Harvard committees and abstain from commenting on issues of the day. A university that feels the need to meet dissent with "more speech" should think twice. Neutrality should be cast aside only when it is incompatible with core university functions. That some university constituents want or expect the school, qua institution, to "acknowledge [their] unique pain"[42] does not qualify—particularly because such demands request not just acknowledgment of pain but substantive agreement with a set of truth claims or political preferences.

Often, however, the reasons for speech will be good enough.[43] For example, schools should not proclaim their anti-racism in order to be seen as seeing the pain of others, but they are fully entitled to justify, and fight for, their affirmative action policies. Such distinctions are unavoidable, although drawing the line between what is necessary and what is not will often be difficult and subjective.

That some institutional speech is appropriate, however, does not mean it carries no costs. A second principle, therefore, is that when universities feel compelled to speak their mind, they should commit at the same time to the aggressive pursuit of an institutional culture that *assures* dissenters that they need not fear reprisal. At the bare minimum, universities must immediately eschew reprisal itself. A university cannot demote, reassign, investigate, or sack dissenters, even (or better yet, especially) when popular sentiment regards their dissent as contemptuous, racist, or unconcerned with the truth.

Beyond this basic requirement, however, a university that takes an institutional position should actively and simultaneously affirm not only that it is open to but that it (to use the language of the Kalven Committee) "embrace[s], [is] hospitable to, and encourage[s] the widest diversity of views"[44]—including whatever views triggered its speaking out. It must do so likewise when its declaration is internally motivated rather than triggered by the radioactive speech of others. Tom Ginsburg has proposed, for example, that for every campus office of diversity and inclusion there should be an office of academic freedom, organized along parallel lines.[45] Even if one resists Ginsburg's willingness to meet bureaucratization with further bureaucratization, affirmative university commitments to open dialogue should come at the same level of intensity, frequency, and performativity as the university's own declarations of what it thinks about its various core values. A university that takes sides when necessary but promises no reprisal can provide robust academic freedom—but only if its promises are made *in a way that dissenters can credit.*

A final recommendation is directed to faculty who hold heterodox views. Their task is easy to articulate and hard to enact: They must be brave enough to speak their minds. This burden falls particularly on faculty protected by tenure—which is by no means an ironclad guarantee against reprisal but is also far from nothing. As long-term dissenters have long known, this expectation comes with no guarantees that speakers will not come to feel uncomfortable or even fearful in their own institutions. Risk, discomfort, and social stigma may well be necessary costs paid for the intellectual culture we desperately need.

No one ever guaranteed, or should guarantee, that dissent would be easy or without social cost. Universities must do their utmost to reassure dissenters in their midst that they are protected, by keeping silent when they can and actively promoting dissent when they feel compelled to speak. But to get to a university culture committed to genuine and robust academic freedom, those who reject the consensus must gird our loins and say what we think.

Notes

1. Kristine L. Bowman and Katharine Gelber, "Responding to Hate Speech: Counterspeech and the University," *Virginia Journal of Social Policy and the Law* 28, no. 3 (2021): 260, https://papers.ssrn.com/sol3/papers.cfm?abstract_id=4180723.

2. Gabriel Jack Chin et al., "Beyond Black and White: Transcript of the Free People of Color Symposium Discussing Campus Approaches to Race in Twentieth Century West Coast Universities and a Racial Justice Audit Template for Universities," *Social Justice Law Review* 27, no. 2 (2023): 75–124, https://escholarship.org/uc/item/9888r91c.

3. Adrienne Lu, "The Apolitical University," *Chronicle of Higher Education*, December 2, 2022, https://www.chronicle.com/article/the-apolitical-university.

4. Komi German and Sean T. Stevens, *Scholars Under Fire: 2021 Year in Review*, Foundation for Individual Rights and Expression, 2022, https://www.thefire.org/sites/default/files/2022/03/02150546/Scholars-Under-Fire-2021-year-in-review_Final.pdf.

5. Erwin Chemerinsky and Howard Gillman, *Free Speech on Campus* (New Haven, CT: Yale University Press, 2017).

6. For example, see Association of American Law Schools, "Law School Solidarity and Antiracism Statements," https://www.aals.org/about/publications/antiracist-clearinghouse.

7. David French, "What the University Presidents Got Right and Wrong About Antisemitic Speech," *New York Times*, December 10, 2023, https://www.nytimes.com/2023/12/10/opinion/antisemitism-university-presidents.html.

8. Jason Willick, "Colleges Went All In on Progressive Politics. Israel Is Spurring a Rethink," *Washington Post*, June 6, 2024, https://www.washingtonpost.com/opinions/2024/06/06/harvard-stanford-israel-neutrality.

9. Jonathan Feingold, "Reclaiming Equality: How Regressive Laws Can Advance Progressive Ends," *South Carolina Law Review* 73, no. 3 (Spring 2022): 723–57, https://scholarship.law.bu.edu/cgi/viewcontent.cgi?article=2840&context=faculty_scholarship.

HOW INSTITUTIONAL SPEECH ERODES ACADEMIC FREEDOM   79

10. Conor Friedersdorf, "The Princeton Faculty's Anti-Free-Speech Demands," *The Atlantic*, August 4, 2020, https://www.theatlantic.com/ideas/archive/2020/08/what-princeton-professors-really-think-about-defining-racism/614911.

11. Anemona Hartocollis, "Princeton Fires Tenured Professor in Campus Controversy," *New York Times*, May 23, 2022, https://www.nytimes.com/2022/05/23/us/princeton-fires-joshua-katz.html.

12. *Burson v. Freeman*, 504 US 191 (1992).

13. Ira Harkavy, "The Role of Universities in Advancing Citizenship and Social Justice in the 21st Century," *Education, Citizenship and Social Justice* 1, no. 1 (March 2006): 5–37, https://journals.sagepub.com/doi/10.1177/1746197906060711; and Brian L. Heuser, "A Critique of 'Principled Neutrality,'" *Inside Higher Ed*, May 2, 2023, https://www.insidehighered.com/opinion/views/2023/05/02/critique-principled-neutrality.

14. *Wooley v. Maynard*, 430 US 705 (1977).

15. Keith E. Whittington, "Free Speech and the Diverse University," *Fordham Law Review* 87, no. 6 (2019): 2453–77, https://ir.lawnet.fordham.edu/cgi/viewcontent.cgi?article=5608&context=flr.

16. Robert P. George, "Universities Shouldn't Be Ideological Churches," *The Atlantic*, June 15, 2023, https://www.theatlantic.com/ideas/archive/2023/06/university-statements-political-issues-abortion-princeton/674390.

17. Bowman and Gelber, "Responding to Hate Speech," 259–60.

18. Keith E. Whittington, "Academic Freedom and the Mission of the University," *Houston Law Review* 59, no. 4 (2022): 821–41, https://houstonlawreview.org/article/35603-academic-freedom-and-the-mission-of-the-university.

19. Kalven Committee, "Report on the University's Role in Political and Social Action," University of Chicago, Office of the Provost, November 11, 1967, https://provost.uchicago.edu/sites/default/files/documents/reports/KalvenRprt_0.pdf.

20. Jenny Martinez, letter to Stanford Law School Community, March 22, 2023, https://law.stanford.edu/wp-content/uploads/2023/03/Next-Steps-on-Protests-and-Free-Speech.pdf.

21. Shilo Brooks et al., "Princeton Principles for a Campus Culture of Free Inquiry," James Madison Program in American Ideals and Institutions, 2023, https://jmp.princeton.edu/princeton-principles-campus-culture-free-inquiry.

22. Noah Feldman et al., "Report on Institutional Voice in the University," Harvard University, 2024, https://provost.harvard.edu/sites/hwpi.harvard.edu/files/provost/files/institutional_voice_may_2024.pdf.

23. Noah Feldman and Alison Simmons, "Harvard Should Say Less. Maybe All Schools Should.," *New York Times*, May 28, 2024, https://www.nytimes.com/2024/05/28/opinion/university-statements-harvard-kalven.html.

24. Feldman et al., "Report on Institutional Voice in the University."

25. Alan M. Garber et al., letter to members of the Harvard community, May 28, 2024, https://www.harvard.edu/president/news/2024/institutional-voice.

26. Kalven Committee, "Report on the University's Role in Political and Social Action."

27. Feldman et al., "Report on Institutional Voice in the University."

80 THE FREE INQUIRY PAPERS

28. George Leef, "Fighting the Spread of Critical Race Theory," *National Review*, February 9, 2022, https://www.nationalreview.com/corner/fighting-the-spread-of-critical-race-theory.

29. Sigal Ben-Porath, "Against Endorsing the Chicago Principles," *Inside Higher Ed*, December 10, 2018, https://www.insidehighered.com/views/2018/12/11/what-chicago-principles-miss-when-it-comes-free-speech-and-academic-freedom-opinion.

30. Azhar Majeed, "The Misapplication of Peer Harassment Law on College and University Campuses and the Loss of Student Speech Rights," *Journal of College and University Law* 35, no. 2 (2009): 404–16, https://papers.ssrn.com/sol3/papers.cfm?abstract_id=1400300.

31. Feldman et al., "Report on Institutional Voice in the University."

32. Robert Post, "The Kalven Report, Institutional Neutrality, and Academic Freedom," in *Revisiting the Kalven Report: The University's Role in Social and Political Action*, ed. Keith E. Whittington and John Tomasi (Baltimore, MD: Johns Hopkins University Press, forthcoming), https://papers.ssrn.com/sol3/papers.cfm?abstract_id=4516235.

33. Craig Calhoun, "Free Inquiry and Public Mission in the Research University," *Social Research* 76, no. 3 (Fall 2009): 909–10, https://www.jstor.org/stable/40972165.

34. Davarian L. Baldwin, *In the Shadow of the Ivory Tower: How Universities Are Plundering Our Cities* (New York: Bold Type Books, 2021).

35. Herb Childress, *The Adjunct Underclass: How America's Colleges Betrayed Their Faculty, Their Students, and Their Mission* (Chicago: University of Chicago Press, 2019).

36. Thomas Wesley Williamson, E. Shannon Hughes, and Penny L. Head, "An Exploration of Administrative Bloat in American Higher Education," *Planning for Higher Education* 46, no. 2 (January–March 2018): 15–22, https://www.proquest.com/docview/2034196841.

37. Benjamin Ginsberg, *The Fall of the Faculty: The Rise of the All-Administrative University and Why It Matters* (New York: Oxford University Press, 2011).

38. I am indebted to Julie Suk for this observation.

39. Tom Eppes, "Hire Learning: Is a Top Spot in University Communications Right for You?," *Public Relations Tactics*, October 2014, 12, https://bluetoad.com/publication/?m=27649&i=226883.

40. Jennifer Gerarda Brown, "Four Questions About Free Speech and Campus Conflict," *Journal of Dispute Resolution* 2018, no. 2 (2018): 45–55, https://scholarship.law.missouri.edu/cgi/viewcontent.cgi?article=1808&context=jdr.

41. Majeed, "The Misapplication of Peer Harassment Law on College and University Campuses and the Loss of Student Speech Rights," 399–400.

42. Taifha N. Baker, "How Top Law Schools Can Resuscitate an Inclusive Climate for Minority and Low-Income Law Students," *Georgetown Journal of Law and Modern Critical Race Perspectives* 9, no. 2 (Fall 2017): 123–52, https://papers.ssrn.com/sol3/papers.cfm?abstract_id=3989432.

43. Post, "The Kalven Report, Institutional Neutrality, and Academic Freedom."

44. Kalven Committee, "Report on the University's Role in Political and Social Action."

45. Tom Ginsburg, "How to Truly Protect Academic Freedom," *Chronicle of Higher Education*, June 16, 2021, https://www.chronicle.com/article/how-to-truly-protect-academic-freedom.

7

Academic Freedom and the Social Media Veto

*Chad G. Rusthoven, George Yancey, Patricia Nayna Schwerdtle,
and Donald Alexander Downs*

> Promoting science isn't just about providing resources—it's
> also about protecting free and open inquiry. . . . It is about
> ensuring that scientific data is never distorted or concealed to
> serve a political agenda—and that we make scientific decisions
> based on facts, not ideology.
>
> —Barack Obama[1]

A cademic freedom is a classical liberal value that supports open scientific inquiry and expression in the academy. It is central to the truth-seeking mission of the university. As stated in the landmark American Association of University Professors 1940 statement on the principles of academic freedom and tenure, "the common good depends upon the free search for truth and its free exposition."[2] Inherent to arguments for academic freedom is the recognition of human fallibility, which applies even to the most accomplished minds. Indeed, the ethos of science and the promise of social progress are predicated on the constant checking and questioning of all truth claims, including those that enjoy consensus. Beyond science, free societies have an interest in maintaining cultures of open inquiry and expression given that any idea, no matter how virtuous its origins, may become a basis for oppression if it is not allowed to be questioned.[3]

One of the most famous historical examples of suppression of scientific inquiry and expression is the Roman Catholic Church's persecution of Galileo for promoting the heliocentric model.[4] Notable 20th-century examples include the targeting of American professors for political beliefs during the McCarthyism era and the Soviet ideological campaign against genetics and science-based agriculture known as Lysenkoism.[5] While the advocates of censorship in these cases considered their actions to be justified by the pursuit of their vision of the greater good, these episodes are now widely acknowledged to be egregious examples of intellectual oppression.

Today, there are worrying censorious trends in the modern academy, including cancellation campaigns and high rates of reported self-censorship. In a 2021 survey of US professors in the social sciences and humanities, 70 percent of conservatives, 42 percent of political centrists, and 26 percent of liberals reported self-censorship in teaching and research.[6] In a 2022 Heterodox Academy survey, 63 percent of college students reported that their campus climate prevented them from saying things they believe, primarily for fear of negative reactions or retribution from fellow students.[7] A 2021 report from the Foundation for Individual Rights and Expression (FIRE) reported that academic targeting incidents in American higher education institutions (e.g., demands for investigations, demotion, censorship, suspension, and termination) increased nearly fivefold from 2015 to 2020, with the majority of cases resulting in formal professional sanctions.[8]

In this context, social media has emerged as a powerful organizing platform for ideological suppression, in which calls for censorship can be amplified by combining posts from academics with those of the public, including political activists and interest groups.[9] Academic targeting on social media has culminated in retractions of peer-reviewed articles, the most severe sanction for published scholarship and one that is traditionally reserved for academic misconduct (e.g., falsification, fabrication, and plagiarism) and catastrophic analytic errors.[10]

This chapter explores these trends by examining three high-profile incidents involving social media attacks on peer-reviewed scholarship. This analysis does not address the ultimate validity of the conclusions in the publications at stake; rather, our concern is with the nature and implications of the reactions that took place.

Case 1: Affirmative Action in Medicine

In April 2020, a peer-reviewed article was published in the *Journal of the American Heart Association* by Norman Wang, a faculty cardiologist at the University of Pittsburgh Medical Center.[11] The article reviewed the history of affirmative action initiatives in medical education, including academic performance data from the Association of American Medical Colleges and affirmative action–related legislation and court rulings. The author argued that (1) historical shortfalls in achieving diversity benchmarks in medical education via affirmative action policies may be primarily attributable to upstream failures in the education system, (2) affirmative action admission preferences cause unintentional harm to some students, and (3) a transition to race-neutral policies would be preferable due to legal and efficacy concerns. The article concluded that "ultimately, all who aspire to a profession in medicine and cardiology must be assessed as individuals on the basis of their personal merits, not their racial and ethnic identities."[12]

After initially receiving minimal online attention, in late July 2020, the article became the focus of numerous condemnations on Twitter, many of which included the hashtag #RetractRacists.[13] In early August, the journal published a statement indicating that its editors were contacted by the author's employer and notified of "many misconceptions and misquotes"; providing two examples, the journal retracted the article without author agreement and published an apology with a pledge to improve its peer-review processes to prevent future missteps.[14] The author's employer removed him from his position as the electrophysiology fellowship program director and reportedly barred the author from contact with students and trainees, stating that his presence made learners "inherently unsafe."[15]

Case 2: Mentorship in Academia

In November 2020, a group of researchers from New York University Abu Dhabi published a peer-reviewed research article in the high-profile scientific journal *Nature Communications*.[16] The study analyzed three million junior-senior coauthor pairings and subsequent article citations (a common metric of academic success that counts the number of times an article is formally referenced by other scholarly articles). Using coauthorship as a proxy for informal mentorship, the article reported that, compared to other potential gender pairings, female-female junior-senior pairings were correlated with fewer subsequent citations for both authors. The publicly available 62-page initial peer-review and author response document demonstrates that the authors rigorously defended their analysis and during the peer-review process and provided survey data to support an association between authorship and mentorship.[17]

After publication, the article received significant condemnation on Twitter; critics cited harm to women in academia, and a prominent open letter from a scholar that was posted on Twitter called for its retraction.[18] In December 2020, after an additional post-publication peer-review process commissioned by the journal, the authors retracted the article. In their published retraction letter, the authors acknowledged criticisms related to their conceptualization of mentorship and expressed "deep regret" for the pain their publication caused, though they notably stated their belief that "the key findings of the paper with regards to coauthorship between junior and senior researchers are still valid."[19] The journal published an apology and announced updated guidelines that will "ensure that the review process takes into account the dimension of potential harm" in its assessments of scholarship going forward.[20]

Case 3: Gender Dysphoria in Adolescents and Young Adults

In August 2018, the multidisciplinary science journal *PLOS One* published a peer-reviewed research article titled "Rapid-Onset Gender Dysphoria in Adolescents and Young Adults: A Study of Parental Reports" by Lisa Littman, then a faculty member at the Brown University School of Public Health.[21] Against a backdrop of marked increases in adolescent presentations of gender dysphoria (GD) internationally, particularly among natal females,[22] the study relied on 256 surveys from parents to describe presentations of GD in adolescents and young adults without a prior history of the diagnosis.

The article reported that 69 percent of the youths were in friend groups in which another friend identified as transgender in the same time frame, and 37 percent were in groups in which over half the friends identified as transgender. The majority of the youths had a history of mental health issues or trauma and were highly immersed in social media content promoting transition, and the observed well-being of the child often declined after their GD was announced.

86 THE FREE INQUIRY PAPERS

Based on the observations, the author hypothesized that social-environmental factors could contribute to a developmental pathway for a particular presentation of GD, which might represent a maladaptive coping mechanism for some adolescents. The article acknowledged various limitations inherent to the study design and stated that the research represented an initial descriptive study and that future research was needed.

After its publication, the article received significant social media attention and comments on the journal website, of both support and condemnation. Methodological criticisms focused on biases inherent to targeted surveys of parents who were identified from websites that were considered critical of transgender identification. Others criticized the article's pathologizing framing, including the use of the psychological terminology of *social contagion*,[23] and some condemned the article as transphobic.[24]

Within two weeks, the journal responded by announcing a post-publication peer review.[25] The next day, the author's university replaced an initial press release promoting the study[26] with a statement from the dean of the school of public health noting "concerns that the conclusions of the study could be used to discredit efforts to support transgender youth and invalidate the perspectives of members of the transgender community."[27] These actions were met with pushback from various academics and members of the public, including a petition calling on the university and journal to uphold principles of academic freedom.[28] In an article defending the author and the role of controversial research in general, the former dean of Harvard University's medical school, Jeffrey Flier, stated,

> In all my years in academia, I have never once seen a comparable reaction from a journal within days of publishing a paper that the journal already had subjected to peer review, accepted and published. One can only assume that the response was in large measure due to the intense lobbying the journal received, and the threat—whether stated or unstated—that more social-media backlash would rain down upon *PLOS One* if action were not taken.[29]

In March 2019, the journal published a correction rewording the article title (to "Parent Reports of Adolescents and Young Adults Perceived to Show Signs of Rapid Onset Gender Dysphoria") and reframing its methods, context, and limitations[30]—even though the journal reportedly acknowledged that no errors had been identified.[31] The author lost her consulting position with the state department of health, reportedly following a letter from activists to her employer. Subsequently, her university faculty position was not renewed.[32]

Analysis of Social Media–Driven Suppression of Research and Expression

Each of these articles can be criticized. The affirmative action article positioned itself as a white paper (i.e., a comprehensive policy review with recommendations) but can be criticized for appearing one-sided by not thoroughly exploring the potential institutional benefits of diversity and challenges faced by minority candidates. Regarding the second article on mentorship, one might question the consistent correlation between coauthorship and mentorship or contend that citations are an imprecise metric of success. In the rapid-onset gender dysphoria (ROGD) article, the results should be interpreted cautiously given the acknowledged limitations and potential selection biases related to targeted survey data completed by self-identifying parents; thus, it is an initial hypothesis-generating descriptive study, suggesting further research.

We examine these cases not because the studies are perfect or stand above critique but to highlight how social media can be used as a powerful tool to dictate which ideas and authors may be expeditiously removed from the arena of scholarly discourse. These cases share the following components. First, they were published peer-reviewed articles that included politically sensitive content that could be interpreted as challenges to favored ideological positions in the academy. Second, the publications became targets of article-retraction campaigns via social media. Third, the negative online attacks evoked remarkably rapid responses from journals and universities, including additional post-publication peer review, article retractions (both journal and author driven), pledges to alter journal peer-review processes, and professional consequences from the scholars' institutions such as demotion and nonrenewal.

The cases do not appear to be outliers, as evidenced in running lists of targeting events,[33] and they add context to the aforementioned FIRE report demonstrating an increase in the number of academic targeting incidents since 2015.[34] We believe these trends are profoundly damaging to science and the academic community, and we review five arguments for this position.

Suppressing open inquiry and expression is anti-scientific. A body of scientific knowledge is never final or immutable; it is provisional and always open to modification, expansion, and refinement by new information.[35] The self-correcting nature of science relies on the principle of open inquiry, which enables rigorous vetting of scientific claims from diverse viewpoints. In *Why Trust Science?* Naomi Oreskes criticizes academic monocultures that lack dissenting perspectives, as they can develop collective blind spots that overlook important questions and data that could challenge shared beliefs:

> The greater the number of different points of view included in a given community, the more likely it is that its scientific practice will be objective and that it will result in descriptions and explanations of natural processes that are more reliable.[36]

Similarly, in *On Liberty*, John Stuart Mill underlines the epistemic importance of consistent challenges to our assumptions: "The beliefs which we have most warrant for, have no safeguards to rest on, but a standing invitation to the whole world to prove them unfounded."[37] The responses to the three cases can be examined in light of the scientific principle of open inquiry.

The affirmative action article presented academic performance data from the Association of American Medical Colleges that raised the possibility that some beneficiaries of affirmative action were actually harmed because of higher subsequent academic attrition rates. Because academic attrition can have significant professional, financial, and psychological consequences, medical students affected by affirmative action would benefit from data-driven responses that explore whether the concerns raised are incorrect, addressable, or acceptable on balance—rather than from article retraction. If some policies are encoded as sacred, collective blind spots can overlook areas of potential improvement.

In addition, the article was retracted before the landmark 2023 US Supreme Court decision in *Students for Fair Admissions v. Harvard*, which overturned affirmative action in higher education. This was during a time of vigorous public debate, when public polling and electoral results—such as California Proposition 16 in 2020, which upheld a ban on affirmative action in the public sector, including education—indicated that the majority of Americans support race-neutral admissions policies.[38] The suppression of academic debate by scholars and institutional leaders on a matter of substantial public interest reflects poorly on the health of the academy. As political scientist Keith Whittington has noted, in such cases, we "should not be surprised if the gap is filled by popularizers, ideologues, and charlatans."[39]

In the mentorship article, considering that the authors stand by their observations regarding coauthorship, proponents of open inquiry should welcome criticisms of the article's limitations while inviting replications to confirm or refute findings, explore causes, and work toward addressing identified impediments to female success. This article did not exclude gender bias as a causal factor for observed differences in citations. Moreover, the observation of a numerical difference in article citations would not invalidate other potential benefits of female-female mentor-mentee relationships.

The ROGD study coincided with substantial unexplained increases in adolescent GD among natal females, along with high rates of co-occurring psychological issues.[40] Because of these trends, numerous scholars have called for more research into the etiology and long-term outcomes for this expanding cohort.[41] The ROGD study was an initial survey-based descriptive study on this topic. Descriptive studies represent a lower level of evidence, and the author acknowledged potential biases from self-selecting parental surveys. Nevertheless, such studies serve an established and important scientific role in highlighting new phenomena and generating hypotheses.[42] Observations in the ROGD study could be influenced by parental biases, but parents could also offer novel insights that, if validated by future research, could expand our knowledge and contribute to the care of some patients. A group of scholars calling for more research on the topic summarized the argument for open inquiry:

Unless we are free to discuss, explore, and research differential presentations of gender dysphoria, the range of interventions which might best serve each young person may not be available to them. We do not think that this is good enough for our patients.[43]

Public targeting of scholars will have chilling effects that narrow the range of research and expression. Successful public targeting of scholars like those in the three case studies will have broader chilling effects on other researchers, eroding academic cultures of intellectual tolerance. How can researchers explore controversial ideas when their work and careers can be quickly undone by social media attacks?

Although professional and social sanctions vary, cases such as these serve as powerful warnings to scholars, journal editorial boards, funding bodies, and university leaders of the significant costs associated with challenging sacred ideological positions. If it is widely understood that the road to vindication for controversial ideas may be lined with asymmetric peer-review standards, investigations, personal attacks, isolation from colleagues, and even termination, it is rational to avoid research topics with a certain political valence. Moreover, although retraction campaigns may be intended to support vulnerable groups, they could cause unintended harm to those groups if they discourage fruitful research.

Politicizing science undermines the credibility of academic research. As Jonathan Rauch shows in *The Constitution of Knowledge*, the credibility of knowledge-generating institutions, including the scientific community, journalism, law, and government intelligence agencies, is fundamentally linked to their perceived commitments to rigorous and consistent professional standards, fairness, objectivity, and an ethos of self-correction.[44] If institutions are viewed as compromising these essential commitments for ideological priorities, they will lose the public's trust. For example, the US public's diminishing levels of trust in journalism, which stood at 36 percent in a 2021 Gallup poll, coincided with 83 percent of the public believing there was meaningful political bias in news coverage.[45]

For the scientific community, the consequences of a perception of politicization were observed during the COVID-19 pandemic in the domain of public health, where public opinions on empirical questions often became symbols of political affiliation.[46] The value of maintaining the credibility of the scientific community through an apolitical commitment to objectivity and consistency cannot be overstated.

Science can become politicized when asymmetric standards based on ideological priorities are used for evaluating scientific research and expression.[47] When asymmetric, and at times impossible, standards are used for politically disfavored scholarship and less scrutiny is applied to favored ideas in funding priorities, grant proposals, peer review, and, in some cases, post-publication retraction campaigns, the net effect is to narrow the range of publishable ideas to align with prevailing ideologies. Evidence of this phenomenon can be observed following the social media attacks in our three case examples.

In the case of the affirmative action article, the retraction was requested by the author's university and justified by the journal based on two alleged misquotes, reportedly without providing the author an opportunity to respond or offer corrections.[48] This fails to accord with standard guidelines for article retractions, which are usually limited to academic misconduct and analytic errors that cannot be addressed.[49] It suggests that the retraction decision was motivated by a desire to distance the journal and the university from the author's viewpoint.

Several of the authors of the mentorship article had published a similar study two years earlier in the same journal, albeit without discussing mentorship; it reported that increases in ethnic diversity among coauthors positively correlated with subsequent article citations.[50] That article was lauded in an editorial in the flagship parent journal and received significant positive attention on Twitter.[51] The observation of increased citations with greater ethnic diversity is a valuable contribution to the literature. However, it is reasonable to question whether the earlier article would have been allowed to stand had the results been reversed (i.e., a negative correlation between ethnic diversity and citations) or whether the subsequent mentorship article would have received similar praise if female-female junior-senior coauthor pairings had correlated with more, rather than fewer, subsequent citations.

In response to the ROGD article, an open letter from the Gender Dysphoria Affirmative Working Group suggested that the article was

92   THE FREE INQUIRY PAPERS

"unethical," and an open letter from the Coalition for the Advancement & Application of Psychological Sciences stated that the ROGD concept had "not been subjected to rigorous peer-review processes that are standard for clinical science."[52] It is certainly appropriate to note that ROGD is not a formal clinical diagnosis and that motivated third parties could misrepresent the strengths of what should be considered an exploratory, hypothesis-generating study. Nevertheless, the study itself obtained approval from the institutional review board for ethical study design, and the article underwent extensive formal scrutiny, withstanding an unusual *two* separate peer-review processes.

In a published response to criticisms, the author of the ROGD article provided side-by-side comparisons demonstrating that the study's methods are established in the field and have been used in multiple well-cited papers.[53] The author also asserted that the study faced more intense scrutiny because it was viewed as opening the door to challenges to the preferred gender-affirmative model of care. Subsequently, similar concerns with the current strength of the evidence for managing adolescent GD and with professional intolerance for diverse viewpoints have been raised in various settings, including a landmark National Health Services commissioned independent report in the UK,[54] more cautious clinical guidelines adopted in several European countries,[55] and public statements from leaders of transgender health associations.[56]

Proposed justifications for using asymmetric standards, in these cases and others, often frame the actions as necessary to protect vulnerable populations from potential harm related to scientific research and expression. This harm-avoidance justification has at least three crucial flaws. First, predictions of harm are irrelevant to whether scientific results are true.[57] Second, prioritizing harm avoidance over truth seeking has no limiting principle; almost any result related to human subjects could be inappropriately used to harm some group.[58] Third, because they are not omniscient, scholars cannot predict the net harm or benefit that scientific results and debate will have over time or the potential downstream harms of suppressing new information. The subjective and malleable nature of a policy of harm avoidance will inevitably lead to politicized decision-making, particularly given that some of the most immediate harms that scientific gatekeepers can avoid by suppressing controversial scholarship include the threat of backlash and damage to their own careers and reputations.

Prioritizing harm avoidance over truth seeking represents not only an inversion of the university's core mission but also an inherently politicized framework for assessing scholarship. These issues illustrate why changes in scientific peer-review standards to selectively prioritize subjective assessments of harm, as seen in updated editorial guidelines for the prestigious journal *Nature* and its portfolio of associated academic journals,[59] will distort, politicize, and undermine the credibility of science.

Social media is incompatible with impartial assessments of scholarship on politically sensitive topics. There is a growing body of research on social media's psychological and social effects. Consider, for example, a 2021 study analyzing 100 million pieces of content on controversial topics, which found that users tend to cluster into echo chambers that reaffirm rather than challenge preexisting beliefs.[60] A 2021 study analyzing 2.7 million social media posts from news organizations and US Congress members found that posts expressing out-group animosity resulted in the most engagement.[61] A 2018 study of 126,000 news stories tweeted by three million users found that falsehoods spread significantly further and faster than true stories and were more likely to be associated with reactions of fear and disgust.[62]

When social media dynamics are dominated by confirmation bias, tribalism, and partisan anger in relation to politically sensitive topics, the environments become incompatible with impartial assessments of scholarship. Indeed, it is difficult to imagine incentive structures less conducive to the core standards and practices of a knowledge-generating institution.

Social media targeting campaigns are likely to be unrepresentative of the academic community. When appraising social media's potential influence on science, some numerical context is important. As of 2021, the National Center for Education Statistics estimated there were 1.5 million faculty members in higher education in the US, and the Census Bureau estimated there were 4.7 million Americans with doctoral degrees.[63] Yet creating the impression of widespread outrage related to scholarship on social media may require only a few dozen original posts from a combination of scholars and the public. These dynamics have allowed a relatively small number of people to elicit rapid reactions from the leaders of universities and scientific journals.

In the three cases reviewed here, it is unknown how representative the online responses were of the academic community, but evidence suggests that few scholars support academic targeting. For example, a 2021 study found that only one in 10 academics would support dismissing a professor for controversial expression.[64]

Conclusions and Recommendations

Open inquiry and expression are fundamental to the truth-seeking mission of the academy. Data indicate an increase in targeting of scholars for their research and expression and considerable self-censorship among university faculty and students. Social media has emerged as a powerful organizing platform for condemning ideas that some consider harmful, and academic journals and universities have demonstrated high levels of responsiveness to negative social media attention.

Successful social media pressure campaigns resulting in the retraction of articles and the appearance of expedited professional consequences will influence the topics researchers avoid, the results they submit for publication, and the scholarship that journals will consider. Reactive modifications to peer-review guidelines that incorporate subjective dimensions of harm will result in asymmetric standards that constrict intellectual diversity, distorting the flow of information. Together, these dynamics will result in unintended and unknowable negative downstream effects on the progress of knowledge. Moreover, the perception of politicized science and institutional deference to online outrage undermines public trust in the academy as an objective knowledge-generating body.

University leadership and journal editorial boards must consider these emerging dynamics and their internal commitments to open inquiry and expression. Institutions should establish policies for dealing with controversies before incidents occur, allowing leaders to point to clear, consistent standards. Although social media allows a relatively small number of people to loudly call for punishing scholars, academic leaders are under no obligation to give in to such demands.[65] Strong statements in support of academic freedom can diffuse controversies by foreclosing the possibility of successful cancellation.[66]

For university leaders, the Chicago statement on freedom of expression, which has been formally adopted by over 100 US universities, provides an outstanding template for principled support of open inquiry and expression.[67] Endorsing institutions could also consider addenda to this statement outlining their support for academic freedom in the face of the unique challenge of social media and other forms of online outrage.

For scientific journals, the Committee on Publication Ethics provides guidelines for article retractions, which are recommended only for the most significant instances of academic misconduct and major analytic errors that irreparably corrupt the study findings.[68] Article corrections are recommended for less significant errors, whereas standard nonpunitive discourses (e.g., editorials, letters to the editor, and author responses) should be used to debate controversial topics. No equivalent to the Chicago statement for academic journals currently exists. However, similar principles could be adopted and, ideally, featured in mission statements and editorial guidelines. These may include:

- A commitment to open inquiry and scholarly expression as fundamental to the truth-seeking mission of the scientific community;

- A commitment to consistent standards in peer-review processes, including avoiding asymmetric standards based on subjective considerations such as predictions of harm or the political, ideological, or religious implications of the scholarship; and

- Standardized processes for handling negative social media attention and other modes of outrage directed at scholarship. Formal actions should generally be limited to substantive allegations of misconduct and significant analytic errors. When investigations are initiated, expedited reactions should be avoided, allowing adequate time to consider all relevant information. Communications to the public during deliberation, if necessary, should be limited and refer to adherence to predetermined standards.

96 THE FREE INQUIRY PAPERS

The trends examined here should concern all who have an interest in the success of the academy. The university's mission is not to make people feel comfortable, but rather to advance and disseminate knowledge. This requires consistent, principled commitments to open inquiry and expression. In the words of the 1974 Report of the Committee on Free Expression at Yale, a.k.a. the Woodward Report,

> The history of intellectual growth and discovery clearly demonstrates the need for unfettered freedom, the right to think the unthinkable, discuss the unmentionable, and challenge the unchallengeable. To curtail free expression strikes twice at intellectual freedom, for whoever deprives another of the right to state unpopular views necessarily also deprives others of the right to listen to those views.[69]

Notes

1. Barack Obama, "Obama's Remarks on Stem Cell Research" (speech, White House, Washington, DC, March 9, 2009), https://www.nytimes.com/2009/03/09/us/politics/09text-obama.html.

2. American Association of University Professors, "1940 Statement of Principles on Academic Freedom and Tenure," 1940, https://www.aaup.org/Report/1940-Statement-Principles-Academic-Freedom-and-Tenure.

3. Dana Villa, *Socratic Citizenship* (Princeton, NJ: Princeton University Press, 2001).

4. Alan Cowell, "After 350 Years, Vatican Says Galileo Was Right: It Moves," *New York Times*, October 31, 1992, https://www.nytimes.com/1992/10/31/world/after-350-years-vatican-says-galileo-was-right-it-moves.html.

5. Svetlana A. Borinskaya, Andrei I. Ermolaev, and Eduard I. Kolchinsky, "Lysenkoism Against Genetics: The Meeting of the Lenin All-Union Academy of Agricultural Sciences of August 1948, Its Background, Causes, and Aftermath," *Genetics* 212, no. 1 (May 2019): 1–12, https://academic.oup.com/genetics/article/212/1/1/6087971; and Ellen Schrecker, "Political Tests for Professors: Academic Freedom During the McCarthy Years" (paper presented at the University Loyalty Oath: A 50th Anniversary Retrospective Symposium, Berkeley, CA, October 7, 1999).

6. Eric Kaufmann, *Academic Freedom in Crisis: Punishment, Political Discrimination, and Self-Censorship*, Center for the Study of Partisanship and Ideology, https://cspicenter.org/wp-content/uploads/2021/03/AcademicFreedom.pdf.

7. Steven Zhou and Nicole Barbaro, *Understanding Student Expression Across Higher Ed: Heterodox Academy's Annual Campus Expression Survey*, Heterodox Academy, March 2023, https://heterodoxacademy.org/reports/2022-campus-expression-survey-report.

8. Komi German and Sean T. Stevens, *Scholars Under Fire: 2021 Year in Review*, Foundation for Individual Rights and Expression, 2022, https://www.thefire.org/sites/default/files/2022/03/02150546/Scholars-Under-Fire-2021-year-in-review_Final.pdf.

9. Sean T. Stevens, Lee Jussim, and Nathan Honeycutt, "Scholarship Suppression: Theoretical Perspectives and Emerging Trends," *Societies* 10, no. 4 (December 2020): 82, https://www.mdpi.com/2075-4698/10/4/82.

10. Lee Jussim, "The Threat to Academic Freedom . . . from Academics," December 27, 2019, https://psychrabble.medium.com/the-threat-to-academic-freedom-from-academics-4685b1705794; and Committee on Publication Ethics, "Retraction Guidelines," November 2019, https://publicationethics.org/node/19896.

11. Norman C. Wang, "Diversity, Inclusion, and Equity: Evolution of Race and Ethnicity Considerations for the Cardiology Workforce in the United States of America from 1969 to 2019," *Journal of the American Heart Association* 9, no. 7 (2020), https://www.ahajournals.org/doi/10.1161/JAHA.120.015959.

12. Wang, "Diversity, Inclusion, and Equity."

13. Altmetric, "Diversity, Inclusion, and Equity: Evolution of Race and Ethnicity Considerations for the Cardiology Workforce in the United States of America from 1969 to 2019," https://ahajournals.altmetric.com/details/78188527/twitter/page:5; and Zachary Robert Caverley, "Dr. Norman C. Wang and Selective Outrage," Quillette, September 22, 2020, https://quillette.com/2020/09/22/dr-norman-c-wang-and-selective-outrage.

14. *Journal of the American Heart Association* and American Heart Association, "Retraction to: Diversity, Inclusion, and Equity: Evolution of Race and Ethnicity Considerations for the Cardiology Workforce in the United States of America from 1969 to 2019," *Journal of the American Heart Association* 9, no. 20 (2020), https://www.ahajournals.org/doi/10.1161/JAHA.119.014602; and Barry London, "Diversity, Equity, and Inclusiveness in Medicine and Cardiology," *Journal of the American Heart Association* 9, no. 17 (2020), https://www.ahajournals.org/doi/10.1161/JAHA.119.014592.

15. Donovan Harrell, "Education Department, AAUP Enter Controversy over Professor's White Paper," *University Times*, October 23, 2020, https://www.utimes.pitt.edu/news/education-department-aaup.

16. Bedoor AlShebli, Kinga Makovi, and Talal Rahwan, "Retracted Article: The Association Between Early Career Informal Mentorship in Academic Collaborations and Junior Author Performance," *Nature Communications* 11, no. 5855 (2020), https://www.nature.com/articles/s41467-020-19723-8.

17. Bedoor AlShebli, Kinga Makovi, and Talal Rahwan, "Reviewers' Comments," 2020, https://static-content.springer.com/esm/art%3A10.1038%2Fs41467-020-19723-8/MediaObjects/41467_2020_19723_MOESM2_ESM.pdf.

18. Tania Reynolds, "Retracting a Controversial Paper Won't Help Female Scientists," Quillette, November 23, 2020, https://quillette.com/2020/11/23/retracting-a-controversial-paper-wont-help-female-scientists; and Altmetric, "Retracted Article: The Association Between Early Career Informal Mentorship in Academic

Collaborations and Junior Author Performance," https://nature.altmetric.com/details/94470485/twitter/page:100.

19. Bedoor AlShebli, Kinga Makovi, and Talal Rahwan, "Retraction Note: The Association Between Early Career Informal Mentorship in Academic Collaborations and Junior Author Performance," *Nature Communications* 11, no. 6466 (2020), https://www.nature.com/articles/s41467-020-20617-y.

20. Editorial Board, "Regarding Mentorship," *Nature Communications* 11, no. 6447 (2020), https://www.nature.com/articles/s41467-020-20618-x.

21. Lisa Littman, "Rapid-Onset Gender Dysphoria in Adolescents and Young Adults: A Study of Parental Reports," *PLOS One* 13, no. 8 (2018), https://journals.plos.org/plosone/article?id=10.1371/journal.pone.0202330.

22. Madison Aitken et al., "Evidence for an Altered Sex Ratio in Clinic-Referred Adolescents with Gender Dysphoria," *Journal of Sexual Medicine* 12, no. 3 (March 2015): 756–63, https://academic.oup.com/jsm/article-abstract/12/3/756/6966737; Hayley Wood et al., "Patterns of Referral to a Gender Identity Service for Children and Adolescents (1976–2011): Age, Sex Ratio, and Sexual Orientation," *Journal of Sex & Marital Therapy* 39, no. 1 (2013): 1–6, https://www.tandfonline.com/doi/abs/10.1080/0092623X.2012.675022; and Riittakerttu Kaltiala-Heino et al., "Time Trends in Referrals to Child and Adolescent Gender Identity Services: A Study in Four Nordic Countries and in the UK," *Nordic Journal of Psychiatry* 74, no. 1 (2020): 40–44, https://www.tandfonline.com/doi/full/10.1080/08039488.2019.1667429.

23. *American Psychological Association Dictionary of Psychology*, s.v. "social contagion," accessed March 23, 2024, https://dictionary.apa.org/social-contagion; Vania Martínez, Álvaro Jiménez-Molina, and Mónica M. Gerber, "Social Contagion, Violence, and Suicide Among Adolescents," *Current Opinion in Psychiatry* 36, no. 3 (2023): 237–42, https://www.ncbi.nlm.nih.gov/pmc/articles/PMC10090320/pdf/coip-36-237.pdf; and Stephen Allison, Megan Warin, and Tarun Bastiampillai, "Anorexia Nervosa and Social Contagion: Clinical Implications," *Australian & New Zealand Journal of Psychiatry* 48, no. 2 (2014): 116–20, https://journals.sagepub.com/doi/10.1177/0004867413502092.

24. Altmetric, "Parent Reports of Adolescents and Young Adults Perceived to Show Signs of a Rapid Onset of Gender Dysphoria," https://plos.altmetric.com/details/46597665/twitter; and Meredith Wadman, "New Paper Ignites Storm over Whether Teens Experience 'Rapid Onset' of Transgender Identity," *Science*, https://www.science.org/content/article/new-paper-ignites-storm-over-whether-teens-experience-rapid-onset-transgender-identity.

25. Staff, "Statement by PLOS One Staff," *PLOS One*, August 27, 2018, https://journals.plos.org/plosone/article/comment?id=10.1371/annotation/2a4269d4-90ab-4f26-bf00-1348cc787ca8.

26. Mollie Rappe, "Brown Researcher First to Describe Rapid-Onset Gender Dysphoria," Brown University, August 22, 2018, https://archive.md/M8a3Z#selection-989.0-989.63.

27. News Staff, "Updated: Brown Statements on Gender Dysphoria Study," Brown University, March 19, 2019, https://news.brown.edu/articles/2018/08/gender.

28. Lee Jussim, "Rapid Onset Gender Dysphoria," *Psychology Today*, March 20, 2019, https://www.psychologytoday.com/us/blog/rabble-rouser/201903/rapid-onset-

gender-dysphoria; and iPetitions, "Brown University and PLoS ONE: Defend Academic Freedom and Scientific Inquiry," accessed June 22, 2022, https://www.ipetitions.com/petition/brown-university-and-plos-one-defend-academic.

29. Jeffrey S. Flier, "As a Former Dean of Harvard Medical School, I Question Brown's Failure to Defend Lisa Littman," Quillette, August 31, 2018, https://quillette.com/2018/08/31/as-a-former-dean-of-harvard-medical-school-i-question-browns-failure-to-defend-lisa-littman.

30. Lisa Littman, "Correction: Parent Reports of Adolescents and Young Adults Perceived to Show Signs of a Rapid Onset of Gender Dysphoria," *PLOS One* 14, no. 3 (2019), https://journals.plos.org/plosone/article?id=10.1371/journal.pone.0214157.

31. Jesse Singal, "How Science-Based Medicine Botched Its Coverage of the Youth Gender Medicine Debate," Singal-Minded, July 10, 2021, https://jessesingal.substack.com/p/how-science-based-medicine-botched.

32. Megyn Kelly, "Dr. Lisa Littman on Rapid Onset Gender Dysphoria, the Teen Trans Trend, and Intellectual Rigor," YouTube, October 25, 2021, https://www.youtube.com/watch?v=Hq8ryFVy_LM.

33. Jussim, "The Threat to Academic Freedom . . . from Academics"; David Acevedo, "Tracking Cancel Culture in Higher Education," National Association of Scholars, November 6, 2023, https://www.nas.org/blogs/article/tracking-cancel-culture-in-higher-education; and Noah Carl, "A List of Academic Petitions and Open Letters," Medium, August 24, 2020, https://noahcarl.medium.com/a-list-of-academic-petitions-and-open-letters-995fadc0a088.

34. German and Stevens, *Scholars Under Fire*.

35. Dorian S. Abbot et al., "In Defense of Merit in Science," *Journal of Controversial Ideas* 3, no. 1 (April 2023).

36. Naomi Oreskes, *Why Trust Science?* (Princeton, NJ: Princeton University Press, 2021).

37. John Stuart Mill, "Of the Liberty of Thought and Discussion," in *On Liberty* (London: John W. Parker and Son, 1859), https://www.utilitarianism.com/ol/two.html.

38. *Students for Fair Admissions v. President and Fellows of Harvard College*, 600 US 181 (2023); Conor Friedersdorf, "Why California Rejected Racial Preferences, Again," *The Atlantic*, November 10, 2020, https://www.theatlantic.com/ideas/archive/2020/11/why-california-rejected-affirmative-action-again/617049; Vianney Gómez, "As Courts Weigh Affirmative Action, Grades and Test Scores Seen as Top Factors in College Admissions," Pew Research Center, https://www.pewresearch.org/fact-tank/2022/04/26/u-s-public-continues-to-view-grades-test-scores-as-top-factors-in-college-admissions; and Frank Newport, "Update on Race, College Admissions and Public Opinion," Gallup, February 17, 2023, https://news.gallup.com/opinion/polling-matters/470681/update-race-college-admissions-public-opinion.aspx.

39. Keith E. Whittington, "The Value of Ideological Diversity Among University Faculty," *Social Philosophy and Policy* 37, no. 2 (Winter 2020): 90–113, https://kewhitt.scholar.princeton.edu/sites/g/files/toruqf3716/files/the_value_of_ideological_diversity_among_university_faculty_draft.pdf.

40. Aitken et al., "Evidence for an Altered Sex Ratio in Clinic-Referred Adolescents with Gender Dysphoria"; Wood et al., "Patterns of Referral to a Gender Identity

Service for Children and Adolescents (1976–2011)"; Kaltiala et al., "Time Trends in Referrals to Child and Adolescent Gender Identity Services: A Study in Four Nordic Countries and in the UK"; Nastasja M. de Graaf et al., "Psychological Functioning in Adolescents Referred to Specialist Gender Identity Clinics Across Europe: A Clinical Comparison Study Between Four Clinics," *European Child & Adolescent Psychiatry* 27 (2018): 909–19, https://link.springer.com/article/10.1007/s00787-017-1098-4; Nastasja M. de Graaf and Polly Carmichael, "Reflections on Emerging Trends in Clinical Work with Gender Diverse Children and Adolescents," *Clinical Child Psychology and Psychiatry* 24, no. 2 (2019): 353–64, https://journals.sagepub.com/doi/10.1177/1359104518812924; and Riittakerttu Kaltiala-Heino et al., "Two Years of Gender Identity Service for Minors: Overrepresentation of Natal Girls with Severe Problems in Adolescent Development," *Child and Adolescent Psychiatry and Mental Health* 9 (2015), https://capmh.biomedcentral.com/articles/10.1186/s13034-015-0042-y.

41. De Graaf and Carmichael, "Reflections on Emerging Trends in Clinical Work with Gender Diverse Children and Adolescents"; Kenneth J. Zucker, "Adolescents with Gender Dysphoria: Reflections on Some Contemporary Clinical and Research Issues," *Archives of Sexual Behavior* 48 (2019): 1983–92, https://link.springer.com/article/10.1007/s10508-019-01518-8; Riittakerttu Kaltiala-Heino et al., "Gender Dysphoria in Adolescence: Current Perspectives," *Adolescent Health, Medicine and Therapeutics* 9 (2018): 31–41, https://link.springer.com/article/10.1007/s10508-019-01518-8; and Anna Hutchinson, Melissa Midgen, and Anastassis Spiliadis, "In Support of Research into Rapid-Onset Gender Dysphoria," *Archives of Sexual Behavior* 49 (2020): 79–80, https://link.springer.com/article/10.1007/s10508-019-01517-9.

42. Daniel J. Hoppe et al., "Hierarchy of Evidence: Where Observational Studies Fit In and Why We Need Them," in "Design, Conduct, and Interpretation of Nonrandomized Orthopaedic Studies: A Practical Approach," ed. Mohit Bhandari et al., supplement, *Journal of Bone and Joint Surgery* 91, no. S3 (2009): 2–9, https://journals.lww.com/jbjsjournal/abstract/2009/05003/hierarchy_of_evidence__where_observational_studies.2.aspx.

43. Hutchinson, Midgen, and Spiliadis, "In Support of Research into Rapid-Onset Gender Dysphoria."

44. Jonathan Rauch, *The Constitution of Knowledge: A Defense of Truth* (Washington, DC: Brookings Institution Press, 2021).

45. Megan Brenan, "Americans' Trust in Media Dips to Second Lowest on Record," Gallup, October 7, 2021, https://news.gallup.com/poll/355526/americans-trust-media-dips-second-lowest-record.aspx; and Megan Brenan and Helen Stubbs, "News Media Viewed as Biased but Crucial to Democracy," Gallup, August 4, 2020, https://news.gallup.com/poll/316574/news-media-viewed-biased-crucial-democracy.aspx.

46. Jeffrey M. Jones, "Democratic, Republican Confidence in Science Diverges," Gallup, July 16, 2021, https://news.gallup.com/poll/352397/democratic-republican-confidence-science-diverges.aspx; Vinay Prasad, "Public Health's Truth Problem," *City Journal*, January 19, 2022, https://www.city-journal.org/public-healths-truth-problem; Andrew J. Dolman, "Opposing Views: Associations of Political Polarization, Political Party Affiliation, and Social Trust with COVID-19 Vaccination Intent and Receipt," *Journal of Public Health* 45, no. 1 (March 2023): 36–39, https://academic.

oup.com/jpubhealth/article/45/1/36/6514797; Dannagal G. Young et al., "The Politics of Mask-Wearing: Political Preferences, Reactance, and Conflict Aversion During COVID," *Social Science & Medicine* 298 (2022), https://www.sciencedirect.com/science/article/pii/S0277953622001423; and Kerrington Powell and Vinay Prasad, "The Noble Lies of COVID-19," Slate, July 28, 2021, https://slate.com/technology/2021/07/noble-lies-covid-fauci-cdc-masks.html.

47. Scott Alexander, "Beware Isolated Demands for Rigor," Slate Star Codex, August 14, 2014, https://slatestarcodex.com/2014/08/14/beware-isolated-demands-for-rigor; and Alan Sokal, "How Ideology Threatens to Corrupt Science," *The Critic*, May 22, 2024, https://thecritic.co.uk/how-ideology-threatens-to-corrupt-science.

48. Zach Greenberg, "Pitt's Punishment of Professor over 'Deep Disagreement' with Academic Paper Merits Judicial Intervention," Foundation for Individual Rights and Expression, January 12, 2021, https://www.thefire.org/pitts-punishment-of-professor-over-deep-disagreement-with-academic-paper-merits-judicial-intervention.

49. Committee on Publication Ethics, "Retraction Guidelines."

50. Bedoor K. AlShebli, Talal Rahwan, and Wei Lee Woon, "The Preeminence of Ethnic Diversity in Scientific Collaboration," *Nature Communications* 9 (2018), https://www.nature.com/articles/s41467-018-07634-8.

51. Kendall Powell, "These Labs Are Remarkably Diverse—Here's Why They're Winning at Science," *Nature* 558, no. 7708 (June 7, 2018): 19–22, https://www.nature.com/articles/d41586-018-05316-5; and Altmetric, "The Preeminence of Ethnic Diversity in Scientific Collaboration," https://nature.altmetric.com/details/34018066/twitter.

52. Gender Dysphoria Affirmative Working Group, "An Open Letter to the Owners, Editors, Members, Advertisers, and Others at Psychology Today," December 5, 2018, https://www.gdaworkinggroup.com/letter-to-psychology-today; and Coalition for the Advancement & Application of Psychological Science, "CAAPS Position Statement on Rapid Onset Gender Dysphoria (ROGD)," accessed June 22, 2022, https://www.caaps.co/rogd-statement.

53. Lisa Littman, "The Use of Methodologies in Littman (2018) Is Consistent with the Use of Methodologies in Other Studies Contributing to the Field of Gender Dysphoria Research: Response to Restar (2019)," *Archives of Sexual Behavior* 49 (2020): 67–77, https://link.springer.com/article/10.1007/s10508-020-01631-z.

54. Cass Review, *Independent Review of Gender Identity Services for Children and Young People*, April 2024, https://cass.independent-review.uk/home/publications/final-report.

55. Joshua Cohen, "Increasing Number of European Nations Adopt a More Cautious Approach to Gender-Affirming Care Among Minors," *Forbes*, June 6, 2023, https://www.forbes.com/sites/joshuacohen/2023/06/06/increasing-number-of-european-nations-adopt-a-more-cautious-approach-to-gender-affirming-care-among-minors; *The Economist*, "Britain Changes Tack in Its Treatment of Trans-Identifying Children," November 17, 2022, https://www.economist.com/britain/2022/11/17/britain-changes-tack-in-its-treatment-of-trans-identifying-children; Jathon Sapsford and Stephanie Armour, "U.S. Becomes Transgender-Care Outlier as More in Europe Urge Caution," *Wall Street Journal*, June 19, 2023, https://www.wsj.com/articles/u-s-becomes-transgender-care-outlier-as-more-in-europe-urge-caution-6c70b5e0; and Ty Roush,

"UK Bans Puberty Blockers for Minors," *Forbes*, March 12, 2024, https://www.forbes.com/sites/tylerroush/2024/03/12/uk-bans-puberty-blockers-for-minors.

56. Laura Edwards-Leeper and Erica Anderson, "The Mental Health Establishment Is Failing Trans Kids," *Washington Post*, November 24, 2021, https://www.washingtonpost.com/outlook/2021/11/24/trans-kids-therapy-psychologist; and Abigail Shrier, "Top Trans Doctors Blow the Whistle on 'Sloppy' Care," Free Press, October 4, 2021, https://bariweiss.substack.com/p/top-trans-doctors-blow-the-whistle.

57. Jussim, "Rapid Onset Gender Dysphoria."

58. Flier, "As a Former Dean of Harvard Medical School, I Question Brown's Failure to Defend Lisa Littman."

59. "Science Must Respect the Dignity and Rights of All Humans," *Nature Human Behaviour* 6 (August 2022): 1029–31, https://www.nature.com/articles/s41562-022-01443-2; Nature Portfolio, "Research Ethics," accessed May 27, 2024, https://www.nature.com/nature-portfolio/editorial-policies/ethics-and-biosecurity; Bo Winegard, "The Fall of 'Nature,'" Quillette, August 8, 2022, https://quillette.com/2022/08/28/the-fall-of-nature; Jonathan Rauch, "Nature Human Misbehavior: Politicized Science Is Neither Science nor Progress," Foundation for Individual Rights and Expression, September 14, 2022, https://www.thefire.org/news/nature-human-misbehavior-politicized-science-neither-science-nor-progress; and Sokal, "How Ideology Threatens to Corrupt Science."

60. Matteo Cinelli et al., "The Echo Chamber Effect on Social Media," *Proceedings of the National Academy of Sciences* 118, no. 9 (2021), https://www.pnas.org/doi/full/10.1073/pnas.2023301118.

61. Steve Rathje, Jay J. Van Bavel, and Sander van der Linden, "Out-Group Animosity Drives Engagement on Social Media," *Proceedings of the National Academy of Sciences* 118, no. 26 (2021), https://www.pnas.org/doi/full/10.1073/pnas.2024292118.

62. Soroush Vosoughi, Deb Roy, and Sinan Aral, "The Spread of True and False News Online," *Science* 359, no. 6380 (2018): 1146–51, https://www.science.org/doi/10.1126/science.aap9559.

63. National Center for Education Statistics, "Characteristics of Postsecondary Faculty," August 2023, https://nces.ed.gov/programs/coe/indicator/csc/postsecondary-faculty; and US Census Bureau, "Census Bureau Releases New Educational Attainment Data," February 24, 2022, https://www.census.gov/newsroom/press-releases/2022/educational-attainment.html.

64. Kaufmann, "Academic Freedom in Crisis."

65. Judith Suissa and Alice Sullivan, "The Gender Wars, Academic Freedom and Education," *Journal of Philosophy of Education* 55, no. 1 (February 2021): 55–82, https://academic.oup.com/jope/article/55/1/55/6821527.

66. Robert J. Zimmer, "Statement on Faculty, Free Expression, and Diversity," University of Chicago, Office of the President, November 29, 2020, https://president.uchicago.edu/en/from-the-president/announcements/2006-2021/112920-free-expression; and News Staff, "Message from Chancellor Kent Syverud and Dean David Van Slyke," Syracuse University News, September 13, 2021, https://news.syr.edu/blog/2021/09/13/message-from-chancellor-kent-syverud-and-dean-david-van-slyke.

ACADEMIC FREEDOM AND THE SOCIAL MEDIA VETO   103

67. Foundation for Individual Rights and Expression, "Chicago Statement: University and Faculty Body Support," https://www.thefire.org/chicago-statement-university-and-faculty-body-support.

68. Committee on Publication Ethics, "Retraction Guidelines."

69. Committee on Freedom of Expression at Yale, "Report of the Committee on Freedom of Expression at Yale," Yale College, December 23, 1974, https://yalecollege.yale.edu/get-know-yale-college/office-dean/reports/report-committee-freedom-yale.

8

Do No Anti-Racist Harm:
Medical Education Under Threat

Sally Satel

Twenty-four years ago, I wrote a book called *PC, M.D.: How Political Correctness Is Corrupting Medicine*. One chapter explored "multicultural counseling," a form of therapy that encourages white clinicians to ask themselves, "What responsibility do you hold for the racist, oppressive and discriminating manner by which you personally and professionally deal with minorities?"[1] Another chapter documented flaws in studies purportedly showing that physicians, as a matter of routine, were racially biased against their patients. I devoted another chapter to the quest for social justice in public health. In the epilogue, which I called "The Indoctrinologist Isn't In . . . Yet," I cautioned: "Those who care about the culture and practice of medicine must be alert to the encroachment of political agendas."[2]

Today, the indoctrinologists are officially in, and their campaign to impose social justice ideology has gathered staggering momentum since the killing of George Floyd. Its roots predate May 2020, however.

December 10, 2014, was International Human Rights Day. That afternoon, 3,000 medical students "died" on the lawns and walkways of medical school campuses across the country. The "National White Coat Die-In" was the brainchild of medical students who were moved to demonstrate for racial justice in the wake of the police killings of Michael Brown and Eric Garner. At the die-in, students wearing surgical scrubs and white jackets lay silent for 4.5 minutes, symbolic of the 4.5 hours that Michael Brown's body remained on the street in Ferguson, Missouri, after a white police officer shot him.

A group called White Coats for Black Lives (WC4BL) emerged from the event. Its mission is to "prepare future physicians to be advocates for racial justice,"[3] and one of its core convictions is that "policing is incompatible with health."[4] Most of the major medical schools have a chapter of WC4BL, which describes its job as "dismantling dominant, exploitative systems in the United States, which are largely reliant on anti-Black racism, colonialism, cisheteropatriarchy, white supremacy, and capitalism."[5]

Early in the COVID-19 pandemic, some argued that if hospitals needed to ration ventilators, they should prioritize black patients rather than rely exclusively on standard criteria, such as clinical need or prognosis.[6] After the Floyd murder, an epidemiologist from the Johns Hopkins Bloomberg School of Public Health informed would-be marchers that "the public health risks of not protesting to demand an end to systemic racism greatly exceed the harms of the virus." Days later, 1,200 health professionals cheered her on in an open letter.[7]

The problem, of course, is that the job of epidemiologists is to inform the public about risks. However, there is no way they can quantify the risk of not marching. But even if they could, it is not their job to tell others what risks are worth taking or what their moral prerogatives should be. Yet in each instance above, the experts allowed their own moral commitments, not objective metrics of risk, to shape their advice.

In late 2020, when it came time to distribute the coronavirus vaccine, an assortment of authorities—including legal scholars, public health experts, and state officials—argued for giving high priority to black citizens in the name of "historical injustice." About that historical injustice there can be no doubt, but the Advisory Committee on Immunization Practices of the Centers for Disease Control and Prevention (CDC) concluded that race should supersede age as a prioritization category because the oldest cohort in America is whiter than the general population.[8]

In reality, the risk was massively greater for older people than younger people, a differential that dwarfed the black-white difference. The CDC was well aware of this. One CDC official even said that a race-based allocation plan would result in up to 6.5 percent more deaths, many of whom would be black senior citizens—the highest-risk group. No matter, the official went on to say, "Racial and ethnic minority groups are underrepresented among adults [older than] 65."[9]

As political scientist Yascha Mounk put it, "America's elderly are too white to be considered a top priority for the distribution of the vaccine against Covid." Elevating "health equity" was about to take precedence at the CDC. The agency's loyalty was to an ideal—not, foremost, to saving the most American lives from infection. The massive public outcry that ensued almost surely helped derail the racial-preference plan; the committee revised its recommendation, thereby preventing thousands of deaths.[10]

What's Happened to My Profession?

Today, medical schools are embattled, beset by woke incursions trying to alter medicine's mission to social justice and physicians' identities to activists. In this chapter, I describe their campaign and its implications for medical education and patient care. I conclude that the social justice movement within medicine identifies some real problems—though these issues have been well-known already—but that its remedies show no signs of effectively addressing these issues. In profound ways, they appear to be harming medicine by chilling collegial and academic discourse, eroding standards of excellence, and siphoning precious time and money from medical education.

In important ways, I hardly recognize my profession. It is too early in this worrisome experiment to see a measurable effect on patient well-being, but we must be on high alert for its manifestation.[11]

A Brief History of Necessary Reform

First, some history. Like so many current excesses, the infusion of radical social justice in medicine has noble roots. In the mid-to-late 19th century, the public health field organized itself around technical strategies aimed at the leading causes of death at the turn of the century: cholera, diphtheria, influenza, pneumonia, and tuberculosis. Unfortunately, physicians had little to offer by way of medical treatment, but they worked closely with public health experts to contain epidemics. As drug discoveries mounted—among them penicillin for a broad swath of infections in 1928 (though it was not used until 1942) and the sulfa drugs in the 1930s—the power and prestige of the medical profession grew, and it separated from public health.

Public health cared for populations, while medicine cared for individuals. Within American public health, an occasional champion of European-style social medicine would emerge. Charles-Edward Amory Winslow, a bacteriologist and head of the Yale School of Public Health, was one. He told his colleagues in 1948, referring to both men and women, that

> men should not sicken and die from polluted water, from malaria-breeding swamps, from epidemics of diphtheria, from tuberculosis. Those battles have been, in large measure, won. We must now determine that men shall not be physically and emotionally crippled by . . . social insecurity.[12]

The field took the opposite route, however, dedicating itself to individual-level risks for injury and chronic illness. Surgeons general and public service advertisements exhorted Americans to stop smoking, eat more vegetables, exercise, wear seat belts, and so on. Within the academy, however, theoretical developments inspired by social medicine were underway. In 1950, sociologists and epidemiologists found common interest, for example, in a study of the relationship of fetal and infant mortality to residential segregation.

By the 1970s, a cadre of epidemiologists were studying the psychological, social, and cultural forces that make people more vulnerable to disease and shape their choices regarding health. The term "social determinants of health," which came into general use in the 1990s, captured that formidable notion.[13] Its more abstract cousin, what I call the social production of health, examined how social inequalities affected health, often with a nakedly ideological slant that implied no limit to the profession.[14] Consider some sample quotations from faculty: "The practice of public health is, to a large degree, the process of redesigning society."[15] "Every problem is a public health problem."[16] "A school of public health is like a school of justice." The latter dictum was issued by Harvey V. Fineberg, a former dean of the Harvard T. H. Chan School of Public Health.[17]

Not everyone welcomed the introduction of progressive norms into public health academies. "We have nearly converted the school of public health from an institution committed to developing the scientific bases for disease prevention into one of many arenas for advancing social justice," Philip Cole of the University of Alabama at Birmingham and his colleagues sternly observed in 2000.[18] "Broadly speaking[,] public health is aligned with the left," said the dean of the Boston University School of Public Health, "and there is no sense dancing around it." He appealed to his colleagues to be "a fully inclusive left," "let go of always taking sides," and abandon "the hectoring tone [that] radicalism can entail."[19]

Over the past decade, politicization of public health has moved from oppression more generally to anti-racism. It has also moved into the medical realm. Medical schools are scrambling to respond to charges by leaders in the field that their institutions perpetuate systemic racism. The key allegations are that (1) such racism is the sole, or near-exclusive, driver of disparities in health status and access to care and (2) it accounts for the underrepresentation of black and Hispanic physicians and researchers in medicine—and the health of minority patients depends on diversity in the medical workforce. The campaign to "dismantle racist policies and practices across all of health care," an imperative issued by the American Medical Association (AMA), takes many forms, as described below.[20] None, in my view, show promise in resolving a real problem: the deficits in minority health and access to care.

Ideological Framework

The most influential institutions in the field—the AMA and the Association of American Medical Colleges (AAMC), which plays a significant role in accrediting schools—have diagnosed the problems facing medicine through the lens of racism, politics, and power differentials.

In 2021, the AMA issued a document called *Advancing Health Equity: A Guide to Language, Narrative and Concepts*. The guide condemned several "dominant narratives" in medicine.[21] One is the "narrative of individualism" and its misbegotten corollary, the notion that health is a personal responsibility.[22] A "healthy equity narrative," the guide instructs, would "expose the political roots underlying apparently 'natural' economic arrangements, such as property rights, market conditions, gentrification, oligopolies and low wage rates."[23] The dominant narratives, says the AMA, "create harm, undermining public health and the advancement of health equity; they must be named, disrupted, and corrected."[24]

One form of correction the AMA recommends is "equity-explicit" language.[25] Instead of "individuals," doctors should say "survivors"; instead of "marginalized communities," they should say "groups that are struggling against economic marginalization."[26] We must also be clear that "people are not vulnerable; they are made vulnerable."[27] Accordingly, we should replace the statement, "low-income people have the highest level of coronary artery disease" with "people underpaid and forced into poverty as a result of banking policies, real estate developers gentrifying neighborhoods, and corporations weakening the power of labor movements, among others, have the highest level of coronary artery disease."[28]

As mentioned above, the social determinants of health are real, and our increased awareness of them has been a major advance in medical training over the past 20 or so years. Doctors need to realize, and many surely do, that even their most motivated patients may not be able to afford medication, take time from work to keep an appointment, access reliable transportation to appointments, or understand a complex medical regimen. We must be prepared to let patients know we understand these obstacles and enlist social workers and case managers to help.

However, the AMA guide recklessly stretches context beyond the realm of understanding determinants and clinical outreach. It rebuffs "programmatic fixes," such as the case manager who arranges for a patient's transportation, because such fixes "ignore the social responsibility of corporations and government agencies." With its emphasis on "power relations"[29] and its push to "redistribute power and resources,"[30] the guide reads more like a postmodern manifesto than an actionable blueprint for physicians. In another document, the AMA's *Organizational Strategic Plan to Embed Racial Justice and Advance Health Equity*, the association calls for the "just representation of Black, Indigenous and Latinx people in medical school admissions as well as medical school and hospital leadership ranks."[31]

In July 2022, the AAMC released *Diversity, Equity, and Inclusion Competencies Across the Learning Continuum*, a set of guidelines for advancing health equity in medical curricula. The competencies function as a blueprint for teaching about "intersectionality," "white privilege," "microaggression," and "allyship."[32] The document includes vague but politicized mandates. For example, trainees and professors are to practice "anti-racism and critical consciousness in health care."[33] For students, it means describing the "impact" of "colonization" or "white supremacy" on health. For faculty, it means "participat[ing] in system-level solutions to end racist practices in education and clinical delivery."[34]

Curriculum

Curricular reform in medical schools is underway. At Stanford University School of Medicine, for example, a new "anti-racist" curriculum will instruct students in "confronting white supremacy."[35] Students at Brown University will take a four-week course on racial justice and health inequity to "gain a deep understanding of topic areas such as critical race theory, intersectionality, and the inequities that pervade the US health care system."[36] At Kaiser Permanente Bernard J. Tyson School of Medicine, topics covered will include social identity, intersectionality, power, and privilege; the history of race and racism in medicine and science; and media bias and literacy.[37] Staple readings of the new curricula are *White Fragility* by Robin DiAngelo and *How to Be an Antiracist* by Ibram X. Kendi.[38]

In 2020, the AAMC informed medical schools that they "must employ anti-racist and unconscious bias training and engage in interracial dialogues."[39] In the spring of 2021, the AMA advocated "mandatory anti-racism [training]" as part of its vision that all physicians "confront inequities and dismantle white supremacy, racism, and other forms of exclusion and structured oppression."[40] Now, at least 23 of America's 25 most prestigious medical colleges and universities have some form of mandatory student training or coursework on ideas related to critical race theory, according to CriticalRace.org, which monitors critical race theory curricula and training in higher education.[41]

State legislatures have become involved. California, Maryland, Michigan, Minnesota, and Washington recently passed legislation mandating implicit bias training for at least some categories of health professionals. Michigan requires implicit bias training for health professionals, and Maryland has made it a condition of obtaining a medical license.[42]

Such training often includes the wildly popular Implicit Association Test, a computer-administered reaction-time test purported to measure unconscious prejudice and thus foretell whether an individual will engage in discrimination. The problem, according to abundant research—including by the psychologists who devised the test—is that it has no predictive value regarding how one interacts with minority individuals.[43]

In short, the trainings are useless, a waste of money and time in a curriculum that is already packed. Students need to learn anatomy, physiology, and pharmacology, among other topics. One of my colleagues, who preferred to be unnamed, told me in the fall of 2020 that her school jettisoned lectures in bioethics to make room for the anti-racist curriculum. "Which is ironic," she said, "because that was where students were taught about subjects like the Tuskegee syphilis experiment."[44] What other essential topics are being displaced to accommodate politicized teaching?

Chilled Discourse

The implementation of the social justice agenda has constrained collegial discourse, challenged the maintenance of standards, and suppressed honest analysis of certain problems. In her article "What Happens When Doctors Can't Tell the Truth?," journalist Katie Herzog wrote of

> doctors who've been reported to their departments for criticizing residents for being late. (It was seen by their trainees as an act of racism.) I've heard from doctors who've stopped giving trainees honest feedback for fear of retaliation. I've spoken to those who have seen clinicians and residents refuse to treat patients based on their race or their perceived conservative politics.[45]

In some quarters, there is reflexive attribution of group differences in health to systemic racism. "It's axiomatic at this point," said a colleague who had participated in a group discussion of stress and rising suicide in black youth.[46] The tacit rule was that only fear of police aggression and subjection to racial discrimination were allowable explanations, not the psychological torture of bullying by classmates or the quotidian terror of neighborhood gun violence. The subtle pressure to attribute health differentials to outside forces naturally takes the focus off how patients can be in better control of their own health. It also narrows the scope of understanding myriad other factors.

Two medical cancellations have attracted notice. In 2020, Norman C. Wang—a cardiologist at the University of Pittsburgh School of Medicine who expressed skepticism about mandatory affirmative action after conducting a careful review of the data—was stripped by his department of his directorship of the electrophysiology fellowship and barred from having contact with medical students, residents, or fellows because his views were "inherently unsafe."[47]

His peer-reviewed paper—"Diversity, Inclusion, and Equity: Evolution of Race and Ethnicity Considerations for the Cardiology Workforce in the United States of America from 1969 to 2019," which appeared in the *Journal of the American Heart Association* (*JAHA*) in March 2020—was retracted by the journal without Wang's consent. The American Heart Association, which publishes *JAHA*, tweeted that his article "does NOT represent [the American Heart Association's] values."[48] The cardiologist has sued the university and the American Health Association.[49] (In September 2022, a judge dismissed the university from the case.)[50]

Wang made his case on strong empirical grounds. According to an analysis by economist Mark J. Perry, between 2013 and 2016—the last year for which the AAMC makes data available—medical schools admitted only 8 percent of white college seniors with below-average undergraduate GPAs and below-average MCAT scores. Asian college seniors with those qualifications were offered slots at a rate of 6 percent.[51] At the same time, schools accepted 56 percent of black college seniors with below-average undergraduate GPAs and below-average MCATs and 31 percent of Hispanic students with those scores. This means that a black student in that range was over seven times as likely to gain admission as a white college senior with the same grades and more than nine times as likely to be admitted as a similarly situated Asian senior.

Performance differentials already exist, and compromising standards will almost surely exacerbate the problem. A 2022 study of clinical performance scores by authors from Emory University, Massachusetts General Hospital, and the University of California, San Francisco, among other institutions, analyzed faculty evaluations of internal medicine residents in such areas as medical knowledge and professionalism. On every assessment, black and Hispanic residents were rated lower than white and Asian residents. The authors speculated that these differences were attributable to "bias in faculty assessment, effects of a non-inclusive learning environment, or structural inequities in assessment." They failed to rule out another possibility—namely, suboptimal performance based on suboptimal preparedness of students admitted under affirmative action policies.[52]

In another cancellation, the editor in chief of the *Journal of the American Medical Association* was effectively forced to resign in June 2021 for a somewhat tone-deaf, but otherwise unremarkable, 15-minute podcast on racism in medicine and because of a tweet advertising it.[53] "Although I did not write or even see the tweet, or create the podcast, as editor-in-chief, I am ultimately responsible for them," he said in a statement.

What other examples have escaped attention? "Most in academic medicine who are troubled by this are keeping their heads down and keeping their mouths shut," said my colleague Thomas Huddle, an internist and professor who retired in 2021 from the University of Alabama at Birmingham's medical school, one of few physicians willing to go on the record. "They're deeply afraid of social media mobs and of academic administrative superiors who've taken this stuff on," he said of his colleagues.[54]

The Reflexive Taboo Against Race and Biology. Another topic under excessive scrutiny is the relationship between race and disease. Some worry that putting "genes" and "race" in the same sentence will encourage eugenics and the fiction that races are discrete entities defined by biological traits. With science literacy among the public so tenuous, the worry is not misplaced. But studies involving genes and race are simply about population genetics—for example, the fact that people sharing a geographical ancestry are more likely to have particular gene variants (alleles) in their genome than do people with a different heritage.[55]

Researchers and physicians agree that pharmacogenomics—the elucidation of the relationship between treatment and individuals' unique genomic fingerprint to create personalized therapies—will make the controversy obsolete. But until this gold standard is used widely, group-based

114 THE FREE INQUIRY PAPERS

genetic analysis will have some value. Even with the caveats in mind, genetic heritage can be relevant to medicine with regard to appropriately dosing certain drugs, more accurately predicting responses to those drugs, using clinical decision-making via algorithms (an especially controversial matter that scientists are currently debating in good faith), and determining heightened risk for certain conditions, such as cardiovascular and renal disease.

A recent study in the *Journal of the American Medical Association* uncovered an interesting finding correlated with race. In a sample of about 300 patients at a New York medical center, black patients had stronger expression of the gene that codes for transmembrane serine protease 2, a protein known as TMPRSS2, than did white, Asian, Hispanic, or mixed-race patients.[56] TMPRSS2 sits on the surface of cells lining the nose and is involved with entry of the coronavirus into those cells. Will that finding hold up on replication? Perhaps not. And if it does, the protein likely accounts for a small part of the racial variation in COVID-19 infections, the lion's share being accounted for by social factors.

Still, the investigation yielded potentially useful findings. Science, after all, is provisional, cumulative, and, eventually, self-correcting. Yet this study, too, provoked a swarm of angry responses from doctors and health professionals: "This is sounding way too much like blaming and rings of eugenics."[57] "Race IS NOT genetic."[58] "Stop. . . . Systemic racism is why [black, indigenous, and people of color] are disproportionately harmed by COVID-19."[59] "I think this would hold water if by 'TMPRSS2,' you meant 'racism.'"[60] "Shame on this publication for perpetuating racism."[61] "That's biomedical racism to a T."[62]

A team writing in Health Affairs Blog warned researchers who planned to publish on health disparities to "never offer genetic interpretations of race because such suppositions are not grounded in science." They also proposed that medical journals "reject articles on racial health inequities that fail to rigorously examine racism." The article review process, they say, requires "editors who are well versed in critical race theory."[63] But why? Genetic inquiry across groups is emphatically not "racial science" or scientific racism. The objectivity of research is not a form of complicity in structures of power; it is the very condition for the discovery of treatments that are genuinely universal.

Concerned by the disavowal of such studies, experts spoke up. "For some applications, race may continue to be the best variable to capture the influence on health," wrote John P. A. Ioannidis, Neil R. Powe, and Clyde Yancy in the *Journal of the American Medical Association*. "Quick dismissal," they cautioned, "may worsen outcomes, especially for the most disadvantaged populations."[64]

In the *New England Journal of Medicine*, five genetics experts, who identified themselves as black, declared that ideally, race will be replaced with "genetic ancestry" as a variable in medical research and practice. Until more ancestry data are available, however, "ignoring race" and extrapolating research findings from European-ancestry populations for "the treatment of non-European populations . . . is neither equitable nor safe." The authors also expressed disappointment that some "curricula promote ideologies that downplay the medical achievements of genetic studies."[65] Highly disconcerting as well are reports that the National Institutes of Health is now restricting access to a large genetic database to impede research on genes associated with educational outcomes and intelligence, even when researchers are interested only in health outcomes.[66]

My Near-Cancellation Experience. I had my own encounter with intolerance in academic medicine on January 8, 2021. Via Zoom, I gave a Grand Rounds lecture to the Yale Department of Psychiatry, where I had been a resident for four years and an assistant professor for five. I left New Haven in 1993 to pursue a health policy fellowship in Washington, DC, and eventually joined a think tank there, but I remained a lecturer in the department. My talk was about the year I assisted treatment efforts in Ironton, a small, embattled town in southeastern Ohio that was reeling from the opioid crisis.

I discussed the deaths-of-despair phenomenon and showed photos of haunted industrial landscapes and Ironton's lonely downtown area.[67] I presented national data on the characteristics of individuals who abuse prescription pills and the frequency with which addiction develops. I talked about the culture of prescribing in rural mining towns and the myriad factors that caused the crisis. I closed by highlighting the heroic efforts of Irontonians to boost the economy and the morale of their beloved town.

One month later, I received an email from the chairman of the department, a fine man and brilliant researcher whom I have known since we

116 THE FREE INQUIRY PAPERS

were interns together in the 1980s. He admitted that he had not anticipated "the extent of the hurt and offense that folks would take" to my presence and presentation. He appended an anonymous complaint he had received from an unspecified number of "Concerned Yale Psychiatry Residents."[68]

The residents told the chairman that my talk, coming only two days after the January 6 attack on the Capitol, "was further traumatizing" to them. They wrote that

> the language Dr. Satel used in her presentation was dehumanizing, demeaning, and classist toward individuals living in rural Ohio and for rural populations in general. . . . We find her canon to be beyond a "difference of opinion" worth debate.[69]

They deemed my earlier writing on health disparities a "racist canon." They expressed "shock and disappointment" at the chairman's failure to "take a public stand against" me and questioned *his* commitment to the department's anti-racist agenda. "Will you continue to invite Grand Rounds Speakers with racist and classist mindsets, like Dr. Satel?" the residents asked. Although they requested that the chairman "revoke" my lectureship at Yale, he did not do so.[70]

The Upstream Nonsolution to Health Disparities

I agree that much of black Americans' disadvantage in health and access to care is the cumulative product of legal, political, and social institutions that have historically discriminated, and sometimes continue to discriminate, against them. Systemic racism may indeed have broad explanatory value regarding health disparities, but as an analytic framework, it doesn't yield realistic prescriptions. Just what are physicians supposed to do? Become activists? The AMA's answer is yes. In a strategic plan it released in the spring of 2021, the organization urged doctors to "push upstream to address all determinants of health and the root causes of inequities" and "dismantle structural racism and intersecting systems of oppression."[71]

This is no solution. Physicians cannot—and *should* not—"dismantle racism and intersecting systems of oppression" as part of their clinical mission. To imply that such activity falls within our scope of expertise is to abuse our authority. Doctors can reasonably lobby for policies directly promoting health, such as better coverage for patient care or more services, but we will lose our focus and dilute our efforts to care for patients if we seek to address the perceived root causes of health disparities.

After all, even seasoned policy analysts can't readily tease out strong causal links between health and sprawling upstream economic and social factors. With so many intervening variables at play, reforms in the service of health may well create unwanted repercussions elsewhere in the system. Any physician is free, of course, to pursue progressive reform as a private citizen, but as doctors, we already have a job: to diagnose and treat.

A Word About Health Disparities. Understanding the dynamics behind health differentials is clearly important. However, I question whether disparity eradication should be the focus of physicians' efforts. To be clear, I do think research on health differentials that track with race, wealth, geography, and other variables is important to understand. Where such findings can help physicians be more responsive to their patients, they are valuable. But the reflexive emphasis on regarding outcomes through a racialized lens can obscure basic principles.

For one, disparities are a dynamic of groups—the comparison of cohorts. As such, they are a more legitimate concern for public health. And indeed, aggregate health problems in localized groups are legitimate targets of intervention, inspiring the 1960s Freedom Riders to bring health care to the rural South and today's public health workers to reduce concentrations of diabetes and alcoholism on American Indian reservations.[72] By contrast, individual physicians focus on the patient in front of them. The disparity that concerns them most—or *should* concern them most—is the gap between their patient's current health and the patient's optimal health. How they treat one patient is not measured against their treatment of another.

The disparity mindset is not only inconsistent with physician-level focus; it has intrinsic problems. First, by grouping people by racial or ethnic identity, analysts will miss the variation in health status between subgroups.[73] Second, if both groups improve in tandem, progress will be

118   THE FREE INQUIRY PAPERS

concealed if the differential still remains. Third, it is no victory if groups converge because one group declined in health or, even if merging, both groups still fare poorly.

Notably, diversifying the medical workforce is presumed to be an important remedy for disparities. The premise is often accepted without question, but the data invoked to support that so-called racial concordance (e.g., black patients with black doctors) improves minority health are mixed and generally unimpressive. Either they find no impact of race on the outcome measurement or, if they do, that measurement in question is typically a proxy for health care or health status (i.e., did the subject undergo a screening test? Is their blood pressure controlled?) but not actual health improvement (i.e., did the patient pursue follow-up care and change behavior, such as diet, when indicated?).[74]

Finally, I have seen how other staff, such as nurses and social workers (usually black, given my inner-city experience), can have meaningful relationships with patients, aiding in matters of sticking to treatment regimens and making the clinical environment more welcoming. In short, the task of improving minority health is not completely dependent on the doctor.

Ensuring Alignment with Diversity, Equity, and Inclusion

Medical schools now impose the values of diversity, equity, and inclusion (DEI) on incoming students. A recent report by Do No Harm, a nonprofit dedicated to maintaining integrity in medicine, reviewed the admissions processes at 50 of the top-ranked medical schools in the US and found that of those 50, 36 asked applicants for their views or experience in DEI efforts, including their affinity for specific statements about racial politics and health outcomes.[75]

Such ideological screening is being practiced, for example, at the University of Pittsburgh School of Medicine, which tells applicants, "We are interested in combating all forms of systemic barriers, and would like to hear your thoughts on opposing specifically: systemic racism, anti-LGBTQ+ discrimination, and misogyny." It goes on: "How will you contribute?"[76] The University of Texas Southwestern Medical School wants applicants to demonstrate "how [they] have committed [themselves] to understanding and aiding in the pursuit of equity and inclusion in [their] academic, professional or personal life."[77]

The DEI screening extends to faculty as well. For those seeking promotion and tenure at the University of North Carolina School of Medicine, the school requires a "positive contribution to DEI efforts"—for example, "performing DEI or social justice–focused lectures to students, residents, or peers"—and a DEI statement.[78] Likewise, the Indiana University School of Medicine (IUSM) recently approved a DEI requirement for faculty as a condition of tenure and promotion, prompting legal warnings.[79] (Save for certain religious institutions, US higher education has not had loyalty oaths since the 1950s.)[80] An administrator at IUSM sent an email "requesting" faculty and staff leaders "spend a minimum of 2 hours on DEI focused professional development throughout the 2022 calendar year," with classes available such as "allyship and anti-racism" and fostering "inclusive language at work."[81]

Prescriptions

In the spring of 2022, Amazon Web Services tapped 10 startups as finalists to participate in its health care accelerator focused on health equity. The project uses the word "equity," but in reality, it offers straightforward assistance to reach "health goals" by "addressing social determinants of health." According to Amazon Web Services, the social drivers range from expanding access to medical transport to helping unhoused patients reach housing and health goals. If minority patients are more likely to need the help, then they will benefit disproportionately, but the help is available to all "vulnerable, low income populations" that need it.[82]

Innovations across the country are taking place in this constructive spirit. In California, for example, when patients with colon cancer were treated at an integrated health care system—a point of entry where all aspects of care were delivered under one roof—black patients fared much better than black patients treated in usual settings.[83] As a result, survival rates were the same for blacks and whites.

The Metropolitan Chicago Breast Cancer Task Force reduced mortality by helping women, mainly black women, navigate the health care system.

The Comer Children's Pediatric Mobile Medical Unit brings services to Chicago's South Side, including immunizations, physicals for school, and screenings for vision, hearing, lead poisoning, and anemia.[84] Medical centers partner with inner-city barbershops to help black patrons control diabetes and high blood pressure and prevent heart attack and stroke.[85] These community-based projects may not be the seeds of revolution, but they can improve and save lives.

Another strategy entails young doctors leveraging geography: They should set up practice in a rural minority town. If being anti-racist is their priority, it is probably the best gift they can give. I am skeptical of this happening, however. An analysis by Stanford University researchers in 2019 showed that young physicians have been moving so "sharply to the left" over the past decade and flocking so densely to urban areas—"ideological sorting," the authors called it—that rural areas are suffering from shortages of physicians.[86]

Litigation is another path. Do No Harm urges physicians in conservative states to contact lawmakers and education boards that govern public universities to push back on the DEI competencies through law or regulation.[87] States have the power to regulate medical school standards.[88] Neither the Liaison Committee on Medical Education (LCME) nor its adviser, the AAMC, are the ultimate arbiters. States grant medical licenses. To date, each state in the US recognizes the standards promulgated by the LCME and insists that all doctors obtain their training at LCME-certified schools. Perhaps this trust could be revoked by some states, Do No Harm also speculates, if standards were to depart from core medical competencies.

Do No Harm has also filed complaints with the US Department of Education's Office for Civil Rights against minority-only medical school fellowships.[89] Meanwhile, the Foundation for Individual Rights and Expression wrote a warning letter to the dean of IUSM in the summer of 2022 regarding DEI requirements. The warning said that the requirement "coerces faculty whose academic interests may lie elsewhere . . . to substantially reorient their scholarly pursuits or administrative service to conform with IUSM's ideological preferences."[90]

The Rising Generation: Politics vs. Patients?

In the summer of 2022, incoming medical students at the University of Minnesota recited an oath to "promote a culture of anti-racism" in their white coat ceremony, during which students receive their first white coat in front of family and friends. White coats, the students said, are themselves a "symbol of power, prestige, and dominance," so they would "strive to reclaim their identity as a symbol of responsibility, humility, and loving kindness," "commit to uprooting the legacy and perpetuation of structural violence deeply embedded within the health care system," and "recognize inequities built by past and present traumas rooted in white supremacy, colonialism, the gender binary, ableism, and all forms of oppression."[91]

What are we to make of this? Are these students merely expressing concern for patients using contemporary, if unfortunate, discourse? How many agree with this speech? After all, they are brand-new students, handed a script that the associate dean for undergraduate medical education called "beautiful."[92] Who could desist? Or is this the beginning of an academic career for many of them in which activism will compete with learning medicine?

I am quite pessimistic. Whether critical medical theorists represent the tip of an iceberg or the far tail of a bell curve seems moot, given their formidable influence at elite medical schools. Many deans and chairs are doubtless too intimidated to resist. At the same time, however, many of their youthful colleagues are likely to be sympathetic to the critical justice project.

Some of my colleagues think that the social justice and anti-racism movement in medicine is severely corrupting the field. I am sympathetic to their views. The erosion of standards and the pressure to formulate "correct" interpretations of clinical and research phenomena pose a serious threat to professional integrity and patient care. Other colleagues are less dismayed. While they lament the distraction, they see it as a massive injection of virtue signaling.

I thought of these colleagues when I read about the incoming class of medical students at the University of Michigan Medical School in July 2022. In protest of the speaker, a pro-life OB-GYN physician at the school, many students stood up and walked out during her speech at their white coat ceremony.[93] Dr. Kristin Collier gave a moving speech:

> The suffering you'll see as a physician can either harden you and make you into a burned-out machine, or you can allow the vocation to soften you. It can help you cultivate compassion, love, justice, and mercy. Let medicine do the latter of the two for you.

The walkout was ironic as well, because Dr. Collier's message was one these students would likely embrace, if they had stayed in their seats to hear it. Perhaps the students who left will become wonderful doctors who keep their politics separate from their care of patients. They have four years in which to mature.

Conclusion

Academic medicine is in the midst of a risky institutional experiment. How will the AMA's new call to "focus attention on *inequitable systems, hierarchies, social structure, power relations, and institutional practices*" (emphasis in original) affect the formation of trainees' professional identities?[94] Are we to believe that health is so thoroughly contingent on malign forces that doctors shouldn't bother educating patients about how they can take responsibility for their well-being? How will the adoption of a zealous social justice agenda affect public trust? And will so much hyperbole about racism in medicine be self-fulfilling, exacerbating distrust where it may already exist?

The pragmatic imperatives of clinical practice may be the best buffer against ideology. The surgical suite, the emergency department, and the examining room are the definitive, consequential spheres of clinical intervention.

The famous 19th-century German statesman and physician Rudolf Virchow called physicians the natural "attorney for the poor."[95] In the clinic and at the bedside, good doctors argue as eloquently as any lawyer for the disadvantaged through their specialized knowledge and compassion. In medical journals, they spread knowledge through dispassionate, truth-seeking methods that speak to all. And in the realm of medicine, they do their best work aiding those who are most vulnerable and in need,

DO NO ANTI-RACIST HARM   123

regardless of group affiliation. The best way to be an anti-racist doctor is to be a good doctor.

Notes

1. Sally Satel, *PC, M.D.: How Political Correctness Is Corrupting Medicine* (New York: Basic Books, 2000), 215.

2. Satel, *PC, M.D.*, 231.

3. White Coats for Black Lives, "#BlackLivesMatter: Physicians Must Stand for Racial Justice," *American Medical Association Journal of Ethics* 17, no. 10 (October 2015): 978–82, https://journalofethics.ama-assn.org/article/blacklivesmatter-physicians-must-stand-racial-justice/2015-10.

4. White Coats for Black Lives, "Actions Speak Louder," June 19, 2020, https://whitecoats4blacklives.org/2020/06/19/actions-speak-louder.

5. White Coats for Black Lives, "Our Vision and Values," June 25, 2021, 1, https://whitecoats4blacklives.org/wp-content/uploads/2021/07/WC4BL_Vision_Document_1_.pdf.

6. Harald Schmidt, "The Way We Ration Ventilators Is Biased," *New York Times*, April 15, 2020, https://www.nytimes.com/2020/04/15/opinion/covid-ventilator-rationing-blacks.html.

7. Jennifer Nuzzo (@JenniferNuzzo), "We should always evaluate the risks and benefits of efforts to control the virus. In this moment the public health risks of not protesting to demand an end to systemic racism greatly exceed the harms of the virus," X, June 2, 2020, 2:25 p.m., https://twitter.com/JenniferNuzzo/status/1267885076697812993; and Mallory Simon, "Over 1,000 Health Professionals Sign a Letter Saying, Don't Shut Down Protests Using Coronavirus Concerns as an Excuse," CNN, June 5, 2020, https://www.cnn.com/2020/06/05/health/health-care-open-letter-protests-coronavirus-trnd/index.html.

8. Megan McArdle, "Public Health Bodies May Be Talking at Us, but They're Actually Talking to Each Other," *Washington Post*, December 27, 2020, https://www.washingtonpost.com/opinions/public-health-bodies-may-be-talking-at-us-but-theyre-actually-talking-to-each-other/2020/12/27/2c5064a2-4626-11eb-975c-d17b8815a66d_story.html.

9. Yascha Mounk, "Why I'm Losing Trust in the Institutions," *Persuasion*, December 23, 2020, https://www.persuasion.community/p/why-im-losing-trust-in-the-institutions.

10. Mounk, "Why I'm Losing Trust in the Institutions."

11. See Catherine Salmon and Lee Jussim in this volume for the disastrous effects of infusing science with ideology.

12. Steve Kemper, "C.-E. A. Winslow, Who Launched Public Health at Yale a Century Ago, Still Influential Today," YaleNews, June 2, 2015, https://news.yale.edu/2015/06/02/public-health-giant-c-ea-winslow-who-launched-public-health-yale-century-ago-still-influe.

13. World Health Organization, "Social Determinants of Health," https://www.who.int/health-topics/social-determinants-of-health.

14. Sandro Galea and Bruce G. Link, "Six Paths for the Future of Social Epidemiology," *American Journal of Epidemiology* 178, no. 6 (September 2013): 843–49, https://www.ncbi.nlm.nih.gov/pmc/articles/PMC3775546.

15. Sally Zierler, remarks at the annual meeting of the American Public Health Association, Washington, DC, November 16, 1998. See also Satel, *P.C., M.D.*, 18.

16. Mark Schiller, "PC, M.D.: How Political Correctness Is Corrupting Medicine," *Psychiatric Services* 52, no. 5 (May 2001), https://ps.psychiatryonline.org/doi/epub/10.1176/appi.ps.52.5.691-a; and Satel, *PC, M.D.*, 18.

17. Eric H. Holder Jr., "Attorney General Eric Holder Speaks at the Harvard School of Public Health Event," US Department of Justice, Office of Public Affairs, May 6, 2011, https://www.justice.gov/opa/speech/attorney-general-eric-holder-speaks-harvard-school-public-health-event.

18. Philip Cole, Elizabeth Delzell, and Brad Rodu, "Moneychangers in the Temple," *Epidemiology* 11, no. 1 (January 2000): 84–90, https://www.jstor.org/stable/3703660.

19. Sandro Galea, "Who's Left?," Healthiest Goldfish, March 19, 2021, https://sandrogalea.substack.com/p/whos-left.

20. American Medical Association, "AMA Adopts Guidelines That Confront Systemic Racism in Medicine," June 15, 2021, https://www.ama-assn.org/press-center/press-releases/ama-adopts-guidelines-confront-systemic-racism-medicine.

21. American Medical Association, *Advancing Health Equity: A Guide to Language, Narrative and Concepts*, 2021, 20, https://www.ama-assn.org/about/ama-center-health-equity/advancing-health-equity-guide-language-narrative-and-concepts-0.

22. American Medical Association, *Advancing Health Equity*, 20, 23–24.

23. American Medical Association, *Advancing Health Equity*, 24.

24. American Medical Association, *Advancing Health Equity*, 5.

25. American Medical Association, *Advancing Health Equity*, 6.

26. American Medical Association, *Advancing Health Equity*, 8.

27. American Medical Association, *Advancing Health Equity*, 15.

28. American Medical Association, *Advancing Health Equity*, 20.

29. American Medical Association, *Advancing Health Equity*, 24.

30. American Medical Association, *Advancing Health Equity*, 25.

31. American Medical Association, *Organizational Strategic Plan to Embed Racial Justice and Advance Health Equity*, 2021–23, 6, https://www.ama-assn.org/system/files/ama-equity-strategic-plan-2021-2023.pdf.

32. Association of American Medical Colleges, *Diversity, Equity, and Inclusion Competencies Across the Learning Continuum*, July 2022, 8–11, https://store.aamc.org/diversity-equity-and-inclusion-competencies-across-the-learning-continuum.html.

33. Association of American Medical Colleges, *Diversity, Equity, and Inclusion Competencies Across the Learning Continuum*, 10.

34. Association of American Medical Colleges, *Diversity, Equity, and Inclusion Competencies Across the Learning Continuum*.

35. Stanford Medicine MD Program, "Social Justice & Health Equity Curriculum Thread," 2023, https://med.stanford.edu/md/discovery-curriculum/social-justice-and-health-equity.html.

36. Office of Medical Education, "Confronting Race in the Medical Curriculum," *Medicine@Brown*, https://medicine.at.brown.edu/article/confronting-race-in-the-medical-curriculum.

37. Kaiser Permanente Bernard J. Tyson School of Medicine, "Creating an Inclusive, Supportive Community," https://medschool.kp.org/about/equity-inclusion-and-diversity.

38. Robin DiAngelo, *White Fragility: Why It's So Hard for White People to Talk About Racism* (Boston, MA: Beacon Press, 2018); and Ibram X. Kendi, *How to Be an Antiracist* (New York: One World, 2019).

39. Association of American Medical Colleges, "AAMC Statement on Police Brutality and Racism in America and Their Impact on Health," press release, June 1, 2020, https://www.aamc.org/news/press-releases/aamc-statement-police-brutality-and-racism-america-and-their-impact-health.

40. AMA Center for Health Equity, "The AMA's Strategic Plan for Advancing Health Equity and Justice in Medicine," AMA Ed Hub, October 6, 2022, https://edhub.ama-assn.org/ama-center-health-equity/module/2797271.

41. William A. Jacobson, "Almost All of Top 25 Medical Schools Mandate Race-Based Training and Study, New CriticalRace.org Database Shows," Legal Insurrection, February 21, 2022, https://legalinsurrection.com/2022/02/almost-all-of-top-25-medical-schools-mandate-race-based-training-and-study-new-criticalrace-org-database-shows; and Critical Race Training in Education, "Medical Schools," https://criticalrace.org/medical-schools.

42. Lisa A. Cooper, Somnath Saha, and Michelle van Ryn, "Mandated Implicit Bias Training for Health Professionals—a Step Toward Equity," *JAMA Health Forum* 3, no. 8 (August 2022), https://jamanetwork.com/journals/jama-health-forum/fullarticle/2795358.

43. Nao Hagiwara et al., "A Call for Grounding Implicit Bias Training in Clinical and Translational Frameworks," *The Lancet* 395, no. 10234 (May 2020): 1457–60, https://www.thelancet.com/journals/lancet/article/PIIS0140-6736(20)30846-1; and Erin Dehon et al., "A Systematic Review of the Impact of Physician Implicit Racial Bias on Clinical Decision Making," *Academic Emergency Medicine* 24, no. 8 (August 2017): 895–904, https://onlinelibrary.wiley.com/doi/full/10.1111/acem.13214.

44. Interview with a medical professor, fall 2020.

45. Katie Herzog, "What Happens When Doctors Can't Tell the Truth?," Free Press, June 3, 2021, https://www.thefp.com/p/what-happens-when-doctors-cant-speak.

46. Sally Satel, "Do No Harm: Critical Race Theory and Medicine," *Liberties* 1, no. 4 (Summer 2021), https://libertiesjournal.com/articles/do-no-harm-critical-race-theory-and-medicine.

47. Center for Individual Rights, "Center for Individual Rights Files Suit on Behalf of Professor Removed from His Position for Research on Affirmative Action," December 17, 2020, https://www.cir-usa.org/2020/12/center-for-individual-rights-files-suit-on-behalf-of-professor-removed-from-his-position-for-research-on-affirmative-action.

48. Norman C. Wang, "Diversity, Inclusion and Equity: Evolution of Race and Ethnicity Considerations for the Cardiology Workforce in the United States of America from 1969 to 2019," *Journal of the American Heart Association* 9, no. 7 (March 2020),

https://www.ahajournals.org/doi/10.1161/JAHA.120.015959; *Journal of the American Heart Association*, "Retraction to: Diversity, Inclusion and Equity: Evolution of Race and Ethnicity Considerations for the Cardiology Workforce in the United States of America from 1969 to 2019," August 6, 2020, https://www.ahajournals.org/doi/10.1161/JAHA.119.014602; and Michael O'Riordan, "AHA, Editors and Cardiologists Ask: How Did 'Racist' Paper Make It to Print?," TCTMD, August 5, 2020, https://www.tctmd.com/news/aha-editors-and-cardiologists-ask-how-did-racist-paper-make-it-print.

49. Donovan Harrell, "Lawsuit Filed Against Pitt on Behalf of Cardiology Professor Norman Wang," *University of Pittsburgh University Times* 53, no. 9 (December 18, 2020), https://www.utimes.pitt.edu/news/lawsuit-filed-against.

50. Allison Radziwon, "University Dismissed from Lawsuit Alleging Slander," *Pitt News*, September 8, 2022, https://pittnews.com/article/174797/news/university-dismissed-from-lawsuit-alleging-slander.

51. Mark J. Perry, "New Chart Illustrates Graphically the Racial Preferences for Blacks, Hispanics Being Admitted to US Medical Schools," Carpe Diem, June 25, 2017, https://www.aei.org/carpe-diem/new-chart-illustrates-graphically-racial-preferences-for-blacks-and-hispanics-being-admitted-to-us-medical-schools.

52. Robin Klein et al., "Association Between Resident Race and Ethnicity and Clinical Performance Assessment Scores in Graduate Medical Education," *Academic Medicine* 97, no. 9 (September 2022), https://pubmed.ncbi.nlm.nih.gov/35583954.

53. Amanda Heidt, "Howard Bauchner Leaves *JAMA* Following Podcast Fallout," *The Scientist*, June 2, 2021, https://www.the-scientist.com/news-opinion/howard-bauchner-leaves-jama-following-podcast-fallout-68839.

54. John Murawski, "As Race 'Equity' Advances in Health Care, Signs of a Chilling Effect on Dissent," RealClearInvestigations, August 12, 2021, https://www.realclearinvestigations.com/articles/2021/08/12/as_race_equity_advances_in_health_care_signs_of_a_chilling_effect_on_dissent_789529.html.

55. These variants may code for proteins or enzymes that cause vulnerabilities to certain diseases or determine how robust a response to treatment is likely to be. Race is thus a shorthand for ancestral descent—and the more precise the ancestral origin, the better, as variations in genetic heritage exist even between groups within a geographical region. Genetic admixing—that is, when parents are of different "races" or are mixed race themselves—further complicates the picture to the point where the shorthand of race becomes irrelevant or too crude a category to be of any help at all.

56. Supinda Bunyavanich, Chantal Grant, and Alfin Vicencio, "Racial/Ethnic Variation in Nasal Gene Expression of Transmembrane Serine Protease 2 (TMPRSS2)," *Journal of the American Medical Association* 324, no. 15 (2020): 1567–68, https://jamanetwork.com/journals/jama/fullarticle/2770682.

57. Amanda P. Williams (@KPobgyndoc), "I 🐾 can't 🐾 with 🐾 these 🐾 folks . . . this is sounding way too much like blaming and rings of eugenics," X, September 12, 2020, 8:35 p.m., https://twitter.com/KPobgyndoc/status/1304941701945946112.

58. Rose Olsen (@rose_m_olson), "Race *IS NOT* genetic. @JAMA_current do better," X, September 13, 2020, 11:53 a.m., https://twitter.com/rose_m_olson/status/1305172810244009986.

59. Karen Gibbins (@rayofdiana), "Attributing genetic variants to race (which is

socially constructed) is racist. Stop," X, September 12, 2020, 11:08 p.m., https://twitter.com/rayofdiana/status/1304980349772988416.

60. Taison Bell (@TaisonBell), "I think this would hold water if by 'TMPRSS2' you meant 'racism,'" X, September 13, 2020, 5:08 p.m., https://twitter.com/taisonbell/status/1305252049966239744.

61. Brittani James (@DrBrittaniJ), "This is the definition of biological racism. Shame on this publication for perpetuating racism. You are the problem," X, September 12, 2020, 8:02 p.m., https://twitter.com/DrBrittaniJ/status/1304933362935705602.

62. Usha Lee McFarling, "Troubling Podcast Puts *JAMA*, the 'Voice of Medicine,' Under Fire for Its Mishandling of Race," STAT, April 6, 2021, https://www.statnews.com/2021/04/06/podcast-puts-jama-under-fire-for-mishandling-of-race.

63. Rhea W. Boyd et al., "On Racism: A New Standard for Publishing on Racial Health Inequities," Health Affairs Blog, July 2, 2020, https://obgynrsintranet.ucsf.edu/sites/g/files/tkssra3981/f/wysiwyg/Health%20Equity%20Research%20%20Interest%20Group%20-%20Inaugural%20Meeting%204.27.pdf.

64. John P. A. Ioannidis, Neil R. Powe, and Clyde Yancy, "Recalibrating the Use of Race in Medical Research," *Journal of the American Medical Association* 325, no. 7 (2021): 623–24, https://jamanetwork.com/journals/jama/fullarticle/2775794.

65. Akinyemi Oni-Orisan et al., "Embracing Genetic Diversity to Improve Black Health," *New England Journal of Medicine* 384, no. 12 (March 2021): 1163–67, https://www.nejm.org/doi/full/10.1056/NEJMms2031080.

66. James Lee, "Don't Even Go There," *City Journal*, October 19, 2022, https://www.city-journal.org/article/dont-even-go-there.

67. Anne Case and Angus Deaton, *Deaths of Despair and the Future of Capitalism* (Princeton, NJ: Princeton University Press, 2020), https://press.princeton.edu/books/hardcover/9780691190785/deaths-of-despair-and-the-future-of-capitalism.

68. Yale School of Medicine Department of Psychiatry chairman, email to author, February 4, 2021.

69. Anonymous students, email to Yale School of Medicine Department of Psychiatry chairman, 2021.

70. Anonymous students, email to Yale School of Medicine Department of Psychiatry chairman, 2021.

71. American Medical Association, *Organizational Strategic Plan to Embed Racial Justice and Advance Health Equity*, 8, 48.

72. John Lewis, letter to A. Phillip Randolph, December 14, 1965, https://www.crmvet.org/docs/6512_sncc_wccr-let.pdf; and Randall C. Swaim and Linda R. Stanley, "Substance Use Among American Indian Youths on Reservations Compared with a National Sample of US Adolescents," *Journal of the American Medical Association* 1, no. 1 (2018): 1–11, https://www.ncbi.nlm.nih.gov/pmc/articles/PMC6324282.

73. Jane L. Delgado, "Beyond Diversity—Time for New Models of Health," *New England Journal of Medicine* 386, no. 6 (February 10, 2022): 503–5, https://www.nejm.org/doi/full/10.1056/nejmp2115149.

74. Alexander Raikin and Stanley Goldfarb, "Re-Segregating Healthcare: Finding the Flaws in a Famous—and Dangerous—Study," Do No Harm, August 26, 2022,

https://donoharmmedicine.org/research/2022/re-segregating-healthcare-finding-the-flaws-in-a-famous-and-dangerous-study; and Megan Johnson Shen et al., "The Effects of Race and Racial Concordance on Patient-Physician Communication: A Systematic Review of the Literature," *Journal of Racial and Ethnic Disparities* 5, no. 1 (2018): 117–40, https://pubmed.ncbi.nlm.nih.gov/28275996.

75. Laura L. Morgan, *Only DEI Advocates Need Apply: 72 Percent of Top-Ranked Medical Schools Inject Identity Politics in Key Admissions Process Step*, Do No Harm, August 2022, https://donoharmmedicine.org/research/2022/only-dei-advocates-need-apply.

76. Stanley Goldfarb and Laura L. Morgan, "Top Med School Putting Wokeism Ahead of Giving America Good Doctors," *New York Post*, November 16, 2022, https://nypost.com/2022/09/02/top-med-schools-putting-wokeism-ahead-of-giving-america-good-doctors.

77. Medical School Headquarters, "University of Texas Southwestern Secondary Application," June 2023, https://medicalschoolhq.net/secondary-essays/univeristy-of-texas-southwestern-secondary-application.

78. John D. Sailer, "UNC School of Medicine's Quiet DEI Revolution," National Association of Scholars, December 7, 2021, https://www.nas.org/blogs/article/unc-school-of-medicines-quiet-dei-revolution.

79 Aaron Terr, "Indiana University School of Medicine Approves Ideological Litmus Test for Faculty Seeking Tenure and Promotion," Foundation for Individual Rights and Expression, July 14, 2022, https://www.thefire.org/news/indiana-university-school-medicine-approves-ideological-litmus-test-faculty-seeking-tenure-and.

80. George Leef, "Loyalty Oaths Return with Faculty 'Diversity Statements,'" March 29, 2017, https://www.jamesgmartin.center/2017/03/loyalty-oaths-return-faculty-diversity-statements.

81. Do No Harm, "Things Keep Getting Worse at This Indiana Medical School," July 18, 2022, https://donoharmmedicine.org/2022/07/18/things-keep-getting-worse-at-this-indiana-medical-school.

82. Jeff Kratz, "AWS Announces the 10 Startups Selected for the 2022 AWS Healthcare Accelerator Focused on Health Equity," AWS Public Sector Blog, August 31, 2022, https://aws.amazon.com/blogs/publicsector/aws-announces-10-startups-selected-2022-aws-healthcare-accelerator-health-equity.

83. Kim F. Rhoads et al., "How Do Integrated Health Care Systems Address Racial and Ethnic Disparities in Colon Cancer?," *Journal of Clinical Oncology* 33, no. 8 (March 2015): 854–60, https://ascopubs.org/doi/10.1200/JCO.2014.56.8642.

84. University of Chicago Medicine Comer Children's Hospital, "Pediatric Mobile Medical Unit," https://www.uchicagomedicine.org/comer/conditions-services/mobile-med-unit.

85. Cedars-Sinai Medical Center Newsroom, "Saving Lives in Black Barbershops," July 26, 2021, https://www.cedars-sinai.org/newsroom/saving-lives-in-black-barbershops.

86. Adam Bonica et al., "Ideological Sorting of Physicians in Both Geography and the Workplace," *Journal of Health Politics, Policy and Law* 45, no. 6 (May 2020), https://www.researchgate.net/publication/341752466_Ideological_Sorting_of_Physicians_in_Both_Geography_and_the_Workplace.

87. Greg Piper, "Medical Schools Risk Accreditation for Not Teaching Antiracism 'Competencies,' Med Group Warns," Just the News, July 22, 2022, https://justthenews.com/accountability/watchdogs/medical-schools-risk-accreditation-not-teaching-anti-racism-competencies.

88. USLegal, "State Regulation of Physicians," https://physicians.uslegal.com/state-regulation-of-physicians.

89. Brittany Bernstein, "Pfizer Sued for Discriminating Against White, Asian Fellowship Applicants," *National Review*, September 16, 2022, https://www.nationalreview.com/news/pfizer-sued-for-discriminating-against-white-asian-fellowship-applicants.

90. Aaron Terr, "FIRE Letter to Indiana University School of Medicine, July 11, 2021," Foundation for Individual Rights and Expression, July 11, 2022, https://www.thefire.org/research-learn/fire-letter-indiana-university-school-medicine-july-11-2022.

91. Anthony Gockowski, "Med Students Take 'Anti-Racism' Oath at University of Minnesota," Alpha News, September 2, 2022, https://alphanews.org/med-students-take-anti-racism-oath-at-university-of-minnesota.

92. Gockowski, "Med Students Take 'Anti-Racism' Oath at University of Minnesota."

93. Amanda Jackson and Caroll Alvarado, "Michigan Medical Students Walk Out of Induction Ceremony to Protest Keynote Speaker with Anti-Abortion Views," CNN, July 26, 2022, https://www.cnn.com/2022/07/26/us/medical-student-abortion-protest-university-of-michigan/index.html.

94. American Medical Association, *Advancing Health Equity*, 24.

95. Contagion: Historical Views of Diseases and Epidemics, "Rudolf Virchow, 1821–1902," Harvard Library, CURIOSity Collections, 2023, https://curiosity.lib.harvard.edu/contagion/feature/rudolf-virchow-1821-1902.

9

Lysenkoism Then and Now: A Cautionary Tale of Censorious Social Norms

Catherine Salmon and Lee Jussim

While many believe science to be free of political and ideological contamination, those who know history know better. Trofim Lysenko's catastrophic effect on agriculture in Soviet-era Russia should serve as a cautionary tale. When scientific truth-seeking processes have been unduly infected by ideological requirements and censorious social norms, it leads to widespread belief in falsehoods and, in the extreme, preventable human-caused disasters. Revisiting such events can function like a lighthouse, warning society of dangers that may not be apparent but might be avoided by those who are alert to them.

We do not suggest that America is on the verge of a Lysenko-like disaster, but we do believe that ideological support for censorious social norms is eroding free inquiry and, downstream, scientific validity and credibility, in a wide range of areas. We address social science in this chapter.

Who Was Lysenko?

In the late 1920s and early 1930s, Lysenko became the preeminent agronomist of Josef Stalin's regime by promising that he could increase crop yields during a significant agricultural crisis in the aftermath of the Russian Civil War. His ideas dovetailed perfectly with the Marxist ideology of the day. Just as any person could play any role in society (individuals were less important than the collective and elites were regarded with suspicion), so, too, could plants and animals cooperate for the greater good and be molded as Lysenko wished. He rejected as "Western science" the core of Mendelian genetics—that genes determine many characteristics of living things. Instead, Lysenko argued that plants could be "trained" or

LYSENKOISM THEN AND NOW 131

"educated" to develop traits that they would pass on to the next generation and thus grow abundantly under all conditions. Plants could be taught to bloom in winter; the will of the people could master nature itself!

The idea that anything (plants, people, or whole societies) could be engineered along any means deemed politically justified comported well with the revolutionary Marxist desire to "disrupt" oppressive capitalist systems and replace them with what we now call "social justice." Lysenko told the government exactly what it wished to hear. Plants will conform, just as the people could be made to conform, to the ideological dictates of the state.[1]

Despite being a "biologist," Lysenko claimed that genes did not exist and therefore were not the vehicle by which traits are passed from one generation to the next. These beliefs fit nicely with the Soviet anti–status quo ideology and blank-slate approach—that is, the paradigm that living things including plants and humans are shaped entirely by their experiences. Humans could be "remade" to fit what was best for society, which was often indistinguishable from what was best for Communist Party apparatchiks. The environment was supposedly all that mattered.

As a result of Stalin's backing, Lysenko was put in charge of virtually all food research in the Soviet Union, at which point his oddball theories drove modern genetics underground. Any scientist who questioned Lysenkoism was at risk of being discredited, fired, imprisoned, even murdered.[2] Although prison goes far beyond modern cancel culture, discrediting, public shaming, and being fired for expressing "wrong" ideas are disturbingly modern.

Had Lysenko rigorously tested his ideas on even one or two small plots of land, the horrific folly of what was to come would have been obvious. In fact, his ideas were vigorously critiqued by many biologists outside the Soviet Union (to whom he was and remains a figure of ridicule) and by at least one well-known Soviet geneticist, Nikolai Vavilov, who starved to death in prison as a result. Vavilov was one of hundreds imprisoned for opposing, or merely being suspected of opposing, Lysenko and thus being "enemies of the state."[3] Lysenko did not shy away from using the secret police to silence detractors.

By the time he was exposed as a fraud in the 1960s, Soviet agriculture and biology were devastated, decades behind the Western world. His practices, including forbidding the use of pesticides and fertilizers, resulted in

132 THE FREE INQUIRY PAPERS

disease-ridden, failing crops. The result was death due to starvation for at least seven million Soviet people. In the 1950s, Mao Zedong adopted the same agricultural policies, resulting in the Great Chinese Famine, the deadliest famine in history, which likely claimed 30 million lives.[4]

One might have assumed that such an outcome wouldn't have been possible. Although scientific processes can be filled with all sorts of errors and biases,[5] ideally, eventually, there is enough openness and skepticism in the system that *some* people follow the scientific method to rigorously test popular hypotheses. Other researchers try to replicate results, and when they fail to do so, it can become public knowledge. If such a process had been respected, Lysenko would have been discredited early on, before mass death.

What can we learn from Lysenko's Soviet and Chinese tragedies? Suppressing free inquiry and academic debate results in bad science, invalid results, and movement away from the truths that science is supposed to seek. Science includes rigorous testing of hypotheses, but it is not only about methodological rigor. It also requires the willingness of courageous researchers to skeptically test popular theories and hypotheses and make the results known to other scientists and the general public *no matter whose ox they gore*. Put differently, for the methodological rigor of science to advance truth and inform public policy, science itself must also include openness to vigorous debate, disagreement, and free discussion.

Truth is unlikely to be advanced if scientists fear losing their jobs for studying the wrong topics or obtaining unpopular findings that challenge prevailing theoretical or political narratives. When scientists are punished for finding things that are true, they will more often be silent in the face of social pressure—and truths will remain hidden. When they are rewarded for findings that are false, they are incentivized to produce even more false findings, and journals and other scientific outlets risk becoming littered with misinformation.

Institutional and informal protections of free speech, academic freedom, and open inquiry are necessary even for seemingly inoffensive or anodyne topics because one can never tell when science or the wider society will converge on a fundamentally wrong conclusion. This was the case for decades when the consensus in the medical community was that stress caused ulcers until it was eventually discovered that they are most commonly caused by bacteria. For political hot-button topics, such as abortion, climate change, and identity-based inequalities, protections are even more important because the motivation to silence opponents is often supercharged by the strong emotions and moral self-righteousness that played such an outsized role in the Communist movements of the 20th century. And we know where that led, with tens of millions dead and political, religious, sexual, and economic freedom destroyed.[6]

Modern Echoes of Lysenkoism

Recent cases of Lysenko-like actions are legion. For example, the Foundation for Individual Rights and Expression maintains the Scholars Under Fire Database, which includes hundreds of faculty and students who have been harassed, publicly shamed, and sometimes punished for expressing their views.[7] In the rest of this chapter, we review three cases in detail that reflect modern echoes of academic Lysenkoism.[8]

The Case of Roland G. Fryer Jr. Consider Roland G. Fryer Jr., the youngest black professor to be tenured at Harvard and a recipient of the McArthur Fellowship award in 2011. He recently returned to his teaching and research roles at Harvard after a two-year suspension for ostensibly violating sexual harassment policies. The specifics, other than that the behavior was verbal, were not publicly disclosed. Certain details of several investigations suggest political motives for wanting to sanction Fryer.[9] Since he was an economics professor, one might wonder what aspects of his research might have generated political animus.

Fryer's publications touching on education, race, and inequality often questioned the dogma that race-based education gaps are due to systemic racism, highlighting instead the role of cultural expectations, books in the home, and socioeconomic status in educational achievement, including research on the success of the nonprofit Harlem Children's Zone. He also waded into the data on police shootings with results that undermined the usual narrative that police systematically kill blacks. Challenging the establishment ideology fostered enemies at Harvard, particularly when his work

134 THE FREE INQUIRY PAPERS

highlighted their own deficiencies.[10] As a result, when a former assistant accused him of sexual harassment, his critics had an opportunity.

A special tribunal was set up that included some whose work Fryer criticized. The result was predictable, a two-year suspension. This was considerably more severe than punishments Harvard meted out to faculty in far more egregious cases of sexual harassment, as recently documented by filmmaker Rob Montz.[11]

Bruce Gilley and "The Case for Colonialism." Portland State University Political Science Professor Bruce Gilley came under fire in 2017 when his article "The Case for Colonialism" was published after going through peer review in the advance online edition of *Third World Quarterly*. The result was an explosion of angry rhetoric, including two petitions signed by thousands of academics insisting that the article be retracted, that the journal apologize for publishing it, and that the editors responsible be fired. In fact, 15 members of the journal's 34-member editorial board resigned in protest. The journal issued a defense of the peer-review process, but amid threats of violence against the editorial staff and death threats received by Gilley, he requested that the article be retracted for the safety of the journal's editorial staff. It was later published in *Academic Questions*, a publication of the National Association of Scholars.[12]

"The Case for Colonialism" argued that colonialism was not the unmitigated evil often claimed and that some modern countries would benefit if they chose to reinstitute what he argued were the more beneficial aspects of colonial rule. Gilley marshaled historical evidence in support of claims that, for most of colonial rule, in some countries, people voted with their feet to support colonialism (e.g., by moving to areas that had stronger rather than weaker colonial control) and that, for many countries, both governance and economic capacity were stronger at the end of their colonial periods than at any time since.[13]

We are not evaluating the merits of Gilley's analyses. However, what is clear is that nothing like data fraud or the type of massive data errors typically required for retractions appeared in his paper. Interestingly, Gilley had submitted the paper to the *Journal of Intervention and Statebuilding* before the ill-fated publication in *Third World Quarterly*. Gilley has written that the first time it was submitted,

The editor there, Nicolas Lemay-Hébert, gave it a desk approval and asked me to strengthen the policy-relevant aspects of the paper prior to sending it for peer review. The paper then received one positive and one negative review. Lemay-Hébert then asked his editorial board whether he should publish the paper and was told that it was too politically controversial to publish. The "fear of political backlash" determined the decision not to accept it, he wrote to me by email.[14]

One of the individuals who started one of the petitions suggested that "instruments and systems" should be put in place to prevent people like Gilley from sharing their viewpoints.[15] Shutting down discourse and debate . . . sound familiar? For those who discount death threats on ideological issues, the multiple stabbings of Salman Rushdie in 2022 should be a chilling reminder of the price some pay for speaking against an ideological narrative.

The Society for Personality and Social Psychology's Mandatory Diversity, Equity, and Inclusion Statement. The Society for Personality and Social Psychology (SPSP) is one of the most important and influential professional societies for social and personality psychologists. On its "about" webpage, the organization declares its mission is to "advance the science, teaching, and application of personality and social psychology."[16] Its website also has many statements promoting its supposed embrace of "diversity and inclusiveness of people and ideas."[17] Its emphasis on diversity, equity, and inclusion (DEI) appears throughout.

Whether this should be taken as a serious commitment to diversity of people and ideas, however, is an open question. For example, psychologists David M. Buss and William von Hippel surveyed social psychologists (members of the Society of Experimental Social Psychology) and found that, in 2012, 301 voted for Barack Obama and four voted for Mitt Romney.[18] Figure 1 captures the curious state of "inclusion" at SPSP and throughout the wider academy.[19]

Although the ultimate goals of DEI programs in academia are almost never articulated, much of the rhetoric involves "representation." This is because many historically marginalized or oppressed groups are

Figure 1. "Inclusion" in US Academia and SPSP

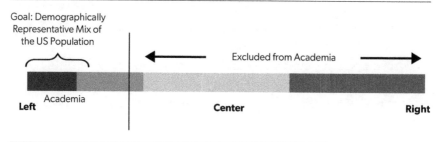

Source: Authors.

underrepresented in the academy. At a minimum, it's reasonable to assume that one can view these programs as seeking adequate representation for these groups. This is captured in the left-hand side of Figure 1. Empirically, however, for reasons that are not fully understood,[20] academia is also functioning to heavily select for people almost exclusively on the political left.

Although SPSP does not hang signs saying, "Non-leftists need not apply," its norms and practices have produced an ideological monoculture. Worse, SPSP has so far done nothing to rectify this sad state of affairs. We suspect that many of its members and most of its leadership would actively reject doing so. This makes sense if most SPSP members see it as a club for those on the left whose goals and purposes include advancing progressive values and ideas. Thus, academic inclusion is functioning to exclude about 80 percent of the population on political grounds.

This is not to declare SPSP worse than much of the rest of academia—it isn't. But at a minimum, it is complicit in a system that effectively excludes most Americans and the ideas they might bring to the table, ironically in the name of inclusion.

"What," you might ask, "does requiring DEI statements have to do with Lysenkoism and censorship?" Quite a lot. First, DEI is plausibly viewed as affirmative action on steroids. It is worth noting here that California voters recently reaffirmed their ban on affirmative action—and California is a majority-minority state (that is, taken together minorities are a majority of the population) and one of the most liberal states in the US. Furthermore, surveys conducted by the Pew Research Center consistently find that majorities, often very large majorities, of representative samples of

Americans from every racial and ethnic group surveyed (including blacks, Hispanics, Asians, and whites) oppose the use of race in both college admissions and employment decisions.[21]

Whether DEI or affirmative action is good policy is hotly debated. To the extent that affirmative action means racial preferences, the US Supreme Court has declared it illegal, at least for college admissions.[22] Our view is that the same illegalization of racial discrimination principles should apply widely. By requiring a DEI statement, SPSP used its power to compel those who would submit to present at its annual convention to endorse a form of affirmative action (which may be illegal and, as we have just documented, most Americans oppose). As such, it engaged in a form of compelled speech and implicitly a form of censorship to advance its political goals, much in the way that many US institutions required loyalty oaths in the McCarthy era. It was not legally compelled speech; it was organizationally compelled speech, which could seriously damage the careers of scholars, particularly untenured scholars who refused to comply. Our view is that compelled speech is almost always a bad idea, especially for a scientific organization that should be embracing robust debate and discussion rather than compelling its members to endorse one side of a debate.

It was also censorship. Many people seem to erroneously believe that censorship is something only the government can do. Any institution, organization, business, group, or individual that successfully prevents the expression or dissemination of an idea has engaged in censorship. The prevention does not need to be *absolute*; a platform that removes a book for sale in response to an outrage mob is engaging in censorship *on that platform*, even if the author can distribute it on other platforms. In the US, private censorship is generally legal; private actors, whether corporate, institutional, or organizational—even social media outrage mobs—can legally censor anything they like. It is still censorship, and our view is that when scientific and academic organizations censor their members' *ideas*, it is corrosive to the truth-seeking mission they supposedly represent.

How did SPSP's DEI mandate constitute censorship? SPSP frames its DEI efforts as part of its "anti-racism" agenda. But anyone unwilling to sign on to its DEI political activism and affirmative action endorsement could have been prevented from presenting their scholarship at SPSP's convention. "Advancing anti-racism" here translates into "state that you agree to

138 THE FREE INQUIRY PAPERS

our political activist agenda or we won't let you speak." That is legal, but it is still censorship. It harms science by limiting the spread of new ideas and protecting establishment ideas from scientific critiques. Inevitably, it is the type of practice that erodes the authority and legitimacy of science.

We see some disturbing echoes of this requirement in Václav Havel's famous 1978 essay, "The Power of the Powerless," in which he exposed and excoriated the Communist systems that ruled over Eastern Europe for most of the 20th century. He wrote:

> The manager of a fruit-and-vegetable shop places in his window, among the onions and carrots, the slogan: "Workers of the world, unite!" Why does he do it? What is he trying to communicate to the world? Is he genuinely enthusiastic about the idea of unity among the workers of the world? Is his enthusiasm so great that he feels an irrepressible impulse to acquaint the public with his ideals? Has he really given more than a moment's thought to how such a unification might occur and what it would mean?
>
> I think it can safely be assumed that the overwhelming majority of shopkeepers never think about the slogans they put in their windows, nor do they use them to express their real opinions. That poster was delivered to our greengrocer from the enterprise headquarters along with the onions and carrots. He put them all into the window simply because it has been done that way for years, because everyone does it, and because that is the way it has to be. If he were to refuse, there could be trouble. He could be reproached for not having the proper decoration in his window; someone might even accuse him of disloyalty. He does it because these things must be done if one is to get along in life.[23]

It is deeply disturbing that a major organization supposedly devoted to psychological science is now implementing norms and practices that echo the oppressive Soviet-era sociopolitical environment that Havel exposed and denounced. As Spinoza once put it, "Freedom is of the first importance in fostering the sciences and the arts."[24]

But there is some good news here. Jonathan Haidt publicly resigned from SPSP in protest,[25] and one of us hosted a testy exchange with some of the SPSP leadership at the time over its DEI mandate.[26] We know of no other public objections. Nonetheless, not long after, SPSP surveyed its members about the DEI mandate and abandoned it.[27] Although we are not expecting the Lysenko-istic turn of academia to evaporate anytime soon, this episode proves it is possible that, sometimes, even relatively modest vocal protests can roll back Lysenkoism.

Conclusions

In this chapter, we have argued that, although we are not facing the type of disaster produced by full-blown Lysenkoism, there are echoes of Lysenkoism throughout the academy, especially with respect to social and political issues. The rise of denunciation, ostracism, and social and organizational forms of censorship as academic norms threatens the validity and credibility of scholarship.

Along with his venality, gaining wealth and power by telling the Communist Party what it wanted to hear, Lysenko's key failing was his inability to separate the ideology of how he wanted the world to be from empirical findings about how the world actually *is*. The academy writ large, with many individual exceptions, seems to be suffering this same failure. It would be bad enough if large numbers of academics had difficulty separating their ideology and values from their scholarship. It is far worse because, so often, these same academics are not merely attempting to pass off ideologically infused scholarship as if it is scientific fact; they are seeking to require others to conform to their narrow ideological dogmas and punishing those who do not.

What can be done? Realistically, these trends have been building for a long time and are not likely to be reversed anytime soon. Furthermore, we doubt that anyone has any sort of magic bullet guaranteed to improve the situation. However, both of us have the experience of working with undergraduates, who have almost never heard of Lysenko or the associated failures and atrocities committed in the name of social justice under Communist regimes. One avenue, then, is for educators to teach these awful histories so that students better understand the potential dangers of ideologically infused science.

Relatedly, we must teach students, in high school and college, the scientific method and its successes over the past two centuries. From reducing famines to advancing modern medicine, science has played an enormous role in expanding lifespans, reducing suffering, and advancing human liberation generally. We believe science has proved far more effective in discerning empirical realities than either the traditional "ways of knowing" or the Marxists' mass movements often favored by some postmodern academics and journalists.

A related small, incomplete solution is for those committed to free inquiry to create new organizations and institutions that prioritize truth over ideology and welcome scholars regardless of their politics. This is practical and could even be fun. If many academic professional organizations have created an environment hostile to free inquiry, one possibility may be to leave them and create entirely new ones.

There is ample precedent for this sort of response. For example, when psychological scientists became disillusioned with the domination of the American Psychological Association by clinicians and practitioners, some broke away and launched what was first called the American Psychological Society and is now the Association for Psychological Science.[28] Such new organizations may not change the minds or behaviors of Lysenko-adjacent academics. However, the mere presence of a home for academics who prioritize truth seeking over ideology and activism could mean that the core values of evidence-based science may be more likely to withstand the current ideological storm.

Notes

1. Zhores A. Medvedev, *The Rise and Fall of T. D. Lysenko* (New York: Columbia University Press, 1969).

2. David Joravsky, *The Lysenko Affair* (Chicago: University of Chicago Press, 2010).

3. William deJong-Lambert, *The Cold War Politics of Genetic Research: An Introduction to the Lysenko Affair* (Dordrecht, Netherlands: Springer, 2012).

4. Sam Kean, "The Soviet Era's Deadliest Scientist Is Regaining Popularity in Russia," *The Atlantic*, December 19, 2017, https://www.theatlantic.com/science/archive/2017/12/trofim-lysenko-soviet-union-russia/548786.

5. Lee Jussim, Jon A. Krosnick, and Sean T. Stevens, eds., *Research Integrity: Best Practices in the Behavioral Sciences* (New York: Oxford University Press, 2022).

6. Stéphane Courtois et al., *The Black Book of Communism: Crimes, Terror, Repression*, trans. Jonathan Murphy and Mark Kramer (Cambridge, MA: Harvard University Press, 1999).

7. Foundation for Individual Rights and Expression, "Scholars Under Fire Database Guide," https://www.thefire.org/research/scholars-under-fire-database/scholars-under-fire-database-guide.

8. For cases of professors punished for expression, see Sean T. Stevens, Lee Jussim, and Nathan Honeycutt, "Scholarship Suppression: Theoretical Perspectives and Emerging Trends," *Societies* 10, no. 4 (December 2020): 82, https://www.mdpi.com/2075-4698/10/4/82#.

9. Glenn Loury, "The Truth About Roland Fryer," March 13, 2022, https://glennloury.substack.com/p/the-truth-about-roland-fryer.

10. Peter W. Wood, "Harvard Cancels a Black Academic Who Debunked Woke Orthodoxy," *New York Post*, March 25, 2022, https://nypost.com/2022/03/25/harvard-cancels-a-black-academic-who-debunked-woke-orthodoxy.

11. Rob Montz, "Why Did Harvard University Go After One of Its Best Black Professors?," Quillette, April 15, 2022, https://quillette.com/2022/04/15/why-did-harvard-university-go-after-one-of-its-best-black-professors.

12. Bruce Gilley, "The Case for Colonialism," *Academic Questions* 31, no. 2 (Summer 2018): 167–85, https://www.nas.org/academic-questions/31/2/the_case_for_colonialism/pdf; and Bruce Gilley, "The Case for Colonialism: A Response to My Critics," *Academic Questions* 35, no. 1 (Summer 2022): 89–126, https://www.nas.org/academic-questions/35/1/the-case-for-colonialism-a-response-to-my-critics/pdf.

13. Gilley, "The Case for Colonialism."

14. Gilley, "The Case for Colonialism: A Response to My Critics."

15. Farhana Sultana, "The False Equivalence of Academic Freedom and Free Speech: Defending Academic Integrity in the Age of White Supremacy, Colonial Nostalgia, and Anti-Intellectualism," *ACME: An International Journal for Critical Geographies* 17, no. 2 (2018): 228–57, https://acme-journal.org/index.php/acme/article/view/1715/1433.

16. Society for Personality and Social Psychology, "About SPSP," https://spsp.org/about-spsp.

17. Society for Personality and Social Psychology, "About SPSP."

18. David M. Buss and William von Hippel, "Psychological Barriers to Evolutionary Psychology: Ideological Bias and Coalitional Adaptations," *Archives of Scientific Psychology* 6, no. 1 (2018): 148–58, https://psycnet.apa.org/fulltext/2018-57934-001.html.pdf.

19. For a review of studies showing that the academy in general and the social sciences in particular are massively skewed to the left, see Nathan Honeycutt and Lee Jussim, "Political Bias in the Social Sciences: A Critical, Theoretical, and Empirical Review," in *Ideological and Political Bias in Psychology: Nature, Scope, and Solutions*, ed. Craig L. Frisby et al. (New York: Springer, 2023).

20. Honeycutt and Jussim, "Political Bias in the Social Sciences."

21. Nikki Graf, "Most Americans Say Colleges Should Not Consider Race or Ethnicity in Admissions," Pew Research Center, February 25, 2019, https://www.

pewresearch.org/fact-tank/2019/02/25/most-americans-say-colleges-should-not-consider-race-or-ethnicity-in-admissions; and Juliana Menasce Horowitz, "Americans See Advantages and Challenges in Country's Growing Racial and Ethnic Diversity," Pew Research Center, May 8, 2019, https://www.pewresearch.org/social-trends/2019/05/08/americans-see-advantages-and-challenges-in-countrys-growing-racial-and-ethnic-diversity.

22. *Students for Fair Admission v. President and Fellows of Harvard College*, 600 US 181 (2023).

23. Václav Havel, "The Power of the Powerless," trans. Paul Wilson, *East European Politics and Societies* 32, no. 2 (May 2018): 353–408.

24. Baruch Spinoza, *Spinoza: Complete Works*, ed. Michael L. Morgan, trans. Samuel Shirley (Indianapolis, IN: Hackett Publishing, 2002).

25. Jonathan Haidt, "When Truth and Social Justice Collide, Choose Truth: Why I'm Resigning from My Professional Society," *Chronicle of Higher Education*, September 23, 2022, https://www.chronicle.com/article/when-truth-and-social-justice-collide-choose-truth.

26. Lee Jussim, "Mandatory Diversity, Equity, and Inclusion Statements at SPSP," Unsafe Science, August 7, 2022, https://unsafescience.substack.com/p/mandatory-diversity-equity-and-inclusion.

27. Lee Jussim, "SPSP Abandons Mandatory DEI Statements," Unsafe Science, July 17, 2023, https://unsafescience.substack.com/p/spsp-abandons-mandatory-dei-statements.

28. Association for Psychological Science, "History of APS," https://www.psychologicalscience.org/about/history-of-aps.

10

Ostrich Syndrome and Campus Free Expression

Sean T. Stevens, Nathan Honeycutt,
Komi Frey, and Andrea Honeycutt

Over the past decade, many college-educated Americans have become more censorious of offensive expression, and the "tolerance gap"—the consistent finding over decades that those with a college education are more tolerant than those without one—has largely evaporated. This represents a profound shift in American attitudes toward free expression,[1] as support for free expression among college graduates has shifted from a clear norm to a contested one.[2] During the same period, college students and faculty have also become more intolerant and censorious.[3] The result? Colleges and universities have become places that discourage vigorous scholarly debate on important issues facing society. This chapter adopts a nonpartisan approach to this festering problem.[4]

There are—and have always been—problems with speech suppression on college campuses. There is also a good amount of evidence that illiberalism among students and faculty has increased over the past decade.[5] Three broad patterns are evident in the data:

1. Attempts to suppress expression on campus are more likely to come from the left of that expression.[6]

2. Politically conservative expression is frequently targeted, but such speech is uncommon on campus.

3. Because the majority of students and faculty identify as left of center, a good amount of the expression targeted for sanction on campus is also likely to be politically left of center.

144 THE FREE INQUIRY PAPERS

None of this is surprising when considering that most people favor censoring speech they deem offensive, hateful, or both[7] and that the majority of students[8] and faculty[9] are politically left of center.

However, partisan interpretations of what kinds of speech are targeted for suppression on campus are common, with liberals and progressives focusing on incidents that target liberal or progressive expression and not conservative expression, and vice versa.[10] This chapter discusses these developments and what we call Ostrich Syndrome (OS), a disposition to ignore or dismiss evidence ("put one's head in the sand") in a way that reinforces one's own partisan beliefs. Niklaus Karlsson, George Loewenstein, and Duane Seppi coined the term "ostrich effect" in 2009 to describe selective attention to information.[11] Our more specific use of the term differs in that a person may move back and forth in his or her receptivity to information.

For conservatives, OS represents an efficient rhetorical fortress that stereotypes colleges and universities as "hotbeds" of "leftist indoctrination" to dismiss partisan arguments they dislike. The efficient rhetorical fortress is able to do this by inculcating the belief that you don't have to listen to liberals, experts, or journalists.[12] This allows conservatives to dismiss academics' viewpoints and concerns because they are "lefties" or "liberals" who are known to have the "wrong opinions." This stereotype of higher education contributes to a view that the ideological skew of academia is the primary problem facing American colleges and universities. Many conservatives have reached this conclusion and appear to remain stuck in what we call Stage 1 of OS.

For liberals or progressives, OS represents a perfect rhetorical fortress.[13] The perfect rhetorical fortress is a more complicated version of the efficient rhetorical fortress that relies on a number of ad hominem comparisons and rhetorical defenses to dismiss any concerns raised about suppression of conservative expression on campus. For instance, a liberal or progressive in Stage 1 of OS often argues that a well-funded cabal of right-wing organizations exaggerates and amplifies such incidents to incite a moral panic about "college kids these days," so there is no reason to be concerned about speech on campus. Unlike most conservatives, however, liberals and progressives are more likely to progress into later stages of OS, in which they acknowledge that there are some legitimate reasons to be concerned about speech on campus but continue to maintain that the problem is being exaggerated.

In this chapter, we first document that current college students and faculty are hostile to free expression and have become increasingly willing to call for its sanction over the past decade. We then delineate the stages of OS and specify and refute examples of arguments made at each stage.

Stage 1 of OS is characterized by ad hominem attacks. In Stage 2, partisans admit there is a problem but claim it has been exaggerated. In Stage 3, they take the problem seriously but raise methodological critiques of how data indicating a problem are collected. Since most conservatives are expected to remain in Stage 1 of OS, the discussion of Stages 2 and 3 primarily focuses on how OS manifests in liberals and progressives.

The State of Free Expression on Campus

Controversies over expression on US college campuses are not new. During the 1950s, suspected Communists' academic freedom was curtailed, and they faced difficulty obtaining tenure; known Communists were often stripped of tenure and fired.[14] The 1960s spawned the Free Speech Movement in Berkeley, California,[15] and protests on campuses across the country that continued into the 1970s.[16] In the 1980s and 1990s, speech codes were implemented, stoking concerns over political correctness.[17] In the past, college administrators were the ones primarily policing speech on campus.[18] In recent years, however, they have gained some unexpected allies: students and faculty themselves.

Numerous surveys from different organizations and polling firms find that large numbers of college students endorse illiberal attitudes. For instance, a majority of students oppose inviting controversial speakers to campus, regardless of whether those speakers' views are liberal or conservative;[19] support establishing free speech zones on campus and restricting students from wearing costumes that could be perceived as reinforcing stereotypes;[20] and believe that other students and professors should be reported to the university if they say something considered offensive.[21] Many students also think colleges should be able to restrict political views they oppose[22] and find it acceptable, to some degree, to shout down a speaker on campus, physically block other students from entering a campus event, or use violence to stop a campus speech.[23]

Not to be outdone, many faculty also report willingness to discriminate against colleagues with different ideological views in making hiring or promotion decisions, during the peer review of papers or grants, or in day-to-day social interactions.[24] For example, a 2024 survey of 6,269 college and university faculty conducted by the Foundation for Individual Rights and Expression (FIRE) asked faculty whether it would adversely affect their hiring decision if an applicant seeking a position in their department was notably conservative or notably liberal. The results were lopsided, with 29 percent responding that it would at least sometimes adversely affect their hiring decision if the applicant was notably conservative (56 percent if including those who indicated "rarely"), while 10 percent said it would at least sometimes adversely affect their hiring decision if the applicant was notably liberal (37 percent if including those who indicated "rarely").[25] Similarly, in a 2022 survey of faculty conducted by FIRE, notable percentages of faculty endorsed illiberal attitudes. Specifically, one-third responded that speech should be restricted if words are intended to be hateful, and a significant portion (ranging from 18 to 36 percent) endorsed their college's administration launching a formal investigation into other faculty members for their controversial expression.[26]

In a 2021 analysis of surveys on free expression, Eric Kaufmann, a professor of politics at University of Buckingham in the UK, assessed support among US faculty and graduate students in the social sciences and humanities for dismissing a colleague whose work yielded unpopular research findings (e.g., that greater ethnic diversity increases societal tension and leads to negative social outcomes).[27] The survey results were encouraging in some ways but troubling in others. Overall, depending on the particular finding in question, only 7 to 18 percent expressed support for dismissal. However, opposition to dismissing a colleague peaked at 52 percent for all but one of the findings asked about. In addition, a significant share of academics claimed to be unsure or neutral on the question of dismissal. Support for dismissal was higher among PhD students compared with faculty, with 49 percent of doctoral students supportive of at least one dismissal campaign compared with just 24 percent of faculty.[28]

These censorious attitudes among students and faculty contribute to a chilling effect: Students and faculty fear social sanction and are reluctant to share their views. For instance, FIRE's annual student survey found that roughly one in five students reported that they self-censored "fairly" or "very" often in 2021 (N = 37,104), 2022 (N = 44,847), and 2023 (N = 55,102). In 2021 and 2022, roughly 60 percent of students also said they were "somewhat" or "very" uncomfortable publicly disagreeing with their professor or expressing an unpopular opinion on their social media account. In 2023, that percentage increased to about 70 percent. Similarly, in 2021 and 2022, roughly half of students felt "somewhat" or "very" uncomfortable when expressing their views on a controversial political topic in class; in 2023, 60 percent of students felt uncomfortable. All these findings were more pronounced among those in the ideological minority on a campus, typically the more moderate and conservative students.[29]

Other data corroborate these findings. Annual administrations of Heterodox Academy's Campus Expression Survey from 2019 to 2021 found that at least one in four students were "somewhat" or "very" reluctant to express their views, in a class of about 20 students, on controversial topics related to politics, race, gender, religion, or sexuality. When asked why, students primarily identified negative reactions from their peers and, to a lesser extent, their professors—including receiving a lower grade because of their views. As with the FIRE surveys, moderate and conservative students reported more reluctance expressing themselves than did liberal students.[30]

Additionally, social science faculty with ideological views that differed from those of most of their colleagues were more than three times as likely to report a hostile climate in their department. These faculty members were also less comfortable expressing those views to colleagues and more likely to say they had refrained from discussing their views in their research or when teaching.[31] In general, conservative faculty and graduate students report more experiences of hostility and greater expectations of being stigmatized by peers or colleagues if their political beliefs were to be revealed.[32]

In FIRE's 2022 faculty survey, more than half of faculty surveyed (52 percent) were "very" or "somewhat" worried about damaging their reputation because someone misunderstood something they said or did. This concern was more pronounced among moderate (56 percent),

148 THE FREE INQUIRY PAPERS

conservative (73 percent), and far-right (78 percent) faculty than among liberal (40 percent) and far-left (38 percent) faculty. This concern is reflected in the rates of self-censorship among faculty, with roughly one-third saying they self-censored "fairly" or "very" often. Self-censorship was again more pronounced among moderate (34 percent), conservative (56 percent), and far-right (76 percent) faculty than among liberal (22 percent) or far-left (14 percent) faculty.

Faculty were also presented with a definition of self-censorship and then asked how often they self-censored in different professional settings.[33] Forty-five percent said it was "very" or "extremely" likely they would self-censor on social media, and another 14 percent said they would likely do so. Forty-four percent said it was "very" or "extremely" likely they would self-censor in official meetings with administrators, faculty, or student groups, and another 17 percent said they would likely do so. Thirty-seven percent said it was "very" or "extremely" likely they would self-censor in publications, talks, interviews, or lectures directed to a general audience, and another 16 percent said they would likely do so. Twenty-five percent said it was "very" or "extremely" likely they would self-censor in academic publications, and another 11 percent said they would likely do so. Finally, when asked if they were more likely to self-censor now compared with September 2020, 38 percent said "much more" or "more" likely, and 53 percent said "about the same."[34]

In the 2024 FIRE faculty survey, a similar pattern emerged. First, the question on "being worried" was split into two separate questions, one asking about losing their job and the second about their reputation. In the first, 38 percent of faculty reported being worried about losing their job because someone misunderstands something they have said or done. In the second, 67 percent of faculty reported being worried about their reputation being damaged because someone misunderstands something they have said or done. Additionally, roughly one in four said they often feel they can't express their opinions because of how students, colleagues, or the administration would respond.[35] All of these findings were substantially more pronounced among conservative faculty.

Qualitative data obtained by asking scholars directly about their personal experiences yield similar results. For instance, nontenured scholars reported being warned by tenured faculty not to pursue controversial research topics until "after they obtain tenure."[36] Other scholars said they would change the topics they cover in class after having witnessed another colleague become embroiled in controversy,[37] having had their own dissenting political views publicly ridiculed,[38] or having faced professional and social ostracism because of them.[39] Socially conservative professors, who tend to embrace traditional religious views, are particularly unpopular in the academy, compared with their more socially liberal counterparts. This also applies to libertarians, a group typically considered right of center due to their pro-capitalist views.[40]

FIRE also maintains two databases—the Campus Deplatforming Database and the Scholars Under Fire Database—that record attempts to suppress speech on campus. For each entry, both databases record who the source of the speech-suppression campaign was (e.g., students, faculty, or activist groups); whether the attempt to suppress speech came from the left or the right of the "controversial" expression; whether there were any petitions for or against the target of the speech-suppression campaign; the administration's public response, if any; and the outcome of the speech-suppression campaign (e.g., a speaker's invitation was revoked, a professor was fired, or no sanction occurred). These databases are valuable because they provide behavioral evidence of who is trying to suppress speech on campus.

The Campus Deplatforming Database tracks attempts to deplatform invited speakers, performances (e.g., comedy shows or plays), film screenings, or artwork.[41] FIRE defines a deplatforming attempt as an effort to censor expression at campus events open to the public. This can include organized campaigns to have a speaker's appearance canceled or spontaneous attempts to disrupt the event while it is in progress. Since 1998, FIRE has recorded more than 1,500 deplatforming attempts.[42] The majority of these attempts target speakers invited to campus by students or faculty or speakers invited to address the college or university during commencement. Performances like *The Vagina Monologues* or drag shows are also frequently targeted by deplatforming campaigns.

From 1998 through 2012, almost three-fifths (297 of 507, or 59 percent) of the deplatforming attempts recorded involved activist organizations. Most of these deplatforming attempts were initiated by the Cardinal Newman Society, a nonprofit that works to promote and defend faithful

Catholic education. The Cardinal Newman Society focused its deplatforming efforts on Catholic colleges and universities, frequently targeting performances of *The Vagina Monologues* or "scandalous" (e.g., pro-choice or pro–gay rights) commencement speakers. During this same period (1998–2012), students were involved in more than a quarter of deplatforming attempts (145 of 507, or 29 percent), student groups were involved in 27 deplatforming attempts (5 percent), and faculty were involved in 34 deplatforming attempts (7 percent).

Over the past decade, however, deplatforming attempts involving on-campus sources have surged. From 2013 to mid-2024, activist organizations, including the Cardinal Newman Society, were involved in 280 deplatforming attempts, or 28 percent of the 1,000 attempts that FIRE recorded during this period. In contrast, students have been involved in 510, or just over half (51 percent), of the deplatforming attempts recorded during this time period; student groups have been involved in about a quarter of these attempts (265, or 27 percent); and faculty have been involved in 128 attempts (13 percent). These campus-initiated deplatforming attempts over the past decade have frequently targeted conservatives such as Ann Coulter, Riley Gaines, Charlie Kirk, Charles Murray, Candace Owens, Ben Shapiro, Matt Walsh, and Milo Yiannopoulos.

The Scholars Under Fire Database includes over 1,000 entries from 2015 to the present. Undergraduate attempts to sanction scholars have increased since 2015, peaking at 82 in 2020. These attempts have since declined to 71 incidents in 2021, 53 in 2022, 25 in 2023, and 11 in the first half of 2024. Likewise, the number of times scholars attempted to sanction other scholars has also increased since 2015, from 10 to a peak of 46 in 2021. Faculty-initiated sanction attempts have since declined, to 21 attempts in 2022, 11 in 2023, and just one in the first half of 2024. Although this database does not attempt to infer the politics of the scholar facing a sanction attempt, it seems reasonable to assume that the majority of the scholars included in the database are politically left of center, given the base rates of faculty and graduate students for political ideology.

The cumulative sum of this behavioral evidence reinforces survey data, suggesting that large portions of college students and faculty are politically intolerant, which helps create a restrictive, stifling speech climate on many campuses. Because incoming students, current graduate students,

OSTRICH SYNDROME AND CAMPUS FREE EXPRESSION   151

and younger faculty are more liberal and ideologically homogeneous than their older counterparts, it is reasonable to predict that such trends will continue and even intensify in the coming years.[43]

The Stages of Ostrich Syndrome

Decades of accumulated evidence of suppression of speech—left, right, and moderate in nature—have drawn decades of partisan interpretations, much of it consistent with OS. This section describes each stage and how it manifests itself among partisans in more detail.

Stage 1. During Stage 1 of OS, partisanship influences what an individual perceives as problematic in a community. In this case, the community is American higher education. A tedious dance ensues, featuring an exaggerated conservative critique of academia and a dismissive, ad hominem liberal counterargument.[44]

As noted above, for conservatives at this stage of OS, the leftward ideological skew in academia is identified as a serious if not intractable problem that undermines their confidence in American higher education. This conservative critique of American higher education is rooted in William F. Buckley's 1951 treatise, *God and Man at Yale: The Superstitions of Academic Freedom*, in which he laments the underrepresentation of conservative views, criticizing Yale as a "hotbed of atheism" and "collectivism."[45] It is not in dispute that academia skews left or that conservative expression is frequently targeted for suppression on campus. Yet there is little evidence that student grades are affected by liberal ideological biases in grading[46] or that the experience of college consistently makes students more liberal.[47]

Research indicates that conservative students perceive and fear that their professors' liberal ideology will lead to grading bias.[48] But it is also reasonable to predict that such bias would occur in disciplines characterized by higher levels of ideological homogeneity.[49] Without consistent evidence that these biases actually affect student grades, it is difficult to argue that this problem is found in all academic disciplines or is prevalent on all college campuses.

152 THE FREE INQUIRY PAPERS

Similarly, the evidence is mixed that the college educated are more likely to identify as politically left of center and support more liberal candidates and policies primarily because of their college experience. Some evidence suggests that students move uniformly left on some issues such as abortion, affirmative action, and same-sex marriage[50] and that those enrolled at liberal arts colleges tend to become more liberal over time, compared with those at other four-year institutions.[51] Yet, other evidence suggests that parental and peer influence are stronger influences on political socialization,[52] and recent studies suggest little to no change in self-identified political ideology after one's first year of college.[53] Thus, although not inaccurate, the conservative critique of academia made in Stage 1 of OS is exaggerated.

A common liberal or progressive ad hominem counterargument made during Stage 1 of OS contends that a nefarious network of right-wing organizations has manufactured a free speech crisis on campus, in which liberal and progressive students and faculty are mischaracterized as highly censorious of and hostile to conservative students and faculty. According to this counterargument, the real problem is the suppression of liberal and progressive expression on campus.[54] It is true that there are right-wing organizations (e.g., Campus Reform, the College Fix, and Professor Watchlist) that amplify examples of conservative expression being suppressed on campus; it is also true that there is not an equivalent group of organizations amplifying incidents when liberal or progressive expression is suppressed on campus. There is also evidence that these right-wing organizations stifle expression of liberal and progressive views.[55]

However, the existence of right-wing organizations whose main purpose is to expose "liberal indoctrination" in American higher education is irrelevant to whether conservative expression is being suppressed on campus. On the contrary, FIRE's Campus Deplatforming Database and Scholars Under Fire Database indicate that it is. Furthermore, notable portions of students—both undergraduate and graduate—and faculty support censoring ideological expression they disagree with. Since most students and faculty identify as politically left of center, it is therefore likely that conservative expression will be targeted for suppression on most campuses.

Stage 2. Presumably, the majority of conservatives remain in Stage 1 of OS. Liberals and progressives who advance to Stage 2 of OS acknowledge that speech is suppressed on a handful of campuses but argue that the problem is still being exaggerated and amplified by the aforementioned organized right-wing network to distract people from larger problems facing higher education. To make this argument, data are often cherry-picked.

For instance, to argue that campuses are generally tolerant of dissenting views and controversial opinions, Mary Anne Franks cited a 2017 Knight and Gallup survey of college students and the general public that found that 70 percent of students preferred an open learning environment in which offensive speech was permitted to one in which certain speech was prohibited.[56] Why is this a good example of someone in Stage 2 of OS? Because the 70 percent figure indicates that about a third of students do prefer a more restrictive speech environment, and citing it implicitly acknowledges that a minority of students may be hostile to free expression. Franks also neglects to mention that the percentage she cited had declined from 78 percent the previous year. Furthermore, the same survey reported that 61 percent of students said that "the climate on my campus prevents some people from saying things they believe because others might find them offensive," an increase from 54 percent the previous year.[57] This data point actually tells us what students think the speech climate is like on their campus, something that the statistic Franks cited does not do.

During Stage 2 of OS, it is also common for liberal or progressive partisans to appeal to political tolerance. According to this argument, college students and the college educated are the most tolerant of offensive expression,[58] and that four years of college experience makes people more tolerant of racist or sexist speech.[59] The problem with the appeal to tolerance is that the findings cited to support it do not refer to current college students.

For instance, to dispel the notion that a large number of students feel they cannot freely express themselves on campus, Aaron Hanlon cited a study by Colin Campbell and Jonathan Horowitz. The problem? Campbell and Horowitz analyzed the 1994 General Social Survey (GSS) and the 1994 Study of American Families and specifically emphasized the limited generalizability of their findings: "The findings roughly reflect the effect of college education from the end of World War II until the Republican

154   THE FREE INQUIRY PAPERS

revolution that elected Newt Gingrich as speaker of the House."[60] Other data commonly cited to support the appeal-to-tolerance argument come from the Ray Franke et al. 2010 study and the 2009 College Senior Survey, meaning the students surveyed started college in the mid-2000s.[61]

A variation on the appeal-to-tolerance argument is citation of GSS data that indicate that each subsequent generation of Americans is more tolerant than the last.[62] However, this interpretation has been questioned in the political science literature for decades because the GSS method of measuring tolerance does not ensure that the survey respondents actually dislike the target they are being asked to tolerate. This makes it difficult to draw conclusions about increases in tolerance, and by proxy support for free expression, over time.[63] Furthermore, the GSS is simply not a good tool for understanding what college students think because it samples households—not people who live in dormitories on college campuses—and in any given year few people age 18 to 22 are sampled.[64]

In other words, it is common for a partisan in Stage 2 of OS to offer a number of arguments that at first glance appear rooted in good evidence that refutes the claim that students have become increasingly censorious of expression on campus. However, citing data from the mid to late 1990s and the 2000s or from surveys that sample the few college students who do not live on campus does not refute the argument that college students have become more supportive of censorship on campus over the past decade.[65] At the same time, not citing data showing that college education has long been associated with higher levels of ideological prejudice[66] and that the tolerance gap has evaporated[67] paints an inaccurate picture of what is currently known about the state of campus free expression.

Stage 3. Liberals and progressives who reach Stage 3 of OS no longer deny that there is a speech-suppression problem on campus and no longer rely primarily on ad hominem arguments about the organized network of right-wing organizations. But they continue to minimize the size and scope of the problem. They do this by either critiquing the methodologies used to collect data supporting the argument that the suppression of speech on campus is a serious problem, or they reinterpret conclusions gleaned from the data in a way that makes it appear like the problems with speech on campus remain limited to a handful of institutions.

One methodological criticism contends that FIRE's Campus Deplatforming Database and Scholars Under Fire Database rely on publicly available information and do not document incidents when a professor is targeted indirectly (e.g., by a state policy banning certain curricula) or when a scholar has reportedly been threatened but there is no way to publicly verify the claim. This first criticism is not really a criticism at all. Why? Although neither database can account for incidents that do not get reported, it is far more likely that both databases are undercounting incidents and therefore underestimating the scope of the problem.[68] The other criticisms demand that the Scholars Under Fire Database measure what it is not designed to account for, because doing so requires tracking information that is not within the scope of the project's methodology.[69]

During this stage, it is also common to encounter the argument that surveying people about self-censorship is flawed because the term has many potential meanings and it is difficult to know what people are thinking when they answer questions about it.[70] This criticism is primarily based on a study that sampled 16 students who completed a survey that included one question from FIRE's 2020 student survey: "On your campus, how often have you felt that you could not express your opinion on a subject because of how students, a professor, or the administration would respond?"[71] These students were purposefully selected from a larger sample of 275 to be interviewed about how they interpreted the question and their experiences with self-censorship on campus.[72] This small sample was created based on its members' personal characteristics.

Certainly, not everyone interprets every survey question in the same way. This variance is accounted for by surveying a large number of people who are selected randomly in some fashion.[73] FIRE's 2022 survey sampled 44,847 students and introduced two new questions asking about feelings that should co-occur with self-censorship.

1. How worried are you about damaging your reputation because someone misunderstands something you have said or done? (Response options: "not at all worried," "not very worried," "worried a little," and "worried a lot")

2. How much pressure do you feel to avoid discussing controversial topics in your classes? (Response options: "no pressure at all," "slight pressure," "some pressure," "a good deal of pressure," and "a great deal of pressure")

Table 1 shows that these questions were both positively correlated: As the frequency of self-censorship increased, so did concern about damaging one's reputation and pressure to avoid discussing controversial topics in class; as concern about damaging one's reputation increased, so did pressure to avoid controversial topics in class.

Another criticism made by liberals and progressives in Stage 3 of OS is that self-censorship is a sign of a campus with a good speech climate.[74] This argument contends that self-censoring a dissenting viewpoint out of fear of social ridicule is desirable and should be the norm. This does not acknowledge the plethora of studies that show that people in higher education are overwhelmingly of one political affiliation, that many of them are keen to target their political opponents, or that social exclusion and ostracism have several negative psychological consequences.[75]

Additionally, the need to maintain one's reputation exerts a heavy influence on one's ability to achieve nearly all the positive incentives in academia, such as obtaining letters of recommendation, interviewing for tenure-track jobs, and receiving promotions.[76] In such a community, it is easy to discourage the expression of certain ideas because humans possess an inherent motivation to forge stable social relationships.[77] As a result, behaviors that can lead to ridicule, exclusion, or ostracism are often avoided.[78] Dissenting views are therefore less likely to be expressed, and this likelihood declines over time until only "hard-core true believers" remain willing to express views widely considered "fringe" or "extreme."[79]

This strong social reputational system fosters a spiral of silence that occurs through formal and informal channels.[80] For instance, peer review of articles and grants is a formal gatekeeping process with many strengths and flaws. These flaws include the encouragement of post hoc analyses by reviewers, nonpublication of null results, and bias in various forms.[81] Informal constraints on this process include advising scholars to wait until they have tenure before pursuing a line of research on a controversial

Table 1. Correlations Between Self-Censorship Survey Items from FIRE's 2022 Student Survey

	Question 1	Question 2
1. Frequency of Self-Censorship	—	—
2. Damage to Reputation	0.23	—
3. Pressure to Avoid Discussion of Controversial Topics	0.46	0.32

Note: All correlations are statistically significant at $p < 0.001$. $N = 44,847$.
Source: Sean T. Stevens, *2022–2023 College Free Speech Rankings: What Is the State of Free Speech on America's College Campuses?*, Foundation for Individual Rights and Expression, 2022, https://www.thefire.org/research-learn/2022-2023-college-free-speech-rankings.

topic, publicly ridiculing dissenting viewpoints, or making career advancement difficult for certain scholars because of their political views. All these encourage self-censorship and discourage the expression of dissenting viewpoints.[82]

Conclusion

In study after study, across different methodologies, researchers find that sizable portions of students and faculty hold intolerant attitudes. They are willing to discriminate against those who disagree with them politically and often harbor bias against more moderate and conservative expression. Students and faculty increasingly attempt to sanction each other, and the tolerance gap between college-educated and noncollege-educated Americans has closed, with the former less likely to support free expression than they were in the past. Finally, the threat to freedom of speech no longer comes mainly from administrators or outside actors; it is now emanating from students and faculty themselves, and it is growing. Scholars, college and university administrators, journalists, and politicians who continue to willfully ignore these realities are in the throes of OS, with their heads planted firmly in the sand.

158 THE FREE INQUIRY PAPERS

Acknowledgments

The authors would like to thank Adam Goldstein, Greg Lukianoff, and Ryne Weiss for comments on earlier versions of this chapter.

Notes

1. See, for example, Lawrence Bobo and Frederick C. Licari, "Education and Political Tolerance: Testing the Effects of Cognitive Sophistication and Target Group Affect," *Public Opinion Quarterly* 53, no. 3 (Fall 1989): 285–308, https://scholar.harvard.edu/files/bobo/files/education.pdf; Anna Boch, "Increasing American Political Tolerance: A Framework Excluding Hate Speech," *Socius* 6 (2020): 1–12, https://journals.sagepub.com/doi/full/10.1177/2378023120903959; Colin Campbell and Jerry Johnson Jr., "Trends in the Association Between a College Education and Political Tolerance, 1976–2016," *Socius* 4 (2018), https://journals.sagepub.com/doi/10.1177/2378023118805858; Dennis Chong, Jack Citrin, and Morris Levy, "The Realignment of Political Tolerance in the United States," October 27, 2021, https://ssrn.com/abstract=3951377; Herbert McClosky and Alida Brill, *Dimensions of Tolerance: What Americans Believe About Civil Liberties* (New York: Russell Sage Foundation, 1983); and Samuel A. Stouffer, *Communism, Conformity, and Civil Liberties: A Cross-Section of the Nation Speaks Its Mind* (New York: Doubleday, 1955).

2. Boch, "Increasing American Political Tolerance"; Chong, Citrin, and Levy, "The Realignment of Political Tolerance in the United States"; and Dennis Chong and Morris Levy, "Competing Norms of Free Expression and Political Tolerance," *Social Research* 85, no. 1 (Spring 2018): 197–227, https://muse.jhu.edu/article/692750.

3. See, for example, Komi German and Sean T. Stevens, *Scholars Under Fire: The Targeting of Scholars for Ideological Reasons from 2015 to Present*, Foundation for Individual Rights and Expression, 2021, https://www.thefire.org/research-learn/scholars-under-fire-targeting-scholars-ideological-reasons-2015-present; Komi German and Sean T. Stevens, *Scholars Under Fire: 2021 Year in Review*, Foundation for Individual Rights and Expression, 2022, https://www.thefire.org/research/publications/miscellaneous-publications/scholars-under-fire/scholars-under-fire-2021-year-in-review-full-text; and Eric Kaufmann, *Academic Freedom in Crisis: Punishment, Political Discrimination, and Self-Censorship*, Center for the Study of Partisanship and Ideology, March 1, 2021, https://cspicenter.org/wp-content/uploads/2021/03/AcademicFreedom.pdf.

4. This chapter was originally drafted in the early half of 2023, before Hamas attacked Israel on October 7, 2023, and Israel's subsequent military operations in Gaza. It has not been updated to reflect that event or the responses on college campuses.

5. See, for example, German and Stevens, *Scholars Under Fire: The Targeting of Scholars for Ideological Reasons from 2015 to Present*; German and Stevens, *Scholars Under Fire: 2021 Year in Review*; Nathan Honeycutt and Laura Freberg, "The Liberal

and Conservative Experience Across Academic Disciplines: An Extension of Inbar and Lammers," *Social Psychological and Science* 8, no. 2 (March 2017): 115–23, https://journals.sagepub.com/doi/abs/10.1177/1948550616667617; Kaufmann, *Academic Freedom in Crisis*; Uwe Peters et al., "Ideological Diversity, Hostility, and Discrimination in Philosophy," *Philosophical Psychology* 33, no. 4 (2020): 511–48, https://www.tandfonline.com/doi/full/10.1080/09515089.2020.1743257; Sean T. Stevens, 2024 *College Free Speech Rankings: What Is the State of Free Speech on America's College Campuses?*, Foundation for Individual Rights and Expression, 2023, https://www.thefire.org/research-learn/2024-college-free-speech-rankings; Sean T. Stevens, 2022–2023 *College Free Speech Rankings: What Is the State of Free Speech on America's College Campuses?*, Foundation for Individual Rights and Expression, 2022, https://www.thefire.org/research-learn/2022-2023-college-free-speech-rankings; Sean T. Stevens and Anne Schwichtenberg, 2021 *College Free Speech Rankings: What Is the State of Free Speech on America's College Campuses?*, Foundation for Individual Rights and Expression, https://www.thefire.org/research-learn/2021-college-free-speech-rankings; and Sean T. Stevens and Anne Schwichtenberg, 2020 *College Free Speech Rankings: What Is the State of Free Speech on America's College Campuses?*, Foundation for Individual Rights and Expression, https://www.thefire.org/research-learn/2020-college-free-speech-rankings

6. The Foundation for Individual Rights and Expression classifies the political motivation for a disinvitation or sanction attempt as relative to the speaker's expression, coming from either their left or their right, rather than inferring the scholar's political orientation.

7. James L. Gibson, "Enigmas of Intolerance: Fifty Years After Stouffer's *Communism, Conformity, and Civil Liberties*," *Perspectives on Politics* 4, no. 1 (March 2006): 21–34, https://www.jstor.org/stable/3688624; John L. Sullivan, James Piereson, and George E. Marcus, "An Alternative Conceptualization of Political Tolerance: Illusory Increases 1950s–1970s," *American Political Science Review* 73, no. 3 (September 1979): 781–94, https://www.jstor.org/stable/1955404; and John L. Sullivan, James Piereson, and George E. Marcus, *Political Tolerance and American Democracy* (Chicago: University of Chicago Press, 1982). See also Jacob Mchangama, *Free Speech: A History from Socrates to Social Media* (New York: Basic Books, 2022).

8. Stevens, 2024 *College Free Speech Rankings*; Stevens, 2022–2023 *College Free Speech Rankings*; Stevens and Schwichtenberg, 2021 *College Free Speech Rankings*; and Stevens and Schwichtenberg, 2020 *College Free Speech Rankings*.

9. José L. Duarte et al., "Political Diversity Will Improve Social Psychological Science," *Behavioral and Brain Sciences* 38 (2015): e130, https://www.cambridge.org/core/journals/behavioral-and-brain-sciences/article/abs/political-diversity-will-improve-social-psychological-science1/A54AD4878AED1AFC8BA6AF54A890149F; Honeycutt and Freberg, "The Liberal and Conservative Experience Across Academic Disciplines"; Nathan Honeycutt, Sean T. Stevens, and Eric Kaufmann, *The Academic Mind in 2022: What Faculty Think About Free Expression and Academic Freedom on Campus*, Foundation for Individual Rights and Expression, 2023, https://www.thefire.org/research-learn/academic-mind-2022-what-faculty-think-about-free-expression-and-academic-freedom; Kaufmann, *Academic Freedom in Crisis*; Mitchell Langbert, "Homogenous: The Political Affiliations of Elite Liberal Arts

College Faculty," *Academic Questions* 31 (2018): 186–97, https://www.nas.org/academic-questions/31/2/homogenous_the_political_affiliations_of_elite_liberal_arts_college_faculty/pdf; Mitchell Langbert, Anthony J. Quain, and Daniel B. Klein, "Faculty Voter Registration in Economics, History, Journalism, Law, and Psychology," *Econ Journal Watch* 13, no. 3 (September 2016): 422–51, https://econjwatch.org/File+download/944/LangbertQuainKleinSept2016.pdf; Mitchell Langbert and Sean T. Stevens, "Partisan Registration of Faculty in Flagship Colleges," *Studies in Higher Education* 47, no. 8 (August 2022): 1750–60, https://www.tandfonline.com/doi/full/10.1080/03075079.20 21.1957815; and Peters et al., "Ideological Diversity, Hostility, and Discrimination in Philosophy."

10. See, for example, William F. Buckley Jr., *God and Man at Yale: The Superstitions of "Academic Freedom"* (Washington, DC: Regnery Publishing, 1951); and John K. Wilson, *The Myth of Political Correctness: The Conservative Attack on Higher Education* (Durham, NC: Duke University Press, 1995).

11. Niklas Karlsson, George Loewenstein, and Duane Seppi, "The Ostrich Effect: Selective Attention to Information," *Journal of Risk and Uncertainty* 38, no. 2 (April 2009): 95–115, https://www.cmu.edu/dietrich/sds/docs/loewenstein/OstrichEffect.pdf.

12. Greg Lukianoff and Rikki Schlott, *The Canceling of the American Mind: Cancel Culture Undermines Trust and Threatens Us All—but There Is a Solution* (New York: Simon & Schuster, 2023).

13. Lukianoff and Schlott, *The Canceling of the American Mind*.

14. David A. Hollinger, "Academic Culture at Michigan, 1938–1988: The Apotheosis of Pluralism," *Rackham Reports* (1988–89): 58–101 (followed by responses from Philip E. Converse, Homer A. Neal, Martha Vicinus, Rudolf Arnheim, and James V. Neal, 102–40); and John Karl Wilson, "A History of Academic Freedom in America" (PhD diss., Illinois State University, Normal, IL, 2014), https://ir.library.illinoisstate.edu/etd/257.

15. Robert Cohen and Reginald E. Zelnik, eds., *The Free Speech Movement: Reflections on Berkeley in the 1960s* (Berkeley, CA: University of California Press, 2002).

16. Simon Hall, "Protest Movements in the 1970s: The Long 1960s," *Journal of Contemporary History* 43, no. 4 (October 2008): 655–72, https://www.jstor.org/stable/40543228.

17. Greg Lukianoff, *Unlearning Liberty: Campus Censorship and the End of American Debate* (New York: Encounter Books, 2014).

18. Greg Lukianoff and Jonathan Haidt, *The Coddling of the American Mind: How Good Intentions and Bad Ideas Are Setting Up a Generation for Failure* (New York: Penguin Press, 2018).

19. Stevens, *2024 College Free Speech Rankings*; Stevens, *2022–2023 College Free Speech Rankings*; Stevens and Schwichtenberg, *2021 College Free Speech Rankings*; and Stevens and Schwichtenberg, *2020 College Free Speech Rankings*.

20. Gallup and Knight Foundation, *Free Expression on Campus: What College Students Think About First Amendment Issues*, 2018, https://knightfoundation.org/wp-content/uploads/2020/01/Knight_Foundation_Free_Expression_on_Campus_2017.pdf; and Knight Foundation, *Free Expression on College Campuses*, May 2019, https://kf-site-production.s3.amazonaws.com/media_elements/files/000/000/351/original/Knight-CP-Report-FINAL.pdf.

21. John Bitzan and Clay Routledge, *2021 American College Student Freedom, Progress and Flourishing Survey*, North Dakota State University, Sheila and Robert Challey Institute for Global Innovation and Growth, https://www.ndsu.edu/fileadmin/challeyinstitute/Research_Briefs/2021_American_College_Student_Survey.pdf; and John Bitzan and Clay Routledge, *2022 American College Student Freedom, Progress and Flourishing Survey*, North Dakota State University, Sheila Robert Challey Institute for Global Innovation and Growth, https://www.ndsu.edu/fileadmin/challeyinstitute/Research_Briefs/2022_American_College_Student_Survey.pdf.

22. Gallup and Knight Foundation, *The First Amendment on Campus 2020 Report: College Students' Views of Free Expression*, May 5, 2020, https://knightfoundation.org/reports/the-first-amendment-on-campus-2020-report-college-students-views-of-free-expression/; and Knight Foundation and Ipsos, *College Student Views on Free Expression and Campus Speech 2022: A Look at Key Trends in Student Speech Views Since 2016*, January 2022, https://knightfoundation.org/wp-content/uploads/2022/01/KFX_College_2022.pdf.

23. Stevens, *2024 College Free Speech Rankings*; Stevens, *2022–2023 College Free Speech Rankings*; Stevens and Schwichtenberg, *2021 College Free Speech Rankings*; and Stevens and Schwichtenberg, *2020 College Free Speech Rankings*.

24. Nathan Honeycutt, "Manifestations of Political Bias" (PhD diss., Rutgers University, New Brunswick, NJ, 2022), https://rucore.libraries.rutgers.edu/rutgers-lib/68409; Nathan Honeycutt and Laura Freberg, "The Liberal and Conservative Experience Across Academic Disciplines: An Extension of Inbar and Lammers," *Social Psychological and Personality Science* 8, no. 2 (2017): 115–23, https://journals.sagepub.com/doi/10.1177/1948550616667617; Yoel Inbar and Joris Lammers, "Political Diversity in Social and Personality Psychology," *Perspectives on Psychological Science* 7, no. 5 (September 2012): 496–503, https://journals.sagepub.com/doi/10.1177/1745691612448792; Kaufmann, *Academic Freedom in Crisis*; and Uwe Peters et al., "Ideological Diversity, Hostility, and Discrimination in Philosophy," *Philosophical Psychology* 33, no. 4 (2020): 511–48, https://www.tandfonline.com/doi/full/10.1080/09515089.2020.1743257.

25. Nathan Honeycutt, Sean T. Stevens, and Laura Freberg, *Faculty Experiences and Perspectives on Free Speech*, forthcoming.

26. Honeycutt, Stevens, and Kaufmann, *The Academic Mind in 2022*.

27. Kaufmann, *Academic Freedom in Crisis*.

28. See Kaufmann, *Academic Freedom in Crisis*.

29. Stevens, *2024 College Free Speech Rankings*. For similar findings, see Stevens, *2022–2023 College Free Speech Rankings*; and Stevens and Schwichtenberg, *2021 College Free Speech Rankings*.

30. Melissa Stiksma, *Understanding the Campus Expression Climate: Fall 2019*, Heterodox Academy, 2020, https://heterodoxacademy.org/wp-content/uploads/2020/07/CES-Fall-2019.pdf; Melissa Stiksma, *Understanding the Campus Expression Climate: Fall 2020*, Heterodox Academy, 2021, https://content.heterodoxacademy.org/uploads/CES-Report-2020.pdf; and Steven Zhou, Melissa Stiksma, and Shelly C. Zhou, *Understanding the Campus Expression Climate: Fall 2021*, Heterodox Academy, March 2022, https://heterodoxnew.wpenginepowered.com/wp-content/uploads/2022/02/CES-

162 THE FREE INQUIRY PAPERS

Report-2022-FINAL.pdf. See also Amy J. Binder and Kate Wood, *Becoming Right: How Campuses Shape Young Conservatives* (Princeton, NJ: Princeton University Press, 2013).

31. Kaufmann, *Academic Freedom in Crisis*.

32. Honeycutt, "Manifestations of Political Bias"; and Nathan Honeycutt and Lee Jussim, "A Model of Political Bias in Social Science Research," *Psychological Inquiry* 31, no. 1 (2020): 73–85, https://www.tandfonline.com/doi/full/10.1080/1047840X.2020.1722600.

33. Self-censorship was defined as refraining from sharing certain views because you fear social (e.g., exclusion from social events), professional (e.g., losing a job or promotion), legal (e.g., prosecution or fine), or violent (e.g., assault) consequences, whether in person or remotely (e.g., by phone or online) and whether the consequences come from state or non-state sources.

34. Honeycutt, Stevens, and Kaufmann, *The Academic Mind in 2022*.

35. Honeycutt, Stevens, and Freberg, *Faculty Experiences and Perspectives on Free Speech*.

36. Sean T. Stevens et al., "Political Exclusion and Discrimination in Social Psychology: Lived Experiences and Solutions," in *The Politics of Social Psychology*, ed. Jarret T. Crawford and Lee Jussim (New York: Routledge, 2018).

37. Marshall School Faculty Council, "Marshall School Report," 2020, https://s3.documentcloud.org/documents/7214117/Marshall-School-Report.pdf.

38. Stevens et al., "Political Exclusion and Discrimination in Social Psychology."

39. German and Stevens, *Scholars Under Fire: The Targeting of Scholars for Ideological Reasons from 2015 to Present*; German and Stevens, *Scholars Under Fire: 2021 Year in Review*; and Stevens et al., "Political Exclusion and Discrimination in Social Psychology."

40. Neil Gross, *Why Are Professors Liberal and Why Do Conservatives Care?* (Cambridge, MA: Harvard University Press, 2013); Kaufmann, *Academic Freedom in Crisis*; Stuart Rothman and S. Robert Lichter, "The Vanishing Conservative—Is There a Glass Ceiling?," in *The Politically Correct University: Problems, Scope, and Reforms*, ed. Robert Maranto, Richard E. Redding, and Frederick M. Hess (Washington, DC: AEI Press, 2009); and George Yancey, *Compromising Scholarship: Religious and Political Bias in American Higher Education* (Waco, TX: Baylor University Press, 2011).

41. These databases are available online. See Foundation for Individual Rights and Expression, Campus Deplatforming Database, https://www.thefire.org/research-learn/campus-deplatforming-database; and Foundation for Individual Rights and Expression, Scholars Under Fire Database, https://www.thefire.org/research/scholars-under-fire-database. All data presented from these databases were current as of June 14, 2024. In the Scholars Under Fire Database, a scholar is defined as anyone who possesses an academic affiliation with a college or university who is primarily involved in teaching or research (e.g., conducting and submitting findings to the peer-review process) and includes professors, lecturers, postdoctoral researchers, and graduate students.

42. The Foundation for Individual Rights and Expression updates the Campus Deplatforming Database regularly. All data reported in this chapter reflect the Campus Deplatforming Database as of June 30, 2024.

43. Kaufmann, *Academic Freedom in Crisis*.

44. See, for example, Buckley, *God and Man at Yale*; and Wilson, *The Myth of Political Correctness*.

45. See Buckley, *God and Man at Yale*; David Horowitz, *Indoctrination U: The Left's War Against Academic Freedom* (New York: Encounter Books, 2007); and Ben Shapiro, *Brainwashed: How Universities Indoctrinate America's Youth* (Nashville, TN: Thomas Nelson, 2010).

46. Edward Burmila, "Liberal Bias in the College Classroom: A Review of the Evidence (or Lack Thereof)," *PS: Political Science & Politics* 54, no. 3 (July 2021): 598–602, https://www.cambridge.org/core/journals/ps-political-science-and-politics/article/abs/liberal-bias-in-the-college-classroom-a-review-of-the-evidence-or-lack-thereof/4015A571030269CF4D8F4031CE697CE3; and Robert Maranto and Matthew Woessner, "Do Gradebooks Lean Left? Relationships Between Grades and Ideology in American Higher Education," *Journal of Open Inquiry in the Behavioral Sciences* (forthcoming).

47. April Kelly-Woessner and Matthew C. Woessner, "My Professor Is a Partisan Hack: How Perceptions of a Professor's Political Views Affect Student Course Evaluations," *PS: Political Science & Politics* 39, no. 3 (July 2006): 495–501, https://www.jstor.org/stable/20451790; Matthew Woessner and April Kelly-Woessner, "I Think My Professor Is a Democrat: Considering Whether Students Recognize and React to Faculty Politics," *PS: Political Science and Politics* 42, no. 2 (April 2009): 343–52, https://www.jstor.org/stable/40647538; and Logan Strother et al., "College Roommates Have a Modest but Significant Influence on Each Other's Political Ideology," *Proceedings of the National Academy of Sciences* 118, no. 2 (2021): e202015514, https://pubmed.ncbi.nlm.nih.gov/33419923. For opposing findings, see Emily Hunt and Phil Davignon, "The Invisible Thread: The Influence of Liberal Faculty on Student Political Views at Evangelical Colleges," *Journal of College and Character* 17, no. 3 (2016): 175–89, https://www.tandfonline.com/doi/abs/10.1080/2194587X.2016.1195750; Ilsa L. Lottes and Peter J. Kuriloff, "The Impact of College Experience on Political and Social Attitudes," *Sex Roles* 31, nos. 1–2 (July 1994): 31–54, https://link.springer.com/article/10.1007/BF01560276; Tali Mendelberg, Katherine T. McCabe, and Adam Thal, "College Socialization and the Economic Views of Affluent Americans," *American Journal of Political Science* 61, no. 3 (July 2017): 606–23, https://onlinelibrary.wiley.com/doi/abs/10.1111/ajps.12265; and Theodore M. Newcomb et al., *Persistence and Change: Bennington College and Its Students After 25 Years* (New York: John Wiley and Sons, 1967).

48. Binder and Wood, *Becoming Right*; Stiksma, *Understanding the Campus Expression Climate: Fall 2019*; Stiksma, *Understanding the Campus Expression Climate: Fall 2020*; and Zhou, Stiksma, and Zhou, *Understanding the Campus Expression Climate: Fall 2021*.

49. See Kaufmann, *Academic Freedom in Crisis*.

50. Matthew Woessner and April Kelly-Woessner, "Why College Students Drift Left: The Stability of Political Identity and Relative Malleability of Issue Positions Among College Students," *PS: Political Science & Politics* 53, no. 4 (October 2020): 657–64, https://www.cambridge.org/core/journals/ps-political-science-and-politics/article/abs/why-college-students-drift-left-the-stability-of-political-identity-and-relative-malleability-of-issue-positions-among-college-students/9569B67D693BBE6A2CDC42292A3237B7.

164 THE FREE INQUIRY PAPERS

51. However, the students who enroll at liberal arts colleges also tend to enter college as more politically liberal. Jana M. Hanson et al., "Do Liberal Arts Colleges Make Students More Liberal? Some Initial Evidence," *Higher Education* 64, no. 3 (September 2021): 355–69, https://link.springer.com/article/10.1007/s10734-011-9498-8.

52. Colin Campbell and Jonathan Horowitz, "Does College Influence Sociopolitical Attitudes?," *Sociology of Education* 89, no. 1 (January 2016): 40–58, https://journals.sagepub.com/doi/10.1177/0038040715617224; Tamkinat Rauf, "How College Makes Liberals (or Conservatives)," *Socius* 7 (2021), https://journals.sagepub.com/doi/10.1177/2378023120982435; Bruce Sacerdote, "Peer Effects with Random Assignment: Results for Dartmouth Roommates," *Quarterly Journal of Economics* 116, no. 2 (May 2001): 681–704, https://www.jstor.org/stable/2696476; and Strother et al., "College Roommates Have a Modest but Significant Influence on Each Other's Political Ideology."

53. Nicholas Havey and Lucas Schalewski, "Political Development away from Home: Understanding How the First Year Influences College Students' Political Orientation Change," *Journal of the First-Year Experience & Students in Transition* 34, no. 1 (Spring 2022): 27–42, https://www.ingentaconnect.com/contentone/fyesit/fyesit/2022/00000034/00000001/art00002;jsessionid=3007lxt3cnl1r.x-ic-live-03; and Strother et al., "College Roommates Have a Modest but Significant Influence on Each Other's Political Ideology."

54. See, for example, Isaac Kamola, "Dear Administrators: To Protect Your Faculty from Right-Wing Attacks, Follow the Money," *Journal of Academic Freedom* 10 (2019): 1–24, https://www.aaup.org/sites/default/files/kamola.pdf; Samantha McCarthy and Isaac Kamola, "Sensationalized Surveillance: Campus Reform and the Targeted Harassment of Faculty," *New Political Science* 44, no. 2 (2022): 227–47, https://www.tandfonline.com/doi/full/10.1080/07393148.2021.1996837; Valerie Scatamburlo-D'Annibale, "The 'Culture Wars' Reloaded: Trump, Anti–Political Correctness and the Right's 'Free Speech' Hypocrisy," *Journal for Critical Education Policy Studies* 17, no. 1 (April 2019): 69–119, https://eric.ed.gov/?id=EJ1214685; and Wilson, *The Myth of Political Correctness.*

55. Hans-Joerg Tiede et al., "Data Snapshot: Whom Does Campus Reform Target and What Are the Effects? An Influential Conservative Website's Strategic Coverage and Its Impact," *Academe* 107, no. 2 (Spring 2021), https://www.aaup.org/article/data-snapshot-whom-does-campus-reform-target-and-what-are-effects.

56. Gallup and Knight Foundation, *Free Expression on Campus*; and Mary Anne Franks, "The Miseducation of Free Speech," *Virginia Law Review Online* 105 (December 2019): 218–42, https://virginialawreview.org/wp-content/uploads/2020/12/Franks_Book.pdf.

57. Gallup and Knight Foundation, *Free Expression on Campus.*

58. See, for example, Bobo and Licari, "Education and Political Tolerance"; and Campbell and Horowitz, "Does College Influence Sociopolitical Attitudes?"

59. Ray Franke et al., *Findings from the 2009 Administration of the College Senior Survey (CSS): National Aggregates,* University of California, Los Angeles, Higher Education Research Institute, Cooperative Institutional Research Program, February 2010, https://www.heri.ucla.edu/PDFs/pubs/Reports/2009_CSS_Report.pdf.

OSTRICH SYNDROME AND CAMPUS FREE EXPRESSION   165

60. Campbell and Horowitz, "Does College Influence Sociopolitical Attitudes?," 44.

61. Franke et al., *Findings from the 2009 Administration of the College Senior Survey* (*CSS*).

62. See, for example, Andrew Hartman, "People Always Think Students Are Hostile to Speech. They Never Really Are.," *Washington Post*, March 15, 2018, https://www.washingtonpost.com/outlook/people-always-think-students-are-hostile-to-speech-they-never-really-are/2018/03/15/cc53cc3a-286c-11e8-bc72-077aa4dab9ef_story.html; Jeffrey Adam Sachs, "The 'Campus Free Speech Crisis' Is a Myth. Here Are the Facts.," *Washington Post*, March 16, 2018, https://www.washingtonpost.com/news/monkey-cage/wp/2018/03/16/the-campus-free-speech-crisis-is-a-myth-here-are-the-facts; and Matthew Yglesias, "Everything We Think About the Political Correctness Debate Is Wrong," Vox, March 12, 2018, https://www.vox.com/policy-and-politics/2018/3/12/17100496/political-correctness-data.

63. See Gibson, "Enigmas of Intolerance"; Sullivan, Piereson, and Marcus, "An Alternative Conceptualization of Political Tolerance"; and Sullivan, Piereson, and Marcus, *Political Tolerance and American Democracy*.

64. Sean T. Stevens and Jonathan Haidt, "The Skeptics Are Wrong Part 1: Attitudes About Free Speech on Campus Are Changing," Heterodox Academy, March 4, 2018, https://heterodoxacademy.org/blog/skeptics-are-wrong-about-campus-speech.

65. See Lukianoff and Haidt, *The Coddling of the American Mind*.

66. P. J. Henry and Jaime L. Napier, "Education Is Related to Greater Ideological Prejudice," *Public Opinion Quarterly* 81, no. 4 (Winter 2017): 930–42, https://www.jstor.org/stable/26801763.

67. Boch, "Increasing American Political Tolerance," 1–12; Campbell and Johnson, "Trends in the Association Between a College Education and Political Tolerance"; and Chong and Levy, "Competing Norms of Free Expression and Political Tolerance."

68. See Kaufmann, *Academic Freedom in Crisis*.

69. See Komi Frey and Sean T. Stevens, "Addressing Criticisms of Scholars Under Fire," Foundation for Individual Rights and Expression, November 3, 2021, https://www.thefire.org/addressing-criticisms-of-scholars-under-fire.

70. Elizabeth Niehaus, "Self-Censorship or Just Being Nice: Understanding College Students' Decisions About Classroom Speech," University of California, National Center for Free Speech and Civic Engagement, https://freespeechcenter.universityofcalifornia.edu/fellows-20-21/niehaus-research; and John K. Wilson, "The Inevitable Problem of Self-Censorship," *Inside Higher Ed*, January 10, 2022, https://www.insidehighered.com/views/2022/01/11/student-self-censorship-fact-not-rampant-campuses-opinion.

71. This question—"Have you personally ever felt you could not express your opinion on a subject because of how students, a professor, or the administration would respond?"—had binary response options ("Yes" and "No") and was subsequently revised to measure frequency of self-censorship in 2021 and 2022 using a five-point scale. See Stevens, *2022–2023 College Free Speech Rankings*; and Stevens and Schwichtenberg, *2021 College Free Speech Rankings*.

72. Niehaus, "Self-Censorship or Just Being Nice."

166 THE FREE INQUIRY PAPERS

73. Paul P. Biemer, "Total Survey Error: Design, Implementation, and Evaluation," *Public Opinion Quarterly* 74, no. 5 (2010): 817–48, https://academic.oup.com/poq/article/74/5/817/1815551.

74. Wilson, "The Inevitable Problem of Self-Censorship."

75. Brock Bastian and Nick Haslam, "Excluded from Humanity: The Dehumanizing Effects of Social Ostracism," *Journal of Experimental Social Psychology* 46, no. 1 (January 2010): 107–13, https://www.sciencedirect.com/science/article/abs/pii/S002210310900208X; and Jean M. Twenge and Roy F. Baumeister, "Social Exclusion Increases Aggression and Self-Defeating Behavior While Reducing Intelligent Thought and Prosocial Behavior," in *The Social Psychology of Inclusion and Exclusion*, ed. Dominic Abrams, Michael A. Hogg, and José M. Marques (New York: Psychology Press, 2004).

76. Lee Jussim et al., "A Social Psychological Model of Scientific Practices: Explaining Research Practices and Outlining the Potential for Successful Reforms," *Psychologica Belgica* 59, no. 1 (2019): 353–72, https://pubmed.ncbi.nlm.nih.gov/31565236; and Sean T. Stevens, Lee Jussim, and Nathan Honeycutt, "Scholarship Suppression: Theoretical Perspectives and Emerging Trends," *Societies* 10, no. 4 (December 2020): 1–21, https://www.mdpi.com/2075-4698/10/4/82.

77. Roy F. Baumeister and Mark R. Leary, "The Need to Belong: Desire for Interpersonal Attachments as a Fundamental Human Motivation," *Psychological Bulletin* 117, no. 3 (1995): 497–529, https://psycnet.apa.org/record/1995-29052-001; and Jonathan Haidt, "The Emotional Dog and Its Rational Tail: A Social Intuitionist Approach to Moral Judgment," *Psychological Review* 108, no. 4 (October 2001): 814–34, https://psycnet.apa.org/record/2001-18918-008.

78. Jean M. Twenge et al., "Social Exclusion Decreases Prosocial Behavior," *Journal of Personality and Social Psychology* 92, no. 1 (January 2007): 56–66, https://pubmed.ncbi.nlm.nih.gov/17201542; and Kipling D. Williams and Steve A. Nida, "Ostracism and Social Exclusion: Implications for Separation, Social Isolation, and Loss," *Current Opinion in Psychology* 47 (October 2022): 101353, https://pubmed.ncbi.nlm.nih.gov/35662059.

79. Jörg Matthes, Johannes Knoll, and Christian von Sikorski, "The 'Spiral of Silence' Revisited: A Meta-Analysis on the Relationship Between Perceptions of Opinion Support and Political Opinion Expression," *Communication Research* 45, no. 1 (February 2018): 3–33, https://journals.sagepub.com/doi/abs/10.1177/0093650217745429?journalCode=crxa; and Noelle-Neumann, "The Spiral of Silence."

80. Duarte et al., "Political Diversity Will Improve Social Psychological Science"; Chris C. Martin, "How Ideology Has Hindered Sociological Insight," *American Sociologist* 47, no. 1 (March 2016): 115–30, https://www.jstor.org/stable/43956979; Noelle-Neumann, "The Spiral of Silence"; and Nicholas Quinn Rosenkranz, "Intellectual Diversity in the Legal Academy," *Harvard Journal of Law & Public Policy* 37 (2014): 137–43, https://scholarship.law.georgetown.edu/facpub/1328.

81. S. I. Abramowitz, B. Gomes, and C. V. Abramowitz, "Publish or Politic: Referee Bias in Manuscript Review," *Journal of Applied Social Psychology* 5, no. 3 (1975): 187–200, https://psycnet.apa.org/record/1976-22323-001; S. J. Ceci, D. Peters, and J. Plotkin, "Human Subjects Review, Personal Values, and the Regulation of Social Science Research," in *Methodological Issues and Strategies in Clinical Research*, ed.

Alan E. Kazdin (Washington, DC: American Psychological Association, 1992); Samir Haffar, Fateh Bazerbachi, and M. Hassan Murad, "Peer Review Bias: A Critical Review," *Mayo Clinic Proceedings* 94, no. 4 (April 2019): 670–76, https://www.mayoclinicproceedings.org/article/S0025-6196(18)30707-9/fulltext; and Douglas P. Peters and Stephen J. Ceci, "Peer-Review Practices of Psychological Journals: The Fate of Published Articles, Submitted Again," *Behavioral and Brain Sciences* 5, no. 2 (June 1982):187–255, https://www.cambridge.org/core/journals/behavioral-and-brain-sciences/article/abs/peerreview-practices-of-psychological-journals-the-fate-of-published-articles-submitted-again/AFE650EB49A6B17992493DE5E49E4431.

82. Stevens et al., "Political Exclusion and Discrimination in Social Psychology"; and Wilson, "A History of Academic Freedom in America."

11

Examining the Tensions Between Free Markets and Free Speech

Brian Knight

"Woke capitalism" is a high-profile and controversial topic that is creating, or at least accelerating, a growing fissure between political conservatives and corporations.[1] It is a flavor of politicized capitalism in which corporate power is used, sometimes coercively, to drive change in the broader society. Although progressive politicized capitalism appears to be ascendant, this does not have to be the case. Other political factions, including conservatives, may and arguably have[2] embraced economic power as a tool to win battles better left to civil exchange or the political process.[3] Regardless of who uses it, economic power, especially when applied coercively, risks further muddying the distinction between politics and the market, both directly and by inviting a legal or regulatory response.

What should the response, if any, be to the rise of politicized capitalism is a challenging question. Politicized capitalism is hard to define, but here is an attempt: when a corporation uses corporate power, resources, or prerogatives in an attempt to induce or compel change in the world in a tangible way that does not directly relate to the corporation's line of business and is not broadly regarded as desirable or at least uncontroversial.[4]

What is immediately apparent from that definition of politicized capitalism is that it is not one thing; it's many things. These distinctions matter for how we view a certain action and determine what, if any, response is appropriate. Getting this analysis right is of no small importance because the challenge politicized capitalism poses has potentially worrisome implications for personal freedom, the proper role of the state, and the functioning of the economy.

For example, one of the most recent high-profile examples of politicized capitalism is Disney's announcement that it would work to oppose laws similar to recently passed Florida legislation limiting how some topics are

TENSIONS BETWEEN FREE MARKETS AND FREE SPEECH   169

discussed in schools.[5] In response, Republican Gov. Ron DeSantis moved to strip Disney of its special tax district in Florida.[6] The governor's action has led to significant disagreement—even among those who profess to be pro-liberty and pro-market—about whether such an act is appropriate.[7]

This chapter illustrates just a few of the diverse issues politicized capitalism poses. Its goal is not to provide a complete definition for the phenomenon or propose appropriate governmental responses, if any exist. Rather, it is to present some plausible scenarios, looking at employment, interactions with (and possible evasions of) controversial laws, and questions around the separation of ownership and control. The goal is to get the reader to think about the different ways such corporate actions might be viewed, their potential effects, whether there is or should be any sort of legally cognizable harm that results, and what, if anything, could or should be done to address that harm.

Politicization and Employment

Politicized corporate action is the most controversial when it comes to the intersection of politics and employment. The phenomenon of someone being "canceled" for having a "bad" political view on social media is well-known. Some evidence shows that significant portions of the American public support the idea that one's political donations could serve as legitimate grounds for being fired, and many Americans worry their political views will harm their employment.[8] Conversely, many firms might suffer legitimate harm by continuing to employ people who express beliefs found objectionable by colleagues and customers, who both appear to increasingly demand that firms align with their values.[9]

What should we make of this issue? Are we sure it is only one issue? Or is it many? To illustrate this point, let me offer a hypothetical. Imagine it is June, Pride Month, in a crowded mall in an affluent suburb. Many of the storefronts are festooned with rainbow patterns and images of LGBTQ+ models. One of those stores, called "Hot Buttons," is a clothing retailer focused on the 15- to 35-year-old demographic. It employs a sales clerk named Jane, who holds conservative religious beliefs. In which of the following cases, if any, should it be acceptable for her employer to fire her?

1. Jane refuses to help find clothes for a customer who identifies as a certain gender, because Jane believes that gender does not match with their birth sex. Jane is fired for refusing to follow the store policy of not discriminating against customers based on gender identity.

2. Jane refuses to wear a "Love Is Love" badge as part of her uniform when Hot Buttons management orders her to because her religious convictions conflict with its implications. She is otherwise happy to fulfill any role and serve any customer to the best of her ability. She is fired because the store owner considers her position bigoted.

3. Same as the second scenario, except Hot Buttons' owner is indifferent to the underlying substantive issue; instead, the owner fires Jane for insubordination because she refuses to wear her uniform in support of an advertising campaign to align the store with a cause popular with its clientele.

4. Same as the second scenario, but Jane's coworkers refuse to work with her, and the owner fires Jane because the owner believes Jane can no longer be effective in her job.

5. Jane wears the "Love Is Love" badge and ably serves all customers but attends a school board meeting on her own time and argues, passionately but respectfully, that student-athletes should only be allowed to compete with others of the same birth sex. The store owner reads news coverage of the meeting, deems Jane's views to be bigoted, and fires her.

6. Same as Scenario 5, except a customer recognizes Jane at the school board meeting and posts her speech on social media, vowing to boycott the store unless Jane is fired. The video goes viral, and the store owner, correctly believing that Jane is now a liability for the store, fires her to placate customers.

7. Same as Scenario 6, but the customer explicitly states that part of their motivation is to intimidate others who share Jane's viewpoint to suppress that speech.

TENSIONS BETWEEN FREE MARKETS AND FREE SPEECH 171

8. Same as Scenario 7, but this time it is the Hot Buttons owner whose explicit goal is chilling similar speech.

These hypotheticals show just a fraction of the complexity surrounding politicized capitalism. All these scenarios involve employment decisions, some relating to Jane's job performance and others to her outside activities. Some touch on Jane's ability to speak freely and not be compelled to speak (by wearing a button), whereas others are far more mundane. In some cases, the store owner is motivated by their own beliefs; in others, the owner seeks to accommodate customers or other employees for purely business reasons. In some cases, the motivation to fire Jane appears to be a desire not to associate with her, while in still others, it is to affect the broader political debate.

And this is just the tip of the iceberg. What if, instead of being motivated by religious beliefs, Jane is motivated by atheistic natural philosophy? What if, instead of a school board meeting, Jane is overheard while eating in a restaurant? What if, instead of speaking respectfully at the school board meeting, Jane is hostile or even derogatory? What if, instead of firing anyone, the owner of a private firm announces they will use firm funds to support or oppose candidates or legislation? What if, instead of an owner, a manager of a public firm decides to fire Jane or spend firm resources? What if, instead of firing an employee, the firm refuses to do business with someone? What if, instead of a clothing store, it is a bank, airline, hospital, or some other essential industry? What if the company receives subsidies from taxpayers? What if the employer treats employees differently for similar conduct based on what side of an issue they were on? What if the motives are mixed or unclear?

Perhaps none of these questions matter and the answer is the same in every case. But reasonable arguments can be made that how we should feel about what happened—and the appropriate legal or regulatory response, if any—will vary based on the facts, circumstances, and competing values at play. To the extent that some government intervention is justified, what those interventions should look like depends on what transpired and who was affected. Is there a harm that should be legally cognizable, and if so, what should redress be?

172   THE FREE INQUIRY PAPERS

For example, is there or should there be a cognizable harm to Jane in the first scenario wherein Jane refuses to help a customer who appears transgender—or is Jane just refusing to do her job of fetching clothes for customers to try on? Is wearing a badge part of her job, as in the second, third, and fourth scenarios, even if it contains a political and ethical statement she disagrees with and is not otherwise essential to her ability to perform her duties? Should it matter whether the company is using the statement as a marketing strategy or whether it reflects the moral views it wants its employees to embrace? Has Jane been harmed in some way, or is this just part of what she signed up for? What if, instead of "Love Is Love," the badge says "Jesus Is Lord" or "Make America Great Again" or "There Is No God"? Should coworkers or customers have an effective veto over whom they work with for normative or culture-fit reasons, or should the logic of antidiscrimination law apply so that coworker and employee preferences against a protected class or characteristic are generally not a valid reason for termination?

Even if you believe that employers should have broad authority to dictate workplace conduct, what about scenarios 5–8? Should employers be able to fire employees for expressing political opinions outside the workplace, including while petitioning government assemblies? Should it matter whether the firm's decision is purely economic? Should it matter whether the intent, by whoever is pushing the issue, is to suppress political speech in pursuit of a political outcome?

To be sure, tensions between economic power and political participation, including speech, are not new. As the legal scholar Eugene Volokh explains, economic coercion targeting votes was prohibited by some states as early as 1839, and several states have laws protecting employees' right to speak to various degrees.[10] These laws are grounded in the need to protect the integrity of both our elections and our broader political process. Volokh also notes, however, that such laws infringe on freedom of association (the idea that the ability to choose whom one enters into relationships with is an important part of individual liberty, albeit not without limitation) and the firm's desire to please customers. So how should we balance these concerns, and should phenomena like social media and increasing polarization influence our calculus?

TENSIONS BETWEEN FREE MARKETS AND FREE SPEECH   173

Interacting with (or Evading) State Laws Through Fringe Benefits

Another area where corporations have chosen or been forced to play a role in a contentious political debate is that of abortion access.[11] One issue that may not seem controversial at first, but that may well become a powder keg, arises when corporations in states where abortion is restricted cover the costs of employees who have to leave the state to obtain an abortion. Depending on one's view, a corporation paying for an employee to leave the state to obtain an abortion is either simply providing a fringe benefit or aiding and abetting the evasion of a law that protects a fetus from being killed.

To illustrate some of the questions that corporations might face, let us return to the mall. Hot Buttons, a national chain, has announced it will cover the cost of both the abortion procedure and travel to a facility where the procedure can legally be done, including out-of-state travel. Barb, a Hot Buttons employee, wishes to have an abortion but is not legally able to under the laws of the state she lives in and where the store is located. Let us assume this process is purely elective without any complicating factors. Imagine the following scenarios.

1. Barb notifies Hot Buttons HR that she would like to avail herself of the abortion coverage benefit. She books plane tickets and schedules an appointment with an out-of-state clinic. When she returns, she submits her receipts and is reimbursed by Hot Buttons.

2. Hot Buttons gives every employee an account to use to travel for any legal medical procedure, without the need to get the travel approved or submit a bill for reimbursement. Barb uses this to book her tickets.

3. Barb takes paid medical leave and travels out of state at her own expense. She then obtains the procedure, and when she returns, she submits the bill for reimbursement for the procedure only, which she receives.

4. Same as the third scenario, but she takes unpaid rather than paid medical leave.

174 THE FREE INQUIRY PAPERS

5. Barb takes paid vacation time to go out of state for a vacation without the intent to have an abortion. While on vacation, Barb decides to have an abortion. When she returns, she submits a bill for reimbursement for the procedure only.

In these examples, is Hot Buttons engaging in corporate political activism? Is it interfering with the democratic process? Or is it simply providing fringe benefits, including health care, to employees? The answer would seem to hinge on what the company and the voters think of abortion.

Many employers are framing their decision to pay for out-of-state abortions as consistent with their policies covering travel for certain medical procedures. From this perspective, providing travel benefits is not particularly political, especially if it provides those benefits for other procedures (as JPMorgan does for organ transplants, for example).[12] In this case, the company can argue that it is not trying to influence or frustrate the democratic process or state laws. Rather, it is allowing employees to get covered care, where such care is legally available.

However, the analogy to other medical procedures is not perfect. Whereas an employee may need to travel out of state for an organ transplant because that is where the organ or the transplant specialist is located, there are not any state prohibitions on this procedure. Conversely, an abortion is unavailable presumably because the state where the employee lives has prohibited her from accessing the procedure. In addition, whereas an employee seeking an organ transplant involves only one party traveling across state lines, an employee traveling to obtain an abortion will presumably be viewed by the employee's home state as involving two parties—the employee and the fetus, the latter of whom the state may view as an independent being vested with rights.[13]

And therein lies the rub: Although a company might view abortion as one medical procedure among many, the laws that prohibit abortion presumably view it as the killing of an entity whom the state has a legitimate interest to protect. An employer may view paying for an employee in Oklahoma to fly to California for an abortion to be on par with sending someone to Cedars-Sinai Medical Center for specialist cancer treatment, but the state and its voters might view it as aiding and abetting something akin to kidnapping, which they believe the state has a legitimate and compelling interest in preventing.

A state's jurisdiction is generally limited to conduct occurring within its borders. As such, it would likely be hard for a state to penalize the firm for paying for an abortion that occurred out of state. However, states that restrict abortions will likely seek to prohibit and penalize those leaving the state and those who assist someone in doing so.

Indeed, whether states can prohibit or penalize someone leaving the state to obtain an abortion will likely be one of the next points of conflict between abortion proponents and opponents. Justice Brett Kavanaugh, in his concurrent opinion in *Dobbs v. Jackson Women's Health Organization*, argues that states could not prohibit someone from leaving the state for an abortion because there is a constitutional right to interstate travel.[14] But this conclusion is not clear, a concern Justices Stephen Breyer, Sonia Sotomayor, and Elena Kagan raised in their dissent.[15] Although there is a general right to interstate travel, there are exceptions in cases in which a crime is being committed involving another person, such as kidnapping.

If states can argue that they can legitimately prohibit someone from leaving the state to obtain an abortion—and that is admittedly a big if—firms providing travel support may risk significant legal exposure. In fact, based on the recent legislative trend to target abortion providers rather than women who have abortions,[16] it is not unreasonable to expect that these states would focus on and seek to harshly penalize those who facilitate the travel—especially if the facilitator is a corporation, which is less likely to be a sympathetic defendant.

If a state could prohibit or penalize leaving the state for an abortion, in which of the earlier scenarios could Hot Buttons face possible liability? Is paying for a procedure that is legal in some states but not others, and travel to those states, sufficient? Should it matter whether the firm specifically covers travel for abortion versus generally covering medical travel costs? What about paid medical leave? Would reimbursing an employee for an abortion after that employee returns home to the restrictive state be enough to give the state jurisdiction?

Whether states can penalize leaving the state for an abortion will likely have to be resolved through either federal legislation or another

Supreme Court case, though even this initial resolution may not prove durable, just as *Roe v. Wade* did not settle the abortion controversy. But in the meantime, it could become one of the most controversial questions surrounding corporate actions that are seen as supporting or facilitating abortion.

Ownership and Control in a Politicized Market

The discussion so far has implicitly treated the company ownership and its managers as one and the same. However, this is frequently not the case. In many companies, the owners authorize others to manage the company for them. The most salient example would be a public company in which potentially millions of investors share ownership of a company that is run by an executive team overseen by a board of directors. Although a firm's leadership is supposed to manage the firm for the shareholders' benefit, there is frequently tension between managers and owners as to what the firm should do. The law generally provides managers with broad protections, provided they can show they were motivated by what they believed was in the shareholders' best interests.

What if Hot Buttons is a publicly traded firm? Then, instead of the owner deciding to fire Jane or pay for an employee's abortion, a manager with a fiduciary duty to shareholders would be making that decision. Should that change the calculus?

What about in cases in which the largest shareholders are not individuals but rather asset managers, like BlackRock and Vanguard, or public pension funds, like the California Public Employees' Retirement System, which invest money provided by individuals but technically own and vote the shares themselves? These large institutional investors have become increasingly important as their share of the equity market has increased significantly over time. They have also become more vocal in their demands that corporations act in ways that further certain policy goals, such as controversial environmental or social policies. Although such moves are often framed as being in the firm's best long-term interest, such claims are often disputed.

What, If Anything, Should Be Done?

Having discussed some examples of what politicized capitalism *might* be, the next question is: "So what?" I do not ask that question flippantly, but rather to highlight that "someone is doing something I dislike" is not, or at least should not be, enough to invoke state power. Rather, there needs to be an actual harm—of the type that the state has a legitimate interest in addressing and legitimate powers to use—before state power can be justified. Even then, involving the state may not be a good idea, because the cure may be worse than the disease.

All that notwithstanding, just because a bar is high does not mean it cannot be cleared. If politicized corporate acts cause concrete harms; threaten to undercut the rights of citizens and the processes, such as peaceful civic engagement or the legitimate application of law, on which the legitimacy of our society rests; or reflect a misuse of property in violation of an agreement or duty, having the government step in to address the problem may be not only justified but also necessary.

In the earlier examples, who is being harmed by the corporation's actions? Arguments can be made that Jane is being harmed by being either forced to speak or penalized for speaking, especially in cases in which she is engaging in the democratic political process on which the legitimacy of our governmental system relies.[17] Arguments can be made that the fetus is being harmed by being removed, without consent, from a state where it was protected. Arguments can be made that the voters of the state where Hot Buttons operates are being harmed by having the democratic process subverted by Hot Buttons contributing to the chilling of speech, using corporate funds to influence elections or elected officials, or aiding in the evasion of state laws. And arguments can be made that the people who provide the money, and bear the economic risk, to buy Hot Buttons stock are being harmed if a manager makes choices that use corporate resources to further his or her political preferences.

Can arguments be made against all these propositions? *Absolutely.* My point in listing them is not to endorse or oppose them, but merely to identify possible arguments that there are legitimate victims of corporate actions in the hypotheticals discussed. But if, for the sake of argument, we take some or all of these propositions as true, what then? Are these the

178 THE FREE INQUIRY PAPERS

types of issues that the state has a legitimate interest in intervening in, and if so, what should it do?

This is an incredibly important question. If the government response is unduly muted, important rights that should be protected by government could remain under threat. Conversely, an excessive or poorly designed response will risk not only harm to employers' legitimate rights but also broader damage to the market system and rule of law.

For example, in the case of Jane losing her job, the response could be something like "make the firm rehire Jane or pay her damages and prohibit similar actions in the future." This would likely be the most targeted solution, but governments often have other options that may have a broader effect. Should the state simply try to redress an individual wrong, or should it try to discourage future behavior via punitive measures? Should it reconsider other benefits provided to the firm, such as a special tax district? Should the state only do so if the firm's behavior is inconsistent with the purpose for which the benefit was granted, or is the punitive effect justification enough?

On the question of abortion, if a state can prohibit someone from leaving the state to obtain an abortion, what, if any, action should the state take against corporations facilitating such trips for their employees? Would a corporation be considered a coconspirator? An accomplice before the fact? Is resorting to criminal law an appropriate response?

What should the state's response be in cases in which the shareholder is the victim of politicized corporate activity? It has long been assumed that dissident shareholders can use the "tools of corporate democracy" to protect themselves from having to fund political speech they disagree with.[18] At worst, such shareholders were presumed to be able to sell their shares if they wished and thereby cease funding the company.[19] As such, although the state may have a legitimate interest in protecting shareholders generally, restricting corporate speech at least was not sufficiently justified to overcome the high hurdle the First Amendment imposed.[20]

Does that logic still hold in a world where the largest investors are giant asset managers who actually own and have voting shares paid for by underlying investors? In the modern world, the average person probably cannot vote all the shares they have paid for, let alone control who gets on a corporate board. They may not even be able to sell their shares if they are invested in an index fund that must cover the entire index. And if their shares are part of retirement or pension funds, they may not be able to exit without significant burden and tax implications. Are traditional tools of corporate democracy still viable in these instances?

Given the increasing distance between individuals who put their money at risk by investing in a company and those who control the company on a day-to-day basis, it is worth asking whether current assumptions about corporate law still hold. For example, are the tools of "corporate democracy" sufficient to allow investors to rein in wayward managers who use corporate resources to further their own political or social preferences at the expense of shareholder value? Of course, a more challenging wrinkle still would be the case in which politicization is in fact good business, but shareholders do not want their property used for that purpose. This question ties into the emerging debate around "stakeholder capitalism" that will likely feature prominently in corporate law discussions for years to come.

Conclusion

Using commerce to try to influence others' behavior, including coercively, is not new. As Volokh noted, laws seeking to prevent employers from using their position of power to prevent employees from voting freely have existed in this country since its early history.[21] In *The Constitution of Liberty*, Friedrich Hayek acknowledged that private commercial relationships could be used to coerce. However, he also noted that a free market could provide a strong defense so long as there were many possible people to deal with and that government intervention to prevent commercial coercion would likely be more coercive than the problem it sought to prevent. Of course, Hayek also assumed that most people in a market would only care about their own ends when doing business. He acknowledged, "We should be very dependent on the beliefs of our fellows if they were prepared to sell their products to us only when they approved of our ends and not for their own advantage."[22]

One wonders what Hayek would make of modern politicized commerce, in which care for another's ends is often front and center. And yet Hayek's concern about the cure being worse than the disease is by no means obsolete. Real and meaningful questions are raised when corporations act to change the world, *especially* if that conduct can be viewed as coercive or a misuse of power or property granted to the corporation for a specific purpose. However, efforts to restrict corporate activity can also implicate important rights such as freedom of speech and freedom of association. These and a host of other prudential concerns recommend caution, though not necessarily acquiescence, in determining how to respond.

This chapter was not meant to propose solutions to these questions but to merely highlight, with a limited number of examples, just how complex and fraught these questions can be. Defenders of liberty will be faced with hard choices going forward about how to react to efforts to use corporate power as a tool of coercion. Unless corporate politicization recedes significantly on its own, we face risks from both politicized commerce and the political response. Assessing how to respond in a principled way that protects core American values and systems is a challenge we as citizens may face. Let us hope we are up to it.

Notes

1. This chapter is a modified and expanded composite of two articles I wrote that ran in *Discourse*. See Brian Knight, "Woke Capitalism Isn't a Thing—It's Many Things," *Discourse*, June 13, 2022, https://www.discoursemagazine.com/p/woke-capitalism-isnt-a-thing-its-many-things; and Brian Knight, "Corporations and Abortion: A Perfect Storm of Controversy," *Discourse*, June 29, 2022, https://www.discoursemagazine.com/p/corporations-and-abortion-a-perfect-storm-of-controversy. It also includes material from a previous blog post of mine. See Brian Knight, "'Corporate Democracy' and Political Activism: Do Previous Assumptions Still Hold?," FinRegRag, April 22, 2021, https://medium.com/finregrag/corporate-democracy-and-political-activism-do-previous-assumptions-still-hold-461b30e7453f.

2. For example, the infamous Hollywood blacklist is arguably an example of economic actors with conservative sympathies using economic power to silence politically unpopular views.

3. Good and bad causes have used economic power as a tool. The question of whether any given cause is virtuous or correct is beyond the scope of this chapter.

4. See Brian Knight and Trace Mitchell, "Private Policies and Public Power: When Banks Act as Regulators Within a Regime of Privilege," *New York University Journal of*

Law and Liberty 13, no. 1 (October 2019): 66–149, https://papers.ssrn.com/sol3/papers. cfm?abstract_id=3466854 (discussing banks seeking to act as de facto regulators by limiting access to services as a tool to force change on politically controversial topics, as opposed to for traditional reasons). See also Saura Masconale and Simone M. Sepe, "Citizen Corp.—Corporate Activism and Democracy," *Washington University Law Review* 100, no. 2 (October 2022): 257–325, https://wustllawreview.org/2022/12/18/ citizen-corp-corporate-activism-and-democracy (discussing the rise of divisive corporate activism where a corporation pursues "divisive moral goods" that are not generally recognized as desirable).

5. Walt Disney Company (@WaltDisneyCo), "Today, our CEO Bob Chapek sent an important message to Disney employees about our support for the LGBTQ+ community: https://bit.ly/3pX8dbd," X, March 11, 2022, 3:16 p.m., https://twitter.com/ WaltDisneyCo/status/1502377943267381249.

6. Arian Campo-Flores and Robbie Whelan, "Florida Gov. DeSantis Seeks to End Walt Disney World's Special Tax District," *Wall Street Journal*, April 19, 2022, https:// www.wsj.com/articles/florida-gov-desantis-seeks-to-end-walt-disney-worlds-special-tax-district-11650381041.

7. Rich Lowry (@RichLowry) "Corporate executives who have bent to woke mobs out of fear should be grateful to Ron DeSantis et al," X, April 23, 2022, 11:38 p.m., https:// twitter.com/RichLowry/status/1518071980364341248; and Robert Tracinski, "This Is How We Get Oligarchs," *Discourse*, May 10, 2022, https://www.discoursemagazine.com/ politics/2022/05/10/this-is-how-we-get-oligarchs.

8. Emily Ekins, "Poll: 62% of Americans Say They Have Political Views They're Afraid to Share," Cato Institute, July 22, 2020, https://www.cato.org/survey-reports/ poll-62-americans-say-they-have-political-views-theyre-afraid-share.

9. See, for example, Victoria Sakal, "Great Expectations: The Evolving Role of Companies in a Post-Election World," Morning Consult, October 2020, https://web. archive.org/web/20230315090633/https://go.morningconsult.com/rs/850-TAA-511/ images/201019_MC_Brands-and-Politics_Report-FINAL.pdf; and Richard Edelman, "The Belief-Driven Employee," Edelman, August 31, 2021, https://www.edelman. com/trust/2021-trust-barometer/belief-driven-employee/new-employee-employer-compact.

10. Eugene Volokh, "Private Employees' Speech and Political Activity: Statutory Protections Against Employer Retaliation," *Texas Review of Law & Politics* 16, no. 2 (Spring 2012): 295–336, https://www2.law.ucla.edu/volokh/empspeech.pdf.

11. The constitutional, legal, and moral status of abortion is obviously highly contested. It is not my intent to take a position on any of those questions. Out of necessity, I am using terminology that is likely not universally accepted, and no endorsement of any position is intended or implied.

12. Allissa Kline, "JPMorgan to Reimburse Employees' Travel Costs for Out-of-State Abortions," *American Banker*, June 24, 2022, https://www.americanbanker.com/ news/jpmorgan-to-reimburse-employees-travel-costs-for-out-of-state-abortions.

13. Multiple states have laws prohibiting causing the death of a fetus or defining "person" for criminal homicide purposes to include fetuses, sometimes from the moment of conception. See National Conference of State Legislatures, "State Laws

on Fetal Homicide and Penalty-Enhancement for Crimes Against Pregnant Women," May 1, 2018, https://web.archive.org/web/20200308213750/https://www.ncsl.org/research/health/fetal-homicide-state-laws.aspx. It remains to be seen how these laws will change post–*Dobbs v. Jackson Women's Health Organization* and whether states will expand criminal laws to encompass other conduct, such as removing a fetus from a state where abortion is restricted or prohibited to obtain an abortion.

14. *Dobbs v. Jackson Women's Health Organization*, 597 US ___, 11 (2022) (Kavanaugh, J., concurring).

15. *Dobbs*, 597 US at 3 (Breyer, Sotomayor, and Kagan, JJ., dissenting).

16. See, for example, Texas Heartbeat Act, S.B. 8, 87th Leg., Reg. Sess. (Tex. 2021) codified at *Texas Health & Safety Code Annual*, §§ 171.201–171.212.

17. See, for example, Masconale and Sepe, "Citizen Corp" (arguing that divisive political activism threatens the political equality of dissenting employees).

18. *First National Bank of Boston v. Bellotti*, 435 US 765, 794–95, 794–95n34 (1978).

19. *Bellotti* at 794–95n34.

20. *Bellotti* at 792–95.

21. Volokh, "Private Employees' Speech and Political Activity," 299n13.

22. Friedrich Hayek, *The Constitution of Liberty* (Chicago: University of Chicago Press, 1960).

PART III.
Keeping Free Inquiry Alive

12

Mobilization for Academic Free Speech: The Wisconsin Model

Donald Alexander Downs

Rivers of ink have been spilled over the seemingly unending crisis of free speech and academic freedom in higher education. Rather than honoring the university's moral charter by fostering the honest and rigorous pursuit of truth through free and open inquiry and the attendant clash of ideas, too many universities have succumbed to ideological echo chambers and repression of speech deemed incongruent with regnant campus beliefs. Many institutions' responses to the war among Israel, Iran, and the Iranian terrorist proxy Hamas that erupted on October 7, 2023, have intensified public scrutiny of the fate of intellectual freedom in academe. It has been a long wait, but after percolating for many years, a reckoning for higher education could be at hand if constructive action is taken.

This chapter discusses my experiences defending free inquiry at the University of Wisconsin–Madison (UW-Madison). I describe a course I taught for years that focused on free speech, Political Science 470. I also focus on the Committee for Academic Freedom and Rights (CAFAR), a movement I was involved with from 1996 to 2016. CAFAR offers a potentially useful model of how to affect internal campus culture through political and intellectual engagement, including interaction with outside sources, and in telling the story of CAFAR, I lay out 10 key strategic points on promoting free inquiry.

How We Got Here in a Nutshell

The speech codes that descended on higher education in the 1980s and 1990s were harbingers of things to come. The codes broadly punished speech, including abstract ideas that "demeaned" or offended individuals and groups based on their racial, gender, ethnic, sexual, and other ascriptive identities. Though many codes were defeated in the courts of law and public opinion, their logic ineluctably metastasized into a broad array of bureaucratic policies and actions that have wounded free inquiry. A short list includes the burgeoning campus bureaucracies that cultivate anti-intellectual sensitivity agendas, students "canceling" and shouting down legitimate and worthy speakers, improper investigations of individuals, the proliferation of "trigger warnings," anonymous complaint systems for reporting any idea a person subjectively considers biased, and official lists of words considered "microaggressions," including even such time-tested and mainstream words or phrases as "America," "merit," "the individual," "illegal immigration," and "anyone can succeed with hard work."[1]

However well motivated, the measures have often led to improper censorship and a chilling effect on honest discourse. Whereas previous historical bouts of improper censorship ended after several years (e.g., the McCarthy era of the 1950s), the new wave of "progressive censorship"— censorship in the name of progressive and "social justice" causes—has now entered its fourth decade. This experience teaches us a classic lesson: Moral ends betray themselves when pursued by unconstitutional, illiberal means that disregard dissenting views and the intellectual differences that naturally characterize human beings as moral and intellectual agents.[2]

The Practical Question Posed. "How did you guys allow this situation to happen?" a friend from outside the university once asked me in genuine bewilderment. How we got here is a complex question, with multiple intellectual, cultural, political, psychological, and historical causes at play, too numerous to discuss in the space allotted to this chapter. They include emergent claims of victimhood and the therapeutic capture of civil rights movements; post-liberal theories of harm, discourse, and the power of language; the emergence of hyper-identity politics and one-sided "social justice" movements that replace the idea of a universality of rights and dignity; egalitarianism's disconnection from liberty and constitutional constraints; growing political homogeneity in faculty; and a decline in the willingness to defend traditional liberal principles of law and rights.[3] These forces have put significant pressure on what the Supreme Court has called our nation's "profound national commitment to the principle that debate on public issues should be uninhibited, robust, and wide-open."[4]

One practical cause stands out: Not nearly enough faculty members and leaders who believe that academic freedom and the pursuit of truth are the first principles of higher education have spoken up and undertaken what is needed to restore these principles to their proper place at the top of the modern university's hierarchy of missions. This shirking of duty is especially disconcerting because some survey research has suggested that a majority of faculty and students actually supported vigorous free speech and inquiry on campus as of 2019, at least in the abstract.[5]

The Wisconsin Free Speech and Academic Freedom Movement. I moved to UW-Madison in 1985 because of Wisconsin's reputation for being intellectually alive. This climate began to change in the late 1980s when, under the chancellorship of Donna Shalala (1988–93), UW-Madison became a national leader in the speech code and censorship movement that was beginning to sweep the nation.[6]

In 1988, the UW System schools' faculty senates, the state legislature, and the Board of Regents approved two codes that limited speech: a student code that applied to all schools in the system and a faculty code that limited speech in the classroom and applied only to the Madison campus. Like many codes, the faculty code punished in-class speech that "demeaned" students based on race, gender, sexual orientation, or the like. The standard for what constituted "demeaning" was subjective, based on how members of the group reacted, however unreasonably. The codes wrought a chilling effect on honest discourse across the campus.

The student code was declared unconstitutional by a federal court in 1991 and was never replaced. But the faculty code remained on the books, just waiting for its time to do mischief.

In recent years, while UW-Madison continues to protect free speech in many worthy ways, it has not been immune to the ideological and bureaucratic forces mentioned in the introduction. This reality poses another stark question: Is internal reform of higher education a viable option in today's world? Or is a broader coalition necessary to win the battle?[7]

Political Science 470: A Way to Teach
the First Amendment in College

In my time at UW-Madison, I saw that students were unfamiliar with the fundamental principles of free speech and free intellectual inquiry.[8] Emotional responses and uninformed presumptions often took precedence over considered judgments, and I decided to teach a large lecture class on the First Amendment to contribute to public knowledge of free speech jurisprudence.

In the spring of 1993, I began teaching a First Amendment class that consisted of 300 students, several of whom were involved in student leadership in various capacities, including student press and government. (These institutional allies later proved invaluable during faculty senate debates.) The idea was to teach students First Amendment basics. I did so until I retired in 2015. As fortune had it, I witnessed many instances in which my passionate students dealt with campus speech they abhorred by applying analytical constitutional reasoning to their responses. This was perhaps the most satisfying aspect of my career. Libertarian philosopher Lester Hunt also taught similar principles in his classes on freedom and liberty, and journalism professor Robert Drechsel reached many students and future allies in his large journalism class on press law.

The Curriculum. The core of my course was First Amendment case law. For many years I used a law school text, *The First Amendment*, by noted constitutional law professors Jesse Choper and Steven Shiffrin, which included selections from key cases accompanied by excellent questions, notes, and legal commentary.[9] I supplemented it with my own lectures and secondary readings. We covered such doctrinal areas as advocating illegal conduct, violence, and revolution; hate speech and fighting words that provoke violent or deeply emotional responses; obscenity and sexual expression; speech in the public forum; heckler's vetoes; symbolic speech and expression intertwined with conduct; academic freedom and free speech on campus; speech compelled by the state and speech by the state; controversial speech by government employees; prior restraints and freedom of the press; and the establishment and free exercise of religion clauses.

188   THE FREE INQUIRY PAPERS

In the last few years, however, I replaced this text with one I wrote, which featured cases, my own commentary, and selections of supplementary material. I did this out of personal interest and a desire to be even more directly involved in the learning process. I also offered the "Downs Text" at no cost to students, a welcome bonus.

Because of the breadth of free speech case law, we spent most of the course on freedom of speech, exploring freedom of religion during the last couple of weeks. Throughout, I stressed freedom of religion as a vital cognate right of intellectual freedom and freedom of conscience. For example, we read the famous 1943 case, *West Virginia State Board of Education v. Barnette*, in which the Supreme Court ruled that a Jehovah's Witness had the right not to salute the American flag in a class ritual at school.[10]

Students need to learn basic facts and principles before they can responsibly engage in critical reasoning. I stressed the foundational cases early on, while adding historical, philosophical, political, and policy-oriented perspectives to build on the foundation as we went along. Students learned what the cases were about and how and why the justices decided as they did. What tests had the Supreme Court used in different doctrinal areas? What underlying principles give substance to the doctrine? Is free speech a good in itself or mainly a vital right to ensure the pursuit of truth or the practice of self-government? Or both? What are its proper limits, and what criteria should be used to make this determination? These questions required students to consider the different factors that shape free speech jurisprudence.

I typically assigned a book that defended free speech from a nonlegal perspective, such as Jonathan Rauch's *Kindly Inquisitors: The New Attacks on Free Thought*, and a book or essays that questioned modern free speech doctrine and theory, such as Catharine MacKinnon's *Only Words*, Stanley Fish's *There's No Such Thing as Free Speech ... and It's a Good Thing Too*, and material on critical race theory.[11]

UW-Madison was the site of numerous free speech and religion controversies between the late 1980s and my retirement in 2016, and I also included cases from our campus to bring the relevance of free speech law and politics home to them.[12] Some UW-Madison campus disputes even led to federal case law, including a 1991 federal decision that struck down the UW System's student speech code and a 2000 US Supreme Court decision that upheld UW-Madison's program of assessing students' fees to fund student groups in a viewpoint-neutral manner.[13] Some of the most prominent academic freedom cases in American history took place at Madison, and I discussed them, including those that led to the "sifting and winnowing" statement by the Regents in 1894 and the university's successful opposition to political pressure to adopt anti-Communist "loyalty oaths" in the early 1950s.[14]

The pivotal midterm exam enabled students to apply their knowledge. It presented a complex take-home hypothetical case that students had to work on and answer like an appellate judge in class a week later, as well as some short-answer questions. I provided extended office hours the week before the exam, during which many students gathered and argued over points and questions. After the exam, I noticed definite improvement in students' understanding and subtlety of thinking.

Fostering free inquiry alone is necessary, but it is not sufficient in an educational institution—nor in life, for that matter. The give-and-take of free inquiry must set the stage for the deployment of logical and evidentiary reasoning that contributes to the critical sifting and winnowing of truth from falsehood and discerning shades of gray when they exist. Without this second step, free inquiry can amount to little more than watching a parade of ideas without coming to a reasoned conclusion that itself must be defended.[15] Political Science 470 emphasized this balance between freedom and critical thinking.

Socratic Inquiry and Emersonian Pursuit. In class we also engaged in the process of questioning and discussing various aspects of the cases and issues before us. In Book I of Plato's *Republic*, Socrates famously challenges Thrasymachus's proposition that justice amounts to whatever serves the interest of those who possess power. Socrates challenges Thrasymachus's theory of justice by striving to demonstrate that justice is a universal or objective principle based on fairness and right that must not be reduced to simple self-interest and power.

Learning First Amendment law and constitutional law encourages students to think beyond their self-interest and predispositions and consider the common good based on the consensually derived constitutional text. I would remind them of what I had said in the early days of the course:

190 THE FREE INQUIRY PAPERS

"What you consider a bad law might be constitutional, and what you consider a wonderful law might be unconstitutional." These counterintuitive points are the beginning of thinking more objectively and dispassionately and of the widening of one's intellectual horizon that is a hallmark of liberal education.

First Amendment jurisprudence teaches a similar message. As Justice Oliver Wendell Holmes Jr.—the godfather of modern free speech doctrine—famously wrote, "If there is any principle of the Constitution that more imperatively calls for attachment than any other it is the principle of free thought—not free thought for those who agree with us but freedom for the thought that we hate."[16]

This brings us to other questions: To what extent are judicial decisions based on judicial will, political ideology, or practical necessity as opposed to jurisprudence? How much should justices consider consequences rather than "pure law" in rendering their decisions? Thrasymachus's theory of justice is reductionist, but its realism is also omnipresent in human action, and idealism shorn of a mature dose of reason can be irresponsible.

We explored the founders' realism in relation to freedom—namely, how the Constitution creates the concentrated power necessary to protect freedom, along with checks and balances to protect freedom from governmental excesses. Power must be brought to bear to protect freedom, including free speech, while counterpower must protect us from the original power.[17] Realism must have its say, though in the proper perspective.

Finally, the course also unavoidably included an Emersonian message of self-reliance, personal growth, and intellectual adventurism, which speaks to the spirit of freedom in a liberal democracy. A free society is premised on the right to one's own thoughts and beliefs and the courage to pursue these goods by exploring new frontiers of learning and discovery. We want minds that are both thoughtful and independent, minds worthy of educated adults who stand for their beliefs while also respecting the rights of others. The most important First Amendment cases, such as *Barnette*, affirm the inalienable duty of ultimately thinking for oneself. As Justice Robert Jackson wrote in this case,

> If there is any fixed star in our constitutional constellation,
> it is that no official, high or petty, can prescribe what shall be

orthodox in politics, nationalism, religion, or other matters of opinion or force citizens to confess by word or act their faith therein.[18]

Nor may any university compel such conformity, though many are trying today.

Whatever success Political Science 470 achieved shows the importance of providing a platform for the presence of free speech principles and law on campus. As juniors and seniors, most of my students already possessed an intellectual foundation that helped them assimilate and analyze the material. Providing a similar experience to freshman and sophomore students in the form of a class or orientation program in logic and critical, evidence-based reasoning would allow their enrichment to begin even earlier. And such a program should be taught by individuals imbued with the spirit of liberty.

Planting the Seeds of CAFAR

In response to the chilling effect on campus, a handful of faculty members formed a small, informal, fledgling free speech counterforce in 1993. To the university's credit, we were tolerated by most colleagues and the administration.

Our minimal presence mattered, and we soon recognized what I consider the first *key strategic point*: It is imperative to get the free speech ball rolling by filling the public space with your voices, lest academic freedom and free speech principles fade from public consciousness. As Alan Bloom wrote in *The Closing of the American Mind*, "Freedom of the mind requires not only, or not even especially, the absence of legal constraints but the presence of alternative thoughts."[19] Attaining public presence is essential to beginning the project of gaining potential allies and sympathizers.

Speaking out consistently can also create a *public persona* for activists that can at least partially immunize them from personal criticism.[20] A key aspect of this effort is to make the academic freedom cause salient to the campus discussion by speaking out in public forums and in the press at every opportunity. We helped make the free speech issue important

192 THE FREE INQUIRY PAPERS

or salient enough to, as sociologists put it, cross the threshold of public attention, much like the drunk driving and domestic violence activists had achieved nationwide in previous decades.[21]

To reach this stage, we used several tools, including bringing in outside speakers who supported our cause. One who came several times was Rauch, the author of *Kindly Inquisitors*, which presents what I consider the best diagnosis available of the new threats to free inquiry at that time and freedom's best defense. No book I taught in any class had a bigger impact on students than Rauch's.[22]

We also quickly realized a *second strategic point*: For free speech mobilization to succeed, you need enough participants who are willing to put in the time and effort that the cause necessitates. And they have to make the cause a *priority*. Motivation and persistence matter. Academic freedom and free speech must matter to you enough to compel you to act in the face of pressure, alienation of certain colleagues, and the demands of other duties.

A *third strategic point* also became clear as our fledgling group struggled on: We discovered the utility of citing examples of the harm and injustice committed by actual cases of censorship and improper investigation. Referring to real cases makes a principle come alive to others, especially those sitting on the fence. ("See? This really happened!") Indeed, some of the most important leaders of our movement had themselves been victimized by the campus speech police. Rather than conforming or hiding from view, they struck back by undertaking constructive action.

These strategic points fell into place at Madison between 1992 and 1995. Then a case under the aegis of the ostensibly dormant faculty speech code changed everything.

The Formation and Activities of CAFAR

In a nutshell, the case involved a secret and illegal investigation of history professor Robert Frykenberg for ostensible gender discrimination and the imposition of improper punishment. Though initially known only by the department and the upper echelons of the administration that enabled it, the case riveted the history department. Stanley G. Payne, a supporter of the investigation's target who soon thereafter would lead our eventual organized resistance group until 2000, portrayed the inquisition as "Soviet" in mentality.[23] The process took place under the reign of the faculty speech code.

Likening the investigation to being crushed by an institutional "Leviathan," Frykenberg hired local attorney Steven Underwood and filed an official complaint with the state's attorney general, leading to a settlement that vindicated him while requiring the university to pay all his legal fees. (Underwood soon became the retained counsel of our group.) Several department members later told me that the crisis could have been resolved quickly and correctly had more leading members of the department stepped forward. History professor John Sharpless, a later stalwart member of our movement who exposed the situation to a broader audience, was a key exception to this critique.

After we found out about the case, other examples of improper and unpublicized investigations and applications of the faculty code came to our attention, including an especially troubling case in the art department that had taken place in 1990. The political scenario regarding this dispute was reminiscent of the Chinese Cultural Revolution. Ultimately, ably assisted by law professor Gordon Baldwin, who became an important member of our group, the professor was vindicated of the spurious charge of racism after a hearing in which Baldwin began by instructing the group that the United States Constitution does not stop outside the door to this room. Despite official vindication, the professor's reputation had been dragged through the mud of rumor, innuendo, and presumptive guilt, and when he asked the administration to show him and make public an official record of his case after it was dropped, he was told the documentation had somehow disappeared.

In another case, Lester Hunt was investigated because a student complained about his quoting the 1950s television show *The Lone Ranger*. Though Hunt was vindicated, the investigation included a threat by an administrator that Hunt could be fired on account of this single statement that was not racist in any way.

Another indefatigable leader of our group was Mary Anderson, a nationally honored scholar of hydrogeology, who had just survived a Kafkaesque drive to unseat her from her position on the University Committee, the leading faculty group that controls the agenda of the faculty senate.

194 THE FREE INQUIRY PAPERS

Anderson's case represented the absurd rabbit hole into which the university had fallen in that time.

After Anderson refused to resign from the committee, the University Committee conducted a trial-like procedure before the entire faculty senate but decided not to provide identities of the accused, the accuser, or any witnesses. The reason for this remarkable version of due process was that Anderson's legal counsel, Gordon Baldwin, had informed the University Committee and the senate that Anderson would sue anyone who slandered her during the procedure. It was like playing basketball without a ball. Needless to say, the process became farcical, and the whole matter was dropped. Later Anderson provided us with essential inside information in our effort to abolish the faculty speech code.

Soon after the history department case was settled in June 1996, a group of over 20 faculty members met for lunch to form an independent group dedicated to furnishing legal support to faculty, students, and staff whose academic freedom or other rights had been violated or wrongly jeopardized. We formed a new nonpartisan group named the Faculty Committee for Academic Freedom and Rights, later dropping the "Faculty" designation to make our eventual acronym "CAFAR." At last, we had an organized, committed group that could stake a stronger claim to campus attention. Our formation exemplified the second strategic point mentioned above: Mobilize, starting with a critical core that can influence and provide cover for those who otherwise would remain silent.[24]

Our mission also included taking public stands on policy matters and actions that affect rights and academic free speech. The Bradley Foundation in Milwaukee generously provided us with $100,000 for legal cases and related expenses, demonstrating how internal campus mobilization can work constructively with external assistance if it does not lose control of its actions.

To our knowledge, no independent campus group like CAFAR existed on any other campus, and even today, I know of no campus group that includes free legal defense in its tool kit. Nationally oriented groups that subsequently have combined policy action and legal defense today are the Foundation for Individual Rights and Expression (FIRE), which started in 1999 and was an ally of CAFAR during our tenure, and the Academic Freedom Alliance, established in 2020. Recently established campus groups now exist at Cornell University, the Massachusetts Institute of Technology (MIT), and other schools.

Right away CAFAR took advantage of a *fourth strategic point*: We sought publicity and saw the media as allies. At the time, the press was overwhelmingly on our side—both the internal student press and the press outside—and we deployed these and related assets many times over the years. The two student newspapers at UW-Madison, the *Badger Herald* and the *Daily Cardinal*, were invaluable allies for two reasons. First, the student press is both a weather vane and influencer of student opinion. Second, speech codes were primarily intended *to serve and protect students*, so student press opposition to the codes provided a standing retort to the administration's claims of paternalistic protection. Without strong student support and partnership with some key student leaders, our success would have been crippled. We returned the favor by publicly and aggressively defending the *Badger Herald* in later years when it came under strong attack for publishing controversial yet clearly constitutionally protected material—for example, David Horowitz's advertisement opposing racial reparations in 2001 and the *Jyllands-Posten* cartoons of Muhammad in 2006.[25]

The first step toward publicity was to issue a public announcement of our formation that included a mission statement:

> We hereby announce the formation of a new faculty group called the [Faculty] Committee for Academic Freedom and Rights. In recent years, faculty members at the University of Wisconsin have been subjected to sometimes alarming threats to their academic freedom and their constitutional rights. These threats, which continue, have come from a variety of sources at departmental, administrative, and campus-wide levels. Such infringements too often wrongfully harm the reputations, rights, and professional goals of individuals, and they do equal damage to the intellectual community. Strong institutional protection of such rights as freedom of speech and inquiry, due process, and equal protection of the law is essential to fostering the principles and goals of a community of scholars.[26]

196 THE FREE INQUIRY PAPERS

The two student newspapers promptly printed our mission statement, and the *Wisconsin State Journal* then ran a sympathetic front-page article on our formation, stunning the administration and gaining us local public notice right off the bat. Jennifer Galloway, the *Wisconsin State Journal* reporter, also mentioned the history department affair. When she asked Jane Hutchison, CAFAR treasurer, why the committee was independent, not part of the university, Hutchison trenchantly replied, "We decided to not involve ourselves with the university because the university is part of the problem."[27]

Our official membership ultimately consisted of about 25 members, but our "executive committee" of a dozen members took most of the initiative. A *fifth strategic point* served us well: Most of our members had established reputations for their research, teaching, and campus involvement. This circumstance was somewhat fortuitous, of course, but it was of genuine value, as it made it difficult for the administration or others to dismiss us as a fringe group. In a related sense, we were aided by the fact that UW-Madison took research and scholarship very seriously, so our efforts to link academic freedom and free speech to the prospects of scholarship met receptive ears in many worthy quarters.

Most importantly, one could trust CAFAR members in the trenches. They relished taking on tough cases, and not a single member ever backed out of a case for fear of criticism. Not once. Such willingness is a *sixth strategic point*: Potential activists must be willing to face criticism from colleagues and others, including erstwhile friends and colleagues who might be allies in other matters. You might have to decide what matters more to you: popularity at the country club or intellectual freedom in academic life. Having CAFAR's fellowship at Madison made this decision easier, while also making the Wisconsin case somewhat sui generis.

Providing legal support in addition to policy activism demonstrated both seriousness on our part and nonpartisanship—an essential attribute—because our clients included individuals from across the political spectrum. In addition, legal support added pressure on the academic freedom side of the administrative incentive structure.[28]

Finally, it was important in itself to provide committed moral and legal support for individuals whose rights were wrongly threatened. Our clients typically thanked us in emotional and appreciative terms for standing with them, often while erstwhile colleagues turned away. Many considered our assistance crucial to protecting their careers and reputations. This personal side of our work must not be undervalued.

Indeed, maintaining the reality and appearance of universalism must be regarded as a *seventh strategic point*: Our policy stands were consciously nonpartisan, and our individual legal clients came from across the ideological spectrum. For example, in 2005 we publicly supported UW-Whitewater when Wisconsin political leaders threatened to defund the university for letting a student group invite controversial anti-American Ward Churchill to campus to speak. CAFAR leaders met with the key legislator behind the threat and wrote the justification that the Whitewater administration presented to the public in a press release.

Wisconsin's Faculty Speech Code

But it was our first policy involvement that propelled us into the vortex of campus policy politics: to seriously revise or abolish the faculty speech code that had sanctioned the accusations and investigations discussed above. This effort took almost three years of struggle that involved expanding networks of internal and external support, and it ended by making us the campus's leading player in the politics of academic freedom and free speech. We were able to link the code to the abuse of improperly accused faculty, thereby turning the faculty speech code into a symbol of oppression and a contradiction of the university's classic commitment to free inquiry.

We began to win the battle of language and symbolic politics. This effort represents an *eighth strategic point*: Frame the issue in the most accurate yet telling way possible, which should include emphasizing the commitment to academic freedom and free inquiry that are likely to be—or should be—founding principles of the institution. For example, we often referred to the official University of Wisconsin Board of Regents' public statement promulgated in the aftermath of a nationally followed academic freedom case in 1894, the core of which is written on a plaque attached to the outside wall of the main entrance to the UW-Madison administration building, Bascom Hall: "Whatever may be the limitations which trammel

198   THE FREE INQUIRY PAPERS

inquiry elsewhere, we believe that the great state University of Wisconsin should ever encourage that continual and fearless sifting and winnowing by which alone the truth can be found."[29]

In 1994, noted economist and education scholar W. Lee Hansen edited a book on the history and politics of the plaque, which was another launching pad of our movement. He, too, became a major leader of CAFAR.[30] We constantly linked this tradition to the abolition of the speech code.

As the 1999 spring semester began, the faculty speech code was the talk of the campus. Student allies were indispensable in spreading the cause, led by undergraduates Jason Shepard and Amy Kasper. The local press was on board, and we nationalized the debate in late 1998 by contacting the *Chronicle of Higher Education*, which published a cover story about the events at Wisconsin that, in turn, sparked more national media coverage.[31] The *New York Times* sent an education reporter to cover the politics and a senate meeting. Several national media sources covered the final vote or its aftermath, along with local media.

We also brought in Rauch and Harvey Silverglate, a cofounder of FIRE and coauthor of an influential book on campus liberty's betrayal with University of Pennsylvania history professor Alan Charles Kors, whom many consider the godfather of the contemporary national campus free speech movement.[32] Silverglate gave a public talk that garnered press attention and wrote a legal brief that we presented to the faculty senate and its top committee, the University Committee.

After a tortuous debate, the faculty senate voted 61–52 on March 1, 1999, to abolish the faculty speech code.[33] This was the first time an American campus had rescinded a speech code without being ordered to do so by a court. In the days after the vote, people I considered on the fence or even in opposition offered congratulations and post hoc support.

Relying on a vote rather than a legal decision compelled us to engage in mobilization and persuasion. This combination had two lasting effects. First, it meant that a senate majority and a large portion of campus opinion had come over to our side. This situation augured well for the future. Second, achieving this victory necessarily entailed the formation of an infrastructure of activists centered on CAFAR that now had a presence on campus. Our leadership played essential roles in ensuing years on numerous pro–academic freedom and due process campus and UW System policies.

We were pleased by the speech code vote in 1999 and gratified by the success we encountered thereafter. But we also learned what I consider a *ninth strategic point*: Fighting to preserve and advance academic freedom and speech is worth it even if you fail. First, it is necessary to keep the idea alive in the world. Second, it is an intrinsic good regardless of outcome. In Kantian terms, it is a deontological good above and beyond its utilitarian aspects. Both dimensions matter. A test we often applied to ourselves along the way: Would each of us be able to sleep well at night in the wake of the choices we made in a challenging situation?

Let me conclude this section by offering a final, *10th strategic point*: Engaging in the fight for free speech and academic freedom on campus can simply be fun! It can awaken you from whatever slumbers to which you might have succumbed, and it can give you the gift of new allies and friends whom you will never forget. It can renew and reenergize your commitment to the calling of higher education and the freedom of diverse and critical inquiry that gives it life.

The Aftermath

Alas, CAFAR's executive committee closed shop in 2016, mainly due to the retirements of key members. The founders of CAFAR, regardless of personal politics, shared a similar vision about intellectual freedom and what threats to take seriously. We were proud of our successes, but we harbored concerns about the future at UW-Madison as we laid our activism to rest.

Though the administration has protected controversial speakers in recent years, I have been informed of administrators wrongly taking students' side in disputes with professors. In one case, a professor was pressured to restructure his entire class to accommodate unreasonable student demands relating to "social justice." (The professor reached out to me after I retired, but he abandoned the effort to resist.) And as The Dispatch revealed in 2020, the university's new bias-reporting program—now run online—led to over a hundred anonymous student complaints against instructors in 2019, many of them ludicrously politicized.[34]

The deployment of principled outside assistance in higher education is now needed more than ever, especially given the outburst and entrenchment of so-called cancel culture. In response, new forms of resistance have arisen involving new well-funded free speech groups at such institutions as Cornell and MIT, aroused alumni and trustees, and outside groups that are adding their weight to FIRE, including Heterodox Academy and the Academic Freedom Alliance, along with several preexisting groups. More such movements have been galvanized since the eruption of the October 7, 2023, conflict in the Middle East. The presence of knowledgeable and committed groups is needed to help campuses enforce the proper lines between protected speech and speech acts that cross the line into criminal acts or violations of proper campus rules.

Legislatures have also entered the fray recently, raising a further set of concerns. Politicians have their own incentives, which are not always friendly to the pursuit of truth.

But if universities abandon their fiduciary responsibility to foster free inquiry, they implicitly open their gates to such outside intervention. When at all feasible, the best remedy to the crisis of free speech and academic freedom in higher education today is for universities to heal themselves.

Notes

1. Among a plethora of sources, see Donald Alexander Downs, *Free Speech and Liberal Education: A Plea for Intellectual Diversity and Tolerance* (Washington, DC: Cato Institute, 2020), chap. 1. Stanford temporarily presented the most extensive and nonsensical microaggression list of all. Susan D'Agostino, "Amid Backlash, Stanford Pulls 'Harmful Language' List," *Inside Higher Education*, January 10, 2023, https://www.insidehighered.com/news/2023/01/11/amid-backlash-stanford-removes-harmful-language-list.

2. The dangers posed by the "moral furies" unmoored from respect for legal limits have been a theme of literature and psychology since Aeschylus's play *Oresteia*.

3. One of the best examples of the literature regarding tectonic forces is Greg Lukianoff and Jonathan Haidt, *The Coddling of the American Mind: How Good Intentions and Bad Ideas Are Setting Up a Generation for Failure* (New York: Penguin Press, 2018). On universalism's decline, see Todd Gitlin, *The Twilight of Common Dreams: Why America Is Wracked by Culture Wars* (New York: Henry Holt Co., 1996).

4. *New York Times v. Sullivan*, 376 US 254, 270 (1964).

5. I analyze surveys up to 2019 in Downs, *Free Speech and Liberal Education*, chap. 6.

6. See also Donald Alexander Downs, *Restoring Free Speech and Liberty on Campus* (New York: Cambridge University Press, 2005); and Downs, *Free Speech and Liberal Education*.

MOBILIZATION FOR ACADEMIC FREE SPEECH   201

7. For example, the "Princeton Principles for a Campus Culture of Free Inquiry" (2023) call for broadening campus movements to include trustees, regents, alumni, and others in the extended campus community while providing guardrails for political involvement, about which the principles are circumspect. Princeton University, James Madison Program in American Ideals and Institutions, "Princeton Principles for a Campus Culture of Free Inquiry," https://jmp.princeton.edu/princeton-principles-campus-culture-free-inquiry.

8. For a classic and influential scholarly summation of this problem at the end of the 1990s, see Alan Charles Kors and Harvey A. Silverglate, *The Shadow University: The Betrayal of Liberty on America's Campuses* (New York: Free Press, 1998).

9. Jesse H. Choper and Steven Shiffrin, *The First Amendment* (St. Paul, MN: Thompson Reuter, 2011).

10. *West Virginia Board of Education v. Barnette*, 319 US 624 (1943).

11. Jonathan Rauch, *Kindly Inquisitors: The New Attacks on Free Thought* (Chicago: University of Chicago Press, 1993); Catharine MacKinnon, *Only Words* (Cambridge, MA: Harvard University Press, 1993); and Stanley Fish, *There's No Such Thing as Free Speech . . . and It's a Good Thing Too* (New York: Oxford University Press, 1994).

12. International relations authority Hans J. Morgenthau has called the method of studying contemporary events through the prism of political theory and universal dilemmas the pedagogy of "higher practicality." Hans J. Morgenthau, "The Purpose of Political Science," in *A Design for Political Science: Scope, Objectives, and Methods*, ed. James C. Charlesworth (Philadelphia, PA: American Academy of Political and Social Science, 1966), 73, 77–78.

13. *UWM Post v. Board of Regents of the University of Wisconsin*, 774 F. Supp. 1163 (E.D. Wis. 1991); and *University of Wisconsin Board of Regents v. Southworth*, 529 US 217 (2000).

14. David E. Cronin and John W. Jenkins, *The University of Wisconsin: A History, 1945–1971* (Madison, WI: University of Wisconsin Press, 1999), 4:92–93.

15. Jonathan Rauch focuses on this second intellectual obligation in his recent magisterial book, which builds on the free inquiry focus of *Kindly Inquisitors*. Jonathan Rauch, *The Constitution of Knowledge: A Defense of Truth* (Washington, DC: Brookings Institution Press, 2021).

16. *United States v. Schwimmer*, 279 US 644 (1929).

17. See, for example, Stephen Holmes, *Passions and Constraint: On the Theory of Liberal Democracy* (Chicago: University of Chicago Press, 1997).

18. *Barnette*, 319 US at 642.

19. Alan Bloom, *The Closing of the American Mind* (New York: Simon & Schuster, 1987), 249.

20. Personalizing of intellectual differences makes tolerance less possible, and it is a feature of the therapeutic ethic to which I alluded, which involves heightened psychological sensitivity. See, for example, Richard Sennett, *The Fall of Public Man* (New York: Knopf, 1977); and Downs, *Free Speech and Liberal Education*, chap. 2.

21. See, for example, Joseph R. Gusfield, *The Culture of Public Problems: Drinking-Driving and the Symbolic Order* (Chicago: University of Chicago Press, 1980).

22. Rauch, *Kindly Inquisitors*.

202 THE FREE INQUIRY PAPERS

23. Donald Alexander Downs and Stanley G. Payne, "The Wisconsin Fight for Academic Freedom," *Academic Questions* 29 (April 2016): 152–60, https://www.nas.org/academic-questions/29/2/the_wisconsin_fight_for_academic_freedom/pdf.

24. See, for example, Timur Kuran, *Private Truths, Public Lies: The Social Consequences of Preference Falsification* (Cambridge, MA: Harvard University Press, 1995). Kuran shows how mobilizing a critical core and ultimately building a bandwagon effect can end up achieving what was previously unthinkable, especially if a crystalizing event or set of events erupts. Kuran's most telling example is the fall of the Soviet Union in 1991. Though the Wisconsin case is small potatoes compared to the historic events that shook Russia, our movement was ultimately astonished at how our eventual successes resembled those Kuran presents.

25. See Downs, *Restoring Free Speech and Liberty on Campus*, chaps. 6 and 7.

26. The CAFAR mission statement was announced in the *Badger Herald* and *Daily Cardinal* in September 1996.

27. Jennifer Galloway, "UW Faculty Defend Free Expression," *Wisconsin State Journal*, November 16, 1996.

28. Incentives can matter more than ideology. See, for example, John Hasnas, "Why Colleges Don't Care About Free Speech," *Wall Street Journal*, February 6, 2022, https://www.wsj.com/articles/college-dont-care-free-speech-ilya-shapiro-treanor-georgetown-cancel-pc-culture-censorship-campus-11644167414.

29. The 1894 case involved Richard Ely, the nation's leading progressive political economist.

30. W. Lee Hansen, ed., *Academic Freedom on Trial: 100 Years of Sifting and Winnowing at the University of Wisconsin–Madison* (Madison, WI: University of Wisconsin Press, 1994).

31. Robin Wilson, "U. of Wisconsin Considers Proposal to Ease Limits on Faculty Speech: Revisions of 17-Year-Old Code Could Signal a Move away from Political Correctness," *Chronicle of Higher Education*, October 2, 1998, https://www.chronicle.com/article/u-of-wisconsin-considers-proposal-to-ease-limits-on-faculty-speech.

32. Kors and Silverglate, *The Shadow University*.

33. The headline on the front page of the *Wisconsin State Journal* the next day read: "Speech Code Is History." The new language in the university rules simply said that no one shall be sanctioned for any statement made in class that is germane to the subject matter.

34. Donald Alexander Downs, "Keep Big Brother off UW Campus," *Wisconsin State Journal*, February 24, 2020, https://madison.com/wsj/opinion/column/donald-downs-keep-big-brother-off-uw-campus/article_3aafcae6-bfb8-5eca-9cfb-a082555308ae.html; and Christian Schneider, "A Year of Discontent on Campus," The Dispatch, February 6, 2020, https://thedispatch.com/p/a-year-of-discontent-on-campus.

13

Make a Bureaucracy to Beat a Bureaucracy? Free Speech Bureaucracies and How to Get Them

Robert Maranto

Today, the solitary inventor, tinkering in his shop, has been overshadowed by task forces of scientists in laboratories and testing fields. In the same fashion, the free university, historically the fountainhead of free ideas and scientific discovery, has experienced a revolution in the conduct of research. Partly because of the huge costs involved, a government contract becomes virtually a substitute for intellectual curiosity. For every old blackboard there are now hundreds of new electronic computers. The prospect of domination of the nation's scholars by Federal employment, project allocations, and the power of money is ever present and is gravely to be regarded.

—Dwight D. Eisenhower[1]

Despite efforts in the 1990s to reinvent the corporation and government,[2] this remains the era of big bureaucracies. I am no mindless basher of bureaucracy. I spent most of my life in public service in the US Office of Personnel Management and in academia, mainly in public universities but also in private universities and colleges. My father spent 35 years in the US Postal Service and a wartime stint in the US Army, and my son worked for a time for a defense agency.

Bureaucracies are not just public-sector phenomena. The private universities and colleges where I taught had management structures and processes resembling those of their public peers: They took federal money and thus had to comply with federal mandates. Influenced even more by isomorphism, their managers tended to copy the "best practices" of their field *whether or not they worked*.

Corporations and foundations are also highly bureaucratic, with many evading market discipline.[3] As with higher education, their bureaucratization often reflects their reliance on government contracts, as Dwight D. Eisenhower astutely observed. Long before "military-industrial complex" became a term, our dense and sometimes dim administrative class spread a broader bureaucratic ideology prizing hyper-specialization and a slavish deference to experts.[4]

In this chapter, I describe what bureaucracies are and do, what they are good at, and where they fall short. I then explain why bureaucracies have inherently problematic relationships with free speech and free inquiry, which makes them ill-suited to fostering excellent teaching and research, particularly sophisticated teaching and non-incremental research. I explore how bureaucratization, especially regarding race and gender issues, threatens free inquiry in ways not foreseen even in the Joseph McCarthy era. Finally, I hint at remedies, which are developed further in the concluding chapter. Such remedies threaten vested interests, particularly those of budget-maximizing bureaucrats,[5] so successful reform will require decades, though there is much to do now to start the process.

What Bureaucracies Are and What They Do

Today it seems odd that in the late 19th and early 20th centuries, bureaucracies were prized for their efficiency. Yet compared with traditional governance by hereditary clans or political spoils systems, bureaucracies often were efficient. Indeed, President George Washington developed bureaucratic structures of government, without which the fledgling nation would have failed. That said, Washington naturally appointed Federalists to office. Andrew Jackson and later presidents more systematically appointed political supporters, to both unite their political party and assure accountability. Arguably, this worked well. Abraham Lincoln made the greatest use of spoils appointees, to keep his Civil War administration from becoming a house divided against itself.[6]

While often used as a synonym for government, bureaucracies are in fact organizations not immediately evaluated by and thus accountable to markets, and they're large enough so that no one leader personally knows and directly controls every employee. This in turn leads to seven other characteristics described by Anthony Downs,[7] Max Weber,[8] and others.

1. Bureaucrats are technical experts in what their agencies do. Civil engineers in state departments of transportation inspect and maintain bridges; the district attorney's lawyers bring cases.

2. Bureaucrats are relatively long-serving, full-time officials. Temporary contract workers don't count. Naturally, this means they invest considerable energy in keeping their jobs and winning promotions.

3. Following from these two characteristics, bureaucrats are hired, promoted, and (at least in theory) sometimes terminated using merit criteria theoretically related to workplace needs. Merit systems offer internal and external legitimacy that, as argued later, bureaucrats do not always merit.

4. Bureaucracy is, at least in theory, impersonal, with people treated according to their formal position in the organization, rather than other forms of status. In theory, bureaucrats are also relatively interchangeable. One sees this in how educational leaders view teachers[9] and how university administrators increasingly view faculty.[10]

5. Lacking a price system (like markets) or charisma (as in many new organizations), bureaucracies are managed by rules, which dominate decision-making.[11]

6. Recordkeeping and paperwork abound, as do routines or standard operating procedures (SOPs) for efficiency and effectiveness.

7. Bureaucracies are hierarchical, with orders flowing down and information flowing up, albeit with substantial hierarchical distortion each way so that those at the top don't really know what goes on

while those at the bottom don't always carry out or even understand orders from on high.[12]

In one of the most insightful treatments of bureaucracy, political scientists Karen Hult and Charles Walcott argue that bureaucracies can work well when two preconditions exist: a high level of goal agreement and a high level of technological stasis and certainty.[13] These permit rules and routines to guide employee efforts in ways that may promote effectiveness and efficiency. For example, everyone wants clean water (goal agreement), and we have a high degree of knowledge (technical certainty) about how to build effective water systems, though sadly, for a range of reasons, some distrust safe public water.[14] Basic tasks such as delivering the mail and coining money are likewise suited for bureaucracies.[15]

Conversely, as Hult and Walcott argue, bureaucracies are ill-equipped for knowledge production, areas that may lack goal agreement and inherently lack technical certainty. Bureaucratic rules and hierarchies impose a single-best way, rather than facilitating many paths in search of discoveries. Bureaucratic rules cannot cure cancer or even homelessness.[16] Notably, in the 19th century, US higher education focused on training ministers and elite networking, missions in accord with imposing orthodoxies. In the early and mid-20th century, higher education missions shifted to producing and disseminating knowledge, missions that, as Princeton Professor Keith Whittington shows, require free speech, free inquiry, and *non*compliance.[17]

Even regarding K–12 and higher education, parents and educators may have legitimate disagreements on the goals and techniques of schooling, which may indeed differ across social and geographic communities. Thus, it is not accurate to say that either Montessori or traditional schooling provides a "good" education; rather, each can be good for some families and educators.[18]

Finally, bureaucracies such as police departments and public schools produce services essential for a free society. Yet their emphases on conformity and compliance can also threaten freedom, including free speech and inquiry.

How Bureaucracies Threaten Free Inquiry

Generally, today's US bureaucracies reflect the triumph of early 20th-century intellectual progressives. As Vincent Ostrom captured in *The Intellectual Crisis in American Public Administration*,[19] the American founders sought a federal republic enabling local and individual initiative, with diversity in public administration fostering and fostered by social diversity. In a free society, no one size fits all. Moreover, rule by any single faction, including an elite faction, would likely degenerate into tyranny.

In short, the founders anticipated the thinking of Alexis de Tocqueville in seeking a localized, diverse society and polity. In contrast, Woodrow Wilson and other progressive bureaucratic thinkers prized centralization and uniformity. In government, this meant clear lines of accountability, with experts imposing the single-best methods in all things, thereby reinforcing the values of the dominant class. The Wilsonian approach empowers institution-based experts—not free speech or free inquiry that could threaten those experts.

Often, experts do more to protect their own turf than to serve society. I am reminded of this multiple times each year when completing two conflict of interest forms, along with three accomplishment reports (for the fiscal year, the calendar year, and the academic year), required by different subunits in the university system. Bureaucracies often prioritize power over efficiency or effectiveness.

Indeed, many bureaucracies become so oriented to compliance that they come to prioritize rules over missions. In what sociologists term "goal displacement," rules *become* the mission. Until the Clinton administration and Congress reinvented federal procurement in the 1990s, it routinely took *six years* for the government to buy software.[20] Prioritizing rules and SOPs over performance created decades-long disasters in such varied places as inner-city schools,[21] US military involvements in Vietnam[22] and Afghanistan,[23] and, of course, universities.[24]

When rules *become* the mission, free inquiry is savaged in three obvious ways. First, the tens of thousands of hours that employees of a given university spend doing paperwork and compliance meetings is time *not* spent teaching or researching. I had a recent reminder of this at an Institutional Review Board (IRB) meeting in which myself and 12 other well-meaning faculty and staff spent 90 minutes—given our collective salaries, over $1,200 in public money—parsing over the compliance rules for a *wine tasting* that a food science professor had conducted for over a decade without incident and that everyone agreed at the onset posed zero risk.[25] Alas, few bureaucrats are familiar with the economic concept of opportunity costs.

Importantly, burgeoning compliance demands mean that everyone is always out of compliance at some time, in some way—particularly those employees who want to get anything done.[26] This empowers unethical leaders to selectively prosecute dissenters, a tendency noted a half century ago by Thomas Sowell[27] and often reported by the Foundation for Individual Rights and Expression (FIRE). A focus on compliance makes every dean a potential Stalin.

Second, as Barry Bozeman, Jan Youtie, and Jiwon Jung find,[28] waiting for approval can delay research, even in emergency cases. This occurred in the development of COVID-19 vaccines when delay proved to be deadly.[29]

Third, as administrative hierarchies grow and top officials with large staffs lose touch with street-level work and workers, bureaucracies come to value process over mission, favoring employees who excel at filling out forms and comforting superiors rather than those teaching and researching. Compliance becomes the organizational raison d'être. What happened a half century ago in New York City Public Schools, where career bureaucrats put defending their turf, budgets, and SOPs over serving students and teachers,[30] is now the norm in higher education. Deans, burgeoning numbers of assistant deans whom political scientist Benjamin Ginsberg dubbed "deanlets," and even provosts and chancellors used to serve in those posts for a few years and then return to teaching and research; they now form a permanent administrative class that, like any *nomenklatura*, promotes its own interests.[31]

It gets worse. In addition to the seven bureaucratic characteristics detailed by Downs, Weber, and others, there are three more that many overlook. First, in the same manner in which firms try to maximize revenues and profits, bureaucracies seek to maximize their budgets. Higher budgets bring job security, opportunities for promotion, and more ability to make a difference in the world—the latter valued by idealistic bureaucrats. Bureaucracies become territorial, guarding their turf from other bureaucracies that might compete.[32] In higher education, it also means that bureaucrats stick together against faculty and students,[33] a frequent complaint voiced in free speech and free inquiry cases chronicled by FIRE.

Second, in part because they produce outputs evaluated by *political* rather than consumer markets, bureaucracies emphasize *loyalty* to other bureaucrats and, at times, external networks such as interest groups and even social media mobs. For example, school systems typically cover up scandals rather than report them, allowing corrupt personnel to stay or quietly resign rather than face law enforcement. Exposing scandals could lead to bad publicity, undermining the electoral prospects of school board members and encouraging businesses to locate elsewhere.[34] Likewise, colleges and universities have for years covered up rather than come clean on admissions and other scandals.[35] In both K–12 and higher education, administrators are incapable of real investigations but all too adept at conducting witch hunts and cover-ups.

Ideological Impacts and Conformity

A third potentially dysfunctional characteristic has to do with bureaucratic ideologies. To be sure, ideologies can promote an organization's mission, providing heuristics for decision-making (including personnel decisions such as promotions) and attracting talented officials who could make more money elsewhere. The Pentagon is staffed largely by conservatives who prioritize national defense; the Environmental Protection Agency is staffed by liberals who value environmental protection. Many such officials could make more money in the private sector but are motivated to work in government in part by ideological incentives.[36]

Yet dedicated and insulated bureaucrats can become too attached to their agency budgets and ideologies, even when those ideologies fail in the real world. Andrew Krepinevich shows how this shaped the US Army's failure in Vietnam.[37] Jonathan Wai and I found comparable failures in US public education.[38] Sometimes, when career bureaucrats strongly dedicated to their organizational ideology clash with political leaders appointed from outside the agency, the politicians hold more realistic, or at least more representative, policy views.[39]

As other chapters in this volume show, this is often the case in higher education, in ways detrimental to free speech and free inquiry. Regarding race, a Minding the Campus series edited by Craig Frisby and me details how common interventions to improve race relations in higher education and corporations contradict psychological research on successful integration and have failed to improve race relations or diversify leadership.[40] Yet reflecting bureaucratic hierarchy and specialization, woke practices have become "best practices" among bureaucrats, who defer to diversity, equity, and inclusion (DEI) "experts." As usual in bureaucracies, dissenters are not considered team players and are thus deemed unsuitable for promotion even when they are right.[41]

Accordingly, organizations pour billions into ineffective and sometimes counterproductive interventions such as diversity training, the Implicit Association Test, and microaggression training because these have assumed the status of best practices—and perhaps because it is easier to implement them than to make more fundamental changes.[42] John McWhorter argues that elite approaches to race have now achieved the status of a religion, providing meaning to some, mainly well-educated (or at least credentialed) white people.[43] Thus, these orthodoxies cannot be questioned, no matter how silly or scientifically unsound.

R. Shep Melnick[44] and Laura Kipnis,[45] among others, argue that the US Department of Education's Title IX bureaucrats and many college officials tasked with implementing Title IX regulations, which have mushroomed under federal pressure, are also ideologically extreme: Many embrace critical theory–oriented approaches to sex supported by few Americans and questioned by science.[46] For example, policies meant to end sexual harassment are in practice overly broad, unpopular, and unconstitutional, abrogating the due process of law, including the rights of the accused to know what they are being charged with, question accusers, and have legal representation.

As bureaucrats with civil service protections, many Title IX bureaucrats are isolated from contrary opinions; they engage networks of leftist interest groups and reporters in making policy and use private "Dear Colleague" letters to colleges that set policy, even though they lack transparency and public input. This largely explains why federal bureaucrats have successfully pushed colleges to adopt rules regarding race and sex that later fail when challenged in court, as when Kipnis suffered a lengthy Title IX complaint for allegedly creating an unsafe environment by *publishing an essay* in the *Chronicle of Higher Education* criticizing a Title IX investigation of another professor. Going beyond higher education, political scientist Darel Paul argues that critical gender theory and other approaches to diversity have been adopted in part to empower new managerial classes staffing bureaucracies, to give them purpose, prestige, and money.[47]

Limitations of free inquiry and free speech also reflect foreign interests. The Network Contagion Research Institute (NCRI) found that universities increasingly receive money from authoritarian regimes including China and Qatar.[48] (An informant in the US Department of Education reports that Iran launders donations through Qatar.) Not surprisingly, NCRI finds that institutions that take more such money have lower FIRE free speech ratings and more reported anti-Jewish incidents.

Whatever the causal mechanism, empirical work by Jay Greene and James Paul shows that the number of bureaucrats who work to promote diversity in higher education has ballooned; they now outnumber history professors, have considerable power, and often use that power to censor, as the powerful always do.[49] In a later work, Greene and Paul analyze diversity bureaucrats' tweets, finding that they tweet three times more about Israel than China, even though the latter is far larger and more repressive toward Muslims and other minorities. While 62 percent of tweets about China are positive, 96 percent of those about Israel are negative.[50]

I argue that the critical theory takeover of key higher education bureaucracies and fields explains opposition to Israel and support for Hamas, despite its horrendous human rights record including a charter that repeatedly calls for killing Jews.[51] At many universities, those who point out these matters face serious risks, as do whistleblowers in any bureaucracy.[52] For better or worse, as I write this, congressional hearings reflect a backlash against higher education institutions that allow free speech in support of a US-designated terrorist organization (Hamas) while heavily policing centrist and conservative speech. Reform will happen, but I believe we in higher education should reform ourselves, rather than being reformed by politicians.

212 THE FREE INQUIRY PAPERS

Fighting Back: Creating a Bureaucracy to Control a Bureaucracy

As prior chapters show, we must restore free inquiry to universities. We can begin by shedding light on the abuses of DEI and other bureaucracies, which cost significant amounts of money while subtracting value through censorship and unneeded processes. There is a pressing need for state legislative and congressional hearings to humanize the toll that attacks on free speech and free inquiry take on individuals and even the broader society, as in the delay of vaccine research in the COVID-19 pandemic.[53] In addition, private groups like FIRE should publicize, perhaps through a YouTube channel, the very real suffering of higher education dissenters and the broader social costs of crushing speech.

As part of a broader public education campaign, the size of DEI and IRB bureaucracies and their impact on higher education should become public knowledge, as suggested by Greene[54] and Greene and Paul.[55] The US Department of Education should issue regular reports with time series tables comparing the numbers of campus bureaucrats to the numbers of teachers and researchers, shaming individual campuses where possible. The long-term goal, as argued earlier, should be to reduce the size of all higher education bureaucracies, returning to the "bad" old days of the 1980s when professors outnumbered administrators and staff and actually required and graded student work. Evidence indicates this would improve both research and teaching.[56]

Yet this is not enough, because ineffective policies have driven out effective ones. Accordingly, we should offer better ways of improving intergroup relations that are centered in the contact hypothesis work of the 1950s and 1960s, which guided successful integration in the US military and other large institutions. Central to successful integration are overarching identities (like American), common goals, transparent standards, and close contact to know those from other groups as individuals.[57] Here, the time is right for the National Science Foundation to issue a report, perhaps authored by Lee Jussim and Musa al-Gharbi, on the effectiveness of DEI-related interventions in improving class mobility and intergroup relations. It could be modeled after Surgeon General Luther Terry's 1964 report summarizing the empirical research on the health effects of cigarette smoking.

Over the long term, publication of such a report could decrease the use of ineffective (and censorious) practices, helping safeguard free inquiry. It would also demonstrate the effective use of empirical work to change dominant practices, perhaps fulfilling some of the equity promises that DEI bureaucracies have failed to deliver. Further, it could begin to disarm the ubiquitous charges of racism greeting anyone who proposes halting ineffective practices.

Fourth, we should exempt the social sciences from IRB oversight. Willy Chertman argues that Congress never intended to include the social sciences.[58] Going further, the federal government could offer researchers a separate fast-track agency to approve research, giving university-level bureaucrats some competition. Going still further, a campus might require attendees at IRB meetings to swipe their ID cards at a meeting's start and end, enabling software to automatically calculate the amount of salary money spent on each meeting. (That could work for all required meetings.)[59]

Fifth, we must do better at K–12 education, teaching students about the importance of free inquiry and the failures of Marxist and other regimes that crushed dissenters in the name of increasing equity. As the authors of Chapters 9 (Catherine Salmon and Lee Jussim) and 17 (Anna I. Krylov and Jay Tanzman) show, it is a travesty that Trofim Lysenko is not a household name. American Birthright or a similar K–12 social studies and history curriculum could help.[60] Ideally, Hollywood might also contribute, because ridicule is sometimes the best form of education. Unfortunately, except for the British film *The Death of Stalin*, it is difficult to think of popular entertainment showing how Marxism works (fails!) in practice.

Sixth, on college campuses, just as the US Department of Education now mandates Title IX–related training, it should also use financial levers to mandate training on free speech and free inquiry for students and faculty. National and state governments should stop funding institutions that threaten free speech and free inquiry and disallow federal grant funding for travel to conferences that require ideological litmus tests and for research published in journals requiring such tests. (After all, taxpayers would not fund trips to venues run by the Ku Klux Klan or pay open access fees for journals run by Hamas—at least not yet.) Such statutes and regulations would not be controversial and would likely survive court

214 THE FREE INQUIRY PAPERS

challenges. The US government should also pay contractors such as FIRE to survey college students and faculty, issuing regular reports on where First Amendment rights are respected and where they are not. Sunshine is the best disinfectant.

Of course, it is one thing to write legislation but quite another to implement it. Here, we can rely on the wisdom of the American founders, who knew that ambition must be made to counteract ambition, helped by public oversight.[61] Accordingly, using the leverage of funding or defunding, governments must insist that higher education institutions have bureaucracies oriented around free inquiry and free speech to counter DEI and other bureaucracies that oppose such freedoms. To take this further, just as we have a US Civil Rights Commission with state-level advisory committees promoting its work—I serve on the one for Arkansas—we need a US First Amendment Commission with its own 50 state advisory committees. If the 14th Amendment has a bureaucracy, so too must the First Amendment. As Downs reminds us,[62] unfortunately, the only way to control a bureaucracy is to create another bureaucracy. More bureaucracies? Sadly, there is no other way.

Without these or similar reforms, US higher education will return, at best, to the real bad old days of the 1800s, when colleges existed to indoctrinate preachers and entertain elite youth or, at worst, to medieval days when indoctrination was the *only* mission, century after century. To paraphrase Winston Churchill, if we do not defeat the current variant of Marxism, we could enter a new dark age, made more enduring by the power of perverted science and bureaucracy. Only Marxists and religious zealots—who are often one and the same—want that.

Notes

1. Dwight D. Eisenhower, "Military-Industrial Complex Speech," Yale Law School, Lillian Goldman Law Library, Avalon Project, 1961, https://avalon.law.yale.edu/20th_century/eisenhower001.asp.

2. Robert Maranto, "The Death of One Best Way: Charter Schools as Reinventing Government," in *School Choice in the Real World: Lessons from Arizona Charter Schools*, ed. Robert Maranto et al. (New York: Routledge, 2001), 39–57.

3. Anthony Downs, *Inside Bureaucracy* (Boston, MA: Little, Brown and Company, 1967).

4. Theodore J. Lowi, *The End of Liberalism: The Second Republic of the United States*, 2nd ed. (New York: W. W. Norton & Company, 1979); Vincent Ostrom, *The Intellectual Crisis in American Public Administration* (Tuscaloosa, AL: University of Alabama Press, 1973); Andrew F. Krepinevich Jr., *The Army and Vietnam* (Baltimore, MD: Johns Hopkins University Press, 1986); Raymond E. Callahan, *Education and the Cult of Efficiency: A Study of the Social Forces That Have Shaped the Administration of the Public Schools* (Chicago: University of Chicago Press, 1962); and Robert Maranto and Jonathan Wai, "Why Intelligence Is Missing from American Education Policy and Practice, and What Can Be Done About It," *Journal of Intelligence* 8, no. 1 (March 2020), https://www.mdpi.com/2079-3200/8/1/2.

5. Downs, *Inside Bureaucracy*; and William A. Niskanen Jr., *Bureaucracy and Representative Government* (Chicago: Aldine-Atherton, 1971).

6. Robert Maranto, "Thinking the Unthinkable in Public Administration: A Case for Spoils in the Federal Bureaucracy," *Administration and Society* 29, no. 6 (January 1998): 623–42; and Robert Maranto, *Beyond a Government of Strangers: How Career Executives and Political Appointees Can Turn Conflict to Cooperation* (Lanham, MD: Lexington Books, 2005).

7. Downs, *Inside Bureaucracy*.

8. Max Weber, "Bureaucracy," in *Classics of Public Administration*, rev. ed., ed. Jay M. Shafritz and Albert C. Hyde (Oak Park, IL: Moore, 1978), 23–28.

9. Maranto and Wai, "Why Intelligence Is Missing from American Education Policy and Practice, and What Can Be Done About It."

10. Benjamin Ginsberg, *The Fall of the Faculty: The Rise of the All-Administrative University and Why It Matters* (Oxford, UK: Oxford University Press, 2011).

11. William G. Ouchi, "Markets, Bureaucracies, and Clans," *Administrative Science Quarterly* 25, no. 1 (March 1980): 129–41.

12. Downs, *Inside Bureaucracy*.

13. Karen M. Hult and Charles Walcott, *Governing Public Organizations: Politics, Structures, and Institutional Design* (Pacific Grove, CA: Brooks/Cole, 1990).

14. Manuel P. Teodoro, Samantha Zuhlke, and David Switzer, *The Profits of Distrust: Citizen-Consumers, Drinking Water, and the Crisis of Confidence in American Government* (Cambridge, UK: Cambridge University Press, 2022).

15. Maranto, *Beyond a Government of Strangers*.

16. Milton Friedman, *Capitalism and Freedom* (Chicago: University of Chicago Press, 1962).

17. Keith E. Whittington, *Speak Freely: Why Universities Must Defend Free Speech* (Princeton, NJ: Princeton University Press, 2018).

18. Jal Mehta and Steven Teles, "Professionalization 2.0: The Case for Plural Professionalism in Education," in *Teacher Quality 2.0: Will Today's Reforms Hold Back Tomorrow's Schools?*, ed. Michael Q. McShane and Frederick M. Hess (Cambridge, MA: Harvard Education Press, 2014).

19. Ostrom, *The Intellectual Crisis in American Public Administration*.

20. Steve Kelman, *Procurement and Public Management: The Fear of Discretion and the Quality of Government Performance* (Washington, DC: AEI Press, 1990).

216 THE FREE INQUIRY PAPERS

21. Charles M. Payne, *So Much Reform, So Little Change: The Persistence of Failure in Urban Schools* (Cambridge, MA: Harvard Education Press, 2008).

22. William R. Corson, *The Betrayal* (New York: W. W. Norton & Company, 1968).

23. Noah Coburn, *Losing Afghanistan: An Obituary for the Intervention* (Stanford, CA: Stanford University Press, 2016).

24. Thomas Sowell, *Black Education: Myths and Tragedies* (New York: McKay, 1972); Ginsberg, *The Fall of the Faculty*; and Jay P. Greene, "DeSantis Calls the Bureaucrats' Bluff," *Washington Examiner*, February 10, 2023, https://www.washingtonexaminer.com/restoring-america/equality-not-elitism/desantis-calls-the-bureaucrats-bluff.

25. Even before our committee got involved, participants were instructed to spit out rather than drink the wine (which totaled just eight ounces), and pregnant women were told not to take part. This meeting was hardly unusual.

26. Robert Maranto, "Why American School Corruption Remains Hidden: Diagnoses and Prescriptions for Reform," *International Journal for Education Law and Policy* 15 (2020): 55–65.

27. Sowell, *Black Education*.

28. Barry Bozeman, Jan Youtie, and Jiwon Jung, "Death by a Thousand 10-Minute Tasks: Workarounds and Noncompliance in University Research Administration," *Administration & Society* 53, no. 4 (April 2021): 527–68, https://journals.sagepub.com/doi/full/10.1177/0095399720947994.

29. Willy Chertman, "It's Time to Review the Institutional Review Boards," Center for the Study of Partisanship and Ideology, June 29, 2022, https://www.cspicenter.com/p/its-time-to-review-the-institutional.

30. David Rogers, 110 *Livingston Street: Politics and Bureaucracy in the New York City School System* (Clinton Corners, NY: Percheron Press, 2006).

31. Ginsberg, *The Fall of the Faculty*; and Greene, "DeSantis Calls the Bureaucrats' Bluff."

32. Downs, *Inside Bureaucracy*; and Niskanen, *Bureaucracy and Representative Government*.

33. Ginsberg, *The Fall of the Faculty*; and Robert Maranto, Catherine Salmon, and Lee Jussim, "Cut Their Pay and Make Them Teach," RealClearEducation, June 9, 2022, https://www.realcleareducation.com/articles/2022/06/09/cut_their_pay_and_make_them_teach_110737.html.

34. Robert Maranto, "A Political Scientist Runs for School Board," *PS: Political Science & Politics* 51, no. 1 (January 2018): 154–58, https://www.cambridge.org/core/services/aop-cambridge-core/content/view/BA938AD1E6442D821082184D8E3439A1/S1049096517001858a.pdf/div-class-title-a-political-scientist-runs-for-school-board-div.pdf; and Maranto, "Why American School Corruption Remains Hidden."

35. Daniel Golden, *The Price of Admission: How America's Ruling Class Buys Its Way into Elite Colleges—and Who Gets Left Outside the Gates* (New York: Three Rivers Press, 2007); and Frederick M. Hess, "Don't Give Campus Admissions Officials a Free Pass in College Admissions Scandals," *Forbes*, October 12, 2021, https://www.forbes.com/sites/frederickhess/2021/10/12/dont-give-campus-officials-a-free-pass-in-college-admissions-scandals.

36. Downs, *Inside Bureaucracy*; and Maranto, *Beyond a Government of Strangers*.

37. Krepinevich, *The Army and Vietnam*.

38. Maranto and Wai, "Why Intelligence Is Missing from American Education Policy and Practice, and What Can Be Done About It."

39. Maranto, *Beyond a Government of Strangers*.

40. Craig Frisby and Robert Maranto, "The Intellectual Fragility of White Fragility," Minding the Campus, August 27, 2020, https://www.mindingthecampus.org/2020/08/27/the-intellectual-fragility-of-white-fragility.

41. Greene, "DeSantis Calls the Bureaucrats' Bluff."

42. Frisby and Maranto, "The Intellectual Fragility of White Fragility."

43. John McWhorter, *Woke Racism: How a New Religion Has Betrayed Black America* (New York: Portfolio Penguin, 2021).

44. R. Shep Melnick, *The Transformation of Title IX: Regulating Gender Equality in Education* (Washington, DC: Brookings Institution Press, 2018).

45. Laura Kipnis, *Unwanted Advances: Sexual Paranoia Comes to Campus* (New York: Harper, 2017).

46. Alice Dreger, *Galileo's Middle Finger: Heretics, Activists, and One Scholar's Search for Justice* (New York: Penguin Books, 2015).

47. Darel E. Paul, *From Tolerance to Equality: How Elites Brought America to Same-Sex Marriage* (Waco, TX: Baylor University Press, 2018).

48. Charles Asher Small et al., "The Corruption of the American Mind: How Foreign Funding in U.S. Higher Education by Authoritarian Regimes, Widely Undisclosed, Predicts Erosion of Democratic Norms and Antisemitic Incidents on Campus," Network Contagion Research Institute and Institute for the Study of Global Antisemitism and Policy, 2023, https://networkcontagion.us/wp-content/uploads/NCRI-Report_The-Corruption-of-the-American-Mind.pdf.

49. Jay P. Greene and James Paul, "Diversity University: DEI Bloat in the Academy," Heritage Foundation, July 27, 2021, https://www.heritage.org/education/report/diversity-university-dei-bloat-the-academy.

50. Jay P. Greene and James Paul, "Inclusion Delusion: The Antisemitism of Diversity, Equity, and Inclusion Staff at Universities," Heritage Foundation, December 8, 2021, https://www.heritage.org/education/report/inclusion-delusion-the-antisemitism-diversity-equity-and-inclusion-staff.

51. Robert Maranto, "Why Students Back Hamas and What Educators Should Do About It," *Star Tribune*, November 8, 2023, https://m.startribune.com/why-students-back-hamas-and-what-educators-should-do-about-it/600318317.

52. Robert Maranto, "Thinking About Low Performers," *PA Times* 31, no. 8 (2008): 10–11; and Allison Stanger, *Whistleblowers: Honesty in America from Washington to Trump* (New Haven, CT: Yale University Press, 2019).

53. Chertman, "It's Time to Review the Institutional Review Boards."

54. Greene, "DeSantis Calls the Bureaucrats' Bluff."

55. Greene and Paul, "Diversity University"; and Greene and Paul, "Inclusion Delusion."

56. Richard Arum and Josipa Roksa, *Academically Adrift: Limited Learning on College Campuses* (Chicago: University of Chicago Press, 2011); Richard Arum and Josipa

218 THE FREE INQUIRY PAPERS

Roksa, *Aspiring Adults Adrift: Tentative Transitions of College Graduates* (Chicago: University of Chicago Press, 2014); and Ginsberg, *The Fall of the Faculty*.

57. Robert Maranto, "Work, Not Woke—Why on Race, U.S. Higher Education Should Copy the U.S. Army," Minding the Campus, March 4, 2021, https://www.mindingthecampus.org/2021/03/04/work-not-woke-why-on-race-u-s-higher-education-should-copy-the-u-s-army.

58. Chertman, "It's Time to Review the Institutional Review Boards."

59. I credit this idea to the late George Denny.

60. Maranto, "Why Students Back Hamas and What Educators Should Do About It."

61. Ostrom, *The Intellectual Crisis in American Public Administration*.

62. Downs, *Inside Bureaucracy*.

14

Can Intellectual Diversity Be Recovered in Academia?

George R. La Noue

A university's ultimate goal should be to assemble faculty and students in exercises to understand the truth about the major problems of human existence. That is why society should and does make such enormous investments in higher education. The issues may range from scientific to philosophical, but the key to analyzing and understanding them is to approach them from different disciplines, methodologies, databases, and values. Without such intellectual diversity, higher education can become an echo chamber of dominant ideologies.

The Framework of Intellectual Diversity

At one time, there was widespread agreement about the role of intellectual diversity and free expression in higher education. In 1940, the American Association of University Professors, working with the Association of American Colleges, issued its famous "Statement of Principles on Academic Freedom and Tenure," which has since been endorsed by more than 250 scholarly and education groups. It asserts that academic freedom is not just to protect individuals or institutions; it also is essential for the common good, which depends on free speech in the search for truth. Consequently, there should be full freedom to conduct research and publish results. Faculty should also have freedom in the classroom to discuss their subject, though they should not "introduce into their teaching controversial matter which has no relation to their subject."[1]

In 1967, the University of Chicago formed the faculty-dominated Kalven Committee to prepare "a statement on the University's role in political and social action." The committee found that the

220 THE FREE INQUIRY PAPERS

mission of the university is the discovery, improvement, and dissemination of knowledge. . . .

Since the university is a community only for these limited and distinctive purposes, it is a community which cannot take collective actions on the issues of the day . . . without inhibiting that full freedom of dissent on which it thrives.[2]

In 1974, after concern about controversial speakers invited to Yale, then-President Kingman Brewster appointed a committee mostly comprising faculty and chaired by the distinguished historian C. Vann Woodward to construct a speech policy. In the classic Woodward Report, the committee reached this consensus:

The primary function of a university is to discover and disseminate knowledge by means of research and teaching. To fulfill this function a free exchange of ideas is necessary not only within its walls but with the world beyond as well. It follows that the university must do everything possible to ensure within it the fullest degree of intellectual freedom. The history of intellectual growth and discovery clearly demonstrates the need for unfettered freedom, the right to think the unthinkable, discuss the unmentionable, and challenge the unchallengeable. To curtail free expression strikes twice at intellectual freedom, for whoever deprives another of the right to state unpopular views necessarily also deprives others of the right to listen to those views.[3]

Federal courts also have been similarly interested in protecting an open intellectual atmosphere on campus. When Paul Sweezy, an economist at the University of New Hampshire, refused to answer questions by that state's attorney general about his lectures and political beliefs, he was found in contempt. Sweezy then appealed to the Supreme Court, which in 1957 articulated a vigorous defense of academic freedom:

The essentiality of freedom in the community of American universities is almost self-evident. No one should underestimate the vital role in a democracy that is played by those who guide and train our youth. To impose any strait jacket upon the intellectual leaders in our colleges and universities would imperil the future of our Nation. No field of education is so thoroughly comprehended by man that new discoveries cannot yet be made. Particularly is that true in the social sciences, where few, if any, principles are accepted as absolutes. Scholarship cannot flourish in an atmosphere of suspicion and distrust. Teachers and students must always remain free to inquire, to study and to evaluate, to gain new maturity and understanding; otherwise, our civilization will stagnate and die.[4]

In 1972, the Supreme Court unanimously struck down a decision by Central Connecticut State College to not certify a chapter of Students for a Democratic Society for use of campus spaces, ostensibly on the grounds that its national organization might engage in violence. Justice Lewis F. Powell wrote in *Healey v. James*,

Yet the precedents of this Court leave no room for the view that, because of the acknowledged need for order, First Amendment protections should apply with less force on college campuses than in the community at large. Quite to the contrary, "[t]he vigilant protection of constitutional freedom is nowhere more vital than in the community of American schools." . . . The college classroom with its surrounding environs is peculiarly the "marketplace of ideas," and we break no new constitutional ground in affirming this Nation's dedication to safeguarding academic freedom.[5]

In 1995, the Court began to develop a doctrine of viewpoint neutrality in public universities, at least regarding the allocation of student activity fees. In protecting students' right to distribute a religious publication, it once again asserted the importance of campus free speech:

The quality and creative power of student intellectual life to this day remains a measure of a school's influence and attainment.

222 THE FREE INQUIRY PAPERS

> For the University [of Virginia], by regulation, to cast disapproval on particular viewpoints of its students risks the suppression of free speech and creative inquiry in one of the vital centers for the Nation's intellectual life, its college and university campuses.[6]

Threats to Intellectual Diversity

Despite the seeming convergence of academic leaders and jurists on free speech, their lofty past affirmations do not describe current realities. In 2021, the Bipartisan Policy Center (BPC), based in Washington, DC, issued the report *Campus Free Expression: A New Roadmap*.[7] The blue-ribbon panel was co-chaired by Jim Douglas, former governor of Vermont, and Chris Gregoire, former governor of Washington state, and included six former or current presidents of various types of colleges and universities, as well as four other specialists. The members took their task seriously and met online weekly. A panel of students was assembled to provide their perspective on campus speech issues. Another group of presidents and trustees was given the final draft for their comments.

The co-chairs' letter prefacing the report states,

> America is suffering a crisis of confidence in many of its leading institutions. Among the most important institutions whose trust among the public has sharply fallen in recent years is higher education. . . .
>
> We believe a major cause is the erosion of a campus culture of free expression and open inquiry.[8]

The report's executive summary begins as follows:

> There is overwhelming survey research and other evidence that the intellectual climate on many college and university campuses is being constrained. Faculty are being deterred from exploring certain subjects and expressing candid opinions even off campus; students are self-censoring; outside

CAN INTELLECTUAL DIVERSITY BE RECOVERED IN ACADEMIA? 223

speakers are disinvited and events are being canceled. Social media has become a megaphone that amplifies campus controversies, increasing their intensity and visibility, compressing time frames for leadership response, and leading to investigation and sanctioning of faculty and students. The traditional understanding of free speech as a liberalizing force is being called into question.

. . . Rather than alleviating the political polarization in our nation today, the inhibition of campus speech is degrading the civic mission of higher education, which is to maintain our pluralistic democracy by preparing students for civic participation as independent thinkers who can tolerate contrary viewpoints and work constructively with those with whom they have principled disagreements.[9]

So why has the United States moved from an era in which higher education was almost universally admired, according to the BPC report, to a period of sharply decreased public trust and the erosion of a campus culture of free expression and open inquiry? There are multiple answers to this question but no simple solutions.

One problem is that academic professional associations, university administrators, faculty senates, and student activists commonly demand institutional commitments to various political causes that leave dissenters in perilous positions. The 1967 Kalven Committee view that such collective actions suppress diverse ideas is now quite archaic.

Of course, people in the academy should have the right to express their political viewpoints. The trend of institutional proclamations, however, becomes more coercive because of the increasing partisan homogeneity of those who control campus discourse. When Everett Ladd and Seymour Lipset wrote *The Divided Academy* in 1975, they found that 37 percent of the faculty older than age 55 identified as Republicans, compared to only 18 percent of those under 35.[10] Thirty years later, a 2005 national survey by Stanley Rothman, S. Robert Lichter, and Neil Nevitte found that 72 percent of all faculty described themselves as liberals and only 15 percent as conservatives; in departments of English literature, philosophy, political science, and religious studies, at least 80 percent of faculty considered themselves liberals, and no more than 5 percent thought of themselves as conservative.[11]

Institutions with selective admissions and large endowments that educate many of America's leaders may be even more one-sided. Mitchell Langbert and his colleagues remeasured the political affiliations of faculty in economics, history, journalism and communications, law, and psychology at elite institutions in 2016. Overall, their research showed professors registered as Democrats outnumbered Republicans by 11.5 to one. There were striking differences among university campuses, however. At Pepperdine, Democrats only slightly outnumbered Republicans (1.2 to one), and at Ohio State, the ratio was 3.2 Democrats to one Republican. Yet at institutions with high-profile professional and graduate programs in those fields, the ratios of Democrats to Republicans were as follows: Harvard, 10 to one; Stanford, 11 to one; Duke, 11 to one; Cornell, 13 to one; University of California, Berkeley, 14 to one; New York University, 16 to one; Yale, 16 to one; Massachusetts Institute of Technology, 19 to one; University of Maryland, 26 to one; Princeton, 30 to one; Columbia, 30 to one; Johns Hopkins, 35 to one; and Brown, 60 to one.[12]

Faculty with similar partisan identifications may not agree on all issues, but there is another powerful campus movement that demands more conformity on values. A new genre of campus bureaucrats who enforce but do not carefully define diversity, equity, and inclusion (DEI) now control de facto speech policy on many campuses. Despite its benign-sounding name, DEI raises many questions about free speech, free assembly, and equal protection on campuses.

The DEI tidal wave has flooded much of higher education. In 2021, the Heritage Foundation completed a survey of DEI officials in 65 universities in the "power five" athletic conferences, which serve 2.2 million students. It found about 3,000 staff members with DEI responsibilities in these institutions. The average was 45.1 DEI officers per campus, and many campuses had more DEI officers than history professors.[13]

DEI bureaucrats generally do not teach or advise students or conduct research. Their mission and duties are to monitor the hiring and evaluation of employees and the admission and conduct of students. They use concepts and procedures that rarely have well-defined boundaries. These bureaucrats are like political commissars who do not produce anything but

CAN INTELLECTUAL DIVERSITY BE RECOVERED IN ACADEMIA? 225

are ideologically empowered to oversee the speech and behavior of those who do. If there was ever a finding that a campus no longer had a DEI problem, they would no longer have a job. So the search for DEI violations is never-ending.

The BPC report states, "While campuses have become more diverse in many ways, they have become increasingly ideologically conformist."[14] A 2020 Gallup poll found that 49 percent of undergraduates say free speech conflicts with diversity and inclusion occasionally and 27 percent said it does so frequently.[15]

Research confirms that few universities are committed to intellectual diversity or even ideological neutrality in advertising for faculty and other positions.[16] But what to do about this problem and who should take action remain unclear. Imposed off-campus remedies may be clumsy and possibly illegal.

What Can Be Done?

Reform can take place through restructuring campus programming, reducing ideological messaging, and, where necessary, bringing litigation.

In his 2021 book *What Universities Owe Democracy*, Ronald J. Daniels, the current president of Johns Hopkins University, noted,

> To a striking degree, our campuses have come to be constructed around the isolated speaker rather than debate or exchange. Classes are predominantly taught by a single teacher or lecturer. Outside speakers brought to campus are just that: speakers. . . . Commencements are memorialized by individual speakers who hold forth to a captive audience. This . . . suggest[s] to our students that the highest ideal of a thinker is proclamation, and that ideas are meant to be developed hermetically and then broadcast to the world rather than cultivated in an ongoing dialogue with others who might disagree or refine them. . . . How can university leaders and faculty complain about how our students don't know how to debate or disagree effectively when we don't even try to reveal to them what it looks like? . . . The bottom line

226 THE FREE INQUIRY PAPERS

then is that university leaders need to be more creative in seeking opportunities to model for our students productive interactions across difference.[17]

President Daniels is right about the harms of overreliance on the single-speaker model. Invited speakers are usually experts in a particular field and paid guests of the campus. Few persons in the audience may have the necessary knowledge to ask serious questions about the speaker's premises or conclusions. There may be conflicts of interest between the inviter and the invitee, whether financial or collegial. Few institutions have rules to avoid such problems or policies requiring that there be diversity of ideological viewpoints among the speakers they invite.

An obvious alternative for the campuses that claim to be "marketplaces of ideas" is to sponsor a series of debates or forums with multiple perspectives, particularly on major public policy issues. The BPC report proclaims, "As a country, we must be better at robustly and respectfully debating difficult policy issues across the political spectrum, and college campuses have an essential role in achieving this civic role."[18] Nearly all students are old enough to vote, and such events might offset the campus partisan imbalance and reassure the public of institutional fairness.

One might assume that such policy debates and forums would feature regularly on campus calendars. Yet my research shows a massive avoidance of that responsibility by colleges and universities. A national stratified survey of 97 campuses and 28 law schools covering 24 major public policy issues in 2014 and 2015 documented that few issues were the subject of institutionally sponsored open debates. Almost no university had any organized program for these debates comparable to campus-sponsored athletic, musical, or theatrical programming.[19] When that same research template was applied to all 35 public and private campuses in North Carolina in the 2018 and 2019 academic years, before COVID-19 struck, the same dismal reality was found.[20]

Both reports covered multiple years and large databases, and both came to the same conclusions. Almost all campuses avoid such events, and no campuses were found that devoted as much staff time and fiscal resources to helping students understand the policy problems that confront them and their country comparable to what they spend on their most minor sports team.

In 2023, Florida became the first state to require its public campuses to sponsor public policy debates. The legislation's preface states,

> The Legislature finds that the advancement of knowledge is the fundamental purpose of the State University System and that such advancement is facilitated by the fearless sifting and winnowing of a wide diversity of views and that the open discussion and debate of contested public policy issues from diverse perspectives provides essential preparation for mature citizenship and an informed exercise of the right to vote.[21]

In addition to forbidding the use of political tests or DEI in hiring on Florida public campuses, the law requires each campus to have an "Office of Public Policy Events" that will organize or stage public policy debates or group forums at least four times a year. Campuses must maintain a searchable, current calendar of such events, and these programs must be accessible to all students, faculty, and staff and be videotaped and preserved.[22]

Nearly three-quarters of all college students attend public institutions, where First Amendment free speech requirements protect them and the institutions' employees. Further, courts have found that if a private campus has made academic freedom part of its contracts, it must honor those obligations.[23] Currently, much campus messaging about speech is purposefully ambiguous, with repressive impact.[24] Microaggressions are not hate speech, and with certain exceptions, hate speech is not illegal. Colleges and universities should make unapologetic statements citing relevant legal authority outlining the distinction between protected and unprotected speech for faculty and students. These statements should be used in orientation for new students, and some faculty may want to include them in their syllabi.

DEI and Title IX bureaucrats have the power of investigation, which can be triggered by a single student's anonymous complaint. Some of the country's most prominent scholars—Laura Kipnis at Northwestern University, Jonathan Haidt at New York University, and Ilya Shapiro at Georgetown University—have faced lengthy investigations for their comments about public policy.

228 THE FREE INQUIRY PAPERS

Almost all campuses have generic statements about academic freedom and due process, but as John Hasnas, professor of business ethics at Georgetown, argues,

> No college or university administrator benefits from a clear distinction between prohibited conduct and protected speech. Deans want the freedom to act quickly to quiet dissension without being burdened by having to draw distinctions between individuals who feel aggrieved by actionable conduct and those who feel aggrieved by intellectual assertions they find repugnant. Similarly, the jobs of the institution's [DEI] bureaucracy staff are infinitely easier if they do not have to make such distinctions, and its mission of stamping out all things that make protected minorities feel unwelcome or unsafe is significantly advanced by ignoring this distinction.[25]

Consequently, Hasnas wants campuses to take a more proactive stance advocating what he calls a "safe harbor provision" that states,

> The University will summarily dismiss any allegation that an individual or group has violated a policy of the university if the allegation is based solely on the individual's or group's expression of his, her, or its religious, philosophical, literary, artistic, political, or scientific viewpoints.[26]

Such a provision would inhibit the perverse incentives now on campus to avoid distinctions between protected and unprotected speech and would keep persons and groups from being the target of punitive investigations of their speech.

Universities today are awash in the language of social justice, racial justice, gender justice, environmental justice, land acknowledgment justice, and, of course, DEI. Required affirmations of those ambiguous concepts are increasing in campus hiring and even in promotion and tenure evaluations.[27]

By 2019, eight of the 10 University of California campuses required DEI statements from all faculty applicants. The DEI-compelled speech mandate can be influential in the employment process. Andrew Gillen found that for a single University of California, Berkeley, life sciences position, 679 of 893 applicants were eliminated because their DEI statements were thought insufficient.[28]

One potential response to this trend is for faculty, trustees, and legislators to demand that terms such as racial and gender justice be carefully defined in ways that do not make universities a further reflection of partisan agendas. Public campuses should have policies forbidding the use of ideological, political, and religious tests by search committees for faculty, staff, and students in hiring, admissions, and access to campus facilities. They should also have a system for monitoring whether parts of the institution are using such tests.[29]

Finally, litigation has been necessary to clarify the gap between campus practices and legal protections. To date, most litigation conflicts over DEI rules have been resolved in favor of free speech. In a 2010 case, Hispanic plaintiffs sued the college for failing to discipline a mathematics professor who criticized "La Raza," immigration, and multiculturalism while lauding Western civilization and Columbus Day. The Ninth Circuit panel, including retired Supreme Court Associate Justice Sandra Day O'Connor sitting by special designation, ruled that the college could not discipline the professor, even though his remarks were inconsistent with its diversity policy. In Chief Judge Alex Kozinski's words,

> The Constitution embraces such a heated exchange of views, even (perhaps especially) when they concern sensitive topics like race, where the risk of conflict and insult is high. . . . Without the right to stand against society's most strongly-held convictions, the marketplace of ideas would decline into a boutique of the banal, as the urge to censor is greatest where debate is most disquieting and orthodoxy is most entrenched. . . . The right to provoke, offend and shock lies at the core of the First Amendment.
>
> This is particularly so on college campuses. Intellectual advancement has traditionally progressed through discord and dissent, as a diversity of views ensures that ideas survive because they are correct, not because they are popular. Colleges

230 THE FREE INQUIRY PAPERS

and universities—sheltered from currents of popular opinion by tradition, geography, tenure and monetary endowments—have historically fostered that exchange. But that role in our society will not survive if certain points of view may be declared beyond the pale.[30]

The University of Michigan, the University of Illinois Urbana-Champaign, the University of Houston, the University of Texas, and Iowa State University have lost in federal courts when Speech First sued them for enforcing ambiguous and overbroad speech and harassment codes. The organization's most recent victory was a unanimous Eleventh Circuit opinion criticizing, in strong terms, a speech code at the University of Central Florida (UCF). The court described UCF's policy in this way:

> The bias-related-incidents policy creates a mechanism by which a UCF student can be anonymously accused of an act of "hate or bias"—*i.e.*, an "offensive" act, even if "legal" and "unintentional," that is directed toward another based on any of a number of characteristics. . . . [UCF] "monitor[s]" and "track[s]" bias-related incidents, "coordinate[s] university resources," marshals a "comprehensive response[]," and, where necessary, coordinates "interventions" among affected parties.[31]

The identities that UCF thought needed protection were race, national origin, religion or non-religion, genetic information, sex, and political affiliation. In a university attended by 55,000 students, implementing that mission could create a lot of work for the DEI bureaucracy.

In perhaps the key exchange in this case's oral argument, the UCF lawyer was asked from the bench whether the following statements would violate the university's discrimination and harassment policy: (1) "Abortion is immoral," (2) "unbridled open immigration is a danger to America on a variety of levels," and (3) "the Palestinian movement is antisemitic."[32] The lawyer replied that he did not think the statements would be proscribed, but he could not say for sure because "the university will consider all the facts and circumstances there."[33] The court responded, "If UCF's own attorney—as one intimately familiar with the University speech policies—can't tell whether a particular statement would violate the policy, it seems eminently fair to conclude that the school's students can't either."[34]

In concurring, Judge Stanley Marcus wrote that UCF's policy

> touches on every conceivable topic that may come up on a college campus. . . . The specter of punishment for expressing unorthodox views on these topics stifles rigorous intellectual debate. And the harm is not limited to professors and students while they are on campus. Our future civic and scientific leaders surely will take these values with them after graduation.[35]

He concluded with this sentence, which is likely to be quoted for some time: "A university that turns itself into an asylum from controversy has ceased to be a university; it has just become an asylum."[36]

The history of civil rights enforcement shows that only significant financial penalties and other sanctions can enforce compliance. In 2020, the University of Washington had to pay $122,000 in legal fees to settle a free speech infringement lawsuit after a federal judge found it used punitive security fees for groups inviting some outside speakers.[37] The University of Iowa more recently faced a stiffer penalty of almost $2 million in legal fees after illegally de-registering some student groups because of their leadership criteria.[38] An occasional financial slap on the wrist may be a useful reminder about public campuses' First Amendment responsibilities. More important, however, is the warning in the BPC report to the whole higher education community that the continued weakening of free expression and intellectual diversity on campuses is eroding public support for higher education institutions and for democracy itself.

Notes

1. Hans-Joerg Tiede, "New Report on Prevalence of AAUP Policies in Higher Ed," Academe Blog, July 20, 2020, https://academeblog.org/2020/07/20/new-report-on-prevalence-of-aaup-policies-in-higher-ed.

2. Kalven Committee, "Report on the University's Role in Political and Social Action," University of Chicago, Office of the Provost, November 11, 1967, https://provost.uchicago.edu/sites/default/files/documents/reports/KalvenRprt_0.pdf.

3. Yale College, Committee on Freedom of Expression at Yale, "Report of the Committee on Freedom of Expression at Yale," December 23, 1974, https://yalecollege. yale.edu/get-know-yale-college/office-dean/reports/report-committee-freedom-expression-yale.

4. *Sweezy v. New Hampshire*, 354 US 234 (1957).

5. *Healy v. James*, 408 US 169, 180 (1972).

6. *Rosenberger v. University of Virginia*, 515 US 819, 835–36 (1995).

7. Bipartisan Policy Center, *Campus Free Expression: A New Roadmap*, November 2021, https://bipartisanpolicy.org/download/?file=/wp-content/uploads/2021/11/BPC-Report-Campus-Free-Expression_A-New-Roadmap.pdf.

8. Bipartisan Policy Center, *Campus Free Expression*.

9. Bipartisan Policy Center, *Campus Free Expression*.

10. Everett Carl Ladd Jr. and Seymour Martin Lipset, *The Divided Academy: Professors and Politics* (New York: McGraw-Hill, 1975).

11. Stanley Rothman, S. Robert Lichter, and Neil Nevitte, "Politics and Professional Advancement Among College Faculty," *The Forum* 3, no. 1 (January 2005), https://www. degruyter.com/document/doi/10.2202/1540-8884.1067/html.

12. Mitchell Langbert, Anthony J. Quain, and Daniel B. Klein, "Faculty Voter Registration in Economics, History, Journalism, Law, and Psychology," *Economic Journal Watch* 13, no. 3 (September 2016): 422–51, https://econjwatch.org/File+download/944/LangbertQuainKleinSept2016.pdf?mimetype=pdf.

13. Jay P. Greene and James D. Paul, "Diversity University: DEI Bloat in the Academy," Heritage Foundation, July 27, 2021, https://www.heritage.org/sites/default/files/2021-07/BG3641_0.pdf.

14. Bipartisan Policy Center, *Campus Free Expression*.

15. Knight Foundation and Gallup, *The First Amendment on Campus 2020 Report: College Students' Views of Free Expression*, 2020, 1, 16–17, https://knightfoundation.org/wp-content/uploads/2020/05/First-Amendment-on-Campus-2020.pdf.

16. Sean T. Stevens and Debra Mashek, "Non-Discrimination Statements at the Institutional Level & What to Do About It," Heterodox Academy, November 27, 2017, https://heterodoxacademy.org/blog/non-discrimination-statements-at-the-institution-level-what-to-do-about-it-part-1; and Sean T. Stevens and Debra Mashek, "Hiring in Higher Ed: Do Job Ads Signal a Desire for Viewpoint Diversity?," Heterodox Academy, December 1, 2017, https://heterodoxacademy.org/blog/hiring-in-higher-ed-do-job-ads-signal-a-desire-for-viewpoint-diversity-part-2.

17. Ronald J. Daniels, Grant Shreve, and Phillip Spector, *What Universities Owe Democracy* (Baltimore, MD: Johns Hopkins University Press, 2021).

18. Bipartisan Policy Center, *Campus Free Expression*, 4.

19. George R. La Noue, *Silenced Stages: The Loss of Academic Freedom and Campus Policy Debates* (Durham, NC: Carolina Academic Press, 2019).

20. George R. La Noue, "Political Reality on North Carolina Campuses: Examining Policy Debates and Forums with Diverse Viewpoints," James G. Martin Center for Academic Renewal, February 17, 2021, https://www.jamesgmartin.center/2021/02/political-reality-on-north-carolina-campuses-examining-policy-debates-and-forums-with-diverse-viewpoints.

CAN INTELLECTUAL DIVERSITY BE RECOVERED IN ACADEMIA? 233

21. Fla. H.B. 931, Postsecondary Educational Institutions (2023), https://www.flsenate.gov/Session/Bill/2023/931/BillText/er/PDF.

22. Fla. H.B. 931, Postsecondary Educational Institutions.

23. Colleen Flaherty, "Divided Wisconsin Supreme Court Backs Marquette Faculty Blogger," *Inside Higher Ed*, July 8, 2018, https://www.insidehighered.com/news/2018/07/09/wisconsin-supreme-court-says-marquette-must-reinstate-professor-it-wanted-fire.

24. George R. La Noue, "DEI Hiring Statements: Common Good Ethics or Partisan Loyalty Oaths?," *Academic Questions* 36, no. 2 (Summer 2023): 23–27, https://www.nas.org/academic-questions/36/2/dei-hiring-statements-common-good-ethics-or-partisan-loyalty-oaths/pdf.

25. John Hasnas, "Free Speech on Campus: Countering the Climate of Fear," *Georgetown Journal of Law & Public Policy* 20 (2022): 996, https://www.law.georgetown.edu/public-policy-journal/wp-content/uploads/sites/23/2022/12/Hasnas.pdf.

26. Hasnas, "Free Speech on Campus: Countering the Climate of Fear," 988.

27. Foundation for Individual Rights and Expression, "FIRE Statement on the Use of Diversity, Equity, and Inclusion Criteria in Faculty Hiring and Evaluation," https://www.thefire.org/research-learn/fire-statement-use-diversity-equity-and-inclusion-criteria-faculty-hiring-and.

28. Andrew Gillen, "The Impact of the Left's Takeover of Academia on the Quality of Higher Education," Areo, April 29, 2020, https://areomagazine.com/2020/04/29/the-impact-of-the-lefts-takeover-of-academia-on-the-quality-of-higher-education; and Robert Maranto and James D. Paul, "Other Than Merit: The Prevalence of Diversity, Equity, and Inclusion Statements in University Hiring," American Enterprise Institute, November 8, 2021, https://www.aei.org/research-products/report/other-than-merit-the-prevalence-of-diversity-equity-and-inclusion-statements-in-university-hiring.

29. George R. La Noue, "Time to Challenge Compelled Speech?," Law & Liberty, March 29, 2022, https://lawliberty.org/time-to-challenge-compelled-speech.

30. *Rodriguez v. Maricopa County Community College District*, 605 F.3d 703, 708 (9th Cir. 2010).

31. *Speech First v. Cartwright*, 32 F.4th 1110 (11th Cir. 2022).

32. *Speech First v. Cartwright*, 32 at 1123.

33. *Speech First v. Cartwright*, 32 at 1131.

34. *Speech First v. Cartwright*, 32 at 1151.

35. *Speech First v. Cartwright*, 32 at 1110.

36. *Speech First v. Cartwright*, 32 at 1110.

37. Katherine Long, "UW to Pay $122,500 in Legal Fees in Settlement with College Republicans over Free Speech," *Seattle Times*, June 18, 2018, https://www.seattletimes.com/seattle-news/uw-to-pay-127000-in-legal-fees-in-settlement-with-college-republicans-over-free-speech.

38. Elizabeth Redden, "Iowa Pays Nearly $2 Million in Christian Student Group Suits," *Inside Higher Ed*, December 7, 2021, https://www.insidehighered.com/quicktakes/2021/12/08/iowa-pays-nearly-2-million-christian-student-group-suits.

15

Merit, Fairness, and Equality: An Alternative to Diversity, Equity, and Inclusion

Dorian S. Abbot, Iván Marinovic,
and Carlos M. Carvalho

Diversity, equity, and inclusion (DEI) bureaucracies are now ubiquitous at universities. However, DEI is in tension with the telos of a university: the pursuit of truth through the production and dissemination of knowledge. DEI programs also violate the moral principles of treating all human beings equally and not using them as mere instruments to achieve sociopolitical ends. To protect universities' integrity, we need an alternative to the DEI agenda.

The widespread adoption of DEI has been facilitated by faculty and administrators who were told that DEI would reduce bias and lead to a fairer system. We propose an alternative to DEI: merit, fairness, and equality (MFE), which aims to deliver on the promise DEI initially made—namely, unbiased selection.[1] MFE acknowledges that biases may affect a selection process and seeks to eliminate them, but it maintains a strict meritocratic framework in which every candidate is treated equally and fairly. Crucially, MFE is concerned primarily with establishing fair processes and would never try to impose quotas or racial preferences, nor would it restrict speech, as DEI often does. In sum, MFE would deliver on the promise that DEI makes but cannot accomplish: It would reduce bias and lead to a fairer system while maintaining strict academic standards, promoting freedom of expression, and advancing universities' core mission.

In this chapter, we lay out MFE in detail and contrast it with DEI. First, we discuss our criticisms of DEI. Then we give an outline for MFE and a guide for practical implementation at a university. Finally, we respond to objections to MFE and draw some conclusions.

Criticism of DEI

DEI is a utopian ideology. It seeks to enforce equality of outcome across identity groups, notably race and sex, although the exact goal is poorly defined because the reference population for determining appropriate representation could be based on the city, state, country, or world. It employs a bureaucracy convinced that "systemic bias" is the main (and often only allowable) explanation for any underrepresentation of women and minorities in activities and scientific disciplines. DEI never considers alternative explanations for underrepresentation in some disciplines (e.g., theoretical physics) other than a conspiracy carried out by the oppressor (i.e., white and Jewish men) against the oppressed.

Like many and perhaps all utopian ideologies, DEI is illiberal. It is becoming increasingly apparent that DEI is fundamentally hostile to free expression and open inquiry.[2] Universities are making official commitments to the DEI doctrine, something unprecedented for institutions previously devoted to the unfettered search for truth. In many places, applicants are asked to sign loyalty oaths to DEI to be considered for faculty or administrative positions. Others are sanctioned for their speech and in some cases even fired.[3] Mandatory DEI training for students and faculty is spreading rapidly across universities, a flagrant violation of the freedom of conscience.[4]

The utopian nature of DEI reaches tragicomic levels in its attempt to create a more "inclusive" environment by codifying and sanctioning "microaggressions"—comments that could upset someone, even unintentionally.[5] This very idea and the arbitrary nature of the list of microaggressions can only produce fear, segregation, and mistrust: exactly the opposite of inclusion. It is also a radical departure from charity, a fundamental principle for any liberal institution.

A crucial factor in the adoption of DEI has been the bait-and-switch method. Stakeholders are promised that DEI will promote "fairness," only to find later that the DEI version of fairness involves explicit discrimination based on race and sex, as well as violations of free speech and academic freedom on campus. One source of this confusion is that the terms "diversity," "equity," and "inclusion" sound good but are not being used with their traditional definitions. Most importantly, equity in the DEI sense does not mean fair and impartial treatment. Instead, it means enforced equal outcomes based on identity group or even preferential outcomes for so-called traditionally oppressed, marginalized, or minoritized identities.

Moreover, when many people agree to increasing diversity, they think they are endorsing diverse perspectives, opinions, and political orientations, which might improve educational outcomes, but this is neither the goal nor the outcome of DEI initiatives. Diversity in DEI is generally restricted to favored identity groups, usually those defined by innate characteristics such as race and sex.

Finally, inclusion is the most counterintuitive of the trio because it often means just the opposite: exclusion of "undesirables" and "deplorables." For example, under DEI, politically conservative Christians can be excluded because of the worry that their perspectives and arguments might upset progressives, homosexuals, or feminists.[6] Ultimately, this exclusion is an attack on Martin Luther King Jr.'s "dream" and the principles of the civil rights movement.

Our primary argument against DEI is ethical: DEI contravenes the basic moral principle that all human beings should be treated equally. It mandates discrimination against applicants based on group membership, which is an affront to their inherent dignity and human rights. Furthermore, DEI treats human beings merely as means to a political end. This shows a surprising disregard for the lessons of history: The catastrophic ideologies of the 20th century also sacrificed individual dignity for the sake of collective social utopias.

DEI encourages identity politics, thereby eroding social cohesion. It is oriented around quotas and set-asides for favored identity groups, which encourages tribalism and balkanization. It teaches that the best way to improve your situation in life is through identity warfare and identity politics activism, rather than diligence and hard work. If we want to see the effects of this type of thinking on a society, look no further than Lebanon or Iraq, where identity politics rules the roost.

DEI heavily uses Herbert Marcuse's concept of repressive tolerance, which asserts that society has not progressed enough to allow the free exchange of ideas, so nonprogressive expression must be restricted.[7] One aspect of this is overt political discrimination through the vilification of nonprogressive perspectives, often via official emails and statements on university websites issued by university leaders and DEI officers. Moreover, attempts to prevent moderates and conservatives from entering the professoriat have become common through DEI statements that compel progressive political speech during the application process.[8]

Additionally, widespread enforcement of DEI ideology through required training and a hostile atmosphere—created by the fear of cancellation by student mobs encouraged by DEI administrators—is forcing moderate and conservative professors out of academia and into industry or retirement. Finally, aggressive use of "bias response teams" chills speech by imposing unconstitutional impediments to free expression, even at public universities.[9]

DEI's antagonism toward free expression extends beyond political discrimination to academic freedom and open inquiry on campus. DEI encourages academics to think of themselves primarily as activists rather than seekers of truth. The truth may not be consistent with the ideology or the social change that is sought, and DEI prioritizes ideology when such a conflict arises. Academics who pursue honest, data-based research that yields findings inconsistent with DEI dogma can be skewered on social media and in letters of denunciation presented to their chairs and deans and eventually sanctioned. (See, for example, the case of Roland Fryer at Harvard University.[10]) They can be deplatformed, disciplined, or dismissed because their findings are not "inclusive" and hearing them might "harm" students.[11] Since universities' fundamental purpose is the production and dissemination of knowledge, "inclusion" defined in this way represents an existential threat to their core mission.

Finally, DEI is bad for the people it claims to help. While most have earned their spot as legitimate members of the academic community, their claim to legitimacy is undermined. DEI infantilizes members of favored groups and discourages them from developing an independent identity based on intellectual perspective rather than innate characteristics. It insulates students and faculty from alternative perspectives and worldviews, so that when they encounter these ideas, they are unable to provide rational counterarguments and instead cry,[12] scream,[13] sputter nonsense, or demand that their interlocutors be silenced.[14]

Outline of MFE

In MFE, all academic decisions are based on academic *merit*. In this way, each applicant and idea is treated *fairly* and not evaluated based on any irrelevant criteria. This promotes the mission of universities: the production of knowledge. It also produces a morally justified approach. In deference to their individual dignity, each person is treated *equally* and given an *equal* shot.

MFE is what many people originally thought DEI was. MFE acknowledges that biases exist and seeks to eliminate them, but it maintains a focus on academic excellence, the pursuit of truth, and the meritocratic selection of students and faculty. MFE seeks to identify and use unbiased predictors of performance in evaluations and is always open to better predictors if they can be identified. The key point, however, is that the metric for success is always academic excellence and the resulting distribution of immutable characteristics among those selected is never taken into account.

An MFE-based hiring or admissions process must strive to treat each applicant equally and impartially. It must therefore avoid any attempt to artificially enforce quotas, targets, or set-asides based on group identity. Ideally, a search would be as blind to non-merit criteria as possible. For example, a hiring committee might not discover the candidates' identity characteristics until the job interview, and an undergraduate admissions committee might never discover them.

Moreover, searches would favor objective criteria over subjective and easily manipulated criteria such as "fit" or "personality." Leaders would encourage a culture in which applicants are not discriminated against for their political beliefs through lectures, directions for hiring initiatives, and training. Crucially, overt political discrimination such as compelled speech through "DEI statements" would be explicitly forbidden. In sum, all candidates would be equally welcome and have equal opportunity to compete and succeed. In other words, universities adopting an MFE approach would actively strive to implement hiring programs consistent with the Constitution and federal law,[15] rather than trying to skirt them.[16]

Part of developing fair hiring and admissions processes is providing appropriate accommodations for people with disabilities and trying to reduce biases that can be clearly identified. A critical examination of biases, however, must be free to identify and attempt to eliminate biases against any group, including those against Asians[17] and men.[18] Similarly, the mere presence of different success rates among different groups, in and of itself, can never be used as evidence that the process is biased. Because no social institution is free from error, it will be necessary to continually refine MFE hiring processes, monitoring for and addressing possible biases introduced by any metrics and algorithms and fixing any weaknesses in the system as a whole.

To effectively pursue the truth, a university must seek and encourage a diversity of viewpoints and opinions. Equality implies that each member of the academic community must have an equal opportunity for expression on campus. No idea should be off-limits simply because it offends someone.

Finally, the ideas generated need to be judged by the academic community based on their merits, not whether some authority deems them to be "disinformation" or even dangerous—and not based on the identity of the people promoting them. Ultimately, the university's goal is to identify those most likely to make contributions to human knowledge and give them a place that most facilitates creating such contributions, not to hand out rewards to individuals based on their status as representatives of some particular identity group and then insulate those individuals from uncomfortable knowledge and ideas.

A variety of other issues surrounding university functioning can be oriented around MFE. Grades in courses must be based on academic performance, with no other factors considered. Speaker invitations must be based on the merit of the speaker's arguments, not their innate attributes. Students should not feel intimidated about expressing politically unpopular opinions in class, and professors should strive to present multiple interpretations if there is legitimate disagreement on an issue. Professors should not force their own ideological commitments on their classes. Scholarly citations and reading lists must be based on the intellectual quality of the cited works, not the authors' identity.

Practical Implementation of MFE

The first step for a university wishing to adopt an MFE framework is to officially enact policies to support it. A good starting point is the "Chicago trifecta" of the Edward Shils report,[19] the Kalven Report,[20] and the "Chicago principles."[21] The Shils report mandates that faculty hiring and promotion decisions be made using only research, teaching, contribution to intellectual community, and service, with a strong preference for research. Each university can tailor such a statement to its own needs—for example, giving preference to teaching—while ensuring that only relevant skills are considered.

Moreover, similar reports could be adopted guaranteeing that admission is based on only past and prospective academic achievement. The Kalven Report mandates that the university, and any of its units, cannot take an official stance on any social or political issue. This should rule out admissions and hiring based on identity characteristics; to do so is to take a social and political stand. So the Kalven Report reinforces the Shils report. But it also protects dissenting scholars who advocate political positions that are unpopular on campus.

This point is taken further by the Chicago principles, which explicitly guarantee all community members the right to make intellectual arguments unmolested and unpunished, even if someone else claims to be deeply offended. The Chicago trifecta provides a strong starting point that any university can adopt to immediately promote MFE on its campus.

After appropriate policies are in place, they must be rigorously enforced. Incoming students and faculty need to be made aware of them, and there must be real consequences for violations. For example, if a department can be shown to have made a hire for non-merit-based reasons, the department chair should be held accountable and, in some cases, even lose their position. If a dean or provost is found to have pressured a department chair to make a non-merit-based hire, they should be held accountable. If students disrupt a seminar because they disagree with the speaker, they should be penalized and in some cases expelled.

This may seem harsh, but strict enforcement of policies with real teeth is necessary in the current situation. (For example, hundreds of law students at Yale University in March 2022 disrupted an intellectual discussion on free expression and physically endangered the participants. They faced no consequences.[22])

The responsibility for enforcing an MFE regime ultimately rests with the university president and the board of trustees that appoints the president. Individuals in these positions need to be selected carefully and take seriously the grave responsibility with which they have been entrusted. Additionally, a university could appoint an officer to oversee and enforce MFE.

Debunking Myths About MFE

A few myths have spread about MFE. Here we debunk them.

MFE does not advance the social good. A university's primary role is the production and dissemination of knowledge. This pursuit has proved to be of immense social good. Universities do not need to apologize for doing their job and try to find some other social benefit to justify their existence. The pursuit of truth is sufficient, and we must be ready to confidently assert this.

Moreover, since DEI impedes the production of knowledge, it actually interferes with the social good that universities do. If we appoint an engineering professor due to identity rather than competence and bridges start falling down, this is counterproductive to social welfare. Meritocracy itself serves the social good. We hire LeBron James to play basketball simply because he is the best, and society as a whole benefits from watching him play, regardless of whether he deserves his gift. Similarly, society benefits when we identify, train, and employ the most talented airplane designers, software engineers, and surgeons. It is true that some young people have advantages that others lack and this can be ameliorated somewhat by making sure everyone has access to high-quality education, but all people benefit when resources are allocated to those best able to exploit and develop them.

Meritocracy is a myth. The objection that meritocracy is a myth is a rhetorical sleight of hand. The claim is that because humans design

242 THE FREE INQUIRY PAPERS

meritocratic evaluations, these evaluations will always have flaws; therefore, we should end meritocratic evaluations altogether and select candidates using other criteria. But this is a logical error: The latter does not follow from the former. Meritocratic evaluations are not perfect, but the way to deal with this is to continually improve them through quantitative analyses, longitudinal studies of eventual success, and careful reflection on potential biases.

To take a practical example, many departments have recently stopped requiring the Graduate Record Examination (GRE) for graduate school admissions. Of course, the GRE is not a perfect predictor of graduate school success, but it's the best one we have.[23] Moreover, it is the only metric rigorously evaluated for bias and proven to be unbiased in predicting later success.[24]

The real myth is that meritocracy is a myth, and it is being spread by people who are fundamentally not interested in producing the best scholars, science, and scholarship.

Diversity is an important aspect of merit. In the 1978 case *Regents of the University of California v. Bakke*, the Supreme Court found that immutable characteristics can be taken into account during admissions only if having a diverse student body can be shown to improve all students' educational experience.[25] Those advocating quotas and set-asides based on identity for "social justice" purposes then switched to arguing that increased diversity would improve the educational experience.

This is a disingenuous argument, however, because it is never extended to diversity of opinion or perspective. In fact, diversity based on immutable characteristics would be useful from an educational perspective only if it could be shown to increase viewpoint diversity. From an educational perspective, it is extremely counterproductive to select a student body that looks different from each other but all thinks alike, which is exactly what DEI attempts to do.

Despite occasional claims to the contrary, a meta-analysis of all available data shows that ethnic, racial, and sex diversity has a negative or neutral impact on team outcomes, whereas diversity in values and perspectives has a neutral or positive impact.[26] There is therefore no outcome-based justification for selecting less qualified candidates simply because they would make a team more diverse in terms of ethnicity, race, or sex.

Respect for diversity of opinions may allow heterodox thinkers or even extremists to spread offensive ideas. Strictly speaking, this last item is not really a myth because MFE allows community members to share views that someone might find offensive. But there is a well-known antidote to bad speech, should it occur: more speech, not suppression of speech. Thomas Jefferson put it best: A university should not be "afraid to tolerate any error so long as reason is left free to combat it."[27]

Moreover, the presence of heterodox opinions on campus is beneficial to all because sometimes they turn out to be right, and even when heterodox opinions are wrong, having to contend with them improves everyone else's arguments. In *On Liberty*, John Stuart Mill reminds us that "he who knows only his own side of the case knows little of that."[28]

Additionally, the most obvious effect that fostering a diversity of views will have is to create a less hostile environment for conservatives and moderates who are routinely subjected to discrimination on campus.[29] Finally, the extremist objection is usually not raised in reference to the 26 percent of sociology faculty and 18 percent of all social science faculty who self-identify as Marxists, which suggests that political bias is built into this objection.[30]

Conclusion

We propose MFE as a framework for student and faculty selection. Unlike DEI, MFE allows a university to address potential biases without violating the fair and equal treatment principle—and without sacrificing freedom of expression. The MFE concept does not belong to us, and we hope that others will adopt it as their own and build on it.

MFE is inherently adaptable to different situations and open to improvement through learning and experimentation. The more universities adopt MFE and share the knowledge generated, the better it will become. Even if a university is unwilling to adopt MFE, individuals can strive to practice it by advocating for merit-based hiring and promotions and freedom of expression on campus.

244 THE FREE INQUIRY PAPERS

Acknowledgments

Three additional authors contributed to this work but cannot reveal their identites due to potential retaliation.

Notes

1. Dorian S. Abbot and Iván Marinovic, "The Diversity Problem on Campus," *Newsweek*, August 12, 2021, https://www.newsweek.com/diversity-problem-campus-opinion-1618419.

2. Foundation for Individual Rights and Expression, "FIRE Statement on the Use of Diversity, Equity, and Inclusion Criteria in Faculty Hiring and Evaluation," June 2, 2022, https://www.thefire.org/issues/fire-statement-on-the-use-of-diversity-equity-and-inclusion-criteria-in-faculty-hiring-and-evaluation.

3. Alex Galbraith, "UCF Professor Fired Following Controversial Tweets About 'Black Privilege' Has Job Reinstated," *Orlando Weekly*, May 20, 2022, https://www.orlandoweekly.com/news/ucf-professor-fired-following-controversial-tweets-about-black-privilege-has-job-reinstated-31635697; and David Acevado, "Tracking Cancel Culture in Higher Education," National Association of Scholars, May 13, 2022, https://www.nas.org/blogs/article/tracking-cancel-culture-in-higher-education.

4. James D. Paul and Robert Maranto, "Other Than Merit: The Prevalence of Diversity, Equity, and Inclusion Statements in University Hiring," American Enterprise Institute, November 8, 2021, https://www.aei.org/research-products/report/other-than-merit-the-prevalence-of-diversity-equity-and-inclusion-statements-in-university-hiring.

5. University of California, Santa Cruz, "Tool: Recognizing Microaggressions and the Messages They Send," November 12, 2014, https://academicaffairs.ucsc.edu/events/documents/Microaggressions_Examples_Arial_2014_11_12.pdf.

6. Dan O'Donnell, "Concordia University Professor Suspended for Criticizing School's Wokeness," WIBA, February 22, 2022, https://wiba.iheart.com/featured/common-sense-central/content/2022-02-22-concordia-university-professor-suspended-for-criticizing-schools-wokeness.

7. Herbert Marcuse, "Repressive Tolerance," in *A Critique of Pure Tolerance*, ed. Robert Paul Wolff, Barrington Moore Jr., and Herbert Marcuse (Boston, MA: Beacon Press, 1965), https://www.marcuse.org/herbert/publications/1960s/1965-repressive-tolerance-1969.pdf.

8. University of California, Santa Cruz, "Tool"; and Abigail Thompson, "A Word From . . .," *Notices of the American Mathematical Society* 66, no. 11 (December 2019): 1778–79, https://www.ams.org/journals/notices/201911/rnoti-p1778.pdf.

9. *Speech First v. Gregory L. Fenves*, 979 F.3d 319 (5th Cir. 2020), https://reason.com/wp-content/uploads/2020/10/SpeechFirstvFenves.pdf.

MERIT, FAIRNESS, AND EQUALITY 245

10. Good Kid Productions, "How Claudine Gay Canceled Harvard's Best Black Professor. (Mini-Doc)," YouTube, March 9, 2022, https://www.youtube.com/watch?v=m8xWOlk3WIw&t=49s&ab_channel=GoodKidProductions.

11. Collen Flaherty, "Victim, or Astronomy's Icarus?," *Inside Higher Ed*, November 4, 2021, https://www.insidehighered.com/news/2021/11/04/astronomer-withdraws-paper-amid-concerns?v2.

12. Carlin Becker, "Hysterical Yale Students Cry and Scream at Their 'Racist' Professor," *Washington Examiner*, September 15, 2016, https://www.washingtonexaminer.com/red-alert-politics/hysterical-yale-students-cry-scream-racist-professor-video.

13. Caroline Downey, "Activists Riot During Campus Speech, Assault Father Who Was Denied Custody of Son After Contesting Transgender Diagnosis," *National Review*, March 3, 2022, https://www.nationalreview.com/news/activists-riot-during-campus-speech-assault-father-who-was-denied-custody-of-son-after-contesting-transgender-diagnosis.

14. Peter Beinhart, "A Violent Attack on Free Speech at Middlebury," *The Atlantic*, March 6, 2017, https://www.theatlantic.com/politics/archive/2017/03/middlebury-free-speech-violence/518667.

15. *Manning Rollerson v. Brazos River Harbor Navigation District of Brazoria County Texas, Now Known as Port Freeport; United States Army Corps of Engineers*, 6 F.4th 633 (5th Cir. 2021), https://www.ca5.uscourts.gov/opinions/pub/20/20-40027-CV0.pdf.

16. Louis K. Bonham, "Fighting Behind Enemy Lines: Three Tactics for Resisting Wokeness from Within," Minding the Campus, December 22, 2021, https://www.mindingthecampus.org/2021/12/22/fighting-behind-enemy-lines-three-tactics-for-resisting-wokeness-from-within.

17. *Students for Fair Admissions v. President and Fellows of Harvard College*, 346 F. Supp. 3d 174 (D. Mass. 2018), https://lawyerscommittee.org/wp-content/uploads/2020/07/Docket-413_SFFA-Memo-in-Sppt-of-SJ.pdf.

18. Mark J. Perry, "Let's Work Together to Challenge the Selective Double Standard for the Enforcement of Title VI and Title IX in Higher Education," Heterodox STEM, March 22, 2022, https://hxstem.substack.com/p/lets-work-together-to-challenge-the.

19. Edward Shils et al., "A Report of the University of Chicago Committee on the Criteria of Academic Appointment," *University of Chicago Record* 4, no. 6 (December 1970), https://provost.uchicago.edu/sites/default/files/documents/reports/shilsrpt_0.pdf.

20. Kalven Committee, "Report on the University's Role in Political and Social Action," University of Chicago, Office of the Provost, November 11, 1967, https://provost.uchicago.edu/sites/default/files/documents/reports/KalvenRprt_0.pdf.

21. Geoffrey R. Stone et al., "Report of the Committee on Freedom of Expression," University of Chicago, 2014, https://provost.uchicago.edu/sites/default/files/documents/reports/FOECommitteeReport.pdf.

22. Aaron Sibarium, "Hundreds of Yale Law Students Disrupt Bipartisan Free Speech Event," Washington Free Beacon, March 16, 2022, https://freebeacon.com/campus/hundreds-of-yale-law-students-disrupt-bipartisan-free-speech-event.

23. Nathan R. Kuncel, Sarah A. Hezlett, and Deniz S. Ones, "A Comprehensive Meta-Analysis of the Predictive Validity of the Graduate Record Examinations:

Implications for Graduate Student Selection and Performance," *Psychological Bulletin* 127 (2001): 162, https://pubmed.ncbi.nlm.nih.gov/11271753; Nathan R. Kuncel and Sarah A. Hezlett, "Standardized Tests Predict Graduate Students' Success," *Science* 315 (2007): 1080–81, https://psycnet.apa.org/record/2007-03168-001; and Nathan R. Kuncel, Khue Tran, and S. H. Zhang, "Measuring Student Character: Modernizing Predictors of Academic Success," in *Higher Education Admissions Practices: An International Perspective*, ed. María Elena Oliveri and Cathy Wendler (Cambridge, UK: Cambridge University Press, 2020), 276–302.

24. Kuncel, Hezlett, and Ones, "A Comprehensive Meta-Analysis of the Predictive Validity of the Graduate Record Examinations."

25. Peter Wood, "Regime Change: Repelling the DEI Assault on Higher Education," National Association of Scholars, June 13, 2022, https://www.nas.org/blogs/statement/regime-change-repelling-the-dei-assault-on-higher-education.

26. Jie Wang et al., "Team Creativity/Innovation in Culturally Diverse Teams: A Meta-Analysis," *Journal of Organizational Behavior* 40, no. 6 (July 2019): 693–708, https://onlinelibrary.wiley.com/doi/abs/10.1002/job.2362.

27. Thomas Jefferson, *The Life and Selected Writings of Thomas Jefferson: Including the Autobiography, the Declaration of Independence & His Public and Private Letters* (New York: Random House, 1998).

28. John Stuart Mill, *On Liberty and Other Essays* (New York: Oxford University Press, 1998).

29. Eric Kaufmann, "Academic Freedom in Crisis: Punishment, Political Discrimination, and Self-Censorship," Center for the Study of Partisanship and Ideology, March 1, 2021, https://www.cspicenter.com/p/academic-freedom-in-crisis-punishment.

30. Neil Gross and Solon Simmons, "The Social and Political Views of American Professors" (working paper, Harvard University Symposium on Professors and Their Politics, Cambridge, MA, 2007), 41, https://www.researchgate.net/publication/228380360_The_Social_and_Political_Views_of_American_Professors.

16

Rhetorical Jujitsu: Leveraging Campus DEI to Promote Ideological Diversity

Richard E. Redding

Today's cancel and censorship culture poses a significant threat to free speech and open inquiry.[1] Colleges and universities, having been captured by progressive thought and professors,[2] are the origin and incubator of this culture. The academy frequently encourages self-censorship, thereby stifling free speech;[3] excludes ideas and people who do not conform to progressive ideology; and indoctrinates students.[4] These students later take this progressive ideology into the workplace, sometimes with the zeal of social justice warriors.[5]

The academy has perpetuated this censorious culture in part through its "diversity" and "diversity, equity, and inclusion" (DEI) projects, which have spread to organizations throughout American society. In the DEI regime, censorship is seen as a worthy pursuit by protecting students and faculty from ideological viewpoints deemed offensive or inaccurate by the politically progressive majority.[6] As Professor Kaleb Demerew points out, this produces a number of pernicious and often unintended effects, including stifling viewpoint diversity, encouraging campus factionalization into favored in-groups versus out-groups and antagonism among such groups, fueling political polarization and feelings of victimization, reducing interaction among groups and individuals with diverse views, and siloing students and faculty in ideological bubbles.[7]

However, DEI's critics have mostly been conservatives sitting outside the academy. The few vocal critics in the academy have often been subjected to withering attacks from colleagues and students, as was the case in 2021 with geophysics professor Dorian S. Abbot at the University of Chicago.[8] The critics' arguments have already persuaded much of the public, as well as some politicians and university board members, which is important in promoting reform. Some states, like Texas and Florida, have passed legislation or promulgated regulations that ban or curtail DEI programs in state universities[9] (a step that perhaps goes too far as a matter of government regulation), and as of early 2024, 13 other states have such legislation pending in the state legislature.[10] But legislation will not pass in all of these states, and 35 states have no such legislation.

Legislation, therefore, is not enough. We also need to persuade the professoriat and university administrators (many of whom are also professors). They control the campus climate and DEI programs and can likely circumvent any legislation or other mandates against DEI. Even those professors and administrators who may be skeptical of DEI and would like to modify it in various ways feel hemmed in by "the constraints on college diversity policymaking [that] come from deeply ingrained institutional norms."[11]

For example, after affirmative action was outlawed in university admissions, some universities simply implemented affirmative action indirectly. They admitted all students who graduated in the top 10 percent of their high school classes, eliminated SAT or ACT test requirements, or based admissions decisions much more on subjective factors such as application essays that discuss the adversities and discrimination that applicants report experiencing.[12]

We will never persuade the academy to jettison its diversity projects. In any case, I agree with the diversity project in principle, just not the ways it has been practiced—that is, all too often through exclusionary programs and policies and in a manner that fails to include ideological diversity.

Rather, we must persuade the academy that DEI should include ideological diversity. The persuasive strategy most likely to convince (some of) the professoriat is to draw on empirical research, conducted by the professors themselves, to show how DEI's values and goals are furthered through ideological diversity and how doing so serves the professors' own personal and professional interests. This rhetorical jujitsu leverages the DEI narrative to show how, on its own terms, the project is compelled to foster ideological diversity.

In this chapter, after highlighting the societal importance of effecting systemic change in the academy and describing current efforts to challenge its DEI project, I outline the contours of a strategy for persuading the professoriat and the psychological research supporting that strategy.

Ultimately, the best way to ensure ideological diversity in the academy is to diversify faculties so that they include not just progressives and liberals but also conservatives, libertarians, and centrists. But this long-term endeavor cannot succeed unless university faculties see ideological diversity as being a relevant component of their DEI project.

Our Cancel Culture: A Long Time Coming from the Academy

The academy has always tilted strongly to the left. But about 25 years ago, ultraprogressive, Marxist, and critical ideologies began to dominate the academic landscape. The young assistant professors and administrators were more liberal and strident in their politics—with 18 percent of professors considering themselves "Marxist" and 25 percent calling themselves "radical";[13] there were virtually no conservatives or libertarians among them.[14] They established a campus culture of ideological hegemony and intolerance that became entrenched in classrooms, as well as in scholarly and professional work.

The ideological capture of the academy produced a left-wing authoritarianism involving restrictions on free speech and academic freedom, censorship, the denouncement or cancellation of speakers and professors, and discrimination against nonprogressive students, faculty, and prospective faculty.[15] Consider these developments in light of the fact that the professoriat produces most of the policy-relevant research in the United States; is often relied on by policymakers for its expertise; has an outsized influence on major professional organizations such as the American Bar Association, the American Medical Association, and the American Psychological Association;[16] produces the next generation of K–12 teachers and shapes public education policy; and is responsible for teaching our future scholars, professionals, executives, and leaders.

Yet conservatives and libertarians outside the academy seemed to care little about what was happening in the ivory tower. Surely, they thought, students were wise enough not to buy their professors' progressive politics—and even if they accepted it as students, they would shed those politics when they went to work in the real world.[17] Certainly, the larger society and corporate America would never accept it. How wrong they were!

250   THE FREE INQUIRY PAPERS

The new professoriat took as its mission the indoctrination of students, hoping the students would later become the foot soldiers in a cultural revolution, as the influential leftist philosophy professor Herbert Marcuse had urged.[18] The indoctrinated students then entered the workforce, where they spread the totalizing and intolerant ideologies in which they had been inculcated. Some of these graduates, particularly in strategic fields like personnel management, used their received ideological views to shape the human resources and philanthropy policies of corporations and nonprofit organizations. Many eventually became the leaders of those organizations.

By starting in the academy, the left was eventually able to capture the main cultural influencers and drivers: education, government, the media and entertainment, and corporate America.[19] As Karl Marx and the socialist educator John Dewey (who more than anyone else was responsible for designing America's public school system) were keenly aware, those who control the educational system control the culture.[20]

Over the past five years, the progressive professoriat and bloated university bureaucracies developed a new vehicle—known as DEI—to advance their ideological agenda. Conceived in the academy, DEI initiatives mushroomed not only there but also, after the 2020 George Floyd murder, in organizations throughout American society. Now, virtually every college, university, major corporation, and nonprofit organization has DEI mission statements, programs, and officers.

DEI is the more aggressive and exclusionary successor to the diversity project that also began in the academy.[21] As with DEI, the diversity imperative spread to organizations throughout society. But diversity meant every kind of (demographic) diversity except for ideological diversity.[22] (I use the term "ideological diversity" rather than "viewpoint diversity" because the views that are suppressed specifically involve sociopolitical, moral, or cultural issues.)

Often, DEI programs operate to suppress open inquiry and marginalize or exclude non-progressives. Thus, conservatives and libertarians sometimes refer to DEI as "discrimination, exclusion, and indoctrination." In many universities—particularly the elite ones—applicants for faculty positions and graduate programs and faculty up for promotion or tenure must or are strongly encouraged to provide a "DEI statement" outlining how they contribute to DEI.[23] University committees often use such statements to screen out those who do not subscribe to progressive ideological dogma and social justice activism in their teaching, scholarship, or other professional activities.[24]

Challenging the Prevailing DEI Narrative

Frontal challenges to the value of DEI are bound to be rejected by university faculty and administrators who, after all, are the ones who designed the DEI policies and programs in the first place. Though much has been written about the lack of ideological diversity on campus, little has been said about how to persuade professors to reorient DEI in favor of ideological diversity. Yet it is the professoriat that plays the pivotal role in shaping DEI and campus culture.

Now is an opportune time to begin persuasive efforts with the professoriat because recent antisemitic events on campus have raised professors' awareness of the broader problem of sociopolitical and ideological conformity and intolerance on campus. Alan Dershowitz, for instance, recently said that the tolerance of antisemitism on college campuses is a direct consequence of their DEI policies.[25] Notably, a study of the tweets of university DEI administrators finds that 96 percent of those about Israel (which are numerous) are negative. By comparison, 62 percent of the tweets about China are positive, even though China is a repressive totalitarian regime that does not tolerate free speech, imprisons dissenters, and practices the forced sterilization of its Muslim minority.[26] Even the liberal commentator Fareed Zakaria lambasted universities for becoming politicized and captured by DEI ideology.[27]

In a relatively strong bipartisan vote by today's standards, the US House of Representatives called for the resignation of the presidents of the Massachusetts Institute of Technology and Harvard after their congressional testimony demonstrated that their concern for the safety and inclusivity of minority groups did not extend equally to Jews.[28] Ironically, the university presidents defended their actions based on the need to protect free speech. Even more indicative of the true nature of DEI is that Harvard President Claudine Gay was a key architect of its ambitious

DEI program,[29] which, no doubt, was one of the factors that propelled her into the Harvard presidency. It is perhaps not surprising that Harvard has the lowest rating of any university in the nation on free speech measures,[30] with its ranking declining during Gay's tenure as a senior university administrator.

We must change faculty attitudes about DEI's meaning and goals so that it encompasses a commitment to ideological diversity that affirmatively includes diverse views in teaching, scholarly work, and university life. It is crucial that universities recruit and hire faculty and graduate students with conservative, libertarian, and centrist viewpoints to create a more ideologically diverse academic landscape. Currently, faculties are ideologically self-replicating, not only because they like to hire those who share their values and so discriminate against those who do not but also because non-progressives are disincentivized from seeking faculty positions because they perceive that the academic climate is hostile to their values and scholarly interests.[31]

Persuading the Professoriat About the Value of Ideological Diversity to DEI

We need a message tailored to the professoriat's values. Nothing is more cherished in the academy than diversity and DEI. Arguments directly challenging these cherished values will likely only have the counterproductive effect of triggering emotional reactions. (One reason diversity training is ineffective in changing attitudes is that it often produces such defensiveness.)[32]

Like everyone else, professors are biased to accept arguments that are consistent with their ideological values because they are so emotionally invested in those values, which play an important role in their professional identity. Highly educated, intelligent people like professors are just as prone to such biases and intolerance,[33] as they can recruit their knowledge and intelligence to construct arguments bolstering their preexisting worldviews.[34] Progressive researchers contend that nonminority group members often do not support DEI because they "perceive that discussions of diversity are not about them . . . [and thus] feel threatening."[35]

Similarly, however, progressive faculty members often do not perceive that DEI should include non-progressives.

Thus, to change faculty attitudes, I suggest a rhetorical jujitsu that leverages their own DEI narrative to show how the goals of DEI compel fostering ideological diversity on campus. We should meet professors where they are and provide a positive narrative as to how ideological diversity is consistent with DEI's values and goals. This is likely to be more persuasive than a negative narrative arguing against DEI.

I am not naive, however. Many will not find this rhetorical jujitsu to be persuasive, particularly given the natural human tendency and psychological need to justify and defend the status quo.[36] A foundational reason why academics favor ideological orthodoxy is that they see their progressive ideology as advancing the interests of marginalized or oppressed groups.[37] Moreover, doing so serves a virtue-signaling and social capital–building function.

Yet leveraging the DEI perspective may persuade traditional free speech liberals and civil libertarians and those still open-minded about what DEI should entail. Moreover, academic fields vary ideologically, so that some—for example, economics, business, and the natural sciences—will be more open to these arguments than others, such as the humanities and social sciences, gender studies, and ethnic studies.[38] We should explain how ideological diversity fits comfortably within DEI, which is an argument that professors should find pleasantly surprising. Messages with surprising or unexpected arguments are more persuasive;[39] this framing may be especially convincing because it may put academics in the psychologically and morally uncomfortable position of feeling hypocritical and unvirtuous by not endorsing ideological diversity.[40]

How the DEI Agenda Advances the Professoriat's Interests. Demerew's recent study of DEI at public and private universities in Texas identifies five prototypical professors and administrators with respect to their attitudes about the implementation of DEI at their institution: (1) the faith-rooted diversifier, (2) the risk manager, (3) the holistic visionary, (4) the public square advocate, and (5) the skeptical pragmatist.[41] Thus, some are true believers in DEI, some see it as a way to manage institutional risk, some take a broader view of diversity but see DEI as one vehicle for advancing certain diversity goals, and some are skeptical of the ideological and political nature of DEI but do subscribe to the goals of diversity and inclusion.[42]

Consider that professors' attitudes about DEI are utilitarian (i.e., shaping behaviors that serve their interests) and serve knowledge (i.e., providing a frame of reference for understanding the world), social identity (i.e., fostering identification with desired groups and mediating their relationships with members of those groups), and self-esteem needs in their academic lives.[43] Because persuasive appeals should be matched to these needs,[44] we must consider the interrelated utilitarian, knowledge, social identity, and self-esteem functions that the DEI project serves for academics.

Subscribing to the DEI agenda serves professors' needs and interests in five ways:

1. It is consistent with the received worldview in academia—which they have internalized—that demographic diversity is vital because it helps marginalized and oppressed groups.

2. It bolsters their self-esteem by making them feel virtuous because they are helping these groups.

3. It supports their social identity by virtue signaling to fellow academics that they are part of the DEI in-group.

4. It serves their interests by enhancing their social and political capital with their colleagues.

5. It serves their interests by hiring faculty and admitting graduate students who share their worldview, because we know from social psychological studies that people want to hire and work with those who are most like themselves attitudinally.[45]

Our persuasive efforts should target the *knowledge* function of professors' DEI attitudes because we can persuade them on that score by drawing on empirical research, discussed later, that the professoriat itself has conducted. Targeting their diversity worldview also simplifies the persuasive message, reducing it to a truism they already accept—that diversity is a good thing—while highlighting the gap between their diversity ideal and their practices and behaviors with respect to the ideologically diverse. We can instill in academics a sense of virtue and self-righteousness in promoting ideological diversity by showing how doing so is consistent with their worldview, so that not promoting it would be to act inconsistently with their virtuous worldview. Invoking guilt in this way is a proven persuasive strategy,[46] and it casts academics in the uncomfortable position of perpetuating the exclusionary status quo. It is especially important, however, to make the point that *promoting ideological diversity need not conflict with the social justice agenda of promoting the interests of marginalized and oppressed groups.*

How Ideological Diversity Advances the DEI Agenda. To consider how ideological diversity might be useful to the DEI agenda, we must understand the values and assumptions underlying the academy's diversity and DEI projects. These projects have focused nearly exclusively on disability, religious diversity (though less so with Christians, especially evangelicals),[47] and, most particularly, demographic diversity vis-à-vis oppressed identity groups.

This focus flows from several key assumptions and associated values underlying DEI. The first assumption is that people's demographic characteristics (and associated cultural backgrounds) are central to their personal identity. The second assumption is that people are often marginalized and discriminated against based on such characteristics. The third assumption is that with demographic diversity comes a diversity of life experiences, values, and ideas, which produces educational benefits.[48] There is also a fourth value underlying DEI, which is the social justice ethos of helping members of these minority groups whom they see as being victims of societal marginalization and oppression.[49] From these assumptions spring the DEI project: giving voice to these identities in pedagogy, scholarship, and university life; fashioning remedies for discrimination; and ensuring sufficient representation of identity groups among faculties and student bodies.

256 THE FREE INQUIRY PAPERS

Importantly, however, a sizable and compelling body of research in behavioral genetics, neuroscience, and social and personality psychology compels the conclusion that the assumptions about the importance of demographic diversity apply equally well—and perhaps even more so—to sociopolitical and ideological diversity. Space constraints do not permit a review of this extensive body of research, which readers can find elsewhere,[50] but the following is a brief précis of this research and its relevance to the key assumptions and values underlying DEI.

First, people's sociopolitical and ideological values are often as important to their psychological makeup and identity as are their demographic characteristics.[51] Ideological beliefs have a robust genetic and neurological basis, suggesting that they may be an essentialist feature of people. Behavior genetic studies show a substantial role for genetics in the sociopolitical attitudes that people develop, with the genetic influence on where people fall on the ideological spectrum being about 45–65 percent and roughly 30 percent on views on specific issues like abortion or gun control. Of course, our genes do not code for such attitudes, but our genetic makeup largely determines our personality, temperament, and cognitive styles, which, in turn, attract us to various ideological viewpoints.[52] Moreover, these traits linked to ideology are correlated with differences in brain structure and function, as shown by studies in the new field of political neuroscience.[53]

Given the strong biological substrate of political and ideological views, people usually do not change their ideological views significantly once they reach young adulthood. Indeed, they are "cultural expressions of a deep-seated genetic divide in human behavioral predispositions"[54] and are relatively resistant to change, with "psychological protection mechanisms developing around those attitudes."[55]

Thus, people's political and ideological beliefs are a core part of their personal identity and psychological makeup; these beliefs influence their view of themselves, their world, and their interpersonal relationships. Not surprisingly, therefore, their ideological views are integral to their sense of meaning, security, and self-esteem.[56] As many studies have shown, ideological and political values serve a psychological function similar to that of religious beliefs, providing a way for people to make sense of the world and a feeling of security and moral purpose. This is particularly the case today, when we seem to have moved from the age of religion to the age of ideology, with our ideological worldviews and tribes serving for many a quasi-religious and social identity function.

Second, people's ideological views affect how they view and relate to others.[57] Likes attract, and opposites repel. This is particularly the case when it comes to attitudes about ideology, politics, and morality. Ideological differences are often a source of prejudice and discrimination because opposing ideological values make us feel uncomfortable. They challenge our worldview and the sense of understanding, purpose, security, and belonging it provides. In fact, studies suggest that ideological-based prejudice is often a more potent source of discrimination than racial prejudice.[58]

It is important to raise awareness that people's ideological values are, to a large extent, an essentialist characteristic just like race or sexual orientation. People often discriminate against those who do not share their ideological values, with the inclination to align with like-minded individuals evident in hiring decisions and interpersonal relationships. Those belonging to the ideological minority in an organization, such as political non-progressives in the academy, also face discrimination.[59]

Third, ideological diversity produces substantial educational and professional benefits and enhances students' ability to work with people of diverse backgrounds.[60] Exposure to diverse perspectives also fosters students' moral development, personal growth, and tolerance of those different from themselves. Cabining off students or marginalized groups from diverse or ideologically uncomfortable views in the name of psychological safety makes students less safe in the long run by stifling their personal development and limiting their understanding of diverse perspectives; this understanding, in turn, reduces anxiety and fear while increasing tolerance.[61] In addition, ideological diversity among faculty enriches scholarly inquiry and leads to a more reliable and representative body of research, particularly on policy-relevant questions and sociopolitical issues; it also allows professors and those they train to better understand and serve the needs of diverse populations.[62]

Using Stories and Metaphors to Persuade. Metaphors and stories are especially powerful persuasive devices, particularly with respect to moral and ideological issues.[63] We ought to back up our empirical arguments with stories describing the costs of ideological hegemony that will resonate with our academic audience and use memorable metaphors to illustrate the relationship between demographic and ideological diversity.[64]

The following accounts illustrate the toll that ideological exclusion and marginalization take on students and young faculty, respectively:

> I remember experiencing a strong ethos of progressive politics in my undergraduate and graduate education. Other political points of view were never aired. Professors would often make denigrating comments about people like me who share my moral values and political views. I always felt marginalized and uncomfortable, and felt under constant pressure to "self-censor"—remembering that it was a very bad feeling to feel that expressing your opinions could reflect negatively on you and be used against you. I never raised my hand in class to offer an alternative viewpoint.[65]

> Many editors of scholarly journals and faculty who are on appointments or tenure committees will, for the most part, not be sympathetic to [your ideas].... Don't volunteer your views... [which is] very difficult ... because we chose to pursue a career relating to ideas, and we care passionately about them.... If you label yourself as [the ideological other] you are likely to invoke a whole set of stereotypes, and everything you say is going to be interpreted in light of them.[66]

The Messenger Is Important. The persuasive power of an argument depends in part on who makes it, and the more frequently an argument is made by trusted experts or colleagues who people think share their values, the more likely it is to be accepted.[67] Appeals to the professoriat for ideological diversity should be made often and mostly by academics and political liberals or progressives, rather than conservatives or nonacademics. People look to their sociopolitical tribe for signals about the attitudes and behaviors they should adopt to virtue signal their badge of loyalty and belonging to the group.[68] We should aim to produce a "respectability cascade" in the professoriat so that the acceptance of ideological diversity will mushroom once faculty members perceive that such diversity is supported by a critical mass of their academic peers.[69]

Diversifying Faculties Is the Long-Term Solution. Ultimately, the best way to ensure ideological diversity in the academy is to diversify faculties so that they include not just progressives and liberals but also conservatives, libertarians, and centrists. Since professors and university administrators (most of whom are also professors) control the curriculum, university programming, faculty hiring, student admissions, and university DEI and free speech policies, it is they who determine whether the campus will be ideologically diverse or hegemonic.

The best way to avoid ideological groupthink on campus, and thereby promote ideological diversity, is to have ideologically diverse faculties. But most faculties are anything but diverse. National surveys show that only 5–10 percent of the professoriat is conservative or libertarian. Of the top-ranked liberal arts colleges, 39 percent have no Republicans on the faculty, and 78 percent of their academic departments have *none* or virtually none.[70] To be sure, conservatives and libertarian students tend to self-select out of an academic career, finding it less appealing than do liberal students, often because they perceive the academic culture to be hostile to their values and worldviews. Moreover, there is documented bias and discrimination against conservatives and libertarians in graduate school admissions and faculty hiring and promotion.[71]

Thus, this long-term endeavor of diversifying faculties is unlikely to succeed unless university faculties see ideological diversity as a relevant component of their DEI project, which should then lead them to hire more ideologically diverse faculty. Specifically, universities should include political orientation and viewpoint diversity within the definition of diversity in their advertising for faculty positions and nondiscrimination statements. Faculty hiring committees should include ideologically diverse members. Academic departments should make affirmative efforts to recruit ideologically diverse professors and graduate students, have ideologically inclusive graduate admissions, and foster an inclusive graduate student environment.[72] We should encourage them to see these efforts as part of the DEI project.

Conclusion

The diversity and DEI projects, both of which began in the academy but then spread to organizations throughout society, are largely responsible for today's censorious and ideologically exclusionary culture. Although diversity, equity, and inclusion are wonderful goals in principle, in practice, they have been used by progressive academics and many of the students they have indoctrinated to enforce a progressive ideological orthodoxy that restricts free speech, shuts down open inquiry on controversial social and political topics, excludes ideologically diverse ideas, and discriminates against non-progressives. This totalizing ideological force has also skewed teaching and policy-relevant research, public policy, the missions and values of professional organizations and corporations, and media and entertainment; all these changes had their genesis in the academy's diversity and DEI projects.

Thus, we cannot ignore what is occurring in our colleges and universities, and although legislative and other outside efforts to rein in DEI are vital for effecting change, it is professors and university administrations who control the campus climate and DEI regimes. The professoriat is unlikely to abandon its strong commitment to DEI, so we need to convince it that the values and goals of DEI are furthered by ideological diversity. To make this case, we can draw on a sizable and compelling body of psychological research demonstrating that the assumptions supporting professors' view that demographic diversity ought to be at the core of DEI apply with equal force to ideological diversity.

Of course, many in the academy will remain unpersuaded by such an argument, mainly because advancing the interests of what they see as marginalized and oppressed groups is a primary goal of their ideological project. Yet this argument is far more likely to persuade the professoriat than simply asserting that DEI is illiberal bunk; plus, it is the principled argument to make. Diversity and inclusion are good things—so long as they include what is probably the most important kind of diversity, particularly for higher education: ideological diversity.

Notes

1. Greg Lukianoff and Rikki Schlott, *The Canceling of the American Mind: Cancel Culture Undermines Trust and Threatens Us All—but There Is a Solution* (New York: Simon & Schuster, 2023).

2. Lee Jussim et al., "The Radicalization of the American Academy," in *The Palgrave Handbook of Left-Wing Extremism*, ed. José Pedro Zúquete (London: Palgrave Macmillan, 2023), 2:343–66; and Richard E. Redding, "Psychologists' Politics," in *Ideological and Political Bias in Psychology: Nature, Scope, and Solutions*, ed. Craig L. Frisby et al. (New York: Springer, 2023), 79–96.

3. See Foundation for Individual Rights and Expression, *The Academic Mind in 2022: What Faculty Think About Free Expression and Academic Freedom on Campus*, 2022, https://www.thefire.org/research-learn/academic-mind-2022-what-faculty-think-about-free-expression-and-academic-freedom; Eric Kaufman, *Academic Freedom in Crisis: Punishment, Political Discrimination, and Self-Censorship*, Center for the Study of Partisanship and Ideology, March 1, 2012, https://www.cspicenter.com/p/academic-freedom-in-crisis-punishment; and S. Zhou, M. Stiksma, and S. C. Zhou, *Understanding the Campus Expression Climate: Fall 2021*, Heterodox Academy, March 2022, https://heterodoxacademy.org/files/CES-Report-2022-FINAL-1.pdf. For a discussion of how this plays out in the academic discipline of psychology, which has had a significant influence on campus free speech issues, see Pamela Paresky and Bradley Campbell, "Psychology's Language and Free Speech Problem," in *Ideological and Political Bias in Psychology: Nature, Scope, and Solutions*, ed. Craig L. Frisby et al. (New York: Springer, 2023), 149–72.

4. Foundation for Individual Rights and Expression, *The Academic Mind in 2022*; Kaufman, *Academic Freedom in Crisis*; and Zhou, Stiksma, and Zhou, *Understanding the Campus Expression Climate*. For student accounts of this indoctrination and self-censorship, see Emma Camp, "I Came to College Eager to Debate. I Found Self-Censorship Instead.," *New York Times*, March 7, 2022, https://www.nytimes.com/2022/03/07/opinion/campus-speech-cancel-culture.html; and Zach Gottlieb, "Listen Up. The Closing of the Teenage Mind Is Almost Complete," *Los Angeles Times*, December 20, 2023, https://www.latimes.com/opinion/story/2023-12-10/los-angeles-high-school-cancel-culture-free-speech.

5. Russell Jacoby, "The Takeover," *Tablet*, December 18, 2022, https://www.tabletmag.com/sections/arts-letters/articles/takeover-russell-jacoby.

6. Kaleb Demerew, "College Diversity Politics and American Higher Education: An Institutional Analysis," *Society* 60, no. 1 (2023): 983–93, https://link.springer.com/article/10.1007/s12115-023-00911-3.

7. Demerew, "College Diversity Politics and American Higher Education."

8. Jussim et al., "The Radicalization of the American Academy."

9. Sneha Dey, "New Anti-DEI Law for Public Texas Colleges Presents Hiring Challenges," *Texas Tribune*, September 22, 2023, https://www.texastribune.org/2023/09/22/texas-universities-chancellors-diversity; and Adrienne Lu, "Here's What Florida's Proposed Anti-DEI Regulations Would Ban," *Chronicle of Higher*

Education, October 12, 2023, https://www.chronicle.com/article/heres-what-floridas-proposed-anti-dei-regulations-would-ban.

10. Rachel Fairbank, "Psychologists Persevere in EDI Work Despite Growing Backlash Against Racial Equity Efforts," *Monitor on Psychology* 55, no. 1 (January/February 2024): 56, https://www.apa.org/monitor/2024/01/trends-anti-equity-diversity-inclusion-laws.

11. Demerew, "College Diversity Politics and American Higher Education," 992.

12. See Rebecca Schneid, "Race-Based College Admissions Are Now Banned, but Texas Schools Have Ways to Ensure Campuses Are Diverse," *Texas Tribune,* July 11, 2023, https://www.texastribune.org/2023/07/11/texas-universities-admissions-affirmative-action.

13. Neil Gross and Solon Simmons, "The Social and Political Views of American College and University Professors," in *Professors and Their Politics,* ed. Neil Gross and Solon Simmons (Baltimore, MD: Johns Hopkins University Press, 2014), 19–52. For example, younger professors are much more willing than senior professors to endorse cancellation and censorship attempts against their colleagues. Kaufman, *Academic Freedom in Crisis.*

14. Redding, "Psychologists' Politics."

15. Redding, "Psychologists' Politics"; and Jussim et al., "The Radicalization of the American Academy."

16. Not only do such professional organizations control much of professional practice (which, in turn, can influence social norms such as those surrounding gender and sexuality), but they also exert an influence on public policy. For example, every year the American Psychological Association (APA) engages in significant lobbying efforts in Congress, provides testimony before House and Senate committees, responds to numerous requests from government agencies for information and guidance, organizes and funds advocacy coalitions, and submits numerous amicus briefs to the US Supreme Court. See American Psychological Association, *Elevating Psychological Science Everywhere,* February 2023, https://www.apa.org/science/about/elevating-psychological-science. The APA also regularly issues press releases on their positions on a wide range of controversial political and social topics, some having little to do with psychological expertise. Nina Silander and Anthony Tarescavage, "Ideological Bias in American Psychological Association Communications: Another Threat to the Credibility of Professional Psychology," in *Ideological and Political Bias in Psychology: Nature, Scope, and Solutions,* ed. Craig L. Frisby et al. (New York: Springer, 2023), 315–42.

17. See Jacoby, "The Takeover." Russell Jacoby noted that in his writings several decades ago, he had argued that "conservatives should awake from their nightmare of radical scholars destroying America and relax; academic revolutionaries preoccupied themselves with their careers and perks. If they made waves, they were confined to the campus pool." But this argument was wrongheaded.

18. Pete Hegseth, *Battle for the American Mind: Uprooting a Century of Miseducation* (New York: Broadside Books, 2022); and Mark R. Levin, *American Marxism* (New York: Simon & Schuster, 2021).

19. Levin, *American Marxism*; Darel E. Paul, *From Tolerance to Equality: How Elites Brought America to Same-Sex Marriage* (Waco, TX: Baylor University Press, 2018); and Christopher F. Rufo, *America's Cultural Revolution: How the Radical Left Conquered Everything* (New York: Broadside Books, 2023).

20. Hegseth, *Battle for the American Mind*; and Levin, *American Marxism*.

21. Peter Wood, *Diversity: The Invention of a Concept* (New York: Encounter Books, 2004).

22. Wood, *Diversity*; and Russell Jacoby, *On Diversity: The Eclipse of the Individual in the Global Era* (New York: Seven Stories Press, 2020).

23. Jussim et al., "The Radicalization of the American Academy"; and James D. Paul and Robert Maranto, "Elite Schools Lead: An Empirical Examination of Diversity Requirements in Higher Education Job Markets," *Studies in Higher Education* 48, no. 2 (2023): 314–28, https://www.tandfonline.com/doi/abs/10.1080/03075079.2022.2134334.

24. Paul and Maranto, "Elite Schools Lead."

25. *Life, Liberty & Levin*, aired December 16, 2023, on Fox News.

26. Jay P. Greene and James D. Paul, *Inclusion Delusion: The Antisemitism of Diversity, Equity, and Inclusion Staff at Universities*, Heritage Foundation, December 8, 2021, https://www.heritage.org/education/report/inclusion-delusion-the-antisemitism-diversity-equity-and-inclusion-staff.

27. *Fareed Zakaria GPS*, aired December 10, 2023, on CNN.

28. See Molly Bohannon, "House Passes Resolution Urging Harvard, MIT Presidents to Resign After Tense Campus Antisemitism Hearing," *Forbes*, December 13, 2023, https://www.forbes.com/sites/mollybohannon/2023/12/13/house-passes-resolution-urging-harvard-mit-presidents-to-resign-after-tense-campus-antisemitism-hearing.

29. Germania Rodriguez Poleo, "How Harvard President Claudine Gay Quietly Built a Diversity Empire as Ivy League's Professor Slam 'Intolerant' School for Bowing to DEI Bureaucracy," *Daily Mail*, December 19, 2023, https://www.dailymail.co.uk/news/article-12881249/Harvard-President-Claudine-Gay-DEI.html.

30. Foundation for Individual Rights and Expression, "2024 College Free Speech Rankings," http://rankings.thefire.org.

31. Richard E. Redding, "Debiasing Psychology: What Is to Be Done?," in *Ideological and Political Bias in Psychology: Nature, Scope, and Solutions*, ed. Craig L. Frisby et al. (New York: Springer, 2023), 929–54; and Redding, "Psychologists' Politics."

32. Frank Dobbin and Alexandra Kalev, "Why Diversity Programs Fail," *Harvard Business Review* (July–August 2016), https://hbr.org/2016/07/why-diversity-programs-fail.

33. See Aino Saarinen et al., "Does Social Intolerance Vary According to Cognitive Style, Genetic Cognitive Capability, or Education?," *Brain and Behavior* 12, no. 9 (September 2022), https://onlinelibrary.wiley.com/doi/epdf/10.1002/brb3.2704.

34. Peter H. Ditto et al., "At Least Bias Is Bipartisan: A Meta-Analytic Comparison of Partisan Bias in Liberals and Conservatives," *Perspectives on Psychological Science* 14, no. 2 (2019): 273–91, https://journals.sagepub.com/doi/10.1177/1745691617746796.

35. Fairbank, "Psychologists Persevere in EDI Work."

36. John T. Jost and John Van der Toorn, "System Justification Theory," in *Handbook of Theories of Social Psychology*, ed. Paul A. M. Van Lange, Arie W. Kuglanski, and E. Tory Higgins (Thousand Oaks, CA: Sage, 2012).

37. See Bradley Campbell and Jason Manning, *The Rise of Victimhood Culture: Micro-aggressions, Safe Spaces, and the New Culture Wars* (New York: Palgrave Macmillan, 2018); and Greg Lukianoff and Jonathan Haidt, *The Coddling of the American Mind: How Good Intentions and Bad Ideas Are Setting Up a Generation for Failure* (New York: Penguin Books, 2018).

38. See Neil Gross and Solon Simmons, "The Social and Political Views of American College and University Professors," in *Professors and Their Politics*, ed. Neil Gross and Solon Simmons (Baltimore, MD: Johns Hopkins University Press, 2014), 19–52.

39. Chip Heath and Dan Heath, *Made to Stick: Why Some Ideas Survive and Others Die* (New York: Random House, 2007).

40. See Anthony R. Pratkanis, "Social Influence Analysis: An Index of Tactics," in *The Science of Social Influence: Advances and Future Progress*, ed. Anthony R. Pratkanis (Philadelphia, PA: Psychology Press, 2007), 17–82.

41. Demerew, "College Diversity Politics and American Higher Education."

42. Demerew, "College Diversity Politics and American Higher Education."

43. Sharon Shavitt and Michelle R. Nelson, "The Role of Attitude Functions in Persuasion and Social Judgment," in *The Persuasion Handbook: Developments in Theory and Practice*, ed. James Price Dillard and Michael Pfau (Thousand Oaks, CA: Sage, 2002), 137–54.

44. Shavitt and Nelson, "The Role of Attitude Functions in Persuasion and Social Judgment."

45. Richard E. Redding and Cory Cobb, "Sociopolitical Values as the Deep Culture in Culturally-Competent Psychotherapy," *Clinical Psychological Science* 11, no. 4 (2023): 666–82, https://journals.sagepub.com/doi/abs/10.1177/21677026221126688?journalCode=cpxa.

46. Robin L. Nabi, "Discrete Emotions and Persuasion," in *The Persuasion Handbook: Developments in Theory and Practice*, ed. James Price Dillard and Michael Pfau (Thousand Oaks, CA: Sage, 2002), 289–308; and Daniel J. O'Keefe, "Guilt as a Mechanism of Persuasion," in *The Persuasion Handbook: Developments in Theory and Practice*, ed. James Price Dillard and Michael Pfau (Thousand Oaks, CA: Sage, 2002), 329–44.

47. George Yancey, *Compromising Scholarship: Religious and Political Bias in American Higher Education* (Waco, TX: Baylor University Press, 2011).

48. Richard E. Redding, "Likes Attract: The Sociopolitical Groupthink of (Social) Psychologists," *Perspectives on Psychological Science* 7, no. 5 (September 2012): 512–15, https://www.jstor.org/stable/44280800.

49. See Campbell and Manning, *Rise of Victimhood Culture*; and Lukianoff and Haidt, *The Coddling of the American Mind*.

50. See Redding and Cobb, "Sociopolitical Values as the Deep Culture in Culturally-Competent Psychotherapy."

51. Redding and Cobb, "Sociopolitical Values as the Deep Culture in Culturally-Competent Psychotherapy."

52. Redding and Cobb, "Sociopolitical Values as the Deep Culture in Culturally-Competent Psychotherapy."

53. Adam Panish and H. Hannah Nam, "The Neurobiology of Political Ideology: Theories, Findings, and Future Directions," *Social and Personality Psychology*

Compass 18, no. 1 (January 2024), https://compass.onlinelibrary.wiley.com/doi/10.1111/spc3.12916?af=R.

54. John R. Alford, Carolyn L. Funk, and John R. Hibbing, "Are Political Orientations Genetically Transmitted?," *American Political Science Review* 99 (2005): 165, https://digitalcommons.unl.edu/cgi/viewcontent.cgi?article=1006&context=poliscifacpub.

55. A. Tesser, "The Importance of Heritability in Psychological Research: The Case of Attitudes," *Psychological Review* 100, no. 1 (1993): 140, https://psycnet.apa.org/record/1993-17572-001.

56. Redding and Cobb, "Sociopolitical Values as the Deep Culture in Culturally-Competent Psychotherapy."

57. Redding and Cobb, "Sociopolitical Values as the Deep Culture in Culturally-Competent Psychotherapy."

58. Redding and Cobb, "Sociopolitical Values as the Deep Culture in Culturally-Competent Psychotherapy."

59. Redding, "Likes Attract"; Redding, "Psychologists' Politics"; and Redding, "Debiasing Psychology."

60. See Redding, "Likes Attract"; Redding, "Psychologists' Politics"; and Redding, "Debiasing Psychology."

61. Lukianoff and Haidt, *The Coddling of the American Mind*.

62. Richard E. Redding, "Sociopolitical Diversity in Psychology: The Case for Pluralism," *American Psychologist* 56, no. 3 (March 2001): 205–15, https://papers.ssrn.com/sol3/papers.cfm?abstract_id=2376451; and Redding, "Debiasing Psychology."

63. George Lakoff and Mark Johnson, *Metaphors We Live By* (Chicago: University of Chicago Press, 1981); and George Lakoff, *Moral Politics: How Liberals and Conservatives Think*, 3rd ed. (Chicago: University of Chicago Press, 2016).

64. See Heath and Heath, *Made to Stick*; and Richard E. Redding, "Lost in Translation No More: Marketing Evidence-Based Policies for Reducing Juvenile Crime," in *A New Juvenile Justice: Total Reform for a Broken System*, ed. Nancy Dowd (New York: New York University Press, 2015), 139–55.

65. Personal communication with the author, September 2, 2023.

66. J. F. G. Shearmur, *Scaling the Ivory Tower: The Pursuit of an Academic Career* (Fairfax, VA: Institute for Humane Studies, George Mason University, 1995), 6.

67. See Dan M. Kahan, "Making Climate-Science Communication Evidence-Based—All the Way Down," in *Culture, Politics and Climate Change: How Information Shapes Our Common Future*, ed. Maxwell Boykoff and Deserai Crow (Philadelphia, PA: Routledge Press, 2014); and Rodney A. Reynolds and J. Lynn Reynolds, "Evidence," in *The Persuasion Handbook: Developments in Theory and Practice*, ed. James Price Dillard and Michael Pfau (Thousand Oaks, CA: Sage, 2002), 427–44.

68. Reynolds and Reynolds, "Evidence"; and Jerold Hale, Brian Householder, and Kathryn Greene, "The Theory of Reasoned Action," in *The Persuasion Handbook: Developments in Theory and Practice*, ed. James Price Dillard and Michael Pfau (Thousand Oaks, CA: Sage, 2002), 259–86.

69. Scott Alexander, "Respectability Cascades," Slate Star Codex, February 4, 2019, http://SlateStarCodex.com/2019/02/04/respectability-cascades.

70. Redding, "Psychologists' Politics."

71. Redding, "Psychologists' Politics."
72. Redding, "Debiasing Psychology."

17

Fighting the Good Fight in an Age of Unreason: A New Dissident Guide

Anna I. Krylov and Jay Tanzman

We live in an age of unreason. The liberal enlightenment, humanism, and democracy are under siege. A once-obscure postmodernist worldview, critical social justice (CSJ) has escaped the academy and is quickly reshaping our institutions and society at large.[1] Long-standing merit-based practices in science are rapidly being subordinated to practices based on the tenets of CSJ theory.[2]

Increasingly, scientists must compete for funding no longer on the basis of scientific merit only but also on the basis of how their proposed research will promote the goals of CSJ. As an example, a National Institutes of Health neurology program requires grant applications to include a "Plan for Enhancing Diverse Perspectives" with the goal to "bring about the culture change necessary to address the inequities and systemic biases in biomedical research."[3] Similarly, funding for fundamental research in chemistry and physics now depends on researchers demonstrating their commitment to "promote equity and inclusion as an intrinsic element to advancing scientific excellence."[4]

In the academy, faculty hiring and administrative appointments are increasingly made on the basis of the candidate's identity.[5] Merit-based admission to schools and universities is being weakened, with standardized tests such as the SAT and ACT being abandoned on "social justice" grounds.[6]

K–12 is affected as well. Some school districts have stopped giving D and F grades to improve "equity."[7] In math classes, activist teachers claim that getting the right answer and showing your work are white supremacist concepts and are advocating, instead, a supposedly anti-racist CSJ pedagogy.[8] Accelerated mathematics programs for gifted students, necessary to prepare them for advanced training and careers in STEM,[9] are being dismantled in the name of "social justice."[10] Many school districts have eliminated honors classes altogether in the name of equity.[11] The resultant weakening of the workforce has already contributed to the fall of the United States from its position as the world leader in science.[12]

In the university, faculty and staff are instructed to use newspeak—neopronouns and other neologisms—in their written and verbal communications for the purpose of "inclusivity."[13] To be avoided are such apparently un-inclusive terms as "straw man argument," "brown-bag lunch," and "picnic."[14] Professional societies and corporations are following suit, proscribing terms such as "field," "dark times," "black market," "double blind study," "nursing mother," "hip hip hooray," "smart phone," "homeless," and "the French."[15]

In biology, an education paper recommends that teachers emphasize the sexual diversity across species in nature, which includes organisms "such as ciliates, algae, and fungi [that] have equal-size gametes (isogamy) and do not therefore have gametic sexes [that is, binary sexes, as mammals do]." This is supposed to promote inclusivity of LGBTQIA2+ students in the classroom.[16]

Chemistry education also needs to be reformed, according to the *Journal of Chemical Education*, which published a virtual diversity, equity, and inclusion (DEI) collection of 67 papers exploring such topics as decolonization of the chemistry curriculum, chemistry and racism, and gender and sexual orientation identities in the chemistry classroom.[17] A recent paper in the same journal describes "a special topic class in chemistry on feminism and science as a tool to disrupt the dysconcious [*sic*] racism in STEM," which explores "the development and interrelationship between quantum mechanics, Marxist materialism, Afro-futurism/pessimism, and postcolonial nationalism." The authors write, "To problematize time as a linear social construct, the Copenhagen interpretation of the collapse of wave-particle duality was utilized."[18] No, Deepak Chopra was not a coauthor of the paper.

In STEM, prospective faculty are asked to pledge their commitment to CSJ ideology and document their activism in advancing DEI.[19] Medical schools are abolishing long-accepted assessments of competency to improve racial parity in residency programs.[20] A pamphlet published by the University of Illinois Chicago School of Public Health claims that public health anti-obesity campaigns are an example of "fatphobia," that public health's "focus on body size is rooted in racism," that "higher weight is not causal to worse health outcomes," and that "focusing on weight ignores systematic injustices."[21] Under the doctrine of gender-affirming care, adolescents are offered life-changing transgender treatments, often after only perfunctory psychological assessment, despite the poor understanding that medicine currently has of the risks and benefits of these treatments.[22]

Free speech itself, the cornerstone of liberal democracy, is under attack. As viewed by CSJ activists, free speech is dangerous, harmful, and equivalent to violence.[23] Adherents of DEI ideology believe that DEI should trump academic freedom.[24] Institutions essential for providing a platform for the marketplace of ideas, information exchange, and debate have largely abandoned their mission in the name of social justice activism. Articles in the press are infused with CSJ ideology.[25] Scientific publishers from *Scientific American* to the flagship journals *Science* and *Nature* have become mouthpieces for CSJ.[26] Universities, whose primary mission is education and truth-seeking, have become complicit in censorship, scholarship suppression, indoctrination, and intimidation.[27]

Universities and professional organizations have compromised their mission as seekers and communicators of objective truths by abandoning traditional institutional neutrality in favor of political activism, taking official positions on elections, police reform, abortion, wars, and other social issues,[28] leaving dissenters out in the cold. Where debate, constructive disagreement, and discussion were once cultivated, conformity and dogmatism—enforced top-down (by CSJ-infused DEI trainings[29]) and bottom-up (by ideologically driven activists[30])—now reign.

On campus, another essential provision of democracy—the presumption of innocence until proven guilty—no longer guides procedures for resolving conflict. Suspensions and terminations of professors without a hearing in response to offense taken by students, faculty members, or administrators have become common.[31] A predictable consequence is that there is now an unprecedented level of self-censorship by students and faculty.[32] Recent changes to Title IX regulations will further erode free speech on campus and the protection of due process.[33]

CSJ adherents accuse dissenters of being indifferent to existing inequalities and historic injustices, being bigots, having nefarious motives, and

270 THE FREE INQUIRY PAPERS

perpetuating existing power structures. We reject these accusations. We oppose the practices of CSJ because they harm everyone, including those groups they purport to elevate.[34] It is precisely because we care about the existing problems in the world and about *real* social justice that we oppose CSJ.

What we are witnessing today—curriculum "decolonization," the elimination of honors classes in schools, the ubiquitous war on merit, the imposition of political litmus tests for academic positions, newspeak, the renaming of everything in sight, and so on—are not isolated excesses perpetrated by a handful of overly zealous but otherwise well-meaning individuals. They are symptoms of a wholesale takeover of our institutions by an illiberal movement that currently has the upper hand.

The current situation is not a pendulum that has swung too far and will self-correct;[35] it is a train hurtling full speed toward a cliff. Those of us unwillingly to go over the edge can either jump off—leave academia (or maybe start up alternative institutions)—or fight to apply the brakes before it is too late. The remainder of this chapter is about the latter course of action.

Why We Should Fight

To put it simply, we should fight because it is the right thing to do. It is not only our duty to the next generation but an opportunity to pay our debt to the previous generations of dissenters who fought against forces of illiberalism to create the free and prosperous world we enjoy today.[36] By fighting, we, too, can fend off the forces of unreason and restore the values of humanism, liberalism, and the Enlightenment. Inaction and submission will only enable the further spread of illiberalism. The history of past illiberal regimes, such as the USSR and Nazi Germany, provide ample lessons and motivation to stand and fight today. The train is gaining momentum; the longer we wait, the harder it will be to stop it. We must act now—while we still can.

Although there are uncanny parallels with totalitarian regimes of the past,[37] we still live in a free, democratic society. Despite the advances of illiberal ideology—manifested by the rise of censorship, the spread of

FIGHTING THE GOOD FIGHT IN AN AGE OF UNREASON 271

cancel culture,[38] and the proliferation of institutionalized structures (such as DEI bureaucracies) to enforce CSJ ideology—the dissenters of today do not face incarceration in prisons, labor camps, and mental hospitals. Nonetheless, we can learn from history.

In his book *To Build a Castle: My Life as a Dissenter*, Vladimir Bukovsky describes his experiences as a dissident who refused to comply with the Soviets and challenged the regime.[39] Bukovsky describes the apathy and complacency of most of the population at that time. People understood the corrupt and inhumane nature of the regime, but they chose to keep their heads down because—as the Russian proverb goes—"No man can splay the stone" (in Russian, плетью обуха не перешибёшь).

Because of this complacency, the economically bankrupt, oppressive, and inhumane Soviet regime lasted as long as it did (over 70 years). But it was the actions of dissidents that ultimately catalyzed its downfall. Consider, for example, the impact of the books by Aleksandr Solzhenitsyn, who told the world the truth about the Soviet regime's atrocities.[40] In addition to meticulously documenting the scale of the atrocities, Solzhenitsyn explained that they came to be not due to deviations from the party line or shortcomings of its individual leaders but as the direct result of Marxist-Leninist ideology.

In Bukovsky's time (the late 1950s to mid-1970s), open dissent was rare. Growing up in the Soviet Union, I (Anna I. Krylov)—like most of my peers—did not even know dissidents existed. It wasn't until perestroika in the late '80s, when I read Solzhenitsyn's books and learned about Andrei Sakharov, that I found out.[41]

Yet it is through the actions of dissidents that the West came to understand the Soviet regime as an "evil empire," and this understanding propelled political forces in the West that ultimately decided the outcome of the Cold War. The dissident movement's impact on the Soviet regime has been illuminated through a series of memoranda of the Central Committee of the Communist Party of the Soviet Union, stolen and published by Bukovsky in his book *Judgment in Moscow: Soviet Crimes and Western Complicity*.[42] The acts of individuals splayed the stone after all.

I was born (in the then-Soviet state of Ukraine) into the luckiest generation in the history of the USSR—the generation that witnessed the fall of the Berlin Wall when they were still young. We could escape to the free

272 THE FREE INQUIRY PAPERS

world, live as free people, and build successful and fulfilling careers in the West. Had the regime lasted another 20 years, my generation would have been yet another in the long list of those whose lives were ruined by the Soviet regime. I feel a personal debt to the dissidents of the day.

Now, it is our turn to be the dissidents and fight the good fight.

Fighting for what is right is not just the right thing to do; it is empowering. Standing up and speaking your mind is liberating, even exhilarating, while hunkering down in fear, hoping the storm will pass, is a bleak experience. Being honest feels good, while being complicit in lies is dispiriting. Fighting the good fight puts you in control, whereas passive submission leaves you helpless. Whether we ultimately win or lose this fight, those who choose to remain silent will look back and ask themselves why they did not act when they could. As German theologian Martin Niemöller wrote after World War II:

> First they came for the socialists, and I did not speak out—because I was not a socialist. Then they came for the trade unionists, and I did not speak out—because I was not a trade unionist. Then they came for the Jews, and I did not speak out—because I was not a Jew. Then they came for me—and there was no one left to speak for me.[43]

Eventually, this illiberal movement, like those of the past, will come for not only the dissidents but also the silent bystanders (and, eventually, its own vocal supporters).

There are myriad excuses, as old as the history of totalitarianism and oppression itself, invoked to justify inaction, complacency, and collaboration. Bukovsky enumerates a few of the more familiar: "What can I do alone?" "I'll be more effective after I get the promotion." "It's not my job; I'm a scientist." "If I don't collaborate, someone else will anyway (and I'll probably do less harm)." These reasons may seem logical, even compelling; however, they are self-deceptions. Not pushing back against bad ideas allows them to spread. Not fighting back against illiberalism allows it to grow. Not standing up for truth permits lies to flourish. Not confronting CSJ ideologists permits them to advance. And when they advance, we lose. *It is a zero-sum game.*

FIGHTING THE GOOD FIGHT IN AN AGE OF UNREASON 273

The choice to fight in the face of potential consequences is personal and not an easy one to make.[44] But as you contemplate whether to act or lay low, consider the importance of truth and integrity in your life. To paraphrase Bari Weiss, worship truth more than Yale:

> Do not lose sight of what is essential. Professional prestige is not essential. Being popular is not essential. Getting your child into an elite preschool is not essential. Doing the right thing is essential. Telling the truth is essential. Protecting your kids is essential.[45]

Sure, no one wants to become a martyr for free speech or experience bullying, ostracism, and professional damage.[46] Cancel culture is real, but the risks are not what dissenters from totalitarian regimes faced historically or face today; cancel culture does not put you in jail. One still can write a dissenting op-ed without the fear of being stripped of their citizenship and expelled from the country, as Solzhenitsyn was for his writings.[47] We still can criticize DEI policies without fear of being put under house arrest, as Sakharov was for his vocal opposition to nuclear weapons and his unwavering defense of human rights.[48] But if we delay, some of the totalitarian nightmares of the past may become a reality.

There are already worrying signs of this totalitarian-style repression in America. Parents opposing CSJ in schools have been accused of terrorism and investigated by the FBI.[49] A journalist who wrote about collusion between the government and social media was paid a surprise home visit by the IRS.[50] A student who questioned the concept of microaggressions[51] at a mandatory training was expelled and forced to "seek psychological services."[52] These incidents in America today are chillingly similar to practices in Russia in the Soviet era, when the KGB routinely investigated dissidents and dissent from Soviet ideology was considered a psychiatric disorder.[53] In the absence of resistance, this illiberal movement, like illiberal movements of the past, will gain ever more power, and we will face ever worse repression and erosion of individual freedom.

Inaction does not guarantee survival, but fighting a successful fight does. The only way to defend yourself against repression by an illiberal ideology is to stop the spread of the ideology.

274   THE FREE INQUIRY PAPERS

The dangers of inaction are real, but how much risk one should take must be a personal decision.[54] Above all, it rarely does any good to get fired. Getting fired is playing into their hands. It's one less enemy in the organization to fight against its ideological capture. Should all the dissidents get fired, the ideology wins. Full stop.

But it's not hopeless. As we elaborate below, there are ways to maximize the impact of your actions and minimize the risks of resistance.

How to Fight

Although there is no surefire road map to solve the current crisis, there are some do's and don'ts. A recently published handbook that we highly recommend, *Counter Wokecraft: A Field Manual for Combatting the Woke in the University and Beyond*—written by an anonymous STEM professor—provides concrete recommendations for staging the resistance.[55] It convincingly explains how small but deliberate actions add up to big change and elaborates on the perils of delaying action. In what follows, we offer our view on how to fight, and we share examples of successful acts of resistance that give us reason for hope. Small contributions add up, so do something rather than nothing. As Gad Saad writes in *The Parasitic Mind: How Infectious Ideas Are Killing Common Sense*:

> The battle of ideas knows no boundaries, so there is plenty to do. If you are a student and hear your professors spouting postmodern nonsense or spewing anti-science drivel, challenge them politely and constructively. If you are a graduate and your *alma mater* is violating its commitment to freedom of speech and freedom of thought, withdraw your donations—and let the school know why. If your Facebook friends are posting comments with which you disagree, engage them and offer an alternative viewpoint.... If you are sitting at your local pub having a conversation about a sensitive topic, do not refrain from speaking your mind. If your politicians are succumbing to suicidal political correctness, vote them out of office.[56]

FIGHTING THE GOOD FIGHT IN AN AGE OF UNREASON 275

Educate yourself; knowledge is power. To effectively counter CSJ ideology, it is crucial to understand its nature and tactics. As two-time Nobel laureate Marie Sklodowska-Curie said, "Nothing in life is to be feared, it is only to be understood. Now is the time to understand more, so we may fear less."[57]

Although Sklodowska-Curie was referring to phenomena of the natural world, the observation applies equally to the world of ideas. By understanding CSJ's origins and tenets, we can fear less—and fight more effectively.

For me (Krylov) and my former compatriots, who were forcibly schooled in Marxism-Leninism and experienced its implementation as socialism firsthand, it is easy to recognize the current illiberal movement's philosophical roots.[58] We recognize the familiar rhetoric and the Orwellian co-option of the language. The Communist Party's media outlet, which disseminated its lies, was called *Pravda* (Правда), which is Russian for "truth"; victims of the Red Terror were called "enemies of the people" (враги народа); Soviet troops invading other countries were called "liberators" (освободители); and nuclear weapons were developed with the slogan "nucleus for the cause of peace" (атом—делу мира). We are used to looking behind the facade of nice-sounding words and seeing their real meaning to those in power.[59]

It is not hard to see that today's "diversity," "equity," and "inclusion" have about as much in common with the noble concepts of diversity, equality, and inclusion as George Orwell's Ministry of Love had to do with love or his Ministry of Plenty had to do with plenty in 1984. (A more fitting operational definition of DEI would be "discrimination, entitlement, and intimidation.") This linguistic tactic is used because it works. It has fooled many STEM academics and ordinary citizens and enabled the illiberal ideology to get its foot in the door. Steven Brint, distinguished professor of sociology and public policy at the University of California, Riverside, relates how activist University of California (UC) administrators used language to gradually alter the mission of the entire UC system:

> "Diversity and Excellence" became a popular slogan at UC. Later, it became "Inclusive Excellence," "Excellence through Diversity," and ultimately, I even heard "Diversity *is* Excellence." George Orwell himself could not have laid out a neater

progression for UC administrators to use language to alter understandings of the university's mission.[60]

As *Counter Wokecraft* explains, the tactics CSJ employs to gain power in our institutions include the use of liberal-sounding "crossover words" to shroud the movement's illiberal aims. The concise essay "DEI: A Trojan Horse for Critical Social Justice in Science" by the same author offers insights into the philosophy that undergirds the CSJ movement and clearly elucidates its aims.[61] For a deeper dive into CSJ, we recommend *Cynical Theories* by Helen Pluckrose and James Lindsay.[62]

Use all existing means of resistance, but first and foremost, the official ones. Mechanisms of resistance are available through existing institutions, even if the institutions themselves are failing to protect their mission.[63] These mechanisms can be exploited to change the institutions from within.

Bukovsky describes how his dissident group worked within the legal boundaries of the Soviet regime.[64] He contrasts this approach with anarchism and revolutionary destructivism, which he argues lead to outcomes that are worse than the original evils. Bukovsky and his dissident comrades structured their activism and resistance within the framework of the Soviet constitution—which many legitimately considered to be a joke. When allowed to speak in court, Bukovsky framed his defense to emphasize the constitutional rights of Soviet citizens, for example, to peacefully demonstrate. Bukovsky attributes their success to this strategy.

As an example of an important victory, he describes how he and his fellow political prisoners managed to resist and ultimately eliminate mandatory "corrective labor" for political prisoners. Following legal protocols, they rolled out a concerted effort of filing official complaints. Although isolated complaints never had any effect (they would be registered, duly processed, and dismissed), by flooding the bureaucratic system with a massive number of such complaints (which *each* had to be properly registered and responded to), they pushed the system beyond its limits. The sheer number of complaints compelled administrative scrutiny of the prison and its officers. And the prisoners won the fight.[65]

FIGHTING THE GOOD FIGHT IN AN AGE OF UNREASON 277

Today, we can work within the system of our universities and professional organizations, even if they have already been ideologically corrupted. We can participate in surveys, communicate our concerns to leadership, nominate candidates committed to liberal principles to committees and leadership, vote against CSJ ideologues, speak up against practices that violate institutions' stated missions,[66] publish well-reasoned opinion pieces,[67] and insist that our institutions adhere to their stated institutional (and legal) commitments to free speech and nondiscrimination, such as being equal opportunity employers.

Counter Wokecraft provides concrete suggestions on how to effectively oppose the advances of the CSJ agenda by simply insisting that standard protocols of decision-making be followed—that is, through formal meetings with organized discussions that adhere to a set agenda, voting by secret ballot, and so on. In short, the existing governance structures and institutional policies can still be used to defend and even restore the institutional mission, even when CSJ activists have undermined the institution's workings. The following success stories illustrate the effectiveness of working within the system.

At the University of Massachusetts, a faculty group fought—and won—against a proposed rewriting of the university mission statement, which would have redefined the purpose of the university as engaging in political and ideological activism rather than pursuing truth.[68]

University of Chicago faculty succeeded in rescinding departmental statements that violated institutional neutrality (by voicing collective support for specific social and political issues in violation of the university's Kalven Report).[69] Also at the University of Chicago, in response to faculty complaints to the institution's Title IX coordinator and general counsel, at least seven programs that gave preferences to specific races or sexes in violation of federal regulations were discontinued.[70]

University of Washington faculty voted down a proposal to require DEI statements for all tenure and promotion candidates.[71] As reported to us, an email campaign initiated by a single faculty member was decisive in defeating the proposal.[72]

At the University of North Carolina (UNC), the board of trustees adopted the Chicago free speech principles and the Kalven Report.[73] The former articulates the university's commitment to free speech and is

278 THE FREE INQUIRY PAPERS

considered a model policy on this issue; the latter ensures institutional neutrality, prohibiting university units from taking stands on moral, political, or ideological issues *unless* they directly affect the institution's mission.[74]

Also at UNC, responding to a faculty petition, the board of governors moved to ban DEI requirements from its hiring and promotion process. The mandate states that the university

> shall neither solicit nor require an employee or applicant for academic admission or employment to affirmatively ascribe to or opine about beliefs, affiliations, ideals, or principles regarding matters of contemporary political debate or social action as a condition to admission, employment, or professional advancement.[75]

In California, mathematicians organized a petition that has, so far, blocked the implementation of radical, CSJ-based revisions to the K–12 math curriculum.[76] At the time of writing, the fight continues.

A new nonprofit, Do No Harm, has been formed to fight the encroachment of identity politics in medicine.[77] Among their successes, filings with the US Department of Education's Office for Civil Rights against two medical schools have eliminated race as a requirement for certain scholarships. As the organization's founder explains, "While the original scholarship was meant for individuals from disadvantaged backgrounds, that worthy goal can and should be met without racial discrimination."[78]

Adverse publicity and mockery, too, can cause universities, which are sensitive to their public image, to roll back woke policies, as the following examples illustrate.

- The Massachusetts Institute of Technology (MIT) administration reversed its decision and reinstated the use of standardized tests for admission,[79] the elimination of which dissidents had mocked.[80]

- The Stanford University "Elimination of Harmful Language Initiative" website, which listed 161 verboten expressions— including "beating a dead horse," "white paper," "insane," and even "American"—was taken down after sustained mockery in the press and on social media. The university's president ultimately disowned the initiative and reaffirmed the university's commitment to free speech.[81]

- At the University of Southern California, the interim provost stated that "the university does not maintain a list of banned or discouraged words" in response to the mockery[82] the university's School of Social Work received following an earlier memorandum it released announcing the cancellation of the word "field" as racist.[83]

- At Texas Tech University, the administration announced it was dropping mandatory DEI statements from the hiring process[84] after details of how these statements influenced hiring decisions had been publicized.[85]

These examples illustrate the maxim that sunlight is the best disinfectant. We can use social media and the press to shine a light on the excesses of CSJ to bring about change.

Pressure from state governments can also force universities to move away from DEI ideology. Facing threats from the state assembly to cut funding, the University of Wisconsin (UW) system has announced it will eliminate mandatory DEI statements for job applicants. As we are writing this chapter, the state assembly is also threatening to eliminate funding for administrative positions at UW dedicated to DEI.[86]

Arizona has also dealt a blow to DEI ideology. The state's board of regents has mandated that public universities drop the use of DEI statements in hiring. The move was in response to a finding by the Goldwater Institute that DEI statements, which were required in over three-fourths of job postings, were being used "to circumvent the state's constitutional prohibition against political litmus tests in public educational institutions."[87]

Organizations such as the Academic Freedom Alliance (AFA) and the Foundation for Individual Rights and Expression (FIRE) have successfully used institutions' own governing policies and bylaws, as well as the law, to defend scores of scholars who have been attacked for their extramural speech and threatened with administrative discipline or firing.[88]

280 THE FREE INQUIRY PAPERS

A movement is afoot to strengthen universities' commitment to academic freedom by encouraging them to officially adopt the Chicago trifecta (the Kalven Report, the Chicago principles, and the Shils report). The "Restoring Academic Freedom" letter, which calls on universities to do so, has garnered 1,700 signatures so far.[89]

Don't play their game; you can't win. We are trained to seek compromises and solutions that bring different groups on board; we seek consensus. That is a fine approach under normal circumstances, when all agents are acting in good faith. But we must recognize that we are up against agents who are driven—knowingly or unknowingly—by an ideology whose goal is to take over the institution. Every compromise with them brings them closer to their goal.[90] Therefore, we must stand our ground.

A major advance in the spread of illiberalism has been the establishment of DEI bureaucracies in our intuitions to enforce CSJ ideology through policy.[91] It is important to understand the power of this system and distinguish the system from the people. A DEI apparatchik can be a nice, well-meaning individual who has been fooled by the movement's deliberately deceptive language;[92] a cynical opportunist who seeks power and career advancement; or a "true believer."

A DEI administrator may be completely unaware of the philosophical origins of CSJ, whose goals the DEI machine has been installed to implement. But just as a Soviet apparatchik need not have read *Das Kapital* to have been an agent enforcing conformity to Marxist doctrine, a DEI apparatchik need not have read the works of the critical theorists Derrick Bell, Kimberlé Crenshaw, Richard Delgado, Jacques Derrida, Michael Foucault, and Antonio Gramsci to be implementing CSJ-inspired ideology. But even participants who are naive about the movement's history, philosophy, or ultimate goals are furthering its aims; they are still cogs in the machine. Do not be fooled by DEI administrators who may naively or deceptively deny that they are advancing CSJ ideology. They are, whether they know or acknowledge it.

The power of the system—the DEI bureaucracy—and its ideological foundation make the motivations of individual participants irrelevant. The story of Tabia Lee illustrates this point.[93] Lee—a black woman who directed a DEI program at a community college in California—questioned anti-racist and gender orthodoxy; declined to join a "socialist network"; objected to land acknowledgments and newspeak terms such as "Latinx," "Filipinx," and neopronouns; and supported a campus event focused on Jewish inclusion and antisemitism. Lee describes her nonorthodox worldview as follows: "I don't have ideological or viewpoint fidelity to anyone. I'm looking for what's going to help people and what will help our students and how we can be better teachers and our best teaching selves."[94]

This attitude was found to be incompatible with DEI ideology. When Lee refused to change her worldview to comply with the orthodoxy, she was terminated from her position.

The establishment of the DEI bureaucracy in our institutions represented a tectonic shift from CSJ as a grassroots movement to CSJ as an official power structure within the university equipped with a massive budget to promote its ideology.[95]

A 2021 report by the Heritage Foundation that documented the size of this new bureaucracy identified 3,000 administrators with DEI responsibilities among the 65 universities they surveyed.[96] This number is in addition to the already-extensive staff of federally mandated Title VI, Title IX, and disability offices, which also perform DEI-related tasks. The new "diversicrats" already outnumber the mandated staffers. For example, the average university examined had 4.2 DEI personnel for every one compliance administrator of the Americans with Disabilities Act. Given the sheer number of DEI officials and their generous salaries (one-third of chief diversity officers are paid more than $200,000 annually),[97] it is unsurprising that DEI budgets are enormous; for example, in 2021, UC Berkeley dedicated $41 *million* to DEI.[98]

The DEI bureaucracy is given official status within the university and is empowered to interfere in faculty hiring, disseminate CSJ ideology by means of mandatory trainings, infuse the ideology into teaching, and curtail academic freedom.[99] Amna Khalid and Jeffrey Aaron Snyder provide insight into the logic and financial incentives behind the DEI machine.

> DEI Inc. is a logic, a lingo, and a set of administrative policies and practices. The logic is as follows: Education is a product, students are consumers, and campus diversity is a customer-service issue that needs to be administered from the top down. ("Chief

diversity officers," according to an article in *Diversity Officer Magazine*, "are best defined as 'change-management specialists.'") DEI Inc. purveys a safety-and-security model of learning that is highly attuned to harm and that conflates respect for minority students with unwavering affirmation and validation.

> *Lived experience, the intent-impact gap, microaggressions, trigger warnings, inclusive excellence.* You know the language of DEI Inc. when you hear it. It's a combination of management-consultant buzzwords, social justice slogans, and "therapy speak." The standard package of DEI Inc. administrative "initiatives" should be familiar too, from antiracism trainings to bias-response teams and mandatory diversity statements for hiring and promotion.[100] (Emphasis in original.)

The DEI bureaucracy is a categorical enemy. Don't deceive yourself into thinking you can work with it to accomplish good for your institution.[101] This bureaucracy is founded on ideas that directly oppose the liberal enlightenment and humanism.[102] Their goals are not your goals; consequently, you cannot ally or compromise with them.

We must instead focus our efforts on stripping the DEI bureaucracy of its power—ideally, ridding the institution of it completely. This will not be an easy fight, but neither is it an impossible dream. State legislatures are already taking action against DEI. As of this writing, 35 states have introduced bills that would restrict or ban DEI offices and staff, mandatory DEI training, diversity statements, and identity-based preferences for hiring and admissions.[103] Recognizing that such bills could go too far and compromise academic freedom, the Manhattan Institute has drafted model legislation that would abolish DEI bureaucracies on campuses while preserving academic freedom.[104] To date, at least one state, Texas, has enacted legislation based on the Manhattan Institute's model.[105]

Another reason to not try working with the DEI bureaucracy is that CSJ ideology leaves no space for rational dialogue. As explained by John McWhorter, Charles Pincourt, Pluckrose, Saad, and others, CSJ is not a rational or empirical worldview but an ideology whose adherents have accepted a set of unfalsifiable tenets that may not be questioned.[106]

FIGHTING THE GOOD FIGHT IN AN AGE OF UNREASON   283

Thus, CSJ ideologues are not open to reasoned arguments that contradict their worldview; it is futile to argue with them. We need, instead, to reason with those of our colleagues who have not yet drunk the Kool-Aid.

Finally, since CSJ's goal is to take over the institution, small compromises with them ultimately lead to large losses for us. Give CSJ an inch, and it will take a mile. Consider, for starters, the following example, in which the dean of the Duke Divinity School made the mistake of conceding to student activists, which led to ever-increasing demands and personal attacks on the dean herself.[107]

"The chickens have come home to roost at Duke's divinity school," writes John Staddon. Elaine Heath, the school's dean, fully allied herself with the CSJ agenda, rolled out a variety of DEI initiatives, issued a self-flagellating editorial admitting the school's "structural sins," and forced nonconforming faculty to resign. Yet despite these concessions, the demands of "marginalized groups" only grew stronger, culminating in uncivil acts, such as the disruption of the dean's state-of-the-school address by "four dissident female students bearing bull-horns and chanting, 'I am somebody and I won't be stopped by nobody,' followed by a rap, [and] a little theatrical performance [of a rude nature]."[108]

Staddon writes:

> There is poetic justice in this incident. Despite the dean's earnest attempts "to provide a welcoming and safe place for students," even after she designed "a space for the work of Sacred Worth, the LGBTQIA+ student group in the Divinity School"—even after disciplining, and losing—Professor Griffiths [a nonconforming faculty member], in spite all this, [said] she has apparently not done enough! The LGBT folk want more, much more, in the form of 15 demands. "We make up an integral part of this community, and yet our needs remain deliberately unheard."[109]

The demands included appointing "a black trans woman or gender non-conforming theologian," as well as "a tenure-track trans woman theologian" and a "tenure-track queer theologian of color, preferably a black or Indigenous person."

284 THE FREE INQUIRY PAPERS

A dissident MIT website, the Babbling Beaver,[110] illustrates the same point by a mock resignation statement by MIT's former president L. Rafael Reif:

> You would think giving them a Women's and Gender Studies Program, hiring six dozen DEI deans and staffers, most of whom couldn't pass 18.01 [MIT's introductory math course] if their lives depended on it, and cancelling invited lecturers to appease shouting Twitter mobs would be enough," lamented the weary lame duck. "But noooo . . . The only thing I accomplished by giving in to the incessant demands was encouraging additional demands, each more strident than the last."[111]

The statement is satire, but the concessions made by the president and the ever-increasing demands were real.

Stories of how CSJ, once it is let in the door, rapidly infiltrates an organization and eventually takes it over are too many to enumerate. We present but one example, in which the process has been meticulously documented. The report, sponsored by the organization Alumni and Donors Unite, explains how CSJ took over the University of San Diego "first gradually then suddenly."

> Gradually, over the course of a decade, CSJ-DEI became sown into the university's fabric through changes in hiring committees and curriculum. Then suddenly in 2020–2021 the administration, outside all normal channels of decision-making, initiated a hostile takeover of [the University of San Diego] and adopted a radical woke agenda into nearly all facets of the university's life.[112]

The devaluation of merit and intellectual honesty in the guise of social justice that we now witness will inevitably lead to the decline of our institutions, if not their destruction.[113] A case in point is the Evergreen State College, which, in 2017, experienced a notorious CSJ uprising on campus.[114] Since then, the university has suffered a 25 percent drop in enrollment and has lost 45 faculty through layoffs and attrition.[115]

FIGHTING THE GOOD FIGHT IN AN AGE OF UNREASON 285

Learn how to recognize and take on categorical enemies. Remember—it is a zero-sum game.

Focus on truth, not partisanship. Do not fear verbal attacks. When you take on CSJ, there is something you will need to come to terms with: You are going to be called names, and your views and beliefs are going to be distorted and misrepresented. These are standard tactics of the CSJ movement. Since the adherents of CSJ have adopted an ideological, rather than a rational, worldview, they cannot rationally defend it, so they use the only tools they have: personal attacks and straw-man arguments. They will call you a "transphobe," racist, misogynist, member of the alt-right, Nazi, and so on, no matter what you say or do. They will deliberately misrepresent your expressions to subvert and discredit them. They will use the motte-and-bailey fallacy to derail conversations.[116] Learn about these tactics so you can anticipate, recognize, and counter them.[117] As Saad explains:

> The name-calling accusations are locked and loaded threats, ready to be deployed against you should you dare to question the relevant progressive tenets. Most people are too afraid to be accused of being racist or misogynist, and so they cower in silence.... Don't fall prey to this silencing strategy. Be assured in your principles and stand ready to defend them with the ferocity of a honey badger.[118]

Because you will be attacked no matter what you believe, what you say, or how carefully you say it, there is no point in affirming you are committed to traditional humanistic, liberal values in your interactions with CSJ ideologues. They don't care. In her essay "I'm a Progressive, Please Don't Hurt Me!" Sarah Haider calls this practice of hedging "throat-clearing" and explains why it is ineffective.[119] She also points out the hidden bigotry of it—that is, the implicit assumption that those on the other side of the aisle are inherently evil. Haider writes:

> Before touching on any perspective that I knew to not be kosher among other Leftists, I tended to precede with some version of

286 THE FREE INQUIRY PAPERS

throat-clearing: "I'm on the left" or "I've voted Democrat my whole life."

I told myself that this was a distinction worth insisting on because 1) it was the truth and 2) because it helped frame the discussion properly—making clear that the argument is coming from someone who values what they value.

But there was another reason too. My political identity reminders were a plea to be considered fully and charitably, to not be villainized and presumed to be motivated by "hate."

The precursor belief to this, of course, is that *actual conservatives should not be taken charitably, are rightfully villainized, and really are motivated by "hate."*

But I'm done sputtering indignantly about being mischaracterized as "conservative," or going out of my way to remind the audience that I really am a good little liberal.[120] (Emphasis in original.)

She goes on to explain that throat clearing is counterproductive because (1) it doesn't work and you won't be spared, (2) it is a tax on energy and attention, (3) it is bad for you, and (4) it is bad for the causes you care about.

So we should stop worrying about our group loyalties and focus on our cause. Truth wears no clothes, so do not try to dress it up in partisan attire. Say what you mean, mean what you say, and move on.

It may be tempting to stay out of the fight to preserve friendships. It is true that some people you thought of as friends may turn against you—privately or even publicly. It has happened to us, and it hurts. But it also lets you know who your real friends are—those who stick up for you regardless of whether they agree with your views. And you will find new friends and allies who share your values. These relationships, forged fighting the good fight, will be enduring and empowering.

Do not apologize. We cannot stress this enough. Your apology will be taken as a sign of weakness and will not absolve you. In fact, it will make matters worse. Apologies to the illiberal mob are like drops of blood in the water to a school of sharks.

Additionally, your apology can be interpreted as an admission of guilt, which can come back to haunt you in the event you need to defend yourself legally or in an administrative proceeding. The AFA advises: "If you confess to an offense you didn't commit, or if you concede to a claim or accusation that is factually inaccurate or not truly an offense, the admission can and will be used against you."[121]

Recognize that the CSJ activists on X, formerly known as Twitter, do not care about your apology; they care about publicly flaying you to sow fear among other potential dissenters.[122] Someone claims to have been offended by your speech? Someone claims it caused them pain? Fine, that's their problem.[123] You know what your views are. And your friends do too. Stay on point.

Build a community and a network. Communities and networks provide moral support, and there is safety in numbers. Some groups already exist. The Heterodox Academy (HxA), for example, provides a platform to organize communities (e.g., HxSTEM is a community of STEM faculty) and connect with colleagues who are open to reasoned debate, as per the HxA statement, which it asks each member to endorse: "*I support open inquiry, viewpoint diversity, and constructive disagreement in research and education.*"[124] The Foundation Against Intolerance and Racism also provides resources and support to those who push back on anti-humanistic policies, especially in schools, universities, and the medical profession.

Organizations like FIRE and the AFA provide educational resources, opportunities to network, and—most importantly—protection, including legal representation. Join and support them. Build groups and act as a group; for example, write an op-ed with a group of coauthors. Ten people are harder to cancel than one. *Counter Wokecraft* describes how to identify the allies among your colleagues and build effective resistance at your workplace.

Stand up for others. Next time, they will do it for you. When you see a colleague being ostracized for what they said, think first, "Which parts of their message do I agree with?" not "Which parts do I disagree with?" If you agree with the main message, say so, and be charitable about imperfect expression. Way too often we hear colleagues justifying their silence with excuses like "I agree with her in general, but she should have been more careful about how she said this or that."

288 THE FREE INQUIRY PAPERS

In response to CSJ takeovers of their professional societies, some—including mathematicians and psychologists—have simply started new ones.[125] Perhaps we need more of this to send a strong message to the old societies that they need to change course. We see the evidence of this strategy's effectiveness. For example, the American Mathematical Society[126] canceled its CSJ-dominated blog shortly after the establishment of the new Association for Mathematical Research, whose apolitical mission is simply to "support mathematical research and scholarship."[127]

In response to increasing ideological influence and censorship in their profession, behavioral scientists founded the Society for Open Inquiry in the Behavioral Sciences in 2022, dedicated to "open inquiry, civil debate, and rigorous standards" in the field.[128] It publishes the *Journal of Open Inquiry in the Behavioral Sciences*, which commits to "free inquiry," "rigorous standards," and "intellectual exchange."[129] Notably, its terms and conditions state that the journal will base retraction decisions strictly on the widely accepted Committee on Publication Ethics guidelines;[130] otherwise, the terms and conditions state, "We will never retract a paper in response to social media mobs, open or private letters calling for retraction, denunciation petitions, or the like."[131]

There is even a new university—the University of Austin (UATX)—established in response to higher education's current CSJ crisis.[132] The message on UATX's website—"We are building a university dedicated to the fearless pursuit of truth"—makes clear what void in the American academy UATX aspires to fill.[133] That the university received over $100 million in donations and over 3,500 inquiries by professors from other institutions within six months of the project's announcement makes clear the demand.[134]

The success of such new initiatives will inspire more educators and scientists to stand up and defend the key principles of science and education. And it will send a strong message to our leadership. Even if we cannot appeal to their sense of duty, the financial considerations ("go woke, go broke")[135] and the effect of negative publicity of the excesses of CSJ (such as demanding DEI loyalty oaths, "decolonizing" the curriculum, renaming everything, and using newspeak)[136] may provide incentives to straighten out their act.

Conclusion

Will we succeed? Will we stop the train before it goes over the cliff? We do not know what will happen if we fight. But we know what will happen if we don't. The task ahead might look impossible, but remember the USSR. It looked like an unbreakable power, yet in the end it collapsed like a house of cards. The Berlin Wall looked indestructible, yet it came down overnight. Recalling his 20 years of experience in the gay marriage debate, Jonathan Rauch told us:

> I can tell you that the wall of received opinion is sturdy and impenetrable . . . until it isn't. And that it's the quiet people in the room who are the swing vote . . . and please *illegitimi non carborundum* [don't let the bastards get you down].[137]

We are not helpless. We have agency, and we should not be afraid to exercise it. We should fight not just because it is the right thing to do but because fighting brings results. If we behave as if we were living in a totalitarian society, it will become a self-fulfilling prophecy.

Afterword

A Russian proverb says, "Fear has big eyes" (у страха глаза велики), meaning that people tend to exaggerate danger. Accordingly, it may feel like resisting the mob will inevitably lead to career damage. But this is not the case; the flip side of risk is reward.

In recognition of her activism—including her publication of "The Peril of Politicizing Science," which "launched a national conversation among scientists and the general public"—Krylov received the inaugural Communicator of the Year Award (in natural sciences and mathematics) from the University of Southern California Dornsife College of Letters, Arts, and Sciences.[138]

In his article "Victory Lap," Lee Jussim, a coeditor of this book, documents that as a result of his public resistance to a mob attack on a colleague falsely accused of racism, his career enjoyed a variety of benefits—

290 THE FREE INQUIRY PAPERS

including additional conference invitations, massive public support for his activism, national attention to his scholarship, and an appointment to a departmental chair (with a commensurate increase in salary), which he was offered *because* he had demonstrated he could take the heat.[139]

Notes

1. Helen Pluckrose and James Lindsay, *Cynical Theories: How Activist Scholarship Made Everything About Race, Gender, and Identity—and Why This Harms Everybody* (Durham, NC: Pitchstone Publishing, 2020); Helen Pluckrose, "What Do We Mean by Critical Social Justice," Counterweight, February 17, 2021, https://web.archive.org/web/20230130044351/https://counterweightsupport.com/2021/02/17/what-do-we-mean-by-critical-social-justice; and Charles Pincourt, "DEI: A Trojan Horse for Critical Social Justice in Science," Merion West, April 8, 2021, https://merionwest.com/2021/04/08/dei-a-trojan-horse-for-critical-social-justice-in-science.

2. Dorian S. Abbot et al., "In Defense of Merit in Science," *Journal of Controversial Ideas* 3, no. 1 (April 2023): 1–26, https://journalofcontroversialideas.org/article/3/1/236.

3. National Institutes of Health, "Plan for Enhancing Diverse Perspectives (PEDP)," May 5, 2023, https://braininitiative.nih.gov/vision/plan-enhancing-diverse-perspectives.

4. Lawrence Krauss, "Now Even Science Grants Must Bow to 'Equity and Inclusion,'" *Wall Street Journal*, October 12, 2022, https://www.wsj.com/articles/science-grants-equity-and-inclusion-energy-department-dei-proposals-hiring-pier-plan-woke-11665153295.

5. Lawrence Krauss, "The New Scientific Method: Identity Politics," *Wall Street Journal*, May 9, 2021, https://www.wsj.com/articles/the-new-scientific-method-identity-politics-11620581262; *The Economist*, "American Universities Are Hiring Based on Devotion to Diversity," February 4, 2023, https://www.economist.com/united-states/2023/02/04/american-universities-are-hiring-based-on-devotion-to-diversity; and John D. Sailer, "How 'Diversity' Policing Fails Science," *Wall Street Journal*, February 6, 2023, https://www.wsj.com/articles/how-diversity-policing-fails-science-equality-equity-education-texas-tech-job-candidates-interview-dei-pronouns-11675722169.

6. National Center for Fair & Open Testing, "Test Optional and Test Free Colleges," https://fairtest.org/test-optional-list; and Editorial Board, "College Testing Bait-and-Switch," *Wall Street Journal*, November 23, 2021, https://www.wsj.com/articles/college-testing-bait-and-switch-university-of-california-sat-janet-napolitano-11637689492.

7. Paloma Esquivel, "Faced with Soaring Ds and Fs, Schools Are Ditching the Old Way of Grading," *Los Angeles Times*, November 8, 2021, https://www.latimes.com/california/story/2021-11-08/as-ds-and-fs-soar-schools-ditch-inequitable-grade-systems.

FIGHTING THE GOOD FIGHT IN AN AGE OF UNREASON 291

8. Sonia Michelle Cintron, Dani Wadlington, and Andre ChenFeng, *Dismantling Racism in Mathematics Instruction*, A Pathway to Equitable Math Instruction, May 2021, https://equitablemath.org/wp-content/uploads/sites/2/2020/11/1_STRIDE1.pdf; and Percy Deift, Svetlana Jitomirskaya, and Sergiu Klainerman, "America Is Flunking Math," Persuasion, May 17, 2021, https://www.persuasion.community/p/why-america-is-flunking-math-education.

9. Percy Deift, Svetlana Jitomirskaya, and Sergiu Klainerman, "As US Schools Prioritize Diversity over Merit, China Is Becoming the World's STEM Leader," Quillette, August 19, 2021, https://quillette.com/2021/08/19/as-us-schools-prioritize-diversity-over-merit-china-is-becoming-the-worlds-stem-leader.

10. National Council of Supervisors of Mathematics and TODOS: Mathematics for ALL, "Mathematics Education Through the Lens of Social Justice: Acknowledgment, Actions, and Accountability," https://www.todos-math.org/assets/docs2016/2016Enews/3.pospaper16_wtodos_8pp.pdf; Rachel Leven, "UC Berkeley Leaders Urge California to Reject Harmful Math Education Proposal," University of California, Berkeley, College of Computing, Data Science, and Society, May 12, 2022, https://data.berkeley.edu/news/uc-berkeley-leaders-urge-california-reject-harmful-math-education-proposal; and Williamson M. Evers and Ze'ev Wurman, "Replace the Proposed New California Math Curriculum Framework," Independent Institute, July 13, 2021, https://www.independent.org/news/article.asp?id=13658.

11. Sara Randazzo, "To Increase Equity, School Districts Eliminate Honors Classes," *Wall Street Journal,* February 17, 2023, https://www.wsj.com/articles/to-increase-equity-school-districts-eliminate-honors-classes-d5985dee.

12. Jeffrey Mervis, "U.S. Science No Longer Leads the World. Here's How Top Advisers Say the Nation Should Respond," *Science,* January 21, 2022, https://www.science.org/content/article/u-s-science-no-longer-leads-world-here-s-how-top-advisers-say-nation-should-respond.

13. University of Pittsburgh, Gender, Sexuality, and Women's Studies Program, "Gender-Inclusive/Non-Sexist Language Guidelines and Resources," https://www.gsws.pitt.edu/resources/faculty-resources/gender-inclusive-non-sexist-language-guidelines-and-resources; and University of Michigan, Information and Technology Services, Words Matter Task Force, "Words Matter Task Force Recommendations," December 8, 2020, https://drive.google.com/file/d/11a8cUt1SCfIxQRBZk_TnRYM5ltENL7LI/view.

14. University of Michigan, Information and Technology Services, Words Matter Task Force, "Words Matter Task Force Recommendations"; Anna I. Krylov, "The Peril of Politicizing Science," *Journal of Physical Chemistry Letters* 12, no. 22 (June 2021): 5371–76, https://pubs.acs.org/doi/full/10.1021/acs.jpclett.1c01475; John McWhorter, "Even *Trigger Warning* Is Now Off-Limits," *The Atlantic,* July 4, 2021, https://www.theatlantic.com/ideas/archive/2021/07/brandeis-language-police-have-suggestions-you/619347; and Ash T. Zemenick et al., "Six Principles for Embracing Gender and Sexual Diversity in Postsecondary Biology Classrooms," *BioScience* 72, no. 5 (May 2022): 481–92, https://academic.oup.com/bioscience/article/72/5/481/6547662. See also Jerry Coyne, "An Ideology-Infused Paper on How to Teach College Biology," Why Evolution

Is True, October 18, 2022, https://whyevolutionistrue.com/2022/10/18/an-ideology-infused-paper-on-how-to-teach-college-biology.

15. We leave as an exercise to the reader's imagination why the word "field" was deemed racist. Anna I. Krylov and Jay Tanzman, "Critical Social Justice Subverts Scientific Publishing," *European Review* 31, no. 5 (October 2023): 527–46, https://www.cambridge.org/core/journals/european-review/article/critical-social-justice-subverts-scientific-publishing/29AF22D23835C74AECDA7964E55812CF; Lawrence Krauss, "Google's 'Inclusive Language' Police," *Wall Street Journal*, January 21, 2022, https://www.wsj.com/articles/google-inclusive-language-cancel-culture-censor-free-speech-offended-woke-micro-aggression-microsoft-11642800484; Pamela Paul, "'Hip Hip Hooray!' Cheering News for Free Speech on Campus," *New York Times*, February 3, 2023, https://www.nytimes.com/2023/02/03/opinion/free-speech-stanford.html; and Nicolas Camut, "Don't Say 'the French' as It's Offensive, AP Says," *Politico*, January 27, 2023, https://www.politico.eu/article/using-labels-the-french-offensive-ap-associated-press-stylebook.

16. Zemenick et al., "Six Principles for Embracing Gender and Sexual Diversity in Postsecondary Biology Classrooms." See also Coyne, "An Ideology-Infused Paper on How to Teach College Biology."

17. Zakiya S. Wilson-Kennedy et al., "Introducing the *Journal of Chemical Education*'s Special Issue on Diversity, Equity, Inclusion, and Respect in Chemistry Education Research and Practice," *Journal of Chemical Education* 99, no. 1 (January 2022): 1–4, https://pubs.acs.org/doi/10.1021/acs.jchemed.1c01219.

18. Michelle Anne C. Reyes et al., "A Special Topic Class in Chemistry on Feminism and Science as a Tool to Disrupt the Dysconcious Racism in STEM," *Journal of Chemical Education* 100, no. 1 (November 2022): 112–17, https://pubs.acs.org/doi/10.1021/acs.jchemed.2c00293.

19. *The Economist*, "American Universities Are Hiring Based on Devotion to Diversity"; Sailer, "How 'Diversity' Policing Fails Science"; Academic Freedom Alliance, "AFA Calls for an End to Required Diversity Statements," press release, August 22, 2022, https://academicfreedom.org/afa-calls-for-an-end-to-required-diversity-statements; and Foundation for Individual Rights and Expression, "FIRE Statement on the Use of Diversity, Equity, and Inclusion Criteria in Faculty Hiring and Evaluation," https://www.thefire.org/issues/fire-statement-on-the-use-of-diversity-equity-and-inclusion-criteria-in-faculty-hiring-and-evaluation.

20. Heather Mac Donald, "The Corruption of Medicine," *City Journal*, Summer 2022, https://www.city-journal.org/the-corruption-of-medicine.

21. Amanda Montgomery, "Public Health Needs to Decouple Weight and Health," University of Illinois Chicago School of Public Health, Collaboratory for Health Justice, October 28, 2021, https://indigo.uic.edu/articles/educational_resource/Public_Health_Needs_to_Decouple_Weight_and_Health/16823341; and Gina Martinez, "University of Illinois Chicago Wants to Ban the Word 'Obesity' Because Focusing on Body Size Is 'Rooted in Racism,'" *Daily Mail*, May 18, 2022, https://www.dailymail.co.uk/news/article-10829285/Woke-experts-warn-word-obesity-RACIST-suggest-people-larger-bodies-instead.html.

FIGHTING THE GOOD FIGHT IN AN AGE OF UNREASON 293

22. Alicia Ault, "Transgender Docs Warn About Gender-Affirmative Care for Youth," Medscape, November 18, 2021, https://www.medscape.com/viewarticle/963269; Cass Review, *Independent Review of Gender Identity Services for Children and Young People*, April 2024, https://cass.independent-review.uk/wp-content/uploads/2024/04/CassReview_Final.pdf; Julia Mason and Leor Sapir, "The American Academy of Pediatrics' Dubious Transgender Science," *Wall Street Journal*, August 17, 2022, https://www.wsj.com/articles/the-american-academy-of-pediatrics-dubious-transgender-science-jack-turban-research-social-contagion-gender-dysphoria-puberty-blockers-uk-11660732791; and Jamie Reed, "I Thought I Was Saving Trans Kids. Now I'm Blowing the Whistle.," Free Press, February 9, 2023, https://www.thefp.com/p/i-thought-i-was-saving-trans-kids.

23. Greg Lukianoff, "Free Speech Does Not Equal Violence: Part 1 of Answers to Bad Arguments Against Free Speech from Nadine Strossen and Greg Lukianoff," Foundation for Individual Rights and Expression, September 1, 2021, https://www.thefire.org/free-speech-does-not-equal-violence-part-1-of-answers-to-bad-arguments-against-free-speech-from-nadine-strossen.

24. Stacy Hawkins, "Sometimes Diversity Trumps Academic Freedom," *Chronicle of Higher Education*, February 28, 2023, https://www.chronicle.com/article/sometimes-diversity-trumps-academic-freedom.

25. Abbot et al., "In Defense of Merit in Science."

26. Jonathan Rauch, "Nature Human Misbehavior: Politicized Science Is Neither Science nor Progress," Foundation for Individual Rights and Expression, September 14, 2022, https://www.thefire.org/nature-human-misbehavior-politicized-science-is-neither-science-nor-progress; Jerry Coyne, "Once Again, Scientific American Distorts Biology, and Now History, to Buttress Its Ideology," Why Evolution Is True, August 29, 2022, https://whyevolutionistrue.com/2022/08/29/once-again-scientific-american-biology-and-now-history-to-buttress-its-ideology; Jerry Coyne, "Scientific American Dedicates Itself to Politics, Not Science; Refuses to Publish Rebuttals of Their False or Misleading Claims," Why Evolution Is True, August 21, 2022, https://whyevolutionistrue.com/2022/08/21/scientific-american-dedicates-itself-to-politics-not-science-refuses-to-publish-rebuttals-of-their-false-or-misleading-claims; Neil Hatfield, Nathanial Brown, and Chad M. Topaz, "Do Introductory Courses Disproportionately Drive Minoritized Students Out of STEM Pathways?," *PNAS Nexus* 1, no. 4 (September 2022): 1–10, https://academic.oup.com/pnasnexus/article/1/4/pgac167/6706685; Joseph L. Graves Jr. et al., "Inequality in Science and the Case for a New Agenda," *Proceedings of the National Academy of Sciences* 119, no. 10 (March 2022), https://www.pnas.org/doi/full/10.1073/pnas.2117831119; Adia Harvey Wingfield, "Systemic Racism Persists in the Sciences," *Science* 369, no. 6502 (July 2020): 351, https://www.science.org/doi/full/10.1126/science.abd8825; H. Holden Thorp, "Inclusion Doesn't Lower Standards," *Science* 377, no. 6602 (July 2022): 129, https://www.science.org/doi/10.1126/science.add7259; Ebony Omotola McGee, "Dismantle Racism in Science," *Science* 375, no. 6584 (March 2022): 937, https://www.science.org/doi/10.1126/science.abo7849; Jeffrey Mervis, "Can U.S. Physics Overcome Its Record of Exclusion?," *Science* 375, no. 6584 (March 2022): 950, https://www.science.org/content/article/why-are-efforts-to-boost-small-number-of-black-us-physicists-failing; Jeffrey

Mervis, "The Toll of White Privilege: How the Dominant Culture Has Discouraged Diversity," *Science* 375, no. 6584 (March 2022): 952, https://www.science.org/content/article/how-culture-of-white-privilege-discourages-black-students-from-becoming-physicists; Melissa Nobles et al., "Science Must Overcome Its Racist Legacy: *Nature*'s Guest Editors Speak," *Nature* 606, no. 7913 (June 2022): 225–27, https://www.nature.com/articles/d41586-022-01527-z; "Tackling Systemic Racism Requires the System of Science to Change," *Nature* 593, no. 7859 (May 2021): 313, https://www.nature.com/articles/d41586-021-01312-4; "Systemic Racism: Science Must Listen, Learn and Change," *Nature* 582, no. 7811 (June 2020): 147, https://www.nature.com/articles/d41586-020-01678-x; and Fauzia Ahmad, "Racism—*Nature* Must Track Diversity of Staff and Publications," *Nature* 582, no. 7813 (June 2020): 488, https://www.nature.com/articles/d41586-020-01825-4.

27. Sean T. Stevens, Lee Jussim, and Nathan Honeycutt, "Scholarship Suppression: Theoretical Perspectives and Emerging Trends," *Societies* 10, no. 4 (October 2020): 82, https://www.mdpi.com/2075-4698/10/4/82; Colleen Flaherty, "Tracking Attacks on Scholars' Speech," *Inside Higher Ed*, August 30, 2021, https://www.insidehighered.com/news/2021/08/31/fire-launches-new-database-tracking-attacks-speech; and Foundation for Individual Rights and Expression, "Worst Colleges for Free Speech," https://www.thefire.org/resources/fires-annual-10-worst-colleges-for-free-speech-lists.

28. Mark McNeilly, "Universities Should Adopt Institutional Neutrality," Heterodox Academy, October 18, 2022, https://heterodoxacademy.org/blog/universities-should-adopt-institutional-neutrality; and Jerry Coyne, "University of Chicago's Kalven Report on Free Speech Featured and Defended in Wall Street Journal Op-Ed," Why Evolution Is True, March 17, 2022, https://whyevolutionistrue.com/2022/03/17/kalven-report-featured-in-wall-street-journal.

29. University of Pittsburgh, Office of Health Sciences Diversity, Equity, and Inclusion, "Diversity, Equity and Inclusion (DEI) Training and Enrichment," https://healthdiversity.pitt.edu/programsinitiatives/diversity-equity-and-inclusion-dei-training-and-enrichment; and Jesse Singal, "What If Diversity Training Is Doing More Harm Than Good?," *New York Times*, January 17, 2023, https://www.nytimes.com/2023/01/17/opinion/dei-trainings-effective.html.

30. Flaherty, "Tracking Attacks on Scholars' Speech."

31. See Foundation for Individual Rights and Expression, "East Georgia College: Professor Fired Without a Hearing over Mysterious 'Sexual Harassment' Charge," https://www.thefire.org/cases/east-georgia-college-professor-fired-without-a-hearing-over-mysterious-sexual-harassment-charge; Foundation for Individual Rights and Expression, "Bennington College: Termination of Professor Without a Hearing," https://www.thefire.org/cases/bennington-college-termination-of-professor-without-a-hearing; Foundation for Individual Rights and Expression, "Orange Coast College: Suspension of Professor Without a Hearing for Political Science Lecture," https://www.thefire.org/cases/orange-coast-college-suspension-of-professor-without-a-hearing-for-political-science-lecture; and Foundation for Individual Rights and Expression, "DePaul University: Professor Suspended for Expression Without Due Process," https://www.thefire.org/cases/depaul-university-professor-suspended-for-expression-without-due-process.

32. Stevens, Jussim, and Honeycutt, "Scholarship Suppression"; Foundation for Individual Rights and Expression, *2020 College Free Speech Rankings: What's the Climate for Free Speech on America's College Campuses?*, https://chronicle.brightspotcdn.com/10/2d/a28062aa41b4bc2acd088fa79da1/2020-college-free-speech-rankings.pdf; and Pomona College, "Perceptions of Speech and Campus Climate: 2018 Gallup Survey of Pomona Students and Faculty," https://www.pomona.edu/public-dialogue/survey.

33. Foundation for Individual Rights and Expression, "Breaking: New Title IX Regulations Undermine Campus Free Speech and Due Process Rights," press release, April 19, 2024, https://www.thefire.org/news/breaking-new-title-ix-regulations-undermine-campus-free-speech-and-due-process-rights.

34. John McWhorter, *Woke Racism: How a New Religion Has Betrayed Black America* (New York: Portfolio, 2021); Thomas Sowell, *Discrimination and Disparities*, rev. ed. (New York: Basic Books, 2019); and Gail Heriot and Maimon Schwarzschild, eds., *A Dubious Expediency: How Race Preferences Damage Higher Education* (New York: Encounter Books, 2021).

35. Charles Pincourt, "The Pendulum and the Ratchet," Woke Dissident Newsletter, February 17, 2022, https://wokedissident.substack.com/p/the-pendulum-and-the-ratchet.

36. Yuval Noah Harari, *Homo Deus: A Brief History of Tomorrow* (New York: HarperCollins, 2018); Steven Pinker, *The Better Angels of Our Nature: Why Violence Has Declined* (New York: Penguin Books, 2011); and Steven Pinker, *Enlightenment Now: The Case for Reason, Science, Humanism, and Progress* (New York: Penguin Publishing Group, 2018).

37. Krylov, "The Peril of Politicizing Science"; Ute Deichmann, "Science and the Ideology of Race in Western Democracies," Heterodox STEM, October 11, 2022, https://hxstem.substack.com/p/science-and-the-ideology-of-race; Anna I. Krylov, "From Russia with Love: Science and Ideology Then and Now," Heterodox STEM, November 28, 2022, https://hxstem.substack.com/p/from-russia-with-love-science-and; SocialImpurity, "On the Communist Origins of Diversity, Equality, and Inclusion Ideology," Heterodox STEM, April 3, 2023, https://hxstem.substack.com/p/on-the-communist-origins-of-diversity; and Izabella Tabarovsky, "The American Soviet Mentality," *Tablet*, June 15, 2020, https://www.tabletmag.com/sections/news/articles/american-soviet-mentality.

38. Krylov, "The Peril of Politicizing Science"; Stevens, Jussim, and Honeycutt, "Scholarship Suppression"; Flaherty, "Tracking Attacks on Scholars' Speech"; Anne Applebaum, "The New Puritans," *The Atlantic*, August 31, 2021, https://www.theatlantic.com/magazine/archive/2021/10/new-puritans-mob-justice-canceled/619818; Anna I. Krylov et al., "Scientists Must Resist Cancel Culture," *Nachrichten aus der Chemie* 70, no. 22 (February 2022): 12–14, https://onlinelibrary.wiley.com/doi/10.1002/nadc.20224120702; and Anna I. Krylov and Jay Tanzman, "Academic Ideologues Are Corrupting STEM. The Silent Liberal Majority Must Fight Back," Quillette, December 18, 2021, https://quillette.com/2021/12/18/scientists-must-gain-the-courage-to-oppose-the-politicization-of-their-disciplines.

39. Vladimir Bukovsky, *To Build a Castle: My Life as a Dissenter*, trans. Michael Scammell Bukovsky (London: André Deutsch, 1978); and Vladimir Bukovsky 1942–2019, website, https://www.vladimirbukovsky.com.

40. Christopher Hitchens, "The Man Who Kept on Writing," Slate, August 4, 2008, https://slate.com/news-and-politics/2008/08/alexander-solzhenitsyn-1918-2008.html.

41. István Hargittai, "His Fate Was Larger Than Himself: Andrei D. Sakharov's Centenary," *European Review* 30, no. 2 (April 2022): 285–300, https://www.cambridge.org/core/journals/european-review/article/his-fate-was-larger-than-himself-andrei-d-sakharovs-centenary/AF67463C6FCA42BFDD5045DFA554CC6D.

42. Vladimir Bukovsky, *Judgment in Moscow: Soviet Crimes and Western Complicity*, trans. Alyona Kojevnikov (n.p.: Ninth of November Press, 2019).

43. US Holocaust Memorial Museum, Holocaust Encyclopedia, "Martin Niemöller: 'First They Came For . . .,'" https://encyclopedia.ushmm.org/content/en/article/martin-niemoeller-first-they-came-for-the-socialists.

44. Charles Pincourt, "What You Can and Should Do," Woke Dissident Newsletter, March 17, 2022, https://wokedissident.substack.com/p/what-you-can-and-should-do.

45. Bari Weiss, "Lincoln Isn't Evil. Neither Is the West. Stand Up to the Woke Lies.," Free Press, February 1, 2021, https://www.thefp.com/p/lincoln-isnt-evil-neither-is-the.

46. Applebaum, "The New Puritans"; Richard Adams, "Kathleen Stock Says She Quit University Post over 'Medieval' Ostracism," *The Guardian*, November 3, 2021, https://www.theguardian.com/education/2021/nov/03/kathleen-stock-says-she-quit-university-post-over-medieval-ostracism; James Damore, "Why I Was Fired by Google," *Wall Street Journal*, August 11, 2017, https://www.wsj.com/articles/why-i-was-fired-by-google-1502481290; and Sam Harris and Antonio García-Martínez, "Corporate Cowardice: A Conversation with Antonio García-Martínez," May 26, 2021, in *Making Sense with Sam Harris*, podcast, MP3 audio, https://www.samharris.org/podcasts/making-sense-episodes/251-corporate-cowardice.

47. Krylov and Tanzman, "Academic Ideologues Are Corrupting STEM."

48. Hargittai, "His Fate Was Larger Than Himself."

49. Maud Maron, "Why Are Moms Like Me Being Called Domestic Terrorists?," Free Press, October 11, 2021, https://www.thefp.com/p/why-are-moms-like-me-being-called.

50. Editorial Board, "The IRS Makes a Strange House Call on Matt Taibbi," *Wall Street Journal*, March 27, 2023, https://www.wsj.com/articles/irs-matt-taibbi-twitter-files-jim-jordan-daniel-werfel-lina-khan-84ee518.

51. Edward Cantu and Lee Jussim, "Microaggressions, Questionable Science, and Free Speech," *Texas Review of Law & Politics* 26, no. 1 (April 2022), https://papers.ssrn.com/sol3/papers.cfm?abstract_id=3822628#.

52. David L. Hudson Jr., "Federal Judge Rules Former Medical Student Cited for Lack of Professionalism Has a Plausible Retaliation Claim," First Amendment Watch, April 13, 2021, https://firstamendmentwatch.org/federal-judge-rules-former-medical-student-cited-for-lack-of-professionalism-has-a-plausible-retaliation-claim.

53. Bukovsky, *To Build a Castle*; and Bukovsky, *Judgment in Moscow*.

54. Pincourt, "What You Can and Should Do."

55. Charles Pincourt and James Lindsay, *Counter Wokecraft: A Field Manual for Combatting the Woke in the University and Beyond* (Orlando, FL: New Discourses, 2021).

56. Gad Saad, *The Parasitic Mind: How Infectious Ideas Are Killing Common Sense* (Washington, DC: Regnery Publishing, 2020).

57. Today in Science History, "Marie Curie," https://todayinsci.com/C/Curie_Marie/CurieMarie-Quotations.htm.

58. Krylov, "From Russia with Love"; and SocialImpurity, "On the Communist Origins of Diversity, Equality, and Inclusion Ideology."

59. To illustrate the Soviet people's skill in navigating through propaganda, Vladimir Bukovsky writes, "An intelligent-looking little old man wanders down the Arbat and into the Prague to do some shopping, a quiet, subdued little man bothering nobody. 'Aha', he says to himself, 'the sun's shinning [*sic*], the bloody sun's grinning its head off again. They will be calling that a socialist achievement next.' He hates the sight of that sky, that soviet sky. . . . There's a fresh newspaper pinned to the wall—what claptrap are they blathering now? He knows it's claptrap and it sickens him to read it, but still he stops and scans it, if only to feed his rage. 'Aha, the harvest! Unprecedented, as usual, in record time, as usual. So we'll be importing grain from Canada again. Students helping on the collective farms. Oh yes, the usual thing: collective farmers, help the students to fill the nation's granaries! A strike in France. Go on, strike away, you'll strike once too often these days. Student demonstrations dispersed. Send them here to help with potato picking, they'll soon forget about demonstrating.'" Bukovsky, *To Build a Castle*.

60. Steven Brint, "The UC's Corner-Office Revolutionary," Quillette, April 9, 2024, https://quillette.com/2024/04/09/the-ucs-corner-office-revolutionary.

61. Pincourt, "DEI."

62. Pluckrose and Lindsay, *Cynical Theories*.

63. Zaid Jilani, "Our Institutions Keep Undermining Themselves," Persuasion, September 29, 2021, https://www.persuasion.community/p/our-institutions-keep-undermining.

64. Bukovsky, *To Build a Castle*.

65. Bukovsky, *To Build a Castle*, 66.

66. Rauch, "Nature Human Misbehavior"; Anna I. Krylov, Gernot Frenking, and Peter Gill, "Royal Society of Chemistry Provides Guidelines for Censorship to Its Editors," *Chemistry International* 44, no. 1 (January–March 2024): 32–34, https://www.degruyter.com/document/doi/10.1515/ci-2022-0119/html; and Jonathan Haidt, "The Two Fiduciary Duties of Professors," Heterodox Academy, September 20, 2022, https://heterodoxacademy.org/blog/the-two-fiduciary-duties-of-professors.

67. Abbot et al., "In Defense of Merit in Science"; Deift, Jitomirskaya, and Klainerman, "America Is Flunking Math"; Deift, Jitomirskaya, and Klainerman, "As US Schools Prioritize Diversity over Merit, China Is Becoming the World's STEM Leader"; Krylov, "The Peril of Politicizing Science"; Krylov et al., "Scientists Must Resist Cancel Culture"; Krylov and Tanzman, "Academic Ideologues Are Corrupting STEM. The Silent Liberal Majority Must Fight Back"; and Krylov, Frenking, and Gill, "Royal Society of Chemistry Provides Guidelines for Censorship to Its Editors."

68. Group of Signatories of UMB Open Letter, "How to Efficiently Organize an Open Letter to Challenge Your University Administration," Heterodox STEM, March 7, 2022, https://hxstem.substack.com/p/how-to-efficiently-organize-an-open.

69. Dorian S. Abbot, private communication with Anna I. Krylov, 2022.

70. Abbot, communication with Krylov.

298 THE FREE INQUIRY PAPERS

71. Aaron Terr, "Victory: University of Washington Rejects DEI Statement Proposal That Threatened Academic Freedom," Foundation for Individual Rights and Expression, June 15, 2022, https://www.thefire.org/victory-university-of-washington-rejects-dei-statement-proposal-that-threatened-academic-freedom.

72. Stuart Reges, message to Anna I. Krylov on Heterodox STEM forum, October 11, 2022.

73. Jerry Coyne, "UNC Adopts Both of Chicago's Free-Speech Principles," Why Evolution Is True, June 28, 2022, https://whyevolutionistrue.com/2022/07/28/unc-adopts-both-of-chicagos-free-speech-principles.

74. Geoffrey R. Stone et al., "Report of the Committee on Freedom of Expression," University of Chicago, Office of the Provost, https://provost.uchicago.edu/sites/default/files/documents/reports/FOECommitteeReport.pdf; and Kalven Committee, "Report on the University's Role in Political and Social Action," University of Chicago, Office of the Provost, November 11, 1967, https://provost.uchicago.edu/sites/default/files/documents/reports/KalvenRprt_0.pdf.

75. Isabel Vincent, "University of North Carolina Cancels Woke Diversity in Hiring," *New York Post*, February 25, 2023, https://nypost.com/2023/02/25/university-of-north-carolina-cancels-woke-diversity-in-hiring.

76. Evers and Wurman, "Replace the Proposed New California Math Curriculum Framework."

77. Do No Harm, website, https://donoharmmedicine.org.

78. Stanley Goldfarb, "How America's Obsession with DEI Is Sabotaging Our Medical Schools," Free Press, May 2, 2023, https://www.thefp.com/p/how-americas-obsession-with-dei-is.

79. Kathy Wren, "Q&A: Stuart Schmill on MIT's Decision to Reinstate the SAT/ACT Requirement," MIT News, March 28, 2022, https://news.mit.edu/2022/stuart-schmill-sat-act-requirement-0328.

80. Babbling Beaver, "Bowing to Babbling Beaver Mockery MIT Reinstates Math SAT Requirement," March 31, 2022, https://babblingbeaver.com/2022/03/31/bowing-to-babbling-beaver-mockery-mit-reinstates-math-sat-requirement.

81. Paul, "'Hip Hip Hooray!'"

82. Lawrence Krauss, "Apparently Social Work May No Longer Be a Legitimate Field, at Least at USC and in Michigan," Critical Mass, June 13, 2023, https://lawrencekrauss.substack.com/p/apparently-social-work-may-no-longer.

83. Paul, "'Hip Hip Hooray!'"

84. National Association of Scholars, "Victory for Academic Freedom: Texas Tech Ditches Diversity Statements," February 8, 2023, https://www.nas.org/blogs/press_release/victory-for-academic-freedom-texas-tech-ditches-diversity-statements.

85. Sailer, "How 'Diversity' Policing Fails Science."

86. Sarah Lehr, "UW to Eliminate Diversity, Equity and Inclusion Statements for Job Applicants as Vos Threatens Funding Cuts," May 11, 2023, https://www.wpr.org/uw-eliminate-diversity-equity-and-inclusion-statements-job-applicants-vos-threatens-funding-cuts.

87. Ray Stern, "AZ Universities Drop Use of Diversity, Equity and Inclusion Statements in Job Applications," *Arizona Republic*, accessed August 9, 2023, https://

web.archive.org/web/20230809080303/https:/eu.azcentral.com/story/news/politics/arizona-education/2023/08/08/asu-ua-nau-drop-use-of-diversity-statements-in-university-job-applications/70554093007.

88. Foundation for Individual Rights and Expression, website, https://www.thefire.org; and Academic Freedom Alliance, "Public Statements," https://academicfreedom.org/public-statements.

89. Stanford Alumni for Free Speech and Critical Thinking, "Archive—Stanford Concerns," https://www.stanfordfreespeech.org/archives.

90. Pluckrose and Lindsay, *Cynical Theories*; Pincourt, "DEI"; Pincourt, "The Pendulum and the Ratchet"; Pincourt and Lindsay, *Counter Wokecraft*; and Andrew M. Lobaczewski, *Political Ponerology: The Science of Evil, Psychopathy, and the Origins of Totalitarianism* (Otto, NC: Red Pill Press, 2022).

91. Pincourt, "DEI"; *The Economist*, "American Universities Are Hiring Based on Devotion to Diversity"; Pincourt and Lindsay, *Counter Wokecraft*; Katherine Mangan, "What Exactly Is a 'DEI Bureaucracy'?," *Chronicle of Higher Education*, February 14, 2023, https://www.chronicle.com/newsletter/race-on-campus/2023-02-14; Matthew Spalding, "DEI Spells Death for the Idea of a University," *Wall Street Journal*, February 10, 2023, https://www.wsj.com/articles/dei-spells-death-for-the-idea-of-a-university-diversity-equity-inclusion-academia-college-hillsdale-new-college-of-florida-open-discourse-1d2ca552; John Sailer, "How DEI Is Supplanting Truth as the Mission of American Universities," Free Press, January 9, 2023, https://www.thefp.com/p/how-dei-is-supplanting-truth-as-the; and Amna Khalid and Jeffrey Aaron Snyder, "Yes, DEI Can Erode Academic Freedom. Let's Not Pretend Otherwise.," *Chronicle of Higher Education*, February 6, 2023, https://www.chronicle.com/article/yes-dei-can-erode-academic-freedom-lets-not-pretend-otherwise.

92. Pluckrose and Lindsay, *Cynical Theories*; and Pincourt and Lindsay, *Counter Wokecraft*.

93. Ryan Quinn, "A DEI Director Ousted for Questioning DEI?," *Inside Higher Ed*, March 9, 2023, https://www.insidehighered.com/news/2023/03/10/equity-director-targeted-she-says-questioning-antiracist-orthodoxy.

94. Quinn, "A DEI Director Ousted for Questioning DEI?"

95. Mangan, "What Exactly Is a 'DEI Bureaucracy'?"; Sailer, "How DEI Is Supplanting Truth as the Mission of American Universities"; University of California, Berkeley, Division of Equity and Inclusion, "Impact Report 2020–21," 91, https://diversity.berkeley.edu/sites/default/files/ucberkeley-diversity-impact-report_oct29.pdf; Jay Greene and James Paul, "Diversity University: DEI Bloat in the Academy," Heritage Foundation, https://www.heritage.org/education/report/diversity-university-dei-bloat-the-academy; and Johanna Alonso, "Diversity Officer Survey Shows Range of Pay, Budgets, Worries," *Inside Higher Ed*, August 31, 2023, https://www.insidehighered.com/news/quick-takes/2023/08/31/diversity-officer-survey-shows-range-pay-budgets-worries.

96. Greene and Paul, "Diversity University: DEI Bloat in the Academy." In their report, Jay Greene and James Paul write: "The average university has 45.1 people tasked with promoting diversity, equity, and inclusion. Some universities have many more. For example, the University of Michigan has 163 DEI personnel. Nineteen of those people

work in a central office of DEI, headed by a Vice Provost for Equity and Inclusion & Chief Diversity Officer, who is subsequently supported by three people with the title Assistant Vice Provost for Equity, Inclusion & Academic Affairs. Five people are listed in the Multicultural Center, another 24 are found in the Center for the Education of Women, and the LGBTQ Spectrum Center has 12 people. Eighteen people are listed on the Multiethnic Student Affairs website with another 14 found at the Office of Academic Multicultural Initiatives. Moreover, colleges and departments at the University of Michigan have their own DEI staff." See also Mangan, "What Exactly Is a 'DEI Bureaucracy'?"

97. Alonso, "Diversity Officer Survey Shows Range of Pay, Budgets, Worries."

98. University of California, Berkeley, Division of Equity and Inclusion, "Impact Report 2020–21." The report breaks down the total 2021 budget of $41 million: 65 percent was used for compensation (i.e., salaries of the "diversicrats"), 2 percent for materials and supplies, and 24 percent for other operational expenses. Only 9 percent was used for student support (for "student awards, including scholarships and fellowships"). University of California, Berkeley, Division of Equity and Inclusion, "Impact Report 2020–21," 91.

99. National Center for Fair & Open Testing, "Test Optional and Test Free Colleges"; Cintron, Wadlington, and ChenFeng, *Dismantling Racism in Mathematics Instruction*; National Council of Supervisors of Mathematics and TODOS: Mathematics for ALL, "Mathematics Education Through the Lens of Social Justice"; and Zemenick et al., "Six Principles for Embracing Gender and Sexual Diversity in Postsecondary Biology Classrooms." See also Coyne, "An Ideology-Infused Paper on How to Teach College Biology"; Wilson-Kennedy et al., "Introducing the Journal of Chemical Education's Special Issue on Diversity, Equity, Inclusion, and Respect in Chemistry Education Research and Practice"; and Hawkins, "Sometimes Diversity Trumps Academic Freedom."

100. Khalid and Snyder, "Yes, DEI Can Erode Academic Freedom."

101. Quinn, "A DEI Director Ousted for Questioning DEI?"

102. Pluckrose and Lindsay, *Cynical Theories*; Pincourt, "DEI"; Abbot et al., "In Defense of Merit in Science"; Hawkins, "Sometimes Diversity Trumps Academic Freedom"; SocialImpurity, "On the Communist Origins of Diversity, Equality, and Inclusion Ideology"; Saad, *The Parasitic Mind*; Spalding, "DEI Spells Death for the Idea of a University"; Sailer, "How DEI Is Supplanting Truth as the Mission of American Universities"; Khalid and Snyder, "Yes, DEI Can Erode Academic Freedom"; Quinn, "A DEI Director Ousted for Questioning DEI?"; Andrew Sullivan, "Removing the Bedrock of Liberalism," Weekly Dish, May 28, 2021, https://andrewsullivan.substack.com/p/removing-the-bedrock-of-liberalism-826; and Amna Khalid and Jeffrey Aaron Snyder, "How to Fix Diversity and Equity," *Chronicle of Higher Education*, May 27, 2021, https://www.chronicle.com/article/how-to-fix-diversity-and-equity.

103. Chronicle Staff, "DEI Legislation Tracker," *Chronicle of Higher Education*, https://www.chronicle.com/article/here-are-the-states-where-lawmakers-are-seeking-to-ban-colleges-dei-efforts.

104. Christopher F. Rufo, Ilya Shapiro, and Matt Beienburg, "Abolish DEI Bureaucracies and Restore Colorblind Equality in Public Universities," Manhattan Institute, January 18, 2023, https://manhattan.institute/article/abolish-dei-bureaucracies-and-restore-colorblind-equality-in-public-universities.

105. Sean Beeghly, "Texas Governor Signs Bill Banning Diversity Initiatives in Public Universities," Jurist, June 18, 2023, https://www.jurist.org/news/2023/06/texas-governor-signs-bill-banning-diversity-initiatives-in-public-universities.

106. McWhorter, *Woke Racism*; Pincourt, "DEI"; Pincourt and Lindsay, *Counter Wokecraft*; Pluckrose and Lindsay, *Cynical Theories*; and Saad, *The Parasitic Mind*.

107. John Staddon, "Duke Divinity School's Race to the Bottom," James G. Martin Center for Academic Renewal, April 16, 2018, https://www.jamesgmartin.center/2018/04/duke-divinity-schools-race-to-the-bottom.

108. Staddon, "Duke Divinity School's Race to the Bottom."

109. Staddon, "Duke Divinity School's Race to the Bottom."

110. Babbling Beaver is a dissident website that exposes and satirizes the woke at the Massachusetts Institute of Technology (MIT). It disseminates what it calls "Real Fake News"—satirical news-like articles that refer to real programs and events at MIT. Babbling Beaver, website, https://babblingbeaver.com.

111. Babbling Beaver, "MIT President Cancels Himself," February 14, 2022, https://babblingbeaver.com/2022/02/14/mit-president-cancels-himself.

112. Alumni and Donors Unite, "How the Administration Brought CSJ to USD," University of San Diego—a Review, September 2021, https://www.alumnianddonorsunite.org/USD/Content/administration_installed_csj.html.

113. Abbot et al., "In Defense of Merit in Science."

114. Uri Harris, "How Activists Took Control of a University: The Case Study of Evergreen State," Quillette, December 18, 2017, https://quillette.com/2017/12/18/activists-took-control-university-case-study-evergreen-state.

115. Editorial Board, "A Lesson in Campus Consequences," *Wall Street Journal*, January 15, 2020, https://www.wsj.com/articles/a-lesson-in-campus-consequences-11579134145.

116. "The Motte and Bailey rhetorical ploy is explained, for example, in *Counter Wokecraft*. The name comes from a type of medieval castle comprising a motte, a well-reinforced tower, and a bailey, a courtyard around the motte, protected by walls and a ditch. The motte is easy to defend but uncomfortable to stay in. The bailey is more comfortable, but also more vulnerable. 'The Motte & Bailey strategy involves a proponent who wants to advocate a difficult-to-defend, extreme position (the bailey). When (or if) the extreme position is challenged, the proponent retreats to an easily defendable and easily acceptable position (the motte). The key to the strategy is a hidden false equivalency of the extreme and easily defendable positions.' For example, a Woke professor can propose that a faculty search committee advances female candidates. When confronted with objections—e.g., by pointing out to the unfairness of such proposition—the Woke advocate might say: 'What, you do not believe that sexism had held women back and limited their professional advances?' This move—retreat to the motte—aims to destabilize the opponent and to distort the nature of the argument. I witnessed this trick in action—its effectiveness is based on the false equivalency between the uncontroversial claim that sexism affected women in the past and the extreme proposition that female candidates should be given a preferential treatment by the search committee." Anna I. Krylov and Jay Tanzman, "Guest Post: Fighting the Good Fight in an Age of

302 THE FREE INQUIRY PAPERS

Unreason—a New Dissident Guide," Critical Mass, October 2, 2023, https://lawrencekrauss.substack.com/p/guest-post-fighting-the-good-fight.

117. Pincourt and Lindsay, *Counter Wokecraft*.

118. Saad, *The Parasitic Mind*, 187.

119. Sarah Haider, "I'm a Progressive, Please Don't Hurt Me!," Hold That Thought by Sarah Haider, February 10, 2022, https://sarahhaider.substack.com/p/im-a-progressive-please-dont-hurt. See Jerry Coyne, "Sarah Haider on Why You Shouldn't Emphasize Your Liberal Bona Fides," February 11, 2022, https://whyevolutionistrue.com/2022/02/11/sarah-haider-on-why-you-shouldnt-emphasize-your-liberal-bona-fides.

120. Haider, "I'm a Progressive, Please Don't Hurt Me!"

121. Donald Aexander Downs, Robert P. George, and Keith E. Whittington, "So They're Trying to Shut You Up: How to Defend Yourself in a Free-Speech Crisis, Whatever Your Politics," *Chronicle of Higher Education*, October 4, 2021, https://www.chronicle.com/article/a-faculty-first-aid-kit-for-your-free-speech-crisis. For a shorter version, see also Academic Freedom Alliance, website, https://academicfreedom.org.

122. Bari Weiss, "On Decency and Double Standards at Georgetown," Free Press, January 30, 2022, https://www.thefp.com/p/on-decency-and-double-standards-at.

123. Lawrence Krauss, "Why the Easily Offended Are a Threat to Scientific Progress," *National Post*, December 5, 2021, https://nationalpost.com/opinion/lawrence-krauss-the-offence-offensive.

124. Heterodox Academy, "About Heterodox Academy," https://heterodoxacademy.org/about.

125. Association for Mathematical Research, website, https://amathr.org; and Lee Jussim, "Introducing the Society for Open Inquiry in the Behavioral Sciences," Unsafe Science, July 8, 2022, https://unsafescience.substack.com/p/introducing-the-society-for-open.

126. "The American Mathematical Society is dedicated to advancing research and connecting the diverse global mathematical community through publications, meetings and conferences, MathSciNet, professional services, advocacy, and awareness programs." American Mathematical Society, website, https://www.ams.org/home/page.

127. Association for Mathematical Research, website, https://amathr.org.

128. Society for Open Inquiry in Behavioral Science, website, https://openinquirybehavio.wixsite.com/oibs.

129. Society for Open Inquiry in Behavioral Science, website, https://openinquirybehavio.wixsite.com/oibs.

130. Committee on Publication Ethics, "Promoting Integrity in Research and Its Publication," https://publicationethics.org.

131. Researchers.One, "Terms and Conditions of Journal of Open Inquiry in the Behavioral Sciences," https://researchers.one/journals/joibs/terms.

132. Tom Bartlett, "A Controversial College Takes Shape," *Chronicle of Higher Education*, November 2, 2022, https://www.chronicle.com/article/a-controversial-college-takes-shape.

133. An older version of the website reads:

> Universities devoted to the unfettered pursuit of truth are the cornerstone of a free and flourishing democratic society.

> For universities to serve their purpose, they must be fully committed to freedom of inquiry, freedom of conscience, and civil discourse.
>
> In order to maintain these principles, UATX will be fiercely independent—financially, intellectually, and politically.

University of Austin, "Our Principles," accessed June 12, 2023, https://web.archive.org/web/20230613094437/https://www.uaustin.org/our-principles.

134. Bari Weiss, "The New Founders America Needs," *Free Press*, July 10, 2022, https://www.thefp.com/p/the-new-founders-america-needs.

135. Chartered Institute of Marketing, "When Brands Go Woke, Do They Go Broke?," February 3, 2020, https://www.cim.co.uk/content-hub/editorial/when-brands-go-woke-do-they-go-broke.

136. Sailer, "How 'Diversity' Policing Fails Science"; Krylov, "The Peril of Politicizing Science"; McWhorter, "Even *Trigger Warning* Is Now Off-Limits"; and Babbling Beaver, website, https://babblingbeaver.com.

137. Jonathan Rauch, email to authors, August 9, 2022.

138. University of Southern California Dornsife Communication Staff, "Inaugural Communicator of the Year Awards Honor Scholars Who Engage with the Public," March 21, 2022, University of Southern California, Dana and David Dornsife College of Letters, Arts and Sciences, https://dornsife.usc.edu/news/stories/2021-communicator-of-the-year-awards.

139. Lee Jussim, "Victory Lap," *Unsafe Science*, September 17, 2023, https://unsafescience.substack.com/p/victory-lap.

PART IV.
Looking Forward

18

Free Speech Advice for the President of Hypothetical U

Greg Lukianoff and Adam Goldstein

"Does calling for the genocide of Jews violate Penn's rules or code of conduct? Yes or no?"[1]

This was Rep. Elise Stefanik's (R-NY) question to the University of Pennsylvania's then-President Elizabeth Magill during a congressional hearing held by the House Committee on Education and the Workforce on December 8, 2023. It was both rhetorical and entomological, in the sense that Magill was thoroughly pinned down by it, and it was all over but the squirming.

Magill replied: "If the speech turns into conduct, it can be harassment, yes." It's not a terrible answer. It might get you a C on a First Amendment exam, but not an F. But Magill's pose as a staunch, unapologetic defender of even highly unsympathetic speech did suffer from one major flaw: It's wholly incongruous with the entirety of Penn's decision-making regarding campus free speech for years.

Penn had devoted a great deal of effort to stamping out microaggressions and forcing its community members to confront unconscious bias. It has a bias response office (administrators who investigate allegedly offensive speech), with a bias response incident protocol (a list of procedures to be followed if someone says something offensive) that relies on a bias response network within the university to refer reports as they deem appropriate (an often anonymous way for someone to turn someone else in for their speech). It has done everything to subject conservative firebrand Professor Amy Wax to a witch hunt except put her on a scale and see if she weighs the same as a duck.[2] Penn hasn't shown anything resembling hesitation when it comes to punishing speech it doesn't like. That's why, in the Foundation for Individual Rights and Expression's (FIRE) 2024 College Free Speech Rankings, Penn was ranked 247th out of 248 schools, with

306

FREE SPEECH ADVICE 307

an overall score of 11.13 on a standardized scale. Only Harvard, with a score of zero, ranked lower.

And so it was that Magill's invocation of an uncontroversial principle of free expression—the dichotomy between words and actions—managed to antagonize everyone. But it wasn't wrong. The "calls for genocide" Rep. Stefanik referenced weren't some mob of students yelling, "Let's go genocide some Jewish students!" They were chants like "globalize the intifada" (a call to shake off oppression) or "from the river to the sea," coming from a group of students who frequently couldn't identify which river or which sea, let alone have an actionable plan to get there and conduct a genocide. So Magill's response was correct. It just wasn't believable from her brand. Penn is no more in a position to be a martyr for free expression than Ty-D-Bol is in a position to sell cheesesteaks: Nothing about its history should convince anyone to buy it.

It didn't have to be that way. Had President Magill entered that hearing as the head of an institution that had stood up for the right to dissent in prior cases, its decision to do so here would not have alienated as many people. There would have been difficult moments, as there always must be in a free society, but moments pass, and principles endure, if you respect them.

Easy to say, I know. And while it will never be *easy* to manage campus protests, it can become eas*ier* if you understand how a free speech culture views protests and expects us (all of us) to react. Let's try an exercise: Let's walk through how a college president *could* react to campus protests in a way that's consistent with a culture of free speech.

Absolution for Your Anti-Speech Instincts

We sense the guilt in you for traveling down this path. We would like to begin by freeing you from the expectations you are putting on yourself. We understand that university presidents went through a difficult time in the past couple of semesters; usually, their oversight of student speech is somewhere between feckless and malicious, and they rarely suffer the consequences for that. Perhaps some of this advice will help them too.

It is OK to feel uncomfortable with protests. Unless you're a deeply maladjusted individual, people yelling at you will upset you, particularly when

308 THE FREE INQUIRY PAPERS

those people are misinformed or, if they use TikTok, actively mal-informed. That discomfort is normal and is happening because you are a human being with a soul. Good for you, in fact! What is *not OK* is assuming your discomfort means the protest should be stopped.

It is *OK* to feel uncomfortable when you need to stop a protest that has turned into violence, threats, harassment, or criminal activity. As we just said, confrontation is uncomfortable. No healthy person wants to see a student's college career hurt by their bad decisions, whether those decisions are alcohol or arson. But the college has obligations to its other students, its faculty, and its role as a place of inquiry. What is *not OK* is refusing to stop violence, threats, harassment, or criminal activity because you feel uncomfortable.

It is *OK* to feel sympathetic to one point of view or hostile to another. As Edward R. Murrow observed, we are all prisoners of our experiences. Campuses frequently consist of like-minded people. The very reason the Israel-Palestine conflict has been such a big deal on campus is that it's a fight among people on the left, people who generally agree about otherwise divisive issues. What is *not OK* is to rationalize that your sympathy justifies suppressing other viewpoints because your feelings must originate in some underlying universal truth that deserves to be enforced.

It is *OK* to doubt yourself and your decisions and to voice that uncertainty. You are not expected to know all the answers about free speech culture and how to protect it. Liberal democracy is still at a tender age (compared to, say, monarchy), and one of its greatest strengths is the ability to refine ever toward liberty. If you realize you handled something wrong, say so, and explain how you might do it differently in the future. What is *not OK* is believing it is better to double down on a mistake than to project weakness by admitting it.

In short, don't feel guilty for your feelings. Understand them, and act in accordance with the higher principles of free speech culture. Forgive yourself (and others) for doing it imperfectly. Recognize that free speech culture is extraordinarily unnatural. Our instinct is to censor. And yet, it is also our instinct to engage in unrestrained procreation, and most of us have managed to avoid doing that; acting out of principles rather than instinct is what makes civilization possible.

Hypothetical University Protests: Day Zero

Let's imagine you are the president of Hypothetical University, a large private institution in the Northeast. While private institutions are not necessarily restrained by the First Amendment, your institution has long promised students they would have First Amendment rights while they attend. Many courts have enforced promises of free expression as contractual, and in California, a state law prevents colleges from punishing students for speech or conduct that would be protected off campus. Accordingly, HypoU has some legal obligations that limit what actions it may take when there's unrest on campus. (You will come to find that's true of the vast majority of higher educational institutions. You could count on one hand the noteworthy schools that have made their reputation on promising *less* freedom, if you exclude the military academies and highly religious universities.)

Your institution should have rules. And before we even describe them, let's avoid repeating the mistakes of the past: Your rules should be clearly communicated and visibly enforced. The selective enforcement of rules was a major component of the hypocrisy that gave college administrators no moral authority when they needed it. If you persecute professors who use ableist language like "shortsighted" but defend the right to call for the extermination of an ethnic group, you don't look like someone who cares about free speech; you look like a bigot who plays favorites.

We'll say it again because it's that important: Your rules should be clearly communicated and visibly enforced. Clearly communicated to students in orientation and handbooks, and clearly communicated to campus employees (including law enforcement) in manuals and trainings. Visibly enforced by explicitly defending the speech that falls within them and pursuing the speech that falls outside of them.

In these orientations and trainings, you should train administrators to not police speech or signal political orthodoxies but defend and promote speech and discussion. If you have bias response teams or professors who rationalize things like shout downs and student cancellations, this is the time to start getting rid of them—or at least moving them into positions where they won't have student contact. That work should have begun yesterday, but the next best time is today.

310   THE FREE INQUIRY PAPERS

So what are the rules that must be carefully inculcated and respected? Some of these are mandated by the government and required to remain eligible for student loan funding, such as rules against harassment. Those rules require colleges to limit the harm from conduct that is "so severe, pervasive, and objectively offensive, and that so undermines and detracts from the victims' educational experience, that the victim-students are effectively denied equal access to an institution's resources and opportunities."[3]

For example, in October 2023, a Cornell student was arrested for a series of online threats against Jewish students at the school, including threats to slit the throats of the men, sexually assault the women and throw them from a bridge, and "bring an assault rifle to campus and shoot all you pig jews." The school, unsurprisingly, acted: They called law enforcement, who arrested and charged the student.[4]

But that is an extreme example, and it's important to note what the rules do *not* require the college to do to stop harassment: Censor speakers. Your institution is obligated to take action to lessen the adverse effects of the harassment, but the universe of potential options is unlimited; as long as it doesn't materially disadvantage either party's ability to receive their education, that meets the obligation. Some administrators have struggled with the idea that the obligation to act imposed by federal regulations does *not* create an exception to the First Amendment.

This is important because, in response to campus protests, the Department of Education has stated that a college still has an obligation to act when no individual actor has engaged in "severe, pervasive, and objectively offensive" conduct or speech, but the collective action of a group or groups has created a "severe, pervasive, and objectively offensive" environment.[5] For example, if a Jewish student must pass chanting mobs, biased posters, and burning effigies to get to every class, the school's obligation to offer aid to the Jewish student does not automatically mean the students who are chanting can be censored. It is possible for someone to have a First Amendment right to participate in a protest, while at the same time, the institution has to do something to help a student who feels targeted by that activity.

Your institution's guiding star here has to be that no student can be deprived of the value of their educational investment based on an environment toxic toward their race, gender, religion, or national origin or the perception of any of those things. And if a student can reasonably argue that's the climate, the institution has to respond—but the response doesn't necessarily have to be punitive or focused on speech. Columbia attempted this during its own encampment when it said classes must have a remote option.[6] Was that a perfect solution? Probably not, but the Department of Education requires the school to do *something*, not *the perfect thing*.

What other rules should the institution have in place? Presumably, it has "time, place, and manner" restraints on where people can gather, and while generous, they likely prohibit outright living in the outdoor common spaces. For rodent and sewage reasons alone, that's a good rule. Even if we succeed in building a civilization on a culture of free speech, it would be short-lived without indoor plumbing.

There should also be rules against all forms of the "heckler's veto," including shouting down or blocking speakers or other organized actions designed to frustrate the ability to engage in peaceful discussion and debate, especially between people with strong opposing viewpoints. FIRE's College Free Speech Rankings Survey shows that students are becoming increasingly comfortable using their actions to shut down speech. In the 2024 rankings, 45 percent of students said it was at least rarely OK to block other students from attending a speech; a year prior, that was 37 percent.[7] In 2024, 27 percent said violence was at least rarely acceptable to stop a speaker; a year prior, it was 20 percent.

Remember, all these rules have to be *viewpoint* and *content* neutral. Viewpoint neutral means the rule doesn't punish some viewpoints more than others; content neutral means the rule doesn't discriminate among issues. In a First Amendment context, viewpoint discrimination is outright unconstitutional, and content discrimination is presumptively unconstitutional and requires strict scrutiny from a court, generally meaning a loss for the institution. And in a free speech cultural context, making rules based on someone's ideas undermines the goal of encouraging the expression of those ideas.

And to reiterate for the third time: Educating students about these rules is just as important as having them. That education should explain *why* the rules exist and *how* a culture of free expression is meant to operate. That is to say, there are neutral, nonspeech rules about the operation of the campus, and the desire to engage in expression does not create an exception

312 THE FREE INQUIRY PAPERS

to those rules. The goal of a university is to educate its students, and to do that, it has to ensure every student has equal access to its offerings.

There is one more rule we should have: a rule of institutional neutrality. But let's discuss the wisdom of that rule after a couple of days of protest, shall we?

Day One: A Wild Protest Appears!

Imagine that students have started to protest on your campus. To achieve the proper visceral effect, let's assume they're protesting you because they think your salary is too high, and they want to take two-thirds of your salary and invest it in food delivery for the protesters.

You realize, of course, that this is untrue; your imaginary salary is entirely in line with both averages across institutions and the value you bring to HypoU. After all, this entire institution would *literally not exist* if you weren't imagining it right now. It's hard to put a value on that! But they're yelling at you, nonetheless.

A hundred protesters are on the open lawn outside your office, holding signs that read: "TUITION HIKES FOR PAY SPIKES," "EDUCATION OVER COMPENSATION," and "OUR DEBT, YOUR PROFIT." They chant: "Fund our future, not your salary!" From the window, you see curious families on a campus visit for prospective students looking over at the crowd, worried. The protesters chant loudly enough for you to hear but not loudly enough to interfere with classes, and they leave when it gets dark.

From a First Amendment standpoint, nothing's wrong here.

"But the students are wrong!" you might well object. Arguably, the right level of compensation for a college president doesn't have an objective truth. But wrong people have First Amendment rights too.

In fact, you'll come to discover that many of the people on campus are ignorant of something, which is probably why they thought it was a good idea to invest in an education. The First Amendment includes the right to be wrong, because if it didn't, we'd need to appoint an arbiter of truth. That duty would probably fall to Congress, and we're not sure *any* of us would trust the result of that process.

Even if we thought that was a good idea, truth is rarely as simple or as binary as we would like, and the process of refining truth means processing through what, eventually, we see as untruth. Truth is a never-ending process of conjecture and refutation, chipping away at falsity to zero in on, but never quite reach, the truth. The diversity of activity on a modern campus reflects the pursuit of truth down every possible corridor, but the institution's purpose remains the pursuit of truth, and the biggest mistakes begin when we forget that.

"But the protests are in view of the prospective students!" you cry. That's good—the sooner students understand that a free speech culture involves some amount of discord, the better. Students who come to believe that freedom requires an imposed tranquility are the kind who will expect *you* to create that tranquility at the expense of individual rights. If someone decides not to go to HypoU based on this protest, that alone might be a sign they aren't ready to participate in the kind of free speech culture that higher education requires.

So what do you do? (For the sake of our hypothetical, let's assume the board that appoints you isn't available to defend their choice.) You could try talking to the protesters directly, although the Christakises' experience at Yale suggests there's a chance you aren't dealing with intellectually honest (or capable) brokers.[8] You could send letters to them—you know where they live, after all—and include in those letters data indicating your salary is in line with standard compensation. You could make a video walking students through your day, showing them that the job isn't easy and involves a lot of work. College presidents are well compensated, but they aren't the idle rich.

In short, you can try educating them. This *is* an educational institution, after all, albeit an imaginary one. You won't convince all of them, but you'll convince some and introduce all of them to facts that could lead them to question their position in the future. Even if you only succeed in demonstrating that there's an argument on the other side, that's progress.

314   THE FREE INQUIRY PAPERS

Day Two: Civil Disobedience

But for our hypothetical's sake, all the wrong things escalate. Now, the students are *encamped* on the lawn outside your office. How much that changes things depends on your rules. Let's assume the existing "time, place, and manner" rules don't prohibit using tents in outdoor spaces but require them to be removed at night. (That's pretty generous, since usually, there are lots of reasons institutions don't permit tents in various spaces, ranging from the risk of damaging underground sprinkler systems to the labeling on the fertilizer, the risk of obstructing foot traffic, or the occupation of parts of campus that other students also have a right to use.)

You should enforce your rules. (Really, you should *always* enforce your rules; that's how you avoid viewpoint discrimination and favoritism. But especially now.) That's not anti-speech. That's civilization.

It would be tempting to permit the encampment to go on until the crowd has vented its spleen. If that policy of handling protests *ever* worked—and there are strong reasons to suspect it never has[9]—it was before social media as an outrage engine and the "professional outside agitators" like the ones who took over a building during Columbia's protests.[10] For the nonstudent agitator, a campus encampment is an opportunity—an attractive nuisance, like a poorly gated pool.

If you don't enforce the rules here, you should rescind them, because enforcing them in the future opens the institution to accusations of selective enforcement. If you've decided the "time, place, and manner" rules were wrong, then change them. Otherwise, provide adequate notice. Provide due process. And enforce the rules.

Maybe once they're told that encampments break the rules, the students will say, "Oh! I didn't realize that. Let me take my banner and my tent, and I'll just be off, then. See you tomorrow, 9:15 a.m. sharp." Sure, why not? We live in a world of infinite possibility, and the odds of this might increase because you took the time to educate them *before* this incident that viewpoint- and content-neutral campus rules will be enforced even when they're engaged in expressive activity.

But it's also possible that some students will not cooperate, and at this point, the crowd is involved in civil disobedience. Civil disobedience is a form of protest using nonviolent unlawful conduct. Erecting encampments contrary to campus rules, occupying a building, or blocking traffic as part of a protest are all forms of civil disobedience.

Does that change anything? No, not in the slightest. Civil disobedience is powerful precisely *because* there are personal stakes to it, and you should still enforce the campus rules. If they won't move the first time you ask, then ask again. If that doesn't work, turn the sprinklers on. If that doesn't work, notify them of the time of their student conduct hearings for breaking the rule against camping in public spaces. If that doesn't work, tell them the exact time law enforcement will show up to start arrests. And if they're still there when the police arrive, they should be arrested for trespassing.

Some will be upset, and others will wear their "martyrdom" as a badge of pride on social media. How being arrested helps the cause is a calculus that a free speech culture puts in the hands of the protester, and you don't have to second-guess that. You're not the president of social change; you're the president of a university.

That isn't the end of your work. You have another opportunity for education, in whatever format you're most comfortable with—letters, op-eds, television interviews, debates, or even mandatory orientation seminars. You could, in theory, require students to complete additional training to avoid being punished under campus rules. (Just don't require them to *agree* with your viewpoints going forward as part of it because that's compelled speech.) Your job is to explain *why* a free speech culture doesn't include violating viewpoint- and content-neutral rules.

We'd start with this: The word "culture" presupposes a society of some form, because to have norms, you have to have a social structure. And those norms have to accommodate the ability to hear other people and live normal lives, or else the society will collapse. If the method of a protest is to *interfere with the operation of society*, then *any culture that values self-preservation*, including a free speech culture, has to *oppose* that method of protest, no matter what viewpoint it expresses. Being on the right side of history is valuable only to societies that make it to the present.

How do you meet your legal obligation to students who feel targeted? For example, let's say student protesters on the HypoU campus do what the protesters at the University of California, Los Angeles, did: Form a human chain to stop a "Zionist" from walking across "their camp," also

316   THE FREE INQUIRY PAPERS

known as the open public lawn of the institution.[11] (Start by enforcing your own rules and having security open the "camp," because blocking students is obviously illegal and absurd.) Then ask the targeted students: How do you feel? What are your needs? What are your fears? What other support would help? Remote classes? Counseling? Additional security? Revised "time, place, and manner" rules? For meeting these anti-harassment obligations, there's no recipe; you just act with compassion and curiosity and do your best.

Day Three: Institutional Neutrality

Having been removed from their encampment hasn't slowed the protests. And now, protesters are calling on you to make a statement of solidarity with their goals of ensuring fair but limited compensation for administrators. (At this point, we're thinking about joining the protests. They're making some good sense!)

Nevertheless, you shouldn't make that statement. Instead, you should have a rule against making these statements—an institutional neutrality rule. Institutional neutrality is the idea that higher education institutions should not take institutional positions on things unless they threaten the university's mission or free inquiry itself.[12]

It's a wise principle in the abstract; universities should be the venue for ideological fights, not weapons in that fight. But it's become far more urgent as movements adopt infinitely intersectional agendas, stacked on each other into an ideological tesseract through which you might adopt a position on sardine imports and come to discover you're unsympathetic to the deforestation of exoplanets.[13] Together, they form an orthodoxy in which the adherents are the Good People and anyone who violates any individual tenet of the faith is a Bad Person.

Your response to this generous invitation should be to decline.[14] Note that the appropriate level of compensation for administrators is a matter of legitimate and robust debate and that you would welcome any proposals to host such a debate, perform any research, or even just hold a forum on the topic. (But . . . please, for anyone coming to the forum, leave your tent at home.)

The first time you attempt this, you will be accused of favoritism because HypoU (like every other university) has probably taken public positions on dozens of other debated issues. Before Harvard adopted its institutional neutrality policy,[15] for example, it stood with the people of Ukraine,[16] insisted Congress should make a pathway to citizenship for children of undocumented immigrants,[17] and reminded us that black lives matter when promising to review how police attend protests.[18] And that cynicism is justified in Harvard's case, which adopted its policy after being criticized for not quite contradicting pro-Palestinian students, activists, and professors in the immediate wake of October 7, in a way that left former institution president Larry Summers feeling "disillusioned and alienated."[19]

You need to take your lumps here because you (or at least, your school) earned them. But if you adopt this policy and stick to it, the climate will improve, and life will become much easier.

"Is the Juice Worth the Squeeze?"

Everything you've read so far is not a "campus in crisis" or chaos or even particularly unusual. It's what free speech on campus looks like: protest, however imperfect. It's not an excuse to shutter a campus or evidence that it isn't working as intended. Be suspicious of people who want to point to protest as a reason to make radical changes. For people who want to restrain speech, *any* incident is adequate justification to propose censorship.

The exercise of free speech emboldens its critics. A protest on campus is an excellent example of this. Those who want to de-prioritize the right of free expression share headlines on social media like so many bloodied shirts, breathless that all this disturbance could have been avoided—*should* have been avoided—if only the administration had been enabled to censor the *right* people at the *right* times.

Tolerating protest is a sign of a functioning free speech culture, however uncomfortable it makes us. At the same time, it can suggest an incomplete free speech culture because protesting is an act of certainty. As Justice Learned Hand cautioned us, "The spirit of liberty is the spirit which is not too sure that it is right; the spirit of liberty is the spirit which seeks

318 THE FREE INQUIRY PAPERS

to understand the mind of other men and women."[20] By its nature, protest is reductive, binary, and one-sided.

An ideal alternative form of speech for a campus community is a dialogue across lines of difference that starts well before a crisis. Dartmouth, for example, has a dialogue project, and it's probably not a coincidence the campus saw less disturbance than its peers after October 7.[21] In a very real sense, campuses should start training their students to question their most deeply held beliefs from the very beginning—and to take seriously the possibility they might be wrong.

Protest should be protected, of course, but hearing people out through debate and discussion, and trying to learn and grow, can make for an even more powerful collegiate experience and certainly contributes to the discovery of truth. And when that doesn't happen, and there's a protest, that's OK too. Perfection is not the standard, and fortunately for your hypothetical career, the bar has not been set exceptionally high.

Notes

1. "Holding Campus Leaders Accountable and Confronting Antisemitism," hearing before the House Committee on Education and the Workforce, December 5, 2023, https://edworkforce.house.gov/calendar/eventsingle.aspx?EventID=409777.

2. *Monty Python and the Holy Grail*, directed by Terry Gilliam and Terry Jones (20th Century Studios, 1975).

3. *Davis v. Monroe County Board of Education*, 526 US 629, 651 (1999).

4. US Attorney's Office, Northern District of New York, "Cornell Student Arrested for Making Online Threats to Jewish Students on Campus," press release, October 31, 2023, https://www.justice.gov/usao-ndny/pr/cornell-student-arrested-making-online-threats-jewish-students-campus.

5. Katherine Knott, "Education Department Steps Up Efforts to Combat Antisemitism," *Inside Higher Ed*, May 8, 2024, https://www.insidehighered.com/news/government/2024/05/08/education-department-provides-new-guidance-antisemitism.

6. Christine Sloan and Ali Bauman, "Columbia University Protests Cause School to Offer Remote Classes for Rest of Semester," CBS News, April 23, 2024, https://www.cbsnews.com/newyork/news/columbia-university-rabbi-says-jewish-students-should-return-to-class-after-passover.

7. Sean T. Stevens, *2024 College Free Speech Rankings: What Is the State of Free Speech on America's College Campuses?*, Foundation for Individual Rights and Expression, 2023, 35, https://www.thefire.org/sites/default/files/2023/09/CFSR%202024_final_updated.pdf.

8. Foundation for Individual Rights and Expression, "Halloween Costume Controversy," https://www.thefire.org/research-learn/halloween-costume-controversy.

9. CBS News, "Crown Heights Riots: 30 Years Later: Looking Back on the Riot That Tore the City Apart," August 19, 2021, https://www.cbsnews.com/newyork/news/crown-heights-riots-30-years-later.

10. Katherine Donlevy and Amanda Woods, "Professional 'Outside Agitators' Behind Illegal Takeover of Columbia University Academic Building: NYPD," *New York Post*, April 30, 2024, https://nypost.com/2024/04/30/us-news/professional-outside-agitators-behind-illegal-takeover-of-columbia-university-academic-building-nypd.

11. Jenny Jarvie, "'Are You a Zionist?': Checkpoints at UCLA Encampment Provoked Fear, Debate Among Jews," *Los Angeles Times*, May 9, 2024, https://www.latimes.com/california/story/2024-05-09/are-you-a-zionist-checkpoints-at-ucla-encampment-provoked-debate-among-jewish-students.

12. Foundation for Individual Rights and Expression, "Adopting Institutional Neutrality," https://www.thefire.org/defending-your-rights/reforming-college-policies/adopting-institutional-neutrality.

13. Or that arresting demonstrators might be an unfair labor practice. Lara Korte, Melanie Mason, and Blake Jones, "California Lawmakers Reject Benefits for Striking Workers over Gaza Protests," *Politico*, June 27, 2024, https://politico.com/news/2024/06/27/california-lawmakers-reject-benefits-for-striking-workers-over-gaza-protests-00165264. Or that climate policies might lead to racial injustice. Beth Gardiner, "Unequal Impact: The Deep Links Between Racism and Climate Change," Yale Environment 360, June 9, 2020, https://e360.yale.edu/features/unequal-impact-the-deep-links-between-inequality-and-climate-change. Or that protests against China's COVID policies don't mention the struggles of the Uyghurs. Vivi E. Lu and Leah J. Teichholtz, "Protestors March Through Harvard Square, Hold Vigil for Victims of Urumqi Fire," *Harvard Crimson*, December 5, 2022, https://www.thecrimson.com/article/2022/12/5/urumqi-fire-march-vigil. None of this is to say that there aren't connections; of course there are. *All* things are connected. But if progress on any issue is gated behind universal agreement on the total orthodoxy of the universe, we end up dividing society, making no progress, and worst of all, preventing the kind of open discussion necessary to find better ways forward.

14. *Wargames*, directed by John Badham (Metro-Goldwyn-Mayer, 1983). ("The only winning move is not to play.")

15. Emma H. Haidar and Cam E. Kettles, "Harvard Will Refrain from Controversial Statements About Public Policy Issues," *Harvard Crimson*, May 28, 2024, https://www.thecrimson.com/article/2024/5/28/harvard-institutional-neutrality-report.

16. Lawrence S. Bacow, "Statement on the Russian Invasion of Ukraine," Harvard University, February 28, 2022, https://www.harvard.edu/president/news-and-statements-by-president-bacow/2022/statement-on-the-russia-ukraine-crisis.

17. Lawrence S. Bacow, "Decision on DACA," Harvard University, June 18, 2020, https://www.harvard.edu/president/news-and-statements-by-president-bacow/2020/decision-on-daca.

18. Lawrence S. Bacow, "HUPD Statement from President Bacow," Harvard University, June 10, 2020, https://www.harvard.edu/president/news-and-statements-by-president-bacow/2020/hupd-statement-from-president-bacow.

19. Ryan Chatelain, "Harvard President Faces Backlash over Response to Hamas Attacks on Israel," NY1, October 11, 2023, https://ny1.com/nyc/all-boroughs/education/2023/10/11/harvard-president-faces-backlash-over-response-to-hamas-attacks-on-israel.

20. Learned Hand, "The Spirit of Liberty," Foundation for Individual Rights and Expression, 1944, https://www.thefire.org/research-learn/spirit-liberty-speech-judge-learned-hand-1944.

21. Dartmouth College, "Dialogue Project," https://dialogueproject.dartmouth.edu.

19

Beyond Free Speech:
The Constitution of Knowledge

Jonathan Rauch

In the spring of 2022, I found myself sitting in a conference room at one of America's great universities. The president was there, plus the provost and half a dozen deans. It was the kind of council that institutions don't assemble unless they are seriously concerned. What was on their minds? One dean put it this way: "There's so much self-censorship happening on our campus that we're self-censoring conversations about self-censorship."

Polls support her contention. The Knight Foundation finds that the percentage of US college students who agreed (strongly or somewhat) that the climate on their campus "prevents some people from saying things they believe because others might find it offensive" rose from 54 percent in 2016 to 65 percent in 2021.[1] The same is true off campus; in a 2023 survey for the Foundation for Individual Rights and Expression (FIRE), two-thirds of Americans agreed that "the political climate these days prevents me from saying things I believe others might find them offensive."[2]

The chill is felt across all ideologies, not just on the right (or left). As of 2023, according to FIRE's polling, about a fourth of conservatives, progressives, and moderates worry about losing their job or career opportunities if they say what they really think. Between 2017 and 2020, the share of Americans saying that the political climate inhibits them from voicing their true beliefs rose by 7 percentage points among conservatives, moderates, and liberals alike—exceeding 50 percent in all three categories.[3]

One study, updated in Chapter 5, estimated that the level of chilling is more than three times the level in the early 1950s, during the McCarthy era.[4] That rather alarming finding is less surprising if you recall that, in the McCarthy era, people knew they could stay out of trouble by avoiding Communism. Today, identifying the trip wires is a matter of guesswork.

322 THE FREE INQUIRY PAPERS

The rules change every day, if indeed there are any rules at all. Without warning, a misplaced pronoun, a lame joke, a misinterpreted comment, or a well-meaning question can bring down a mob calling for your firing or investigation. Even silence is often construed as "violence."

This atmosphere was not what I hoped for three decades ago, when I published my book *Kindly Inquisitors: The New Attacks on Free Thought.* In those days, universities were busy enacting speech codes, and professors were theorizing ingeniously about oppressive speech, discriminatory verbal harassment, and words that wound. For a couple of decades after that book was published, the problem seemed to recede—but now it has come back with a vengeance, in a more insidious and pervasive form. The fight for the open society has changed, and defenders must change with it. Understanding the new landscape means understanding three things.

First, defending free speech is not enough. We must also defend the system of rules and institutions that organizes disagreement and converts it into facts: the Constitution of Knowledge.[5]

Second, our challenge no longer lies primarily in the realm of censorious laws and formal prosecutions. Today's fight is in the culture.

Third, our two constitutions—the US Constitution and the Constitution of Knowledge—rest on the same principles: freedom to inquire, discipline of facts, and viewpoint diversity. All three are under attack, and all three need defending.

Free Speech Isn't Enough

Kindly Inquisitors was a defense of what I called "liberal science," my term for not just technical sciences like physics and biology but the whole rules-based system of public debate and criticism that anchors modern liberal societies to truth. That system, which was born of the same Enlightenment that produced the US Constitution, revolutionized human affairs by overthrowing the authority of priests, princes, politburos, and other rulers to decide what is and is not true. It replaced them with a global social network of critical thinkers hunting for each other's errors and thus sifting haystacks of hypotheses to find needles of knowledge.

Two revolutionary rules lie at the heart of liberal science. The fallibilist rule, *no final say*, bars anyone from claiming he or she can permanently end an argument; instead, everything remains, in principle, open to question. By remaining open to the possibility that even seemingly obvious truths may be wrong, this rule protects free speech and dissent against authoritarian diktat or coercive closure. The empirical rule, *no personal authority*, says that whatever you do to validate your ideas must work for *anyone* who replicates your experiment or traces your logic. By treating persons as interchangeable, this rule allows everyone to participate on the same terms. Truth cannot be tribal, personal, or received by revelation; it must be shared. As the great 19th-century American philosopher Charles Sanders Peirce wrote, "One man's experience is nothing if it stands alone. If he sees what others cannot, we call it hallucination. It is not 'my' experience but 'our' experience that has to be thought of; and this 'us' has indefinite possibilities."[6] Together, the two rules create the unique conditions that make possible an open-ended, universal, self-organizing, ever-expanding search for objective knowledge: liberal science.

In *Kindly Inquisitors*, I also identified three threats to liberal science: one from what I called *fundamentalists*, by which I meant not just dogmatic religious believers but all who see no reason to tolerate what they are certain are wrong ideas; a second from *radical egalitarians*, who think the search for knowledge should favor historically marginalized groups; and a third from *humanitarians*, who want to suppress ideas that they regard as harmful, unsafe, or oppressive. All three lead directly to epistemic authoritarianism: thought policing by politicians, bureaucrats, or activists who use their power to determine what can and can't be said, studied, and concluded. I argued that all three illiberal principles had made headway—often, alas, unopposed—in the academy, in America generally, and in the world.

Three decades later, I wish *Kindly Inquisitors* were obsolete. Instead, it is often cited as prescient. Actually, no crystal ball was needed. The path to today's world of "microaggressions," "words that wound," "silence is violence," and "check your privilege" was well marked.

A generation ago, I wrote that the remedy is for individuals to stand up on behalf of the principles underlying liberal science. We need to insist that giving offense is *never* violence. As Sir Salman Rushdie said, "What is freedom of expression? Without the freedom to offend, it ceases to exist."

We need to insist that oppression, whether real or claimed, does not give any person or group standing to silence others or evade critical examination; you can *inform* an argument by citing someone's marginalized status, but you can't end the argument or disqualify an arguer. We need to insist that subjective ("lived") experience and personal conviction reveal precisely nothing about who is objectively right or wrong; subjecting our views to public criticism and impersonal checking is the *only* legitimate path to objective knowledge. We need to remember that the right to speak freely is conjoined with a duty to be thick-skinned; not taking offense is at least as important as not giving offense.

I still believe all those things. In recent years, though, I have come to believe that in thinking so much about individuals and freedom, I was thinking too little about institutions and rules.

The Constitution of Knowledge

America's Declaration of Independence is a seminal statement of principles, but the founding generation discovered quickly that principles were not enough. Under the Articles of Confederation, the early republic plunged toward chaos; the governing structure wasn't strong enough, balanced enough, or dynamic enough to hold the country together. The founders—especially James Madison—realized that principles, however sound, do not work without *structure*: rules and institutions that incentivize negotiation and compromise and discourage extremism and factionalism. In other words, we needed a *constitution*.

The same thing is true in the epistemic realm—the world of knowledge. There, too, general principles and unstructured autonomy are not enough. Producing knowledge requires organizing disagreements into elaborately structured public conversations in which disparate viewpoints can be rigorously and methodically compared and contested. To do that requires the rules and institutions that together comprise the Constitution of Knowledge.

Like the US Constitution, the Constitution of Knowledge is a structure for organizing disagreement and making collective decisions. It is primarily about constraints and rules, not freedom as such. It requires us to spend years learning how to perform experiments, gather evidence, develop arguments, manage data, structure articles, cite sources, build expertise, and behave civilly. It requires us to remain open to correction, no matter how certain we may feel. It demands that we inquire truthfully and earnestly, following the trail of evidence, and that we forbear from lying, confabulating, and bullshitting, even if doing those things might make us rich and famous. It requires us to aim our aggression against ideas rather than persons, avoiding ad hominem arguments and personal attacks. It bars us from claiming that subjective experience or certainty ever makes us right.

Above all, the Constitution of Knowledge requires us to negotiate across difference. As the US Constitution forces us to compromise in order to make law, so the Constitution of Knowledge forces us to persuade in order to make knowledge. And because humans often resent having to compromise and persuade, the epistemic constitution, like the political one, is not self-maintaining. It isn't "set it and forget it."

From Law to Culture

That was what I didn't fully appreciate a generation ago. Like many people, I assumed that the marketplace of ideas is self-organizing, something that grows up automatically wherever the fallibilist rule and the empirical rule are observed. Justice Oliver Wendell Holmes Jr. famously said, "The best test of truth is the power of the thought to get itself accepted in the competition of the market."[7] I took him to be saying that just speaking freely, just propounding views, tests ideas well enough to identify truth. Step one, free speech. Step two, marketplace of ideas. Voilà: knowledge!

What did I miss?

Free speech is indeed indispensable to rational inquiry, and I was right to emphasize it 30 years ago, when formal college speech codes and theoretical attacks on free expression were at high tide. But, like a mutating virus, the problem morphed. By the late 2010s, the bigger threat to intellectual freedom came in the *social* sphere. If you said something that traduced some invisible boundary, you could lose your friends, your professional standing, your reputation, your job. You could become socially radioactive literally overnight, a phenomenon that came to be known as being *canceled*.

326   THE FREE INQUIRY PAPERS

For most of human history, the main method of getting rid of error was by getting rid of the errant, whether by jailing, exiling, or burning them. "When complete agreement could not otherwise be reached," said Peirce, "a general massacre of all who have not thought in a certain way has proved a very effective means of settling opinion in a country."[8] The Constitution of Knowledge's radical social innovation is to force us to kill our hypotheses instead of each other. Knowledge never reaches us whole; it comes piecemeal through trial and error, so we need to let people be wrong. If someone's idea is debunked, we encourage him or her to learn from the mistake and try again. Cancel culture, by contrast, treats even one error—or even one *alleged* error—as a career-ending crime. It rushes to discredit the person, not the idea.

In 2021, Nadine Strossen, a former president of the American Civil Liberties Union and a prominent First Amendment defender, wrote an important essay titled *Resisting Cancel Culture: Promoting Dialogue, Debate, and Free Speech in the College Classroom*. She argued that free speech defenders need to pivot away from their familiar turf of fighting government censorship and toward the less familiar terrain of culture. Echoing Madison's warning that the Constitution rests ultimately on values, not laws, she wrote:

> If we are to enjoy meaningful freedom of speech, we need a free speech culture. . . .
> . . . Without a vibrant free speech culture, even a strongly enforced First Amendment cannot secure the actual exercise of freedom of speech by individuals who are—understandably—cowed by social pressures.[9]

In academia, a related problem surfaced. A generation ago, conservatives worried that left-wing professors were indoctrinating their students. Though some indoctrination undoubtedly happened (and happens), today the problem is again more subtle and elusive, because, again, it has become more *social*. Today, entire university departments and academic disciplines tilt so uniformly to the political left that many scholars no longer perceive their biases, because no one in their professional orbit challenges them.

One (typical) study, by Mitchell Langbert, sampled liberal arts faculties and found that 78 percent of academic departments "have either zero Republicans, or so few as to make no difference."[10] The ratios of Democrats to Republicans ranged from 1.6:1 in engineering to 56:0 in communications and 108:0 in interdisciplinary studies. Langbert also found that the ratio of registered Democrats to Republicans among academic faculty more than doubled from 4.5:1 in 1999 to 10:1 in 2018. The ratio of political donations is even more lopsided at 21:1, according to findings by Langbert and Sean T. Stevens.[11] Such large imbalances make it possible, even common, for academics in some fields to go through their whole careers, from graduate school to retirement, without ever encountering a right-of-center mentor or colleague. With academics trapped in epistemic bubbles of which they are unaware, disciplines become, in effect, self-indoctrinating.

Outside the academy, in the culture, a parallel form of self-indoctrination has emerged. On social media, recommendation algorithms and user preferences draw people toward extreme viewpoints and isolated communities. Particularly on the political right, but also on the left, cable news and other partisan media create tribal echo chambers. In the physical world, people self-segregate in like-minded partisan communities. Polls find that many Americans not only disagree with the other political party but regard it with fear and even hatred (a phenomenon called *affective polarization*).[12] In those respects and others, social and media dynamics that once encouraged compromise and coexistence are giving way to dynamics that foster isolation, tribalism, and splintered, irreconcilable realities: what the social psychologist Jonathan Haidt has called a "post-Babel" world.[13]

Traditional First Amendment doctrines are well equipped for fighting government censorship but much less capable against social chilling and intellectual monocultures. The marketplace of ideas will not function if people are frightened of speaking their mind or shielded from reasoned disagreement. In today's world, the biggest problem facing freedom of thought and inquiry is not censorship but censure and closure.

328   THE FREE INQUIRY PAPERS

Constitutional Values

The Constitution of Knowledge, unlike the marketplace of ideas, is not a simile, a metaphor, or an analogy. Although it is not written down on parchment and does not have a supreme court, it is a tangible set of rules and norms defining—*constituting*—a real-world community and chartering real-world institutions. It defines a *we*, as in *We, the people.*

We are those who adhere to the Constitution of Knowledge as we go about our professional and intellectual work. We are what I call (with apologies to Karl Rove) the *reality-based community.*[14] If you're reading this chapter, chances are you are one of us.

We can serve in all kinds of realms, from libraries and museums to consultancies and pharmaceutical companies, but the four most import-ant are academia, journalism, law, and government. Without the Consti-tution of Knowledge, academia becomes politicized and cultic, journalism becomes partisan and sensational, law becomes arbitrary and capricious, and government becomes tyrannical and abusive. When politicians can broadcast propaganda, lies, and conspiracy theories; when prosecu-tors can fabricate evidence and false charges; when journalists can print fake news; when scholars can distort or suppress research to suit their politics—then we are in a world where truth has ceased to matter and dis-putes of fact are settled the old-fashioned way: by force, oppression, and deceit. Soon we find our societies untethered from reality and at odds over even basic facts.

Both constitutions—the political and the epistemic—define commu-nities, and both communities share the same basic values, which is why to defend *either* constitution, we must defend *both*. Among their common values, three stand out.

First, *openness*. In the political sphere, openness entails freedom to speak, to vote, to organize, to petition for redress. In the epistemic sphere, openness means freedom to inquire, to experiment, to dissent, to criticize. In both spheres, openness advances progress by ensuring that new ideas and approaches can be tried and old ones can be updated, and it advances freedom by giving individuals room to pursue their ideas and ideals.

Second, *rule by rules*. In the political sphere, we commit to lawfulness: accepting the rule of law and the results of elections, even if we dislike the outcome. In the epistemic sphere, we commit to *factfulness*: subordinating our personal views to established facts and acknowledging the legitimacy of expert consensus, even when we lose the argument. In both spheres, we follow norms and protocols that require us to interact with others on equal and impersonal terms, even if that sometimes means setting our personal interests and ambitions aside.

Third, *pluralism*. In the political sphere, pluralism entails embracing ideological and factional diversity: accepting that a large republic is rife with political disagreement and that no group is entitled to dominate or eliminate the others. Like it or not, we have to share the country. In the epistemic sphere, pluralism means embracing *viewpoint* diversity: not only tolerating but positively welcoming disagreement and dissent and recognizing that, even in principle, disagreement and error are the raw materials for knowledge. We can't learn if our views aren't challenged.

Individual freedom, impersonal rules, pluralism: These are the values our two constitutions share, and these are the values we must defend.

What We—Make That *You*—Can Do

Of course, the practical question is how to translate these values into practical strategies. There's a lot that can be done.

Take universities, for example. There are all kinds of ways they can strengthen openness, factuality, and pluralism. They can adopt the Chicago principles,[15] a strong commitment to free speech. They can include free speech principles in their freshman orientation programs. They can stop investigating students and professors for speech that is protected by the First Amendment. They can rebuff efforts to politicize scholarship and instruction, regardless of anyone's claims about social justice. They can prevent bureaucrats like lawyers, diversity officials, and student-affairs administrators from meddling in scholarly life, especially in the classroom. They can resist efforts by politicians and legislatures to dictate what can and cannot be taught and studied. They can be as committed to ideological diversity as they are to other forms of diversity. They can be as vigilant against anti-conservative discrimination as they are against racism, sexism, and anti-LGBT discrimination. They can

330 THE FREE INQUIRY PAPERS

encourage students to encounter challenging viewpoints and discourage them from invoking "emotional safety" to avoid them. They can encourage students who feel offended to speak directly with students or professors they disagree with, instead of encouraging them to file anonymous "bias incident reports."

I could go on, but the key to winning the cultural fight isn't to follow my prescriptions but for you to develop your own. *Every* member of the reality-based community can do something to shore up the Constitution of Knowledge in his or her own institutional environment. It might be something as small as speaking up in a faculty meeting or as big as founding a new organization, such as the University of Austin or the Academic Freedom Alliance. Cultural activism depends on each of us projecting and defending our values however we can in the institutions we know best and love most.

The Constitution of Knowledge creates more new knowledge every day than humanity accumulated in our first 200,000 years. Linking millions of minds around the world in a collective hunt for error has transformed our capacity as a species, increasing by orders of magnitude the *sapiens* of *Homo*. It can organize experts and institutions on every continent to decode a new virus in a matter of days and design a vaccine in a few days more. It can overturn falsehoods that were ubiquitous for thousands of years—falsehoods like racism, sexism, and homophobia.

For generations, it worked so well that we took it for granted. We got lazy about making the case for it. We assumed that the marketplace of ideas takes care of itself. We thought the advantages of free speech and rigorous criticism were obvious. We relaxed because the courts were on our side. Now we know we were sleepwalking.

The American founders did not make that mistake. They issued the US Constitution with the warning that Benjamin Franklin gave the woman who asked what kind of government the framers had devised: "A republic ... if you can keep it."[16] Most of the founders, in one way or another, warned that what Madison called "parchment barriers"—words on paper—cannot by themselves stand against the "encroaching spirit of power."[17] As he said at the Virginia ratifying convention, "Is there no virtue among us? If there be not, we are in a wretched situation. No theoretical checks—no form of government can render us secure."[18]

In other words, culture and values are upstream of law. We must understand, embrace, and defend the culture and the values on which *both* our constitutions depend.

Notes

1. Knight Foundation, *College Student Views on Free Expression and Campus Speech 2022*, January 2022, https://knightfoundation.org/reports/college-student-views-on-free-expression-and-campus-speech-2022.

2. Survey results provided to the author by the Foundation for Individual Rights and Expression.

3. Even among self-identified "strong liberals," 42 percent agreed that they are fearful of expressing their true views—a startling 12-point increase from three years earlier. Emily Ekins, "Poll: 62% of Americans Say They Have Political Views They're Afraid to Share," Cato Institute, July 22, 2020, https://www.cato.org/survey-reports/poll-62-americans-say-they-have-political-views-theyre-afraid-share.

4. James L. Gibson and Joseph L. Sutherland, "Americans Are Self-Censoring at Record Rates," *Persuasion*, July 31, 2020, https://www.persuasion.community/p/americans-are-self-censoring-at-record.

5. See Jonathan Rauch, *The Constitution of Knowledge: A Defense of Truth* (Washington, DC: Brookings Institution Press, 2021).

6. Philip P. Wiener, ed., *Charles S. Peirce: Selected Writings* (Mineola, NY: Dover Publications, 1966), xx.

7. *Abrams v. United States*, 250 US 616 (1919).

8. See C. S. Peirce, "The Fixation of Belief," *Popular Science Monthly* 12, no. 1 (1877): 1–15, https://philarchive.org/rec/PEITFO.

9. Nadine Strossen, *Resisting Cancel Culture: Promoting Dialogue, Debate, and Free Speech in the College Classroom*, American Council of Trustees and Alumni, February 1, 2021, 8, 15, https://www.goacta.org/resource/resisting-cancel-culture.

10. Mitchell Langbert, "Homogenous: The Political Affiliations of Elite Liberal Arts College Faculty," *Academic Questions* 31, no. 2 (Summer 2018), https://www.nas.org/academic-questions/31/2/homogenous_the_political_affiliations_of_elite_liberal_arts_college_faculty.

11. Mitchell Langbert and Sean T. Stevens, "Partisan Registration and Contributions of Faculty in Flagship Colleges," National Association of Scholars, January 17, 2020, https://www.nas.org/blogs/article/partisan-registration-and-contributions-of-faculty-in-flagship-colleges.

12. See, for example, Thomas B. Edsall, "The Politics of Delusion Have Taken Hold," *New York Times*, May 31, 2023, https://www.nytimes.com/2023/05/31/opinion/politics-partisanship-delusion.html; and Pew Research Center, "As Partisan Hostility Grows, Signs of Frustration with the Two-Party System," August 9, 2022, https://www.pewresearch.org/politics/2022/08/09/as-partisan-hostility-grows-signs-of-frustration-with-the-two-party-system.

332 THE FREE INQUIRY PAPERS

13. Jonathan Haidt, "Why the Past Ten Years of American Life Have Been Uniquely Stupid," *The Atlantic*, May 2022, https://pressbooks.pub/dunicklm/chapter/why-the-past-ten-years-of-american-life-have-been-uniquely-stupid.

14. Rove is generally understood to be the unnamed Bush administration official who was quoted in 2004 using the term "reality-based community" derisively. See Ron Suskind, "Faith, Certainty and the Presidency of George W. Bush," *New York Times*, October 17, 2004, https://www.nytimes.com/2004/10/17/magazine/faith-certainty-and-the-presidency-of-george-w-bush.html.

15. University of Chicago, "Free Expression," https://freeexpression.uchicago.edu.

16. James McHenry, diary, September 18, 1787, James McHenry Papers, Library of Congress (63.02.00), https://www.loc.gov/exhibits/creating-the-united-states/convention-and-ratification.html#obj8.

17. *Federalist*, no. 48 (James Madison).

18. James Madison, "Judicial Powers of the National Government, 20 June 1788," Founders Online, https://founders.archives.gov/documents/Madison/01-11-02-0101.

20

Conclusion:
How to Bring Back Free Inquiry

Robert Maranto, Lee Jussim, Catherine Salmon, and Sally Satel

In this volume, we have established three key realities. First, free inquiry is essential for democracy, science, and individual justice. It is part of an institutional and attitudinal system, what Jonathan Rauch refers to in Chapter 19 as "the Constitution of Knowledge." Free inquiry enables modernity.

Second, free inquiry in the United States is under threat, more so than at any time since the McCarthy era (as Joseph L. Sutherland and James L. Gibson show in Chapter 5) and likely more so than at any time since the 1800s, when ethnic and political mob violence was common. Increasingly, people fear saying what they think, and scientists are told what they can and cannot study. We have forgotten the lessons of US history, as Jonathan Zimmerman discusses in Chapter 3, and the deadly lessons of Lysenkoism and other political currents in the Soviet Union and China, as detailed by Catherine Salmon and Lee Jussim in Chapter 9 and Anna I. Krylov and Jay Tanzman in Chapter 17. The success of denunciation and demonization by social media mobs has incentivized a whole generation to attempt to impose new norms, values, and rules on others. As a result, previous norms, values, and rules have changed quickly—and not for the better.

Third, today's taboos are developed and enforced not by outsiders but by students, professors, and bureaucracies *within* higher education. Indeed, the steady growth in censorious bureaucracies and the explosive growth of social media enabled apex predators in free speech ecosystems, creating a chilling effect on speech and inquiry and likely causing local and regional extinctions of free thought. Threats to free inquiry increasingly affect the business, academic, and even scientific sectors such as medicine and medical schools (as Sally Satel shows in Chapter 8)—which affects us all.

334   THE FREE INQUIRY PAPERS

This conclusion explores immediate and long-term ways to restore free inquiry. The good news is that our society and higher education system do remain largely free. As Krylov and Tanzman point out, restoring free inquiry here is almost infinitely easier than the work of Soviet dissidents confronting Communism. To those who despair, our first admonition is to have *hope!* Hope enables agency. Agency enables action.

Short-Term and Midterm Efforts

Here, gleaned from various contributors, we editors recommend the following short-term and midterm actions and tactics for legislators, alumni, and higher education leaders, actions that can enable long-term reforms.

Sponsor Campus Debates on Contentious Topics. State legislators and others should encourage and possibly fund campus debates on issues such as elections, abortion, the Hamas-Israel war, drugs, guns, foreign policy interventions, policing, Marxism (such as whether the Cuban and Venezuelan models should be emulated), and, most importantly for our purposes, the diversity, equity, and inclusion (DEI) divide. As George R. La Noue documents in Chapter 14, campus debates are now rare and sometimes interrupted midstream or aborted even before they have a chance to take place. Familiarizing students with the culture of debate would encourage a climate of free thought and free inquiry. The goal is for students to use social pressure to derail their colleagues' efforts at cancellations. Institutions could even require courses in debate.

We also recommend developing a national database of debates and debate cancellations, created by the US Department of Education or a free speech nonprofit such as the Foundation for Individual Rights and Expression (FIRE). We need to make it a national issue that higher education, the segment of society that should be most open to free discourse, has become a debate desert, which has serious implications for democracy. Sadly, institutions led by "educators" who have spent their entire careers in higher education have far worse free speech climates than do those whose leaders have more varied life experience, a searing indictment of academia.[1]

To draw attention to the issue, one could, for instance, commission a national poll or repackage and expand existing FIRE polls to measure the degree to which secondary and college students are exposed to debates at their educational institutions. If at many institutions the result is rarely or never, then one can question whether such institutions should receive public funding from our ideologically diverse taxpayers.

Humanize the Canceled. FIRE or a similar organization should publicize the stories of those who have been canceled, perhaps using YouTube or other social media, to humanize the victims of this trend. This could include historic free speech activists like the still-active Mary Beth Tinker of *Tinker v. Des Moines*, noted in Zimmerman's chapter. Too many of these figures have been dehumanized, allowing others to ignore their ideas. Telling their stories is a necessary counterbalance to attempts at demonization in the pursuit of justifying social ostracism.

Hold Hearings on Bureaucratic Attempts to Limit Free Speech and Open Inquiry. There is another important tool that can bring light to this issue. State legislatures and the US Congress should hold hearings to highlight attempts by university bureaucrats (sometimes in collaboration with the media and Big Tech) and higher education leaders to limit free speech. Such hearings could personalize university administrators' roles in producing censorious norms and practices, ideally leading to demotions in some cases, thus offering bureaucrats incentives to avoid such behavior.

We now have evidence that such hearings can work. In the wake of Hamas's October 7 attack on Israel, the presidents of the Massachusetts Institute of Technology (MIT), the University of Pennsylvania, and Harvard University faced congressional scrutiny over antisemitism on their campuses. When pressed on whether calls for committing genocide against Jews violated their policies, all three university presidents claimed vigorous protections for controversial speech while parroting the refrain that context matters.[2] This was, in fact, the technically correct response because, unless speech calls for imminent violence directed at a specific person, their policies protect it, as Greg Lukianoff and Adam Goldstein describe in Chapter 18. The problem was not that they espoused the wrong policies; it was that all three institutions (especially Harvard and Penn) had

336 THE FREE INQUIRY PAPERS

completely miserable track records of actually defending faculty engaging in speech far short of calling for genocide.

For example, Harvard effectively ousted a biology professor, Carole Hooven, for claiming that sex was biological and binary. Penn spent years investigating Amy Wax and considering revoking her tenure because she argued that immigration should be restricted to Europeans. MIT canceled a talk on exoplanets by contributor Dorian S. Abbot because he had previously advocated that colleges should employ academic merit in admissions and hiring.[3]

These are not isolated incidents. In 2023, Harvard earned the worst FIRE rating for free speech ever recorded, coming in dead last at 248th in the US, just behind Penn's 247th rating.[4] MIT's ranking was not as terrible, at 136th, but this is not the ranking of a university implementing the robust protections for speech and academic freedom professed by its president before Congress.

Quite simply, professors and students are afraid to say what they think. As a professor at one of these institutions complained privately:

> [My university] is worse than the FIRE rating since many professors are punished for their findings. And this is kept under the radar. It's common for deans to tell professors they are fired, the professor says they will go public, so then the university pays them to go away.[5]

Seemingly, prestigious US universities are using bureaucratic soldiers to re-create the climates of fear found in totalitarian and authoritarian systems—or in Sicily under the Mafiosi. Research and teaching cannot work well in such environments. If we fail to tell these stories and hold leaders accountable, then behaviors that undermine education will continue to metastasize.

Given the tendencies of higher education bureaucrats,[6] congressional hearings could be a crucial step in making bullying and censorship riskier than allowing free inquiry, by exposing institutional hypocrisy, as Lukianoff and Goldstein describe in Chapter 18. Ideally, over time, governing boards will develop standard operating procedures to demote administrators, including college presidents, who use their bureaucratic power

HOW TO BRING BACK FREE INQUIRY 337

to limit rather than safeguard free speech and free inquiry rights (or who simply fail to do so when they could have). The terminations of just a few higher education leaders could send a message throughout the industry, helping reshape current culture.[7]

We are already seeing evidence of that happening. After the disastrous congressional hearing, Harvard's and Penn's presidents both resigned.

Repair or Reduce Higher Education Bureaucracies That Limit Free Speech. We must reform and downsize higher education bureaucracies, which, as previously noted, have strong incentives to limit free speech and often serve as a college president's personal Praetorian Guard. We should begin by downsizing or even eliminating DEI bureaucracies, which have grown exponentially and expanded their missions in ways detrimental to free inquiry.

Additionally, as Robert Maranto suggests in Chapter 13, state and federal governments should encourage or even require colleges and universities to develop free inquiry bureaucracies to counter their DEI and Title IX bureaucracies, with the risk of losing government funding if they fail to do so. Such bureaucracies could thwart infringements on academic freedom and open inquiry. For example, they could have the power to summarily dismiss spurious accusations against academics, whether they come from online mobs or DEI bureaucracies, thereby preempting at least some attempts at deplatforming, dis-invitations, investigations, and punishments for protected speech on controversial topics.

Furthermore, such free inquiry bureaucracies could train students and professors on the importance of free speech during orientation. One activity of such bureaucracies should be to strongly encourage departments and whole institutions to develop their own versions of the Chicago free speech principles (as has one of our departments) and the Kalven Report on maintaining institutional neutrality (discussed in Chapter 6 by Aaron Saiger) and to otherwise embrace the merit, fairness, and equality principles outlined in Chapter 15 by Abbot, Iván Marinovic, and Carlos M. Carvalho.

Teach Free Speech and Open Inquiry. Colleges and universities should require a foundational course on free speech and open inquiry and

338 THE FREE INQUIRY PAPERS

support faculty training in this area. State legislatures could strongly encourage colleges to require an introductory class on free speech and free inquiry, to help students adjust to college life, perhaps modeled on the University of Wisconsin's First Amendment class, as Donald Alexander Downs describes in Chapter 12. Relatedly, colleges could sponsor student and faculty training regarding how to be a free speech activist. These could help counter the thousands of courses, often in schools of education, that teach students how to *limit* free speech and free inquiry. Such courses could be fairly inexpensive if many components were online as in most existing training, including (demonstrably ineffective) diversity training.[8]

End Public Funding for Higher Education Organizations That Require Political or Ideological Statements of Faith. Three other steps would rest on federal (or state) legislation or perhaps on new US Department of Education regulations. Governments should deny public funds to travel to conferences sponsored by groups that demand that research adhere to particular ideologies (with certain exemptions for faith-based institutions and groups). Governments should deny public funds to higher education institutions that require political or ideological statements of faith, such as DEI statements, for job applicants or promotion (again, with certain exemptions for faith-based institutions). And governments should deny public funds to research published in journals that require political or ideological statements of faith or specific demographic requirements in restricting research questions. In tandem, these three steps would rapidly erode the ideological and demographic blacklists that are rapidly dominating research, as when a journal editor recently told one of us he could not submit for publication quantitative research on black principals because he is not black.

Add Ideology to the List of "Protected Classes." Another step would be to add ideology to the list of "protected classes" in admissions and personnel systems to restore some pluralism to academic institutions and departments that skew heavily left. Unlike ideological monocultures, pluralism is directly related to open inquiry because it widens the universe of ideas acceptable for study and consideration.

Because surveys consistently show roughly equal proportions of people identify as Democrats or Republicans,[9] and more identify as moderates and conservatives than as liberals,[10] most academic institutions would fail a "disparate impact" test applied to political identities. Disparate impact measures whether hiring (or other) practices disproportionately affect a protected group.[11] Although passing this test is not sufficient to prove discrimination, it is a first step. As such, this could motivate lawsuit-averse administrators (which is to say, most of them) to adopt procedures designed to increase pluralism in their institutions. This would also encourage development of specialized law firms, privatizing some of the regulatory efforts to encourage free speech and free inquiry.

Of course, this could have unanticipated consequences. Some might shift their reported ideological affiliation just to sue for damages, as indeed some have with their reported racial or ethnic group.[12] Accordingly, this might be an area in which to move gradually, with experimentation on the state and local level.

Evaluate DEI Interventions. Many attempts to regulate speech and inquiry reflect critical theory–oriented efforts to enhance equity, in part by improving class mobility. Unfortunately, many widely used practices simply fail to work.[13] Accordingly, we propose that the National Science Foundation enlist researchers from across the ideological spectrum who have publicly stated widely different views about the value of DEI programs to issue a report on the effectiveness of DEI-related interventions in improving class mobility and intergroup relations. This could be modeled after Surgeon General Luther Terry's 1964 report summarizing the empirical research on the health effects of cigarette smoking. Terry never sought to punish speech by tobacco executives; rather, over time, he defeated it in open discourse.

Fight Bad Speech with Counter-Speech. Likewise, it seems to us that the best way to defeat widespread support for Hamas on elite college campuses is not to criminalize such speech and make its proponents martyrs but to confront it with factual and at times satirical counter-speech. Why should the Babylon Bee have all the fun?[14] Over the long term, this could decrease the use of ineffective (and censorious) practices, helping

340 THE FREE INQUIRY PAPERS

safeguard free inquiry. It could also demonstrate the effective use of empirical work to change public and social practice.

Reform Institutional Review Boards. Institutional review boards (IRBs) were created to protect human subjects in research, particularly in light of failures to do so such as in the Tuskegee syphilis study. However, participating in most social science research does not present legitimate threats to physical or mental health. Increasingly, IRBs are limiting research not to protect subjects but for ideological reasons. Accordingly, Congress should remove many types of social science from IRB jurisdiction.

Long-Term Institutional Reforms

We end with a proposal for two sets of interlocking, long-term institutional reforms.

Improve Public Education on Pluralism and the First Amendment. To paraphrase James Madison, laws and even constitutions are mere paper barriers without public support. Unfortunately, support for free speech and free inquiry was never as strong as we would like, and considerable evidence indicates that, at least among elites, these values are fading fast, a potentially calamitous development. For example, one prominent university press editor confided they could not consider publishing this volume, in part because their own reviewers thought this volume's approach to free inquiry was "ideologically driven." (That is a direct quote, which struck us as particularly amusing because the editors and contributors span the ideological spectrum.) An editor at another prominent university press said they liked the idea of the volume but their junior staff would never permit the press to publish a book supporting free inquiry.

Such decisions happen thousands of times each day, with remarkably little attention; thus, science dies in darkness. To counter this, our most important long-term reforms would remake K–12 education standards and curricula to highlight pluralism and the First Amendment. We must do more, pushing public education to address *why* 20th-century fascist and Communist alternatives did not merely fail but failed with disastrous consequences for humanity.

Relatedly, Congress and the president should declare November 9 (the anniversary of the fall of the Berlin Wall) a national holiday marking the end of the Cold War, to facilitate teaching about how Marxism failed in 20-odd countries. Indeed, "Fall of the Wall Day" could be paired with Martin Luther King Jr. Day, Juneteenth, and July 4 as one of four Freedom Day holidays. This would provide historical references so students might see how new higher education institutions like bias-response teams resemble Communist institutions like the Stasi in the German Democratic Republic (Communist East Germany), where citizens were paid to inform on their neighbors and family members so that no one could ever trust anyone.

As part of November 9 festivities, educational institutions on all levels could sponsor surviving victims of Communism to tell their stories, including new victims from Hong Kong and Caracas. We should likewise encourage taxpayer-funded media like PBS to sponsor documentaries on the KGB, the Holodomor (both particularly relevant given current events), Mao Zedong's Cultural Revolution, and Democratic Kampuchea's Year Zero. Without this knowledge, we are raising a generation apt to repeat some of history's greatest mistakes, centralizing power to ensure "right" thinking.

In addition, we need a permanent, national institutional presence to highlight the importance of the First Amendment, just as the bipartisan US Civil Rights Commission and its 50 state-level advisory committees, which issue regular reports, highlight the importance of the 14th Amendment. A US First Amendment Commission, created by Congress, would provide an institutional home for supporters of free speech (and freedom of religion), educate the public and policymakers on how these rights make the US unique and have enabled every social movement in US history, and offer regular reports about how to safeguard those rights. Ideally, such a commission would provide each political party, and the press, a stake in protecting First Amendment rights, even for their opponents. Indeed, arguably, the First Amendment and the values it encourages are key national features separating the US from Russia and China, parts of our national identity that should transcend party lines. Those values need an institutional home.

342 THE FREE INQUIRY PAPERS

Create New Institutions of Higher Learning. On the higher education front, an additional possibility, albeit a resource-intensive one, would be to establish new institutions dedicated to the robust exploration of ideas and the search for truth, such as the recently established University of Austin, which was flooded with job applications as soon as plans for it were announced. Given the infrastructure of a research university, creating several satellite campuses for the University of Austin would be more cost-effective than creating brand-new universities.

A cheaper and more feasible option would be for public university systems to dedicate some of their campuses entirely to the classically liberal values of merit-based admissions and hiring and clearly state that they prioritize free and open inquiry and discourse over social justice indoctrination and activism. These distinct institutions would need distinct accreditors that respect their missions, rather than having to conform to the dictates of existing accreditors, some of which are captured by critical theory.[15]

Such education markets would then enable students, faculty, and donors to vote with their feet and dollars. Ultimately, through their choice of practitioners, the public can decide which type of institutions should train the new generations of doctors, lawyers, scientists, professors, educators, journalists, and citizens.

Individual and Collective Action

While much of what we say concerns policymakers and institutions, we end this closing chapter where we began it, with a plea for individual agency and collective action. We urge those whose freedoms are threatened to band together with others, as professors recently did at Harvard,[16] for both their sanity and their long-term success. Without emotional and material support and friendly advice, organized censors will pick us off one at a time; indeed, the social isolation produced by the COVID-19 pandemic enabled such bureaucratic behavior at campuses like Stanford, where administrators closed many student organizations and forced others to endorse DEI principles, ultimately undermining social trust in the manner of totalitarian regimes.[17]

Yet history rarely moves in straight lines, and it is not too late to change direction. The current antipathy toward free inquiry can, and must, be changed for both education and democracy to survive. The stakes are that high.

Notes

1. Robert Maranto and Martha Bradley-Dorsey, "Yelling FIRE on Campus: Higher Education Free Speech Leaders and Laggards," *Academic Questions* 36, no. 1 (Spring 2023): 23–33, https://www.nas.org/academic-questions/36/1/yelling-fire-on-campus-free-speech-leaders-and-laggards.

2. Yascha Mounk, "The Universities That Don't Understand Academic Freedom," *The Atlantic*, December 8, 2023, https://www.theatlantic.com/ideas/archive/2023/12/harvard-mit-upenn-free-speech-congressional-hearings/676278.

3. Greg Lukianoff and Rikki Schlott, *The Canceling of the American Mind* (New York: Simon & Schuster, 2023), 74, 206–7; and Robert Maranto, Catherine Salmon, and Lee Jussim, "Cut Their Pay and Make Them Teach," RealClearEducation, June 9, 2022, https://www.realcleareducation.com/articles/2022/06/09/cut_their_pay_and_make_them_teach_110737.html.

4. Sean T. Stevens, 2024 *College Free Speech Rankings: What Is the State of Free Speech on America's College Campuses?*, Foundation for Individual Rights and Expression and College Pulse, 2023, https://www.thefire.org/research-learn/2024-college-free-speech-rankings.

5. Personal communication, October 12, 2023.

6. Anthony Downs, *Inside Bureaucracy* (Boston, MA: Little, Brown, 1967).

7. Maranto, Salmon, and Jussim, "Cut Their Pay and Make Them Teach."

8. Musa al-Gharbi, "Diversity Is Important. Diversity-Related Training Is Terrible.," September 16, 2020, https://musaalgharbi.com/2020/09/16/diversity-important-related-training-terrible.

9. Jeffrey M. Jones, "U.S. Party Preferences Evenly Split in 2022 After Shift to GOP," Gallup, January 12, 2023, https://news.gallup.com/poll/467897/party-preferences-evenly-split-2022-shift-gop.aspx.

10. Lydia Saad, "U.S. Political Ideology Steady; Conservatives, Moderates Tie," Gallup, January 17, 2022, https://news.gallup.com/poll/388988/political-ideology-steady-conservatives-moderates-tie.aspx.

11. US Department of Justice, Civil Rights Division, *Title VI Legal Manual*, https://www.justice.gov/crt/fcs/T6Manual7#C.

12. David E. Bernstein, *Classified: The Untold Story of Racial Classification in America* (New York: Bombardier Books, 2022).

13. Craig Frisby and Robert Maranto, "Diversity Training Is Unscientific, and Divisive," *Academic Questions* 34, no. 2 (Summer 2021): 41–45, https://www.nas.org/academic-questions/34/2/diversity-training-is-unscientific-and-divisive.

14. Babylon Bee, "Harvard Crew Team Unveils New U-Boat," November 3, 2023, https://babylonbee.com/news/harvard-crew-team-unveils-new-u-boat.

15. Robert Manzer, "The American University's Path to Illiberalism," American Enterprise Institute, April 20, 2023, https://www.aei.org/research-products/report/the-american-universitys-path-to-illiberalism.

16. Rahem D. Hamid and Elias J. Schisgall, "More Than 70 Harvard Faculty Form Council on Academic Freedom, Co-Led by Steven Pinker," *Harvard Crimson*, April 14, 2023, https://www.thecrimson.com/article/2023/4/14/pinker-academic-freedom-council.

17. CSPAN-3, "Campus Free Speech," October 29, 2023; and Ginevra Davis, "Stanford's War on Social Life," *Palladium*, June 13, 2022, https://www.palladiummag.com/2022/06/13/stanfords-war-on-social-life.

About the Authors

Dorian S. Abbot is an associate professor in the geophysical sciences department at the University of Chicago. In his research, he uses mathematical and computational models to understand and explain fundamental problems in earth and planetary sciences. He has worked on problems related to climate, paleoclimate, planetary dynamics, planetary habitability, and exoplanets. Abbot is a member of the Council of the Faculty Senate at the University of Chicago, a cofounder of the faculty group UChicago Free, a founding member of the Academic Freedom Alliance, and a cofounder and moderator of the Heterodox Academy STEM community. He has written and spoken extensively on issues related to academic freedom. Abbot was awarded the 2021 Hero of Intellectual Freedom Award by the American Council of Trustees and Alumni and the 2022 Courage Award by the Heterodox Academy.

Graeme Auton has been a professor of political science at the University of Redlands in Redlands, California, since 1987. Since 2008, he has also been affiliated with the graduate program in national security studies at California State University, San Bernardino. He received a PhD in political science at the University of California, Santa Barbara, in 1976. Auton has also been a NATO research fellow and a Ford Postdoctoral Fellow at Harvard University's Weatherhead Center for International Affairs. In the early 1990s, he worked for the US Arms Control and Disarmament Agency in Washington, DC; Brussels, Belgium; and Vienna, Austria, focusing on European security and arms-control issues. In 2006, he was a Fulbright Hayes Fellow in the Russian Far East. In 2007, he was a Senior Fulbright Scholar at Kyung He University in Seoul, South Korea. Most of Auton's published work focuses on international security issues and the international politics of Europe and Northeast Asia. His most recent scholarly article (in Columbia University's *Journal of International Affairs*) looked at the contagiousness of regional conflict in the Middle

346 THE FREE INQUIRY PAPERS

East. In recent years, Auton has expressed growing concern about the overall trajectory of a deeply politicized higher education establishment in the United States.

Akeela Careem is a PhD candidate in social psychology at Rutgers University–New Brunswick. She has a master's in social psychology and a bachelor's in finance. Her research focuses on various areas of political psychology, including political protest, social movements, and authoritarianism.

Carlos M. Carvalho is professor of statistics and the La Quinta Centennial Professor of Business at the University of Texas at Austin. He develops statistical models for causal inference and empirical finance. He is the director of the Salem Center for Policy. Carvalho received a PhD in statistics from Duke University. His research focuses on Bayesian statistics in complex, high-dimensional problems with applications ranging from economics to genetics. Before moving to Texas, he was on the faculty at the University of Chicago Booth School of Business.

Donald Alexander Downs is the Alexander Meiklejohn Emeritus Professor of Political Science and Emeritus Affiliate Professor of Law and Journalism at the University of Wisconsin–Madison. Before teaching at Wisconsin, he taught at the University of Michigan and the University of Notre Dame. Downs has written articles and award-winning books about academic freedom; free speech; campus politics; American politics; political and legal thought and movements; citizenship; domestic violence, psychiatry, and criminal law; and the relationship among the military, the university, and civic education. His most recent books are *Free Speech and Liberal Education: A Plea for Intellectual Diversity and Tolerance* (2020) and *The Value and Limits of Academic Speech: Philosophical, Political, and Legal Aspects* (2018), coedited with Chris W. Surprenant. He served as secretary and then president of the Committee for Academic Freedom and Rights from 1996 to 2016 and as faculty adviser to the Open Inquiry Project at the Institute for Humane Studies from 2015 to 2019. He currently serves on the Academic Affairs Committee of the Academic Freedom Alliance. In 2013, he won the Jeane Kirkpatrick Prize for Academic Freedom.

ABOUT THE AUTHORS 347

Komi Frey is the director of faculty outreach at the Foundation for Individual Rights and Expression (FIRE). She graduated with highest honors from the University of California, Davis, and then received her PhD in social psychology from the University of California, Riverside, where she was a National Science Foundation Graduate Research Fellow. At FIRE, her goal is to build a coalition of faculty who will defend free speech and inquiry at higher education institutions nationwide. She is also a visiting scholar at the University of Pennsylvania, where she conducts research with the Adversarial Collaboration Project.

James L. Gibson is the Sidney W. Souers Professor of Government in the department of political science at Washington University in St. Louis and Professor Extraordinary in Political Science at Stellenbosch University (South Africa). Gibson's research interests are in law and politics, comparative politics, and American politics. His newest book is *Democracy's Destruction? Changing Perceptions of the Supreme Court, the Presidency, and the Senate After the 2020 Election* (2024).

Adam Goldstein is the vice president of strategic initiatives at the Foundation for Individual Rights and Expression, where he researches and writes about free expression and the First Amendment. In his time at FIRE, he has worked in research, public advocacy, campus rights, and policy reform, and he contributed research to *The Coddling of the American Mind* and *The Canceling of the American Mind*. For 13 years, Goldstein was an attorney with the Student Press Law Center, giving legal assistance to over 15,000 students, parents, and others. While at the center, he coauthored its legal textbook, *Law of the Student Press*. In the past, he taught student media law for Michigan State University's Graduate School of Education, advocated for domain name owners in arbitration, and blogged about First Amendment and civil rights issues on the Huffington Post. Goldstein is a graduate of Fordham University School of Law and Fordham College at Lincoln Center, and he is licensed to practice in New York and the District of Columbia.

348 THE FREE INQUIRY PAPERS

Andrea Honeycutt is a doctoral student in education policy in the Department of Education Reform at the University of Arkansas. As a data analyst at the Foundation for Individual Rights and Expression, she studied issues related to the health of higher education institutions and wrote and presented on college students' mental health and its relationship to free speech. Currently, her research is focused on evaluating long-term spending and staffing changes in higher education.

Nathan Honeycutt is the manager of polling and analytics at the Foundation for Individual Rights and Expression. His research has primarily investigated political diversity and discrimination among university faculty and students. Honeycutt has published articles on political bias, political polarization, scientific integrity, and censorship in higher education, and he is a founding member of the Society for Open Inquiry in the Behavioral Sciences.

Lee Jussim is a distinguished professor of psychology at Rutgers University, where he recently completed his second term as department chair and is currently serving as acting chair for the anthropology department. He has published over 100 articles and chapters and seven books. His scholarship addresses stereotypes, prejudice, expectancy effects, and accuracy; how dysfunctional academic norms, including in peer review, methods, and political biases, threaten the validity of much work produced by the social sciences; and, more recently, radicalization in academia and the wider society. His book, *Social Perception and Social Reality: Why Accuracy Dominates Bias and Self-Fulfilling Prophecy* (2012), contested the psychological canon that social perception was mostly bias, and he received the Association of American Publishers Awards for Professional and Scholarly Excellence for best book in psychology in 2012. He is a founding member of the Academic Freedom Alliance and the Society for Open Inquiry in the Behavioral Sciences, which aspires to be an antidote to the denunciatory, censorious turn in academia. He also writes essays on social science and academia at Unsafe Science on Substack.

Brian Knight is the director of innovation and governance and a senior research fellow at the Mercatus Center at George Mason University. His research focuses on numerous aspects of financial regulation, including the creation of pro-innovation regulatory environments, the role of federalism in fintech regulation, the use of digital assets for financial transactions, the role of regulation for credit markets and consumer protection, and the provision of capital to businesses. Before joining Mercatus, Knight worked for the Milken Institute, where he headed up the FinTech and Capital Access programs. He has experience working for a broker-dealer with a focus on the emerging online private-placement market, and he was the cofounder of CrowdCheck, a company providing due-diligence and disclosure services to companies and intermediaries engaged in online private offerings. Knight received a law degree from the University of Virginia and a bachelor's degree from the College of William & Mary.

Anna I. Krylov is the University of Southern California associates chair in natural sciences and a professor of chemistry. She received her professional training from Moscow State University, the Hebrew University of Jerusalem, and the University of California, Berkeley. Krylov's work, which includes more than 300 papers and 300 invited talks, has received numerous international awards. She is a fellow of the American Chemical Society, the American Physical Society, the Royal Society of Chemistry, and the American Association for the Advancement of Science, and she is an elected member of the American Academy of Sciences and Letters, the International Academy of Quantum Molecular Science, and the Academia Europaea. An outspoken advocate of freedom of speech and academic freedom, Krylov is a founding member of the Academic Freedom Alliance. Her paper "The Peril of Politicizing Science," which launched a national conversation on the growing influence of political ideology over STEM, has received over 100,000 views.

George R. La Noue is a legally trained political scientist who is now an emeritus professor of political science and public policy at the University of Maryland, Baltimore County. He is the author of *Silenced Stages: The Loss of Academic Freedom and Campus Policy Debates* (2019) and many law review, public administration, and political science articles. He has served as a litigation expert or consultant for three federal agencies and more than 30 private clients in federal court cases.

350 THE FREE INQUIRY PAPERS

Greg Lukianoff is an attorney, a *New York Times* bestselling author, and the president and CEO of the Foundation for Individual Rights and Expression (FIRE). He is the author of *Unlearning Liberty: Campus Censorship and the End of American Debate, Freedom from Speech*, and *FIRE's Guide to Free Speech on Campus*. He coauthored *The Coddling of the American Mind: How Good Intentions and Bad Ideas Are Setting Up a Generation for Failure* with Jonathan Haidt. Most recently, Lukianoff coauthored *The Canceling of the American Mind: Cancel Culture Undermines Trust and Threatens Us All—but There Is a Solution* with Rikki Schlott. Lukianoff is also an executive producer of *Can We Take a Joke?* (2015), a feature-length documentary that explores the collision among comedy, censorship, and outrage culture, both on and off campus, and of *Mighty Ira: A Civil Liberties Story* (2020), an award-winning feature-length film about the life and career of former American Civil Liberties Union Executive Director Ira Glasser. Lukianoff has been published in the *New York Times*, the *Wall Street Journal*, the *Washington Post, Los Angeles Times*, the *Boston Globe*, and numerous other publications. He frequently appears on TV shows and radio programs, including the *CBS Evening News, The Today Show*, and NPR's *Morning Edition*. In 2008, he became the first-ever recipient of the Playboy Foundation's Freedom of Expression Award, and he has testified before both the US Senate and the House of Representatives about free speech issues on America's college campuses.

Robert Maranto is a political scientist serving as the 21st Century Chair in Leadership in the Department of Education Reform at the University of Arkansas. He researches administrative reform generally and education reform in particular while editing the *Journal of School Choice*. He has served on his local school board and in other public posts and is a founding member of the Society for Open Inquiry in Behavioral Science. With others, he has produced over 100 refereed publications and 16 scholarly books, including *COVID-19 and Schools: Policymakers, Stakeholders, and School Choice* (2024); *Educating Believers: Religion and School Choice* (2021); *President Obama and Education Reform* (2012); and *The Politically Correct University* (2009). Maranto has also penned more than 200 commentaries for venues including the *Wall Street Journal, The Hill*, and *National Review*. He is now working on a book about his experiences as an education

ABOUT THE AUTHORS 351

reformer serving on his local school board, tentatively titled *School Board Confidential.*

Iván Marinovic is an associate professor of accounting at the Stanford Graduate School of Business. He is an applied game theorist who studies contract theory and information transmission in capital markets. Marinovic is a cofounder of the Stanford Classical Liberalism Initiative and the Stanford Academic Freedom Alliance. He is also a cofounder of the Accounting and Economics Society.

Jonathan Rauch, a senior fellow at the Brookings Institution in Washington, DC, is the author of eight books and many articles on public policy, culture, and government. His latest book, published in 2021 by the Brookings Press, is *The Constitution of Knowledge: A Defense of Truth*, a spirited and deep-diving account of how to push back against disinformation, canceling, and other new threats to our fact-based epistemic order. That book builds on his 1993 defense of open and fact-based discourse, *Kindly Inquisitors: The New Attacks on Free Thought*. He is a contributing writer for *The Atlantic* and recipient of the 2005 National Magazine Award, the magazine industry's equivalent of the Pulitzer Prize. In 2018, he published *The Happiness Curve: Why Life Gets Better After 50*, a lauded account of the surprising relationship between aging and happiness. Other books include *Denial: My 25 Years Without a Soul*, a memoir of his struggle with his sexuality, and *Gay Marriage: Why It Is Good for Gays, Good for Straights, and Good for America*, published in 2004 by Times Books (Henry Holt).

Richard E. Redding is the Ronald D. Rotunda Distinguished Professor of Jurisprudence, professor of psychology and education, and an associate dean for academic affairs at Chapman University. Redding has written extensively on the importance of viewpoint and sociopolitical diversity in teaching, research, and professional practice. Notable publications include *Ideological and Political Bias in Psychology: Nature, Scope, and Solutions* (2023); "Sociopolitical Values at the Deep Culture in Culturally-Competent Psychotherapy," in *Clinical Psychological Science* (2023); "Likes Attract: The Sociopolitical Groupthink of (Social) Psychologists," in *Perspectives on Psychological Science* (2012); *The Politically Correct University: Problems, Scope,*

352 THE FREE INQUIRY PAPERS

and Reforms (2009); and "Sociopolitical Diversity in Psychology: The Case for Pluralism," in *American Psychologist* (2001). He is also the founding president of the Society for Open Inquiry in the Behavioral Science. Redding holds a PhD from the University of Virginia, an MS from Vanderbilt University, and a JD from Washington and Lee University.

Chad G. Rusthoven (chad.rusthoven@gmail.com) is a radiation oncologist and an associate clinical professor at the University of Colorado School of Medicine. He is an active medical researcher and serves in leadership on national clinical trials in the field of oncology. He is also a member of the national Academic Freedom Alliance.

Aaron Saiger is a professor of law at Fordham Law School, where he has taught since 2003 and where he was the dean's distinguished research scholar in 2017–18. He writes and teaches on administrative law and regulatory policy, education law and policy, and local government. He received his PhD from the Woodrow Wilson School of Public and International Affairs at Princeton University and his JD from Columbia University. He was a law clerk to the Honorable Ruth Bader Ginsburg of the United States Supreme Court (2001–02) and the Honorable Douglas H. Ginsburg of the United States Court of Appeals for the District of Columbia Circuit (2000–01). Saiger's most recent administrative law scholarship has appeared in the *Vanderbilt Law Review* and the *Boston University Law Review*. His forthcoming book, *Schoolhouse in the Cloud*, will be published by the Oxford University Press.

Catherine Salmon received a BSc in biology in 1992 and a PhD in evolutionary psychology in 1997 from McMaster University in Canada. After several years as a postdoctoral researcher at Simon Fraser University in Vancouver, she joined the faculty at the University of Redlands in Southern California, where she is currently a professor in the psychology department and the director of the human-animal studies program. She is the coauthor of *The Secret Power of Middle Children* (2012) and *Warrior Lovers: Erotic Fiction, Evolution and Female Sexuality* (2003). Her primary research interests include parental investment and sibling conflict; male and female sexuality, particularly as expressed in pornography and other erotic genres;

ABOUT THE AUTHORS   353

and human-animal interactions. She chaired her university's institutional review board for 10 years and was the editor in chief of the journal *Evolutionary Behavioral Sciences* from 2017 through 2023. She is a founding member of the Society for Open Inquiry in Behavioral Science.

Sally Satel is a senior fellow at the American Enterprise Institute; the medical director of a local methadone clinic in Washington, DC; and a lecturer at Yale University School of Medicine. She earned a BS from Cornell University, an MS from the University of Chicago, and an MD from Brown University. After completing her residency in psychiatry at Yale University School of Medicine, she was an assistant professor of psychiatry from 1988 to 1993. From 1993 to 1994, she was a Robert Wood Johnson Foundation Health Policy Fellow with the Senate Labor and Human Resources Committee.

Patricia Nayna Schwerdtle is a global public health academic based in the Faculty of Medicine at Heidelberg University's Heidelberg Institute of Global Health in Germany. She is also affiliated with Monash University in Australia. Her research for a PhD focuses on climate change–related migration and health. She has worked in the field of emergency and medical humanitarian assistance since 2007 and was formerly vice president on the board of Médecins Sans Frontières (Doctors Without Borders) in Australia. She is well published in the fields of climate change and health, climate change adaptation for health, humanitarian assistance, and health professions education. She has been affiliated with Counterweight (UK), Do Not Divide Us (UK), and the Heterodox Academy (US). She advises governments, nongovernmental organizations, and universities on climate change and health and on building climate-resilient, migrant-inclusive, and environmentally sustainable health systems.

Sean T. Stevens has a PhD in social psychology from Rutgers University and is the chief research advisor for the Foundation for Individual Rights and Expression. For almost two decades, his research has focused on understanding how moral convictions produce motivated reasoning in the political domain and how this motivated reasoning can distort research in the social sciences. Recently, he has begun investigating the psychological

354 THE FREE INQUIRY PAPERS

factors that motivate support for censorship and self-censorship. He is also a member of the Best Practices in Science Movement and works to promote scientific-integrity practices in the social sciences.

Joseph L. Sutherland is the inaugural director of the Center for AI Learning, a newly established center at Emory University that promotes scholarly AI literacy, research, and community. He maintains faculty affiliations in the Department of Quantitative Theory and Methods and the Empathetic AI for Health Institute at Emory University. He is a fellow of the Weidenbaum Center on the Economy, Government, and Public Policy at Washington University in St. Louis.

Jay Tanzman is a statistical consultant working in biostatistics, epidemiology, social sciences, and educational research. He has published criticisms of the statistical practices in the social sciences and has been an outspoken advocate for improving the statistical methods employed in experimental psychology. He uses statistical insights to assist scientists in fighting false claims of discrimination in STEM fields. Previously, he held academic positions at Loma Linda University and the University of California, Los Angeles.

George Yancey is a professor at the Institute for Studies of Religion and in the sociology department at Baylor University. He has published several research articles on institutional racial diversity, racial identity, atheists, cultural progressives, academic bias, and anti-Christian hostility. His books include *One Faith No More: The Transformation of Christianity in Red and Blue America* (2021); *Compromising Scholarship: Religious and Political Bias in American Higher Education* (2017); *So Many Christians, So Few Lions: Is There Christianophobia in the United States?* (2014); and, with Michael Emerson, *Transcending Racial Barriers: Toward a Mutual Obligations Approach* (2010).

Jonathan Zimmerman is a professor of history of education and the Berkowitz Professor in Education at the University of Pennsylvania. A former Peace Corps volunteer and high school teacher, Zimmerman is the author of *Free Speech and Why You Should Give a Damn* (illustrated by cartoonist Signe Wilkinson) and eight other books. He is also a columnist at the *Philadelphia Inquirer* and a frequent contributor to the *Washington Post*, the *New York Review of Books*, and other popular newspapers and magazines. Zimmerman taught for 20 years at New York University, where he received its Distinguished Teaching Award in 2008.

Index

AAMC. *See* Association of American Medical Colleges

Abbot, Dorian S., 247, 336

Abortions, 178, 181n11
  access to, 173–74
  employers paying for out-of-state, 173–75
  Supreme Court overturning right to, 62–64

Academia
  academic achievement undermined by, 16
  conservatives critiquing, 151–52
  DEI programs in, 135–36
  exclusion from, 136
  the left influencing, 136, 141n19, 151, 249–50, 326
  Lysenkoism and, 139
  mentorship in, 84–85
  professors forced out of, 237
  reputation and, 156
  See also Universities

Academic achievement, 16, 240

Academic community, social media not representing, 94–96

Academic departments, without Republicans, 327

Academic freedom, 10–11, 71, 197, 219, 280
  the academy restricting, 249
  administrators and, 65–66, 74

of Communists, 145
culture of, 75
of faculty, 73
in higher education, 184
institutional speech and, 63
of professors, 67
program to promote, 76–78
scholars protected by, 29–30
scientific inquiry supported by, 82
Sweezy defending, 220
universities denying, 62, 64
See also Committee for Academic Freedom and Rights

Academic Freedom Alliance (AFA), 194, 279, 287

Academic inquiry, bias and, 31

Academic performance, 84, 88–89, 239

Academic priorities, democratic priorities clashing with, 9–11

Academic Questions (publication), 134

Academic research, credibility of, 90–93

The Academy
  academic freedom and restricted by, 249
  free speech restricted by, 249
  political viewpoints expressed within, 223

357

358 THE FREE INQUIRY PAPERS

self-censorship in, 83

Activist organizations, deplatforming attempts by, 149–50

Ad hominem attacks, 145

Administrative appointments,
candidate identity affecting,
267

Administrative jobs, growth in, 73

Administrators, 64, 73, 209, 309
academic freedom and, 65–66, 74
faculty influenced by, 68, 74–75
intellectual life shaped by, 72
speech policed by, 145
standard operating procedures
to demote, 336
student organizations closed
by, 342
students sided with by, 199
UC affected by, 275–76
virtue signaling by, 9
See also DEI administrators

Admissions, 89, 238–39
academic achievement as base
of, 240
affirmative action in, 248
conservatives discriminated
against by, 259
DEI bureaucracy monitoring, 224
merit and, 267

Adolescents, GD in, 85–87

Advancing Health Equity (AMA),
108–9

Advisory Committee on Immunization Practices, of CDC, 105

AFA. See Academic Freedom
Alliance

Affective polarization, 52, 327
ideological, 52, 54
partisan, 52, 54
self-censorship in relation to, 51,
52, 55

Affirmative action, 87, 91, 112–13
academic performance and,
88–89
in admissions, 248
DEI compared with, 136–37
in medicine, 83–84
students affected by, 84

Alumni and Donors Unite (organization), 284

AMA. See American Medical
Association

Amazon Web Services, 119

American Association of University
Professors, 219

American Health Association, 112

American Mathematical Society, 287

American Medical Association
(AMA), 108–10, 116, 122

American Psychological Association (APA), 140, 262n16

American Psychological Society.
See Association for Psychological Science

Anarchism, 276

Anderson, Mary, 193–94

Anti-harassment obligations, 315

Anti-obesity campaigns, fatphobia
and, 268–69

Anti-racism, 137–38
public health and, 108
universities and, 64, 75–76

University of Minnesota and, 121

Antisemitism, 251, 335

Anti-speech instincts, 307–8

Anti-war expression, Supreme
Court protecting, 23

Anti-war resistance, 22

APA. *See* American Psychological
Association

Arizona, public universities in, 279

Army (US), 209

Article retractions guidelines, by
Committee on Publication
Ethics, 95

Articles of Confederation, 324

Association for Mathematical
Research, 287

Association for Psychological Science "American Psychological
Society," 140

Association of American Colleges,
219

Association of American Medical
Colleges (AAMC), 84, 88, 108

Authoritarianism, censorship and,
35

Babbling Beaver (website), 284,
301n110

Badger Herald (newspaper), 195

Baldwin, Davarian, 73

Baldwin, Gordon, 193, 194

Bartholet, Elizabeth, 13

Beauharnais v. Illinois (Supreme
Court), 14

Behavioral scientists, censorship
of, 288

Berlin Wall, 271–72, 289, 341

Bias, 39, 110, 239, 259
academic inquiry and, 31
in faculty, 113
grading, 151
of professors, 252–53

Bias response teams, 237, 306, 341

Bias trainings, implicit, 39, 110

Biology, race and, 113–15

Bipartisan Policy Center (BPC),
222–23, 225–26

Birth control campaigns, 24

Bloom, Alan, 191

Bozeman, Barry, 208

BPC. *See* Bipartisan Policy Center

The Bradley Foundation, 194

Brain structure, ideology and, 256

Brewster, Kingman, 220

Britain, parliamentary democracy
in, 11

Brown, Michael, 104

Brown University, 85, 110

Buckley, William F., 151

Bukovsky, Vladimir, 272, 297n59
corrective labor avoided by,
276
Judgment in Moscow by, 271
To Build a Castle by, 271

Bureaucracies, 203–5, 208–9
free inquiry, 337
progressives reflected in, 207
Title IX, 337
See also DEI bureaucracies

Bureaucrats, higher education,
336–37

Buss, David M., 135

CAFAR. *See* Committee for Academic Freedom and Rights
Caldwell, Christopher, 13–14
Calhoun, Craig, 73
Campbell, Colin, 153–54
Campus culture, professors shaping, 251
Campus debates, on contentious topics, 334–35
Campus Deplatforming Database (FIRE), 149, 152, 155
Campus Expression Survey, by Heterodox Academy, 147
Campus Free Expression (BPC), 222–23
Campus practices, legal protections contrasted with, 229
Campuses
  antisemitism on, 251
  free expression on, 145–51
  free inquiry attacked on, 28
  free speech attacked on, 21, 28
  policy debates sponsored by, 227
  presumption of innocence lacked on, 269
  See also Protests
Cancel culture, 247, 249, 273, 325–26
Cancellation, 83, 113, 185, 335
  DEI administrators encouraging, 237
  experience of near-, 115–16
  national database of debates and, 334
  of Wang, 112

Candidate identity, hiring and administrative appointments affected by, 267
Cardinal Newman Society, 149–50
Carlson, Taylor, 51
"The Case for Colonialism" (Gilley), 134
CDC. *See* Centers for Disease Control and Prevention
Censorship
  authoritarianism and, 35
  of behavioral scientists, 288
  DEI and, 247
  First Amendment fighting, 327
  of gay and lesbian Americans, 24
  minorities oppressed through, 33
  open inquiry threatened by, 247
  progressive, 185
  by SPSP, 137–38
  See also Self-censorship
Centers for Disease Control and Prevention (CDC), 105
Central Committee of the Communist Party of the Soviet Union, 271
Central Connecticut State College, 221
Chemistry education, 268
Chertman, Willy, 213
Chicago principles, 240, 277, 329–30, 337
Chicago statement, on free expression, 95
Chilled discourse, 111–13
Chilling effect, 90, 185, 186, 191, 333
  faculty and students

INDEX 361

contributing to, 147
public targeting of scholars
creating, 90
of social justice, 106
China, 211, 251
Choper, Jesse, 187
Chronicle of Higher Education, 10,
198, 211
Churchill, Ward, 197
Churchill, Winston, 214
Civil disobedience, 314–16
Civil liberties, 53, 54
Civil rights, free speech and, 34
Civil Rights Commission (US), 214,
341
Class mobility, 339
Clinical practice, ideology buffered
against through, 122
Clinton administration, 207
The Closing of the American Mind
(Bloom), 191
Coalition for the Advancement &
Application of Psychological
Sciences, 92
Coauthorship, 85, 87, 89
Code of conduct, at University of
Pennsylvania, 306
Cold War, 271, 341
Cole, Philip, 108
Collection action, individual action
and, 342–43
College Free Speech Rankings
(FIRE), 306, 311
College Senior Survey (2009), 154
Colleges, structural leftist funda-
mentalism ingrained in, 8

Collier, Kristin, 121–22
Columbia University, 314
Comer Children's Pediatric Mobile
Medical Unit, 120
Committee for Academic Freedom
and Rights (CAFAR), 184, 199
formation and activities of,
192–97
planting the seeds of, 191–92
publicity for, 195
Committee on Publication Ethics
guidelines, 95, 288
Communications offices, 74
Communicator of the Year Award,
from University of Southern
California Dornsife College
of Letters, Arts, and Sciences, 289
Communist institutions,
bias-response teams resembling, 341
Communist Party, 8, 131, 138–39,
275
Communist Party of the Soviet
Union, Central Committee
of the, 271
Communists, academic freedom
of, 145
Compelled speech, 137, 237, 238
Compliance rules, IRB parsing,
207–8
Conformity, ideological impacts
and, 209–11
Congressional hearings, for higher
education bureaucrats,
336–37

Conservative expression, higher education suppressing, 152, 153, 154

Conservative parties, success of, 15

Conservative students, grading bias feared by, 151

Conservatives, 144, 237, 249
  academia critiqued by, 151–52
  admissions discriminating against, 259
  DEI excluding, 250–51
  free speech associated with, 22
  hostility toward, 147

The Constitution, 63–64, 322, 324–25, 328, 330–31
  First Amendment of, 14, 21, 34, 178, 189–90, 227
  free thought called for in, 190
  heated exchange of views embraced by, 229

Constitution of Knowledge, 324–25, 326, 328, 330–31, 333

The Constitution of Knowledge (Rauch), 90

The Constitution of Liberty (Hayek), 179

Constitutional law, students learning, 189–90

Cornell University, Jewish students threatened at, 310

Corporate universities, institutional speech and, 67

Corrective labor, Bukovsky avoiding, 276

Counter Wokecraft (anonymous), 274, 276, 277, 287, 301n116

COVID-19 pandemic, 90–91, 105, 114

Critical race theory, 35–36, 110

Critical social justice (CSJ), 275
  DEI administrators advancing, 280
  free speech opposed by, 269
  K–12 math curriculum revised for, 278
  merit-based practices subordinating, 267
  professional societies and, 288
  without space for rational dialogue, 282
  University of San Diego taken over by, 284

Critical theory, at higher education, 211

Crossman, Richard, 6, 8

CSJ. *See* Critical social justice

Culture
  of academic freedom, 75
  campus, 251
  cancel, 247, 249, 273, 325–26
  free speech, 308, 313, 315, 317–18
  law and, 325–27
  See also Cancel culture

Curricular reform, in medical schools, 110

Cynical Theories (Pluckrose and Lindsay), 276

Daily Cardinal (newspaper), 195

Daniels, Ronald J., 225–26

Dartmouth University, dialogue project at, 318

The Death of Stalin (film), 213

Debates, campus, 334–35

Declaration of Independence, 324

"Decree for the Protection of the German People" (Nazi law), 33

DEI. *See* Diversity, equity, and inclusion

"DEI" (anonymous), 276

DEI administrators
cancellation encouraged by, 237
CSJ advanced by, 280
Israel opposed by, 251

DEI bureaucracies, 228, 230, 234, 281–82
downsizing, 337
equity promises not delivered on by, 213
hiring and admissions monitored by, 224

DEI personnel, at University of Michigan, 299n96

DEI programs, in academia, 135–36

DEI screening, of faculty, 119

DEI statements, 119, 136–37, 250–51, 277
compelled speech and, 237
UC requiring, 228–29
UW dropping, 279

Demerew, Kaleb, 247, 253

Democracy, 225–26
collapse of, 11–14
free inquiry and, 6
Haidt on, 7
liberal, 308
parliamentary, 11
populism and, 15

threats to, 14–17

Democratic priorities, academic priorities clashing with, 9–11

Democrats, faculty dominating, 327

Demographic characteristics, DEI and, 255

Demographic diversity, 255–56

Department of Education (US), 210, 213–14, 278, 310–11

Deplatforming attempts, 149–50

Dershowitz, Alan, 251

DeSantis, Ron, 35, 169

Dewey, John, 250

Dialogue project, at Dartmouth University, 318

DiAngelo, Robin, 110

Disney, 168–69

Disparate impact, 339

Diversification, of faculty, 259

Diversity
demographic, 255–56
extremism and, 243
merit and, 242–43
narrative of, 251–52
sexual, 268
sociopolitical, 256
within student body, 242
See also Ideological diversity; Intellectual diversity

Diversity, equity, and inclusion (DEI), 118–19, 135–36, 139, 210–12, 224–25, 260
affirmative action compared with, 136–37
censorship and, 247

conservatives and libertarians
excluded by, 250–51
criticism of, 235–38
demographic characteristics
and, 255
evaluating, 339
free expression opposed by, 237
hiring and, 278
identity politics encouraged by,
236
ideological diversity advancing,
248–49, 252–53, 255
Journal of Chemical Education
publishing on, 268
legislation opposing, 248
MFE contrasted with, 234, 238,
243
open inquiry suppressed by,
250–51
as Orwellian, 275
professors advanced by, 253–55
social justice and, 16
state legislatures opposed by, 282
Diversity, Equity, and Inclusion Com-
petencies Across the Learning
Continuum (AAMC), 109–10
"Diversity, Inclusion, and Equity"
(Wang), 112
Diversity trainings, 16–17, 39
The Divided Academy (Lipset), 223
Do No Harm (nonprofit), 118, 120,
278
Dobbs v. Jackson Women's Health
Organization (Supreme
Court), 175, 181n13
Douglas, Jim, 222

Douglas, William O., 14
Douglass, Frederick, 23–24, 33
Downs, Anthony, 205
Duke Divinity School, 283
Duncan, Kyle, 69–70

Economic power, political partici-
pation in tension with, 172
Educational experience, social
justice influencing, 242
Edward Shils report, 240
Egalitarianism, 30
Eisenhower, Dwight D., 203, 204
"Elimination of Harmful Language
Initiative" website, 278
Elite politics, 11–14
Emersonian pursuit, 189
Empirical rule, 323
Employers, out-of-state abortions
paid for by, 173–75
Employment, politics and, 169–72
The Enlightenment, 322
Environmental Protection Agency,
209
Essentialist characteristics, ideo-
logical values as, 257
Evergreen State College, 284
Expression, 94
Chicago statement on freedom
of, 95
social media suppressing, 87–90
suppression of, 88–91
Extremism, diversity and, 243

Faculty, 65
academic freedom of, 73

administrators influencing, 68, 74–75

bias in, 113

chilling effect contributed to by, 147

DEI screening of, 119

Democrats dominating, 327

diversification of, 259

ideological diversity lacked by, 259

illiberalism of, 143

intolerant attitudes held by, 157

marginalization experienced by, 258

newspeak used by, 268

partisanship of, 224

at Princeton University, 70

promotion processes for, 278

on public health, 107

self-censorship by, 94, 269

social science, 147

University of North Texas terminating, 17

virtue signaling by, 9

See also Hiring; Professors; Scholars

Faculty adjuncts, 73–74

Faculty speech code, 192–94, 197–98

Fallibilism, 7

Fallibilist rule, 323

Fatphobia, anti-obesity campaigns and, 268–69

FBI, 273

Federalist 10 (Madison), 12

Federalist 51 (Madison), 12

Federalists, 204

Fineberg, Harvey V., 107

FIRE. *See* Foundation for Individual Rights and Expression

First Amendment, of the Constitution, 14, 21, 34, 66, 178, 187–90, 214

censorship fought by, 327

public education on, 340–41

students protected by, 227, 309

The First Amendment (Choper and Shiffrin), 187

First Amendment Commission (US), 341

First Amendment rights, 309, 312

Flier, Jeffrey, 86

Florida

Disney and, 168–69

House Bill 7 in, 35

State University System in, 227

Floyd, George, 63, 104, 105, 250

Foundation for Individual Rights and Expression (FIRE), 83, 120, 146–48, 156, 194, 208

Campus Deplatforming Database by, 149, 152, 155

College Free Speech Rankings by, 306, 311

educational resources, opportunities to network, and protection provided by, 287

political motivation classified by, 159n6

Scholars Under Fire Database by, 133, 149–50, 152, 155

Student Survey by, 157

Franke, Ray, 154
Franklin, Benjamin, 330
Franks, Mary Anne, 153
Free expression, 29–30, 96, 222–23, 307
  on campuses, 145–51
  Chicago statement on, 95
  DEI opposing, 237
  in higher education, 219
  students protected by, 21
Free inquiry. *See specific topics*
Free inquiry bureaucracies, Title IX bureaucracies countering, 337
Free intellectual inquiry, 187
Free speech, 29–30, 50, 187, 199
  the academy restricting, 249
  campuses attacking, 21, 28
  cancel culture threatening, 247
  civil rights and, 34
  conservatives associated with, 22
  CSJ opposing, 269
  Douglass supporting, 23–24
  free inquiry compared with, 6
  hearings on bureaucratic attempts to limit, 335–36
  in higher education, 184
  higher education bureaucrats reducing, 337
  importance of campus, 221–22
  marketplace of ideas and, 325
  during protests, 33
  social justice advocates limiting, 28
  Supreme Court on, 34
  teaching, 337–38

  threats to, 14–17
  Tinker arguing for, 21–22, 26
  at UW-Madison, 188–89
  virtue signaling shutting down free inquiry and, 15–16
Free speech culture, 308, 313, 315, 317–18
Free Speech Movement, 145
Free thought, the Constitution calling for, 190
Freedom and Tolerance Surveys, 53, 59n14
Freedom of expression. *See* Free expression
Freedom of religion, 188
Freedom of speech. *See* Free speech
Freedom Riders, 117
Fringe benefits, state laws interacted with through, 173–76
Frisby, Craig, 210
Fryer, Roland G., Jr., 133–34
Frykenberg, Robert, 192–93
Fundamentalism, 323
  intellectual diversity threatened by, 11
  postmodern approaches resembling, 9
  structural leftist, 8

Galileo, 82
Galloway, Jennifer, 196
Garner, Eric, 104
Gay, Claudine, 251–52
Gay and lesbian Americans, censorship of, 24
Gaza, 158n4

GD. *See* Gender dysphoria

Gender dysphoria (GD)
  in adolescents, 85–87
  rapid-onset, 87, 89, 92
  in young adults, 85–87

Gender Dysphoria Affirmative
  Working Group, 92

Gender identity, 170

General Social Survey (GSS), 53,
  153–54

Genetics, Lysenko denying, 130–31

Georgia, 36

Al-Gharbi, Musa, 16, 212

Gibson, James L., 60n18

Gillen, Andrew, 229

Gilley, Bruce, 134

Ginsberg, Benjamin, 208

Ginsburg, Tom, 77

Goal displacement, 207

God and Man at Yale (Buckley), 151

The God That Failed (Crossman),
  6, 8

Goldwater Institute, 279

Government-speech doctrine, 67

Grading, on academic performance, 239

Grading bias, conservative students fearing, 151

Graduate Record Examination
  (GRE), 242

Grand Rounds Speakers, 115–16

GRE. *See* Graduate Record
  Examination

Great Chinese Famine, 132

Greene, Jay, 211, 299n96

Gregoire, Chris, 222

Groups, restriction of free inquiry
  empowering wrong, 37–38

GSS. *See* General Social Survey

Haider, Sarah, 285–86

Haidt, Jonathan, 227, 327
  on democracy, 7
  on protests, 5
  SPSP resigned from by, 139

Hamas, 64, 158n4, 184, 211, 335, 339

Hanlon, Aaron, 153–54

Hansen, W. Lee, 198

Harassment, of students, 310

Harlem Children's Zone (nonprofit), 133

Harm avoidance, 93

Harms, free inquiry limited to
  avoid, 30–31

Harvard University, 70–71, 76, 86,
  251–52, 307, 335
  Fryer suspended from, 133–34
  Hooven ousted by, 336
  institutional neutrality adopted
  at, 317

Hasnas, John, 228

Havel, Václav, 138

Hayek, Friedrich, 179–80

Healey v. James (Supreme Court),
  221

Health Affairs Blog, 114

Health differentials, systemic racism and, 111–12

Health disparities, 116–18

Heath, Elaine, 283

Heckler's veto, 311

Heliocentric model, 82

Heritage Foundation, 225, 281

Herzog, Katie, 111

Heterodox Academy (HxA), 83, 147, 287

Higher education, 2, 10, 198, 211
  academic freedom in, 184
  conservative expression suppressed by, 152, 153, 154
  free expression in, 219
  free speech in, 184
  progressive politics in, 258
  See also Academia; The academy; Rules; Students; Universities

Higher education bureaucrats, 336–37

Higher education organizations, public funding of, 338

Hippel, William von, 135

Hiring, 238–39, 259
  candidate identity affecting, 267
  DEI and, 278
  DEI bureaucracy monitoring, 224
  non-merit-based, 240
  See also DEI statements

Hirsch, E. D., 16

Hoffer, Eric, 7

Hollywood blacklist, 180n2

Holmes, Oliver Wendell, Jr., 22–23, 190, 325

Holodomor famine, 6

Home education, 13

Honeycutt, Nathan, 29

Hooven, Carole, 336

Horowitz, Jonathan, 153–54

Hostility, toward conservatives, 147

House Bill 7 (Florida), 35

House Committee on Education and the Workforce, 306

House of Representatives (US), 251

How to Be an Antiracist (Kendi), 110

Huddle, Thomas, 113

Hult, Karen, 206

Human subjects, IRB protecting, 340

Humanitarians, 323

Hunt, Lester, 193

Hutchison, Jane, 196

HxA. *See* Heterodox Academy

IAT. *See* Implicit Association Test

Identity politics, 236, 278

Ideological diversity, 256
  DEI advanced by, 248–49, 252–53, 255
  educational and professional benefits of, 257
  faculty lacking, 259
  professors served by, 248
  social justice not conflicting with, 255

Ideological impacts, conformity and, 209–11

Ideological statements of faith, 338

Ideological values, as essentialist characteristics, 257

Ideology, 139, 268–69
  brain structure and, 256
  clinical practice buffering against, 122
  illiberal, 270–71, 273, 275
  institutions taken over by, 280
  liberal, 151

Marxist, 130–31
Marxist-Leninist, 271
political, 150–52
progressive, 247, 260
as protected class, 338–39
religion and, 257
social justice, 104
truth over, 140
See also Critical social justice;
  Diversity, equity, and inclusion
Illiberal attitudes, students endors-
  ing, 145–46
Illiberal ideology, 270–71, 273, 275
Illiberalism, of faculty, 143
"I'm a Progressive" (Haider), 285
Implicit Association Test (IAT), 37,
  111, 210
Implicit bias trainings, 39, 110
Inclusivity, 268
Indiana University School of Medicine (IUSM), 119, 120
Individual action, collection action
  and, 342–43
Inquiry, threats to, 14–17
Institutional neutrality
  Harvard University adopting, 317
  rules on, 316
  at University of Chicago, 277
Institutional Review Boards (IRB),
  212
  compliance rules parsed by,
    207–8
  human subjects protected by,
    340
  social sciences excluded from,
    213

Institutional speech, 65, 66, 77
  academic freedom and, 63
  corporate universities and, 67
  pedagogical justification for, 75
  universities eschewing, 62–63
Institutions
  Communist, 341
  creating new, 342
  ideology taking over, 280
  private, 309
  universities as, 72–74
*The Intellectual Crisis in American
  Public Administration*, 207
Intellectual diversity
  framework for, 219–20
  fundamentalism threatening, 11
  threats to, 222–25
Intellectual honesty, 284
International Human Rights Day,
  104
Intolerant attitudes, students and
  faculty holding, 157
Ioannidis, John P. A., 115
IRB. *See* Institutional Review Boards
Ironton (Ohio), 115
Israel, 16, 158n4, 184, 211, 251
Israel-Hamas war, 64
Israel-Palestine conflict, 308
IUSM. *See* Indiana University
  School of Medicine
"I've Been to the Mountaintop"
  (King), 32–33

Jackson, Andrew, 204
Jackson, Robert, 190–91
Jacoby, Russell, 262n17

JAHA. See Journal of the American Heart Association

January 6 (attacks), 25, 116

Jefferson, Thomas, 243

Jewish students, Cornell University threatening, 310

Johns Hopkins University, 225–26

Journal editorial boards, 94–95

Journal of Chemical Education, 268

Journal of Intervention and Statebuilding, 134

Journal of Open Inquiry in the Behavioral Sciences, 288

Journal of the American Heart Association (JAHA), 84, 112

Journal of the American Medical Association, 113, 115

Journalism, public trust in, 90

Judgment in Moscow (Bukovsky), 271

Jung, Jiwon, 208

Jussim, Lee, 29, 212, 289–90

K–12 education, 213, 267–68, 340

K–12 math curriculum, CSJ revising, 278

Kaiser Permanente Bernard J. Tyson School of Medicine, 110

Kalven, Harry, Jr., 68–69

Kalven Committee, 68, 70–71, 74, 76–78, 219–20, 223

Kalven Report, 240, 277, 337

Das Kapital (Marx), 280

Karlsson, Niklaus, 144

Kasper, Amy, 198

Kaufmann, Eric, 14, 146

Kavanaugh, Brett, 175

Kendi, Ibram X., 110

KGB, 273

Khalid, Amna, 281

Kindly Inquisitors (Rauch), 192, 322–23

King, Martin Luther, Jr., 32, 40, 236

Kipnis, Laura, 10, 210, 211, 227

Knight Foundation, 321

Knoll, Johannes, 56

Knowledge, free inquiry allowing advancement of, 38–39

Koestler, Arthur, 8

Kors, Alan Charles, 198

Kozinski, Alex, 38–39, 229

Krepinevich, Andrew, 209

Krylov, Anna I., 289

Kuran, Timur, 202n24

Ladd, Everett, 223

Langbert, Mitchell, 224, 327

Law, culture and, 325–27

LCME. *See* Liaison Committee on Medical Education

Lee, Tabia, 280

The Left

    academia influenced by, 136, 141n19, 151, 249–50, 326

    anti-constitutional temper of, 13–14

    cultural influencers and drivers controlled by, 250

Leftists, 8, 136, 285–86

Legal protections, campus practices contrasted with, 229

Legislation, DEI opposed through, 248

Lemay-Hébert, Nicolas, 135
"Letter from a Birmingham Jail" (King), 40
Liaison Committee on Medical Education (LCME), 120
Liberal arts colleges, 152
Liberal democracy, 308
Liberal ideology, of professors, 151
Liberal science, 322–23
Liberals, 144, 152, 153
Libertarians, 249, 250–51
Liberty versus oppression, 5
Lichter, S. Robert, 223
Lincoln, Abraham, 204
Lindsay, James, 276
Lipset, Seymour, 223
Littman, Lisa, 85
Loewenstein, George, 144
The Lone Ranger (television show), 193
Lukianoff, Greg, 5
Lysenko, Trofim, 130–32, 139, 213
Lysenkoism, 82, 133

Madison, James, 12, 324, 326, 330, 340
Magill, Elizabeth, 306–7
Maher, Bill, 17
Management, ownership contrasted with, 176
Manhattan Institute, 282
Mann, Thomas, 8
Mao Zedong, 132
Maranto, Robert, 16
Marcus, Stanley, 231
Marcuse, Herbert, 236, 250

Marginalization, students and faculty experiencing, 258
Mariupol (Ukraine), 5
Marketplace of ideas, 325, 330
Marshall, Thurgood, 34
Martinez, Jenny, 69–70
Marx, Karl, 250, 280
Marxism, 130–31, 213, 214, 249, 341
Marxist-Leninism, 271, 275
Massachusetts Institute of Technology (MIT), 251, 278, 284, 301n110, 335, 336
Matthes, Jörg, 56
McCarthy, Joseph, 204, 333
McCarthyism, 33–34, 82, 137, 185, 321
McWhorter, John, 16, 210
Medical schools, 110, 268
Medical students, incoming, 121
Medical workforce, diversifying, 118
Medicine
    affirmative action in, 83–84
    identity politics in, 278
    social justice movement within, 106
Melnick, R. Shep, 16, 210
Mentorship, 84–85, 91
Merit
    admissions and, 267
    diversity and, 242–43
    social justice devaluing, 284
Merit, fairness, and equality (MFE), 238–39
    DEI contrasted with, 234, 238, 243
    myths about, 241–43

practical implementation of, 240–41

social good and, 241

Merit-based practices, CSJ subordinated by, 267

Meritocracy, 241–42

Meso-level environment, 55–56

Metaphor, as persuasive device, 257–58

Metropolitan Chicago Breast Cancer Task Force, 119

MFE. *See* Merit, fairness, and equality

Microaggressions, 185, 227, 273, 306

Mill, John Stuart, 38, 88

Miller, Geoffrey, 15–16

Minding the Campus (series), 210

Minorities, censorship oppressing, 33

MIT. *See* Massachusetts Institute of Technology

Moderates, 237

Modernity, free inquiry enabling, 333

Montgomery Police Department, 34

Montz, Rob, 134–39

Moral furies, 200n2

Morgenthau, Hans J., 201n12

Motte and Bailey rhetorical ploy, 301n116

Mounk, Yascha, 105

Multicultural counseling, 104

Murrow, Edward R., 308

Mutz, Diana C., 59

Mystal, Elie, 13

Name-calling accusations, 285

National Association of Scholars, 134

National Health Services, 92

National Institutes of Health, 267

National Science Foundation, 212, 339

"National White Coat Die-In," 104

Nationalist parties, success of, 15

Nature (journal), 269

Nature Communications (journal), 84

Nature Human Behaviour (journal), 30

NCRI. *See* Network Contagion Research Institute

Negy, Charles, 10–11

Neopronouns, 268

Network Contagion Research Institute (NCRI), 211

Neutrality, 76

as ideal but often impossible, 68–71

principled, 72–75

speech trumping university operations and, 75

See also Institutional neutrality

Nevitte, Neil, 223

New England Journal of Medicine, 115

New York City Public Schools, 208

New York Times (newspaper), 34, 198

New York Times v. Sullivan, 34

New York University Abu Dhabi, 84

Newspeak, faculty using, 268

Niemöller, Martin, 272

Nietzsche, Friedrich, 5
Noelle-Neumann, Elisabeth, 56
Northwestern University, 10

Obama, Barack, 82
O'Connor, Sandra Day, 229
October 7, 2023, attacks, 64, 184, 200, 317–18, 335
Office for Civil Rights, of US Department of Education, 278
Office of Personnel Management (US), 203
Office of Public Policy Events, 227
Ohio State, 224
Oklahoma, critical race theory banned in, 35–36
On Liberty (Mill), 38, 88, 243
Open inquiry, 3, 94–95, 288
    censorship threatening, 247
    DEI suppressing, 250–51
    hearings on bureaucratic attempts to limit, 335–36
    suppression of, 88–91
    teaching, 337–38
The Open Society and Its Enemies (Popper), 7
Opioid crisis, Ironton affected by, 115
Oppression, liberty versus, 5
Oreskes, Naomi, 88
Orwell, George, 275
Ostrich Syndrome (OS), 144, 151–57
Ostrom, Vincent, 9, 207
Ownership, management contrasted with, 176

The Parasitic Mind (Saad), 274
Parliamentary democracy, in Britain, 11
Partisanship, 151
    of faculty, 224
    speech suppression and, 143
    truth and, 285–86
    See also Affective polarization; Conservatives; The left; Progressives
Patton, Greg, 26
Paul, James, 211, 299n96
Payne, Stanley G., 192
PBS (media), 341
PC, M.D. (Satel), 104
Peirce, Charles Sanders, 323, 326
The Pentagon, 209
Pepperdine University, 224
"The Peril of Politicizing Science" (Krylov), 289
Perry, Mark J., 112
Pew Research Center, 136
Pharmacogenomics, 113
Planned Parenthood, 24
Plato, 189
PLOS One (journal), 85, 86
Pluckrose, Helen, 276
Pluralism, 329–30
    progressives distrusting, 9
    public education on, 340–41
    within US government, 13
Polarization, affective. *See* Affective polarization
Policy debates, campuses sponsoring, 227

Political and ideological beliefs, 256–57

Political ideology, 150–52

Political participation, economic power in tension with, 172

Political repression, self-censorship and, 60n21

Political Science 470 (course), 184, 187–89, 191

Political statements of faith, 338

Political tolerance, liberals and progressives appealing to, 153

Political viewpoints, the Academy and expression of, 223

Politicized capitalism, 168, 171, 177

Politicized market, ownership and control in, 176

Politics
  elite, 11–14
  employment and, 169–72
  identity, 236, 278
  progressive, 249, 258
  See also Partisanship

Popper, Karl, 7

Populism, democracy and, 15

Portland State University, 134

Postmodern approaches, fundamentalism resembled by, 9

Powe, Neil R., 115

Powell, Lewis F., 221

"The Power of the Powerless" (Havel), 138

Pravda (Правда) (media outlet), 275

Prescriptions, 119–20

Presumption of innocence, campuses lacking, 269

"Princeton Principles for a Campus Culture of Free Inquiry" (Princeton University), 201n7

Princeton University, 70, 201n7

Principled neutrality, exceptions to, 72–75

Private institutions, First Amendment rights at, 309

Professional organizations, public policy influenced by, 262n16

Professional societies, CSJ and, 288

Professors, 64–65, 82, 239
  academia forcing out, 237
  academic freedom of, 67
  bias of, 252–53
  campus culture shaped by, 251
  DEI advancing, 253–55
  ideological diversity serving, 248
  liberal ideology of, 151
  as Marxists and radicals, 249
  McCarthyism targeting, 82
  progressive politics of, 249, 258
  respectability cascade in, 258
  self-censorship by, 83
  social justice affecting, 199
  students indoctrinated by, 250, 326
  See also specific professors

Progressive censorship, 185

Progressive ideology, students indoctrinated with, 247, 260

Progressive norms, at public health academies, 107–8

Progressive politics, 249, 258

Progressives, 144, 152, 286
  bureaucracies reflecting, 207

pluralism distrusted by, 9
political tolerance appealed to
by, 153
Pro-life speaker, protest of, 121–22
Promotion processes, for faculty,
278
Propaganda, Soviet people navigat-
ing, 297n59
Protected class, ideology as, 338–39
Protests, 309–14
free speech culture tolerating,
317–18
free speech during, 33
Haidt on, 5
of pro-life speakers, 121–22
at UC, 316
Public education, on pluralism and
First Amendment, 340–41
Public funding, of higher education
organizations, 338
Public health, 104, 107–8, 117
Public health academies, progres-
sive norms at, 107–8
Public persona, 191–92
Public policy, professional organi-
zations influencing, 262n16
Public policy issues, 226
Public trust, in journalism, 90
Public universities, in Arizona, 279
Publicity, for CAFAR, 195

Race, 63, 113–15, 126n55
Racism, 111–12, 116
See also Anti-racism
Radical egalitarians, 323
Radicals, 249

Ramaswamy, Vivek, 16
Rapid-onset gender dysphoria
(ROGD), 87, 89, 92
"Rapid-Onset Gender Dysphoria
in Adolescents and Young
Adults" (Littman), 85
Rauch, Jonathan, 90, 192, 198,
201n15, 322–23, 333
Reality-based community, 328, 330
Red Scare, 33–34, 48
Red Terror, 275
*Regents of the University of California
v. Bakke* (Supreme Court),
242
Reif, L. Rafael, 284
Religion, ideology and, 257
Religious publication, students
distributing, 221
Report of the Committee on Free
Expression at Yale "Wood-
ward Report," 96
Representation, 135–36
Repressive tolerance, 236
Republic (Plato), 189
Republican state governments, free
inquiry threatened by, 35
Republicans, academic depart-
ments without, 327
Resistance, official means of,
276–80
Resisting Cancel Culture (Strossen),
326
Respectability cascade, in profes-
sors, 258
"Restoring Academic Freedom"
(letter), 280

376 THE FREE INQUIRY PAPERS

#RetractRacists, 84

Revolutionary destructivism, 276

Rodriguez v. Maricopa County Community College District, 38–39

ROGD. *See* Rapid-onset gender dysphoria

Rogowski, Jon, 51

Roman Catholic Church, 82

Rothman, Stanley, 223

Rules, 310

    compliance, 207–8

    on institutional neutrality, 316

    selective enforcement of, 309, 314

    as viewpoint and content neutral, 311

Rushdie, Salman, 323

Russia, Ukraine invaded by, 5–6

Russian Civil War, 130

Saad, Gad, 274, 285

Safe harbor provision, 228

Sakharov, Andrei, 271, 273

Sanger, Margaret, 24

Satel, Sally, 104

Schenck, Charles, 22

Scholars, 134

    academic freedom protecting, 29–30

    compelled speech damaging, 137

    public targeting of, 90

Scholars Under Fire Database (FIRE), 133, 149–50, 152, 155

Scholarship on sensitive topics, social media and, 93

School choice, 13

Science (journal), 269

Science, politicizing, 90–93

Scientific American (publisher), 269

Scientific inquiry, academic freedom supporting with, 82

Scientific method, 140

Scientific research, asymmetric standards evaluating, 91, 92–93

Self-censorship, 54, 58n4, 147–48, 157, 258, 321

    in the academy, 83

    affective polarization in relation to, 51, 52, 55

    by faculty, 94, 269

    increase in, 48, 156

    political repression and, 60n21

    predictors of, 60n20

    by professors, 83

    rise of, 50

    social fear driving, 57

    social justice affected by, 39–40

    as spiral of silence, 56

    by students, 94, 155–56, 222, 269

Self-indoctrination, through social media, 327

Self-reliance, 190

Seppi, Duane, 144

Settle, Jaime, 51

Sexual diversity, teachers emphasizing, 268

Shalala, Donna, 186

Shapiro, Ilya, 227

Sharpless, John, 193

Shepard, Jason, 198

Shermer, Michael, 35

Shiffrin, Steven, 187
Sikorski, Christian von, 56
Silverglate, Harvey, 198
Sklodowska-Curie, Marie, 275
Snyder, Jeffrey Aaron, 281
Social contagion, 86
Social determinants of health, 107, 109
Social good, MFE and, 241
Social justice, 66, 131, 185, 268
    chilling effect of, 106
    under Communist Party, 139
    DEI and, 16
    educational experience influenced by, 242
    free inquiry and, 28, 30–37, 40
    ideological diversity not conflicting with, 255
    merit devalued by, 284
    "perceived harms" justifying, 36
    professors affected by, 199
    public health and, 104
    self-censorship affecting, 39–40
    See also Anti-racism; Critical social justice
Social justice advocates, free speech limited by, 28
Social justice ideology, 104
Social justice movement, within medicine, 106
Social media, 333
    academic community not represented through, 94–96
    expression suppressed by, 87–90
    pressure campaigns on, 94
    research suppressed by, 87–90

scholarship on sensitive topics and, 93
self-indoctrination through, 327
Social media giants, 7
Social medicine, 107
Social production of health, 107
Social reputational system, spiral of silence fostered by, 156–57
Social science faculty, 147
Social sciences, IRB excluding, 213
Socialism, 275
Society for Open Inquiry in Behavioral Science, 3, 288
Society for Personality and Social Psychology (SPSP), 135–36
    censorship by, 137–38
    exclusion from, 136
    Haidt resigning from, 139
Sociopolitical diversity, 256
Socrates, 189–90
Socratic inquiry, 189–91
Solzhenitsyn, Aleksandr, 271, 273
SOPs. *See* Standard operating procedures
Soviet people, propaganda navigated by, 297n59
Soviet regime, 271–72
Soviet Union (USSR), 271, 273
Sowell, Thomas, 208
Speech
    administrators policing, 145
    compelled, 137, 237, 238
    counter-, 63–65, 339–40
    neutrality and university operations trumped by, 75

See also Free speech; Institutional speech

Speech codes, 184–85, 192–94, 197–98, 230–31

Speech First, UCF sued by, 230

Speech suppression, partisanship and, 143

Spiral of silence, 156–57

SPSP. *See* Society for Personality and Social Psychology

Staddon, John, 283

Stalin, Josef, 6, 130–31

Standard operating procedures (SOPs), 205

Stanford Law School, 69

Stanford University, 66, 278

State laws, fringe benefits interacting with, 173–76

State legislatures, 282, 334

State University System, in Florida, 227

"Statement of Principles on Academic Freedom and Tenure" (American Association of University Professors), 219

Stefanik, Elise, 306–7

STEM, 268–69

Stevens, Sean T., 29, 327

Stories, as persuasive device, 257–58

Stouffer, Samuel, 48, 49, 58n4

Strossen, Nadine, 326

Structural leftist fundamentalism, colleges and universities ingrained with, 8

Student body, diversity within, 242

Student newspapers, 195–96

Student organizations, administrators closing, 342

Student services professionals, 74

Students, 112–13, 187, 283, 307, 310, 311–13

administrators siding with, 199

affirmative action affecting, 84

chilling effect contributed to by, 147

constitutional law learned by, 189–90

deplatforming attempts by, 150

First Amendment protecting, 227, 309

free expression protecting, 21

grading bias feared by conservative, 151

harassment of, 310

illiberal attitudes endorsed by, 145–46

intolerant attitudes held by, 157

marginalization experienced by, 258

"National White Coat Die-In" participated in by, 104

open learning environment preferred by, 153

professors indoctrinating, 250, 326

progressive ideology indoctrinating, 247, 260

religious publication distributed by, 221

self-censorship by, 94, 155–56, 222, 269

trigger warnings demanded by, 26

Students for a Democratic Society, 221

Students for Fair Admissions v. Harvard (Supreme Court), 89

Study of American Families (1994), 153

Suffrage rights campaigns, 24

Summers, Larry, 317

Suppression, of free inquiry, 11–14

Supreme Court (US)
  anti-war expression protected by, 23
  Beauharnais v. Illinois at, 14
  Dobbs v. Jackson Women's Health Organization at, 175, 181n13
  on free speech, 34
  Healey v. James at, 221
  Regents of the University of California v. Bakke at, 242
  right to abortions overturned by, 62–64
  Students for Fair Admissions v. Harvard at, 89
  Tinker v. Des Moines at, 21
  West Virginia State Board of Education v. Barnette at, 188

Sutherland, Joseph L., 51

Sweezy, Paul, 220

Sweezy v. New Hampshire, 57

Systemic racism, 111–12, 116

Teachers, sexual diversity emphasized by, 268

Tenure, 82

Terry, Luther, 212, 339

Texas Tech University, 279

Third World Quarterly (journal), 134

Thrasymachus, 189–90

Throat-clearing, 285–86

TikTok, 308

Tinker, Mary Beth, 21–22, 26, 335

Tinker v. Des Moines (Supreme Court), 21, 335

Title IX, 210–11, 227, 269

Title IX bureaucracies, free inquiry bureaucracies countering, 337

To Build a Castle (Bukovsky), 271

Tocqueville, Alexis de, 207

Tolerance, of dissent, 65–68

Tolerance gap, 143

Totalitarian-style repression, in US, 273

Trigger warnings, 26, 185

The True Believer (Hoffer), 8

Trump, Donald, 14

Truth
  over ideology, 140
  partisanship and, 285–86
  pursuit of, 184, 186, 188

Truth seeking, 63, 66, 71, 82, 92–95, 122

Turchin, Peter, 11–12, 14

Turner, Nat, 23

Twitter, 84, 85
  See also X

UATX. *See* University of Austin

UC. *See* University of California

UCF. *See* University of Central Florida

Ukraine, Russia invading, 5–6

Unbiased selection, 234

UNC. *See* University of North Carolina

Underwood, Steven, 193

United States (US)
  free inquiry under attack in, 2–3, 333
  totalitarian-style repression in, 273
  See also Florida; Supreme Court

Universities, 5–6
  academic freedom denied at, 62, 64
  anti-racism and, 64, 75–76
  climates of fear at, 336
  institutional speech eschewed by, 62–63
  as institutions, 72–74
  mission and method of, 62
  openness, factuality, and pluralism strengthened at, 329–30
  publicity and mockery affecting, 278
  race opined on by, 63
  structural leftist fundamentalism ingrained in, 8
  See also Administrators; Admissions; Campuses; Faculty; Students; *specific universities*

University leadership, 94–95

University of Austin (UATX), 288, 302n133, 342

University of Buckingham, 146

University of California (UC)
  administrators affecting, 275–76
  DEI statements required by, 228–29
  protests at, 316

University of California, Berkeley, 229, 299n96

University of California, Los Angeles, 315–16

University of Central Florida (UCF), 10–11, 230–31

University of Chicago, 68, 219, 247, 277

University of Illinois Chicago School of Public Health, 268

University of Iowa, 231

University of Massachusetts, 277

University of Michigan, 25, 121, 299n96

University of Minnesota, 121

University of New Hampshire, 220

University of North Carolina (UNC), 277–78

University of North Carolina School of Medicine, 119

University of North Texas, 17

University of Pennsylvania, 335
  code of conduct at, 306
  Kors presenting to University Committee at, 198
  Wax investigated by, 336

University of Pittsburgh Medical Center, 84

University of Pittsburgh School of Medicine, 118

University of San Diego, 284
University of Southern California, 26, 279
University of Southern California Dornsife College of Letters, Arts, and Sciences, 289
University of Texas Southwestern Medical School, 118
University of Washington, 231
University of Wisconsin (UW), 197, 279, 338
University of Wisconsin–Madison (UW-Madison), 184, 186, 188–89, 196
University operations, 73, 75
Unwillingness to speak one's mind, change in levels of, 49
US Army, 209
US Department of Education, 210, 213–14, 278, 310–11
US First Amendment Commission, 341
US government, pluralism within, 13
US House of Representatives, 251
US Office of Personnel Management, 203
USSR, 6. *See* Soviet Union
Utopian ideologies, 235
UW. *See* University of Wisconsin
UW-Madison. *See* University of Wisconsin–Madison

The Vagina Monologues, 150
Vavilov, Nikolai, 131
"Victory Lap" (Jussim), 289–90
Virchow, Rudolf, 122–23

Virtue signaling, 9–10, 15–16, 253, 254
Virtue Signaling (Miller), 15–16
Volokh, Eugene, 172, 179

Wai, Jonathan, 16
Walcott, Charles, 206
Wang, Norman C., 112
Warren, Earl, 57
Warren Harding Junior High School, 21
Washington, George, 204
Washington Post, 17
Wax, Amy, 306, 336
WC4BL. *See* White Coats for Black Lives
Weber, Max, 205
Weiss, Bari, 273
West Virginia State Board of Education v. Barnette (Supreme Court), 188, 190
"What Happens When Doctors Can't Tell the Truth?" (Herzog), 111
What Universities Owe Democracy (Daniels), 225–26
White coat ceremony, at University of Minnesota, 121
White Coats for Black Lives (WC4BL), 104–5
White Fragility (DiAngelo), 110
Whittington, Keith, 89, 206
Why Trust Science? (Oreskes), 88
Wilson, Woodrow, 9, 207
Winslow, Charles-Edward Amory, 107

382 THE FREE INQUIRY PAPERS

Wisconsin State Journal, 196
Woke capitalism, 168
Woodward, C. Vann, 220
Woodward Report, 220
  See also Report of the Committee
    on Free Expression at Yale
World War II, 272

X "Twitter," 287

Yale Department of Psychiatry, 115
Yale School of Public Health, 107
Yancy, Clyde, 115
Young adults, GD in, 85–87
Youtie, Jan, 208

Zakaria, Fareed, 251

Правда. *See Pravda*

The American Enterprise Institute for Public Policy Research

AEI is a nonpartisan, nonprofit research and educational organization. The work of our scholars and staff advances ideas rooted in our commitment to expanding individual liberty, increasing opportunity, and strengthening freedom.

The Institute engages in research; publishes books, papers, studies, and short-form commentary; and conducts seminars and conferences. AEI's research activities are carried out under four major departments: Domestic Policy Studies, Economic Policy Studies, Foreign and Defense Policy Studies, and Social, Cultural, and Constitutional Studies. The resident scholars and fellows listed in these pages are part of a network that also includes nonresident scholars at top universities.

The views expressed in AEI publications are those of the authors; AEI does not take institutional positions on any issues.

BOARD OF TRUSTEES

DANIEL A. D'ANIELLO, *Chairman*
Cofounder and Chairman Emeritus
The Carlyle Group

CLIFFORD S. ASNESS
Managing and Founding Principal
AQR Capital Management LLC

PETER H. COORS
Chairman of the Board
Molson Coors Brewing Company

HARLAN CROW
Chairman
Crow Holdings

RAVENEL B. CURRY III
Chief Investment Officer
Eagle Capital Management LLC

KIMBERLY O. DENNIS
President and CEO
Searle Freedom Trust

DICK DEVOS
President
The Windquest Group

ROBERT DOAR
President
American Enterprise Institute

BEHDAD EGHBALI
Managing Partner and Cofounder
Clearlake Capital Group LP

MARTIN C. ELTRICH III
Partner
AEA Investors LP

TULLY M. FRIEDMAN
Managing Director, Retired
FFL Partners LLC

CHRISTOPHER B. GALVIN
Chairman
Harrison Street Capital LLC

HARVEY GOLUB
Chairman and CEO, Retired
American Express Company
Chairman, Miller Buckfire

FRANK J. HANNA
CEO
Hanna Capital LLC

JOHN K. HURLEY
Founder and Managing Partner
Cavalry Asset Management

DEEPA JAVERI
Chief Financial Officer
XRHealth

JOANNA F. JONSSON
Vice Chair, Capital Group
President, Capital Research
 Management Company

MARC S. LIPSCHULTZ
Co-CEO
Blue Owl Capital

JOHN A. LUKE JR.
Chairman
WestRock Company

BOB MURLEY
Senior Adviser
UBS

PAT NEAL
Chairman of the Executive Committee
Neal Communities

ROSS PEROT JR.
Chairman
Hillwood Development Company

GEOFFREY S. REHNERT
Co-CEO
Audax Group

MATTHEW K. ROSE
Retired CEO/Chairman
BNSF Railway

EDWARD B. RUST JR.
Chairman Emeritus
State Farm Insurance Companies

WILSON H. TAYLOR
Chairman Emeritus
Cigna Corporation

WILLIAM H. WALTON
Managing Member
Rockpoint Group LLC

WILL WEATHERFORD
Managing Partner
Weatherford Capital

EMERITUS TRUSTEES

THE HONORABLE
RICHARD B. CHENEY

JOHN FARACI

ROBERT F. GREENHILL

BRUCE KOVNER

KEVIN B. ROLLINS

D. GIDEON SEARLE

OFFICERS

ROBERT DOAR
President

JASON BERTSCH
Executive Vice President

JOHN CUSEY
Senior Vice President for
External Relations

KAZUKI KO
Vice President;
Chief Financial Officer

KATHERYNE WALKER
Vice President of Operations;
Chief Human Resources Officer

MATTHEW CONTINETTI
Senior Fellow; Director, Domestic
Policy Studies; Patrick and Charlene
Neal Chair in American Prosperity

YUVAL LEVIN
Senior Fellow; Director, Social,
Cultural, and Constitutional Studies;
Beth and Ravenel Curry Chair in Public
Policy; Editor in Chief, National Affairs

KORI SCHAKE
Senior Fellow; Director, Foreign and
Defense Policy Studies

MICHAEL R. STRAIN
Senior Fellow; Director, Economic
Policy Studies; Arthur F. Burns Scholar
in Political Economy

RESEARCH STAFF

SAMUEL J. ABRAMS
Nonresident Senior Fellow

BETH AKERS
Senior Fellow

J. JOEL ALICEA
Nonresident Fellow

JOSEPH ANTOS
Senior Fellow Emeritus

LEON ARON
Senior Fellow

KIRSTEN AXELSEN
Nonresident Fellow

JOHN BAILEY
Nonresident Senior Fellow

KYLE BALZER
Jeane Kirkpatrick Fellow

CLAUDE BARFIELD
Senior Fellow

MICHAEL BARONE
Senior Fellow Emeritus

MICHAEL BECKLEY
Nonresident Senior Fellow

ERIC J. BELASCO
Nonresident Senior Fellow

ANDREW G. BIGGS
Senior Fellow

MASON M. BISHOP
Nonresident Fellow

DAN BLUMENTHAL
Senior Fellow

KARLYN BOWMAN
Distinguished Senior Fellow Emeritus

HAL BRANDS
Senior Fellow

ALEX BRILL
Senior Fellow

ARTHUR C. BROOKS
President Emeritus

RICHARD BURKHAUSER
Nonresident Senior Fellow

CLAY CALVERT
Nonresident Senior Fellow

JAMES C. CAPRETTA
Senior Fellow; Milton Friedman Chair

TIMOTHY P. CARNEY
Senior Fellow

AMITABH CHANDRA
Nonresident Senior Fellow

LYNNE V. CHENEY
Distinguished Senior Fellow

YVONNE CHIU
Jeane Kirkpatrick Fellow

JAMES W. COLEMAN
Nonresident Senior Fellow

PRESTON COOPER
Senior Fellow

ZACK COOPER
Senior Fellow

KEVIN CORINTH
Senior Fellow; Deputy Director, Center on Opportunity and Social Mobility

JAY COST
Gerald R. Ford Nonresident Senior Fellow

DANIEL A. COX
Senior Fellow; Director, Survey Center on American Life

SADANAND DHUME
Senior Fellow

GISELLE DONNELLY
Senior Fellow

ROSS DOUTHAT
Nonresident Fellow

COLIN DUECK
Nonresident Senior Fellow

MACKENZIE EAGLEN
Senior Fellow

NICHOLAS EBERSTADT
Henry Wendt Chair in Political Economy

MAX EDEN
Senior Fellow

JEFFREY EISENACH
Nonresident Senior Fellow

ANDREW FERGUSON
Nonresident Fellow

JESÚS FERNÁNDEZ-VILLAVERDE
John H. Makin Visiting Scholar

JOHN G. FERRARI
Nonresident Senior Fellow

JOHN C. FORTIER
Senior Fellow

AARON FRIEDBERG
Nonresident Senior Fellow

JOSEPH B. FULLER
Nonresident Senior Fellow

SCOTT GANZ
Research Fellow

R. RICHARD GEDDES
Nonresident Senior Fellow

ROBERT P. GEORGE
Nonresident Senior Fellow

EDWARD L. GLAESER
Nonresident Senior Fellow

JOSEPH W. GLAUBER
Nonresident Senior Fellow

JONAH GOLDBERG
Senior Fellow; Asness Chair in Applied Liberty

JACK LANDMAN GOLDSMITH
Nonresident Senior Fellow

BARRY K. GOODWIN
Nonresident Senior Fellow

SCOTT GOTTLIEB, MD
Senior Fellow

PHIL GRAMM
Nonresident Senior Fellow

WILLIAM C. GREENWALT
Nonresident Senior Fellow

JIM HARPER
Nonresident Senior Fellow

TODD HARRISON
Senior Fellow

WILLIAM HAUN
Nonresident Fellow

FREDERICK M. HESS
Senior Fellow; Director, Education Policy Studies

CAROLE HOOVEN
Nonresident Senior Fellow

BRONWYN HOWELL
Nonresident Senior Fellow

R. GLENN HUBBARD
Nonresident Senior Fellow

HOWARD HUSOCK
Senior Fellow

DAVID HYMAN
Nonresident Senior Fellow

BENEDIC N. IPPOLITO
Senior Fellow

MARK JAMISON
Nonresident Senior Fellow

FREDERICK W. KAGAN
Senior Fellow; Director, Critical Threats Project

STEVEN B. KAMIN
Senior Fellow

LEON R. KASS, MD
Senior Fellow Emeritus

JOSHUA T. KATZ
Senior Fellow

L. LYNNE KIESLING
Nonresident Senior Fellow

KLON KITCHEN
Nonresident Senior Fellow

KEVIN R. KOSAR
Senior Fellow

ROBERT KULICK
Visiting Fellow

PAUL H. KUPIEC
Senior Fellow

DESMOND LACHMAN
Senior Fellow

PAUL LETTOW
Senior Fellow

DANIEL LYONS
Nonresident Senior Fellow

NAT MALKUS
*Senior Fellow; Deputy Director,
Education Policy Studies*

JOHN D. MAURER
Nonresident Fellow

ELAINE MCCUSKER
Senior Fellow

BRUCE D. MEYER
Nonresident Senior Fellow

BRIAN J. MILLER
Nonresident Fellow

CHRIS MILLER
Nonresident Senior Fellow

THOMAS P. MILLER
Senior Fellow

M. ANTHONY MILLS
*Senior Fellow; Director, Center
for Technology, Science, and
Energy*

FERDINANDO MONTE
Nonresident Senior Fellow

CHARLES MURRAY
*F. A. Hayek Chair Emeritus in
Cultural Studies*

STEPHEN D. OLINER
Senior Fellow Emeritus

BRENT ORRELL
Senior Fellow

TOBIAS PETER
*Senior Fellow; Codirector,
AEI Housing Center*

JAMES PETHOKOUKIS
*Senior Fellow; Editor, AEIdeas
Blog; DeWitt Wallace Chair*

ROGER PIELKE JR.
Senior Fellow

EDWARD J. PINTO
*Senior Fellow; Codirector,
AEI Housing Center*

DANIELLE PLETKA
Distinguished Senior Fellow

KENNETH M. POLLACK
Senior Fellow

KYLE POMERLEAU
Senior Fellow

ROBERT PONDISCIO
Senior Fellow

RAMESH PONNURU
Nonresident Senior Fellow

ROB PORTMAN
*Distinguished Visiting Fellow in
the Practice of Public Policy*

ANGELA RACHIDI
Senior Fellow; Rowe Scholar

NAOMI SCHAEFER RILEY
Senior Fellow

WILL RINEHART
Senior Fellow

DALIBOR ROHAC
Senior Fellow

CHRISTINE ROSEN
Senior Fellow

JEFFREY A. ROSEN
Nonresident Fellow

MICHAEL ROSEN
Nonresident Senior Fellow

IAN ROWE
Senior Fellow

MICHAEL RUBIN
Senior Fellow

PAUL RYAN
*Distinguished Visiting Fellow
in the Practice of Public Policy*

SALLY SATEL, MD
Senior Fellow

ERIC SAYERS
Nonresident Fellow

CHRISTOPHER J. SCALIA
Senior Fellow

DIANA SCHAUB
Nonresident Senior Fellow

ANNA SCHERBINA
Nonresident Senior Fellow

GARY J. SCHMITT
Senior Fellow

MARK SCHNEIDER
Nonresident Senior Fellow

DEREK SCISSORS
Senior Fellow

NEENA SHENAI
Nonresident Fellow

DAN SLATER
Nonresident Fellow

SITA NATARAJ SLAVOV
Nonresident Senior Fellow

THOMAS SMITH
Nonresident Fellow

VINCENT H. SMITH
Nonresident Senior Fellow

CHRISTINA HOFF
SOMMERS
Senior Fellow Emeritus

CHRIS STIREWALT
Senior Fellow

BENJAMIN STOREY
Senior Fellow

JENNA SILBER STOREY
Senior Fellow

RUY TEIXEIRA
Nonresident Senior Fellow

SHANE TEWS
Nonresident Senior Fellow

MARC A. THIESSEN
Senior Fellow

JOSEPH S. TRACY
Nonresident Senior Fellow

SEAN TRENDE
Nonresident Fellow

BORIS VABSON
Nonresident Fellow

TUNKU VARADARAJAN
Nonresident Fellow

STAN VEUGER
Senior Fellow

ALAN D. VIARD
Senior Fellow Emeritus

DUSTIN WALKER
Nonresident Fellow

PHILIP WALLACH
Senior Fellow

PETER J. WALLISON
Senior Fellow Emeritus

MARK J. WARSHAWSKY
Senior Fellow

MATT WEIDINGER
Senior Fellow; Rowe Scholar

ADAM J. WHITE
*Senior Fellow; Laurence H. Silberman
Chair in Constitutional Governance*

BRAD WILCOX
Nonresident Senior Fellow

THOMAS CHATTERTON
WILLIAMS
Nonresident Fellow

SCOTT WINSHIP
*Senior Fellow; Director,
Center on Opportunity and
Social Mobility*

AUDRYE WONG
Jeane Kirkpatrick Fellow

JOHN YOO
Nonresident Senior Fellow

BENJAMIN ZYCHER
Senior Fellow

www.ingramcontent.com/pod-product-compliance
Lightning Source LLC
Jackson TN
JSHW022303130325
80721JS00002B/3